LIBRARY
HOWARD COMMUNITY COLLEGE
10901 LITTLE PATUXENT PARKWAY
COLUMBIA, MD 21044-3197

Intersectionality & Higher Education

THEORY, RESEARCH, & PRAXIS

Donald Mitchell, Jr., Editor

with Charlana Y. Simmons & Lindsay A. Greyerbiehl, Associate Editors

Foreword by Susan R. Jones

PETER LANG
New York • Bern • Frankfurt • Berlin
Brussels • Vienna • Oxford • Warsaw

Library of Congress Cataloging-in-Publication Data

Intersectionality & higher education: theory, research, & praxis /
edited by Donald Mitchell, Jr., Charlana Y. Simmons, Lindsay A. Greyerbiehl.
pages cm
Includes bibliographical references.
1. Minorities—Education (Higher)—United States. 2. Education, Higher—
Social aspects—United States. 3. Multicultural education—United States.
4. Identity (Psychology) 5. Racism in education—United States.
6. Educational equalization—United States. I. Mitchell, Donald II. Simmons, Charlana
III. Greyerbiehl, Lindsay IV. Title: Intersectionality and higher education.
LC3731.I566 378.19820973—dc23 2014024782
ISBN 978-1-4331-2589-8 (hardcover)
ISBN 978-1-4331-2588-1 (paperback)
ISBN 978-1-4539-1407-6 (e-book)

Bibliographic information published by **Die Deutsche Nationalbibliothek**.
Die Deutsche Nationalbibliothek lists this publication in the "Deutsche
Nationalbibliografie"; detailed bibliographic data are available
on the Internet at http://dnb.d-nb.de/.

The paper in this book meets the guidelines for permanence and durability
of the Committee on Production Guidelines for Book Longevity
of the Council of Library Resources.

© 2014 Peter Lang Publishing, Inc., New York
29 Broadway, 18th floor, New York, NY 10006
www.peterlang.com

All rights reserved.
Reprint or reproduction, even partially, in all forms such as microfilm,
xerography, microfiche, microcard, and offset strictly prohibited.

Printed in the United States of America

Advance praise for Intersectionality & Higher Education

"*Intersectionality & Higher Education: Theory, Research, & Praxis* is such an important read for new and more seasoned educators on the student affairs and higher education scholar-practitioner continuum. It engages readers on multiple levels and adds to our understanding of intersectionality not only as an area of study, but as a tool that can and should be used to improve our work. The text covers a diverse range of identities, highlighting narratives of often unheard communities, and integrating race, gender, class, sexuality, and nativity in new ways. The contributing authors manage to hold on to the complexity of intersectionality, while also creating accessible space for scholars and practitioners to understand, engage, and explore intersectional concepts. Collectively, this work urges us to be reflective about the structures that reinforce our experiences of oppression and privilege as well as the experiences of others, and provides us with thoughtful strategies that can ultimately lead us to more equitable communities."

—Kimberly A. Griffin, Associate Professor, University of Maryland, College Park

"This book illustrates the potential for the lens of intersectionality to inform how higher education scholars and practitioners respond to changing identities in the U.S. population. The authors illuminate the experiences of underexplored identities in higher education, call for us to recognize that no one can be reduced to one or two identities, and provide us with the tools to do so. Importantly, the contributors reveal the role of privilege as well as marginality in shaping higher education experiences and illustrate how higher education personnel can address the complexities of simultaneously experiencing both conditions. To advance intersectionality's potential to influence social transformation, the book demonstrates how this lens can foster more inclusive environments for faculty, practitioners, and students from diverse social and economic backgrounds. Together, the authors offer many empirical examples of how higher education personnel can effect institutional change in this direction. This book pushes faculty, scholars, and students to expand the ways that we develop theory, conduct research, and create culturally responsive teaching and learning environments in higher education. "

—Anne-Marie Núñez, Associate Professor, The University of Texas at San Antonio

Intersectionality
& Higher Education

This book is part of the Peter Lang Education list.
Every volume is peer reviewed and meets
the highest quality standards for content and production.

PETER LANG
New York • Bern • Frankfurt • Berlin
Brussels • Vienna • Oxford • Warsaw

Contents

Illustrations

FIGURES

TABLES

Foreword

SUSAN R. JONES

Intersectionality as a framework for analyzing and understanding higher education has attracted scholars, researchers, and practitioners because of its explanatory
and elucidating power in addressing the complexities of what we experience to be
higher education in contemporary times. Many years ago, noted higher education
and student development scholar Arthur Chickering commented that we "should
hold the many theories available to us with tenuous tenacity and maintain a tough-
minded and inquiring mind regarding theories" (Thomas & Chickering, 1984,
p. 399). This continues to be good advice, particularly when embracing newer
theoretical constructs and frameworks that become so popular so quickly that they
run the risk of becoming "buzzwords" as well as being "catchy and convenient"
(Davis, 2008, p. 75). Intersectionality has garnered the attention of scholars and
practitioners in higher education and inspired them to define, understand, and
apply it to various educational issues, institutional contexts, and student populations. Indeed, *Intersectionality & Higher Education: Theory, Research, and Praxis*
represents a comprehensive and creative effort, with a diverse array of chapters
covering a wide range of topics and perspectives on intersectionality in higher
education.

Many in higher education were initially drawn to intersectionality because
it emphasized linking identity to structures of privilege and oppression (Jones &
Abes, 2013). As sociologist and leading scholar on intersectionality Bonnie
Thornton Dill wrote, "To a large extent, intersectional work is about identity"

(Dill, McLaughlin, & Nieves, 2007, p. 630). However, to only see intersectionality as being about identity is to ignore its historical and disciplinary origins and intent and thereby miss the mark of its full analytic power. Higher education scholars have been relatively unsophisticated in the application of intersectionality because they overemphasized its identity applications. In fact, intersectionality is only about identity when structures of inequality are foregrounded and identities considered in light of social issues and power dynamics. As Patricia Hill Collins (2009) wrote:

> In recent years, intersectional analyses have far too often turned inward, to the level of personal identity narratives, in part, because intersectionality can be grasped far more easily when constructing one's own autobiography. This stress on identity narratives, especially individual identity narratives, does provide an important contribution to fleshing out our understandings of how people experience and construct identities within intersecting systems of power. Yet this turning inward also reflects the shift within American society away from social structural analyses of social problems. (p. ix)

More recent writings about intersectionality negotiate the tensions in defining what intersectionality is and is not, with one scholar addressing the "theoretical, political, and methodological murkiness" (Nash, 2008, p. 1) in intersectionality. Intersectionality is referred to as a framework, theory, or approach to social activism (Warner & Shields, 2013, p. 804), as a theory of marginalized subjectivity or a generalized theory of identity (Nash, 2008), as theoretical interventions (Dill & Zambrana, 2009), and as "a method, and a disposition, a heuristic and analytic tool" (Carbado, Crenshaw, Mays, & Tomlinson, 2013, p. 303). Scholars of intersectionality are now arguing for a more complex understanding of intersectionality which acknowledges the complexity and definitional murkiness involved. In fact, Davis (2008) suggested that the ambiguities of intersectionality contain its core contributions. She wrote, "paradoxically, precisely the vagueness and open-endedness of 'intersectionality' may be the very secret of its success" (Davis, 2008, p. 69). Finally, in an essay mapping the intellectual history and movements of intersectionality, Carbado, Crenshaw, Mays, and Tomlinson (2013) advised "understanding intersectionality as a work-in-progress" and that rather than focusing on what intersectionality *is*, it is more productive "to assess what intersectionality *does*" (p. 304). This is a provocative suggestion, and various approaches are represented in the chapters in *Intersectionality & Higher Education*.

What exactly does intersectionality enable those of us who work in higher education to *do*? In an essay on the promise of intersectionality in higher education, Museus and Griffin (2011) suggested that it enables a more accurate reflection of the diversity in higher education, facilitates the centering of voices and experiences of those at the margins, foregrounds the relationship between social identities and inequality, and avoids perpetuation of inequality (pp. 9–11). Taken together, the chapter authors in this book employ intersectionality in advancing a more complex and holistic understanding of intersectional theories, research, and practices in higher education.

The scope of this text is reflected in its organizational structure. The volume is divided into three sections addressing theory, research, and praxis, and each chapter offers the reader a perspective on the application of intersectionality to a particular topic relevant to the contemporary context of higher education. The nine chapters in the theory section attend to historical legacies of intersectionality, theories of identity and identity models informed by intersectionality, and particular groups with undertheorized identities, such as indigenous peoples, undocumented students, LGBTQ students, and academics. The eight chapters in the research section enable readers to consider what it means to conduct intersectional research. The examples provided are studies guided by intersectionality in relation to research design as well as in specific intersections. The section on praxis includes six chapters that highlight specific initiatives and programs designed with intersectionality as a guiding framework and emphasize the importance of building alliances and coalitions, safe spaces, empowerment, and systemic change.

Of course, at the heart of intersectionality is the integration of theory, research, and praxis. Theory and research without practice (in the name of social change) are vacuous, and practice without theory and research is often misguided and ill informed. This text may, of course, be read sequentially, section by section, but it is important to note that each chapter stands alone and contributes to an understanding of intersectionality in and of itself as well as in relation to other chapters. The chapters call the reader to question what might be taken for granted, where power lurks in campus policies and practices, which populations are missing from the larger discourse in higher education and thereby are not well understood, and to more deliberately critique structures of inequality. As a whole, these chapters ask readers to reconsider our generation and consumption of theory, research, and our educational practices in light of core tenets of intersectionality that insist on a macro analysis of structures of power, privilege, and oppression and to assure that theory, research, and practice are inexorably linked in the service of social transformation and equity. The volume is a unique and important contribution, one that encourages those in higher education to put intersectionality to work in ways that advance social justice and a more equitable society.

Intersectionality is a "work-in-progress...animated by the imperative of social change" as aptly described by Carbado et al. (2013, pp. 304, 312). As such, we should hold it with "tenuous tenacity" (Thomas & Chickering, 1984, p. 399) because it has much to offer in the arena of higher education yet is only as good as what it *does*. *Intersectionality & Higher Education: Theory, Research, and Praxis* equips the field of higher education with an important and useful text that should increase the likelihood of theorists, researchers, and practitioners *doing* intersectionality well.

Susan R. Jones
The Ohio State University
Columbus, Ohio

REFERENCES

Carbado, D. W., Crenshaw, K. W., Mays, V. M., & Tomlinson, B. (2013). Intersectionality: Mapping the movements of a theory. *Du Bois Review, 10*, 303–312.

Collins, P. H. (2009). Foreword: Emerging intersections—building knowledge and transforming institutions. In B. T. Dill & R. E. Zambrana (Eds.), *Emerging intersections: Race, class, and gender in theory, policy, and practice* (pp. vii–xiii). New Brunswick, NJ: Rutgers University Press.

Davis, K. (2008). Intersectionality as buzzword: A sociology of science perspective on what makes a feminist theory successful. *Feminist Theory, 9*, 67–85.

Dill, B. T., McLaughlin, A. E., & Nieves, A. D. (2007). Future direction of feminist research: Intersectionality. In S. N. Hesse-Biber (Ed.), *Handbook of feminist research* (pp. 629–637). Thousand Oaks, CA: Sage.

Dill, B. T., & Zambrana, R. E. (2009). Critical thinking about inequality: An emerging lens. In B. T. Dill & R. E. Zambrana (Eds.), *Emerging intersections: Race, class, and gender in theory, policy, and practice* (pp. 1–21). New Brunswick, NJ: Rutgers University Press.

Jones, S. R., & Abes, E. S. (2013). *Identity development of college students: Advancing frameworks for multiple dimensions of identity.* San Francisco, CA: Jossey-Bass.

Museus, S. D., & Griffin, K. A. (2011). Mapping the margins in higher education: On the promise of intersectionality frameworks in research and discourse. In S. D. Museus & K. A. Griffin (Eds.), *Using mixed-method approaches to study intersectionality in higher education: New directions for institutional research* (pp. 5–13). San Francisco, CA: Jossey-Bass.

Nash, J. C. (2008). Re-thinking intersectionality. *Feminist Review, 89*, 1–15.

Thomas, R., & Chickering, A. W. (1984). Education and identity revisited. *Journal of College Student Personnel, 25*, 392–399.

Warner, L. R., & Shields, S. A. (2013). The intersections of sexuality, gender, and race: Identity research at the crossroads. *Sex Roles, 68*, 803–810.

Acknowledgments

We would like to thank those who made the publication of this text possible. First, we thank all of the chapter authors who helped shape this volume through their writings and peer reviews. Second, we thank Dr. Susan R. Jones for contributing the Foreword. Third, we thank Dr. Gregory S. Goodman, our series editor, for investing in our vision for the text. Fourth, we thank Chris Myers, Stephen Mazur, Sophie Appel, and Phyllis Korper—all at Peter Lang—for all that they brought to the production of this volume. Finally, we thank a host of family, friends, and colleagues, whose love and support keep us going each day.

Introduction

DONALD MITCHELL, JR.

Living with and navigating multiple, intersecting identities is not a new phenomenon (Yuval-Davis, 2013). Perhaps W. E. B. Du Bois's (1903/2010) artic-ulation of double consciousness was an expression of the intersection of being both American and an American of African descent and the complexities of navigating those identities. And perhaps Martin Luther King, Jr.'s difficult decision to dis-tance himself from civil rights activist Bayard Rustin—who openly identified as gay (Branch, 1989)—captured the complexities and intersections of religion, pol-itics, and social justice. However, using the term *intersectionality* to discuss these experiences was introduced by Kimberlé Crenshaw, a scholar of law, critical race theory, and Black feminist thought, in 1989. She used intersectionality to explain the experiences of Black women who, because of the intersection of race and gen-der, are exposed to exponential forms of marginalization and oppression.

In addition to Crenshaw, other women of color scholars have also contrib-uted to the widespread recognition of intersectionality, such as Patricia Hill Collins, Bonnie Thornton Dill, Ange-Marie Hancock, and bell hooks. Because of increased recognition and appreciation for intersectionality as a framework, it is now used more broadly to define (a) the intersecting identities of individuals beyond women of color (e.g., Strayhorn, 2013), (b) power relations among groups (e.g., Yuval-Davis, 2013), and (c) research paradigms used to design empirical studies exploring multiple and interlocking identities (e.g., Griffin & Museus, 2011; Hancock, 2007). Intersectionality now garners attention in education, law, philosophy, political science, psychology, and sociology, and scholarly conversations about intersectionality and its multiple meanings now span the globe. While scholars of higher education (e.g., Griffin & Museus, 2011; Jones & Abes, 2013; Strayhorn, 2013) have begun documenting intersectionality within certain higher education contexts, it has received limited attention in the field of higher education overall. However, the liberal or progressive nature of higher education (Solow, 2004), in conjunction with rapid demographic shifts occurring in U.S. higher education, will probably encourage higher education researchers and practitioners to become further immersed in intersectionality discourse.

Underrepresented racial/ethnic minorities (i.e., African Americans, Hispanic Americans, Native Americans, Pacific Islanders) will collectively make up the majority of the U.S. population by 2025 (Malcolm, Dowd, & Yu, 2010). In addition, men are receiving fewer degrees than their women counterparts (Sax, 2008). Yet women remain underrepresented in science, technology, engineering, and mathematics (STEM) disciplines, are paid less across disciplines, and are less likely to receive promotions in comparison to men within U.S. higher education contexts (Ginther & Hayes, 2003; Glazer-Raymo, 2003). These trends and complexities affect U.S. higher education as we know it, and further explorations of these intricacies are warranted because they ultimately affect the nation and the world. If the United States is to stay competitive in an increasingly "flat world" (Friedman, 2005), students from all backgrounds must receive their fair share of degrees awarded in all disciplines from the associate to the doctoral level. Without diversity in the ivory towers, the United States is inevitably at risk of further eroding its economic prosperity and leaving national needs unfulfilled.

Intersectional explorations and practices can serve as gateways for exploring, interpreting, documenting, and, most importantly, providing solutions to the social concerns facing U.S. higher education institutions. For example, college students' social and academic integration into university life is an area of inquiry that could benefit from the tenets of intersectionality. According to Strayhorn (2012), academic and financial variables, together, account for approximately 40% of postsecondary outcomes. He then goes on to note that a sense of belonging is a salient variable that is often overlooked in postsecondary outcomes. Perhaps what Strayhorn conveys is that overlooking students' unique identities and needs stifles their sense of belonging and may negatively affect retention and graduation rates.

Accordingly, research, policies, and practices that recognize the relevance of intersectionality may be important in improving educational outcomes for current and future college students. Without these advancements in practice, colleges and universities may continue to fall short in giving every student a fair chance to achieve learning outcomes; they must recognize students' continuous need to navigate spaces in an attempt to belong and begin to deconstruct oppressive forces on colleges campuses. For example, students are often confused when they are invited to join all-encompassing, identity-based groups, because the invitation sometimes marginalizes or de-emphasizes other facets of their identity (Renn, 2011). When students of mixed Black and White racial backgrounds are asked to join Black students' unions—even though they may have never identified solely as Black—they may not find those unions as adequate or necessary support systems (Renn, 2011). These types of experiences often affect college students' social integration, which, in turn, influences their academic outcomes, because social and academic integration are interrelated (Pascarella & Terenzini, 2005).

As access expands, demographics shift, and institutions become more diverse across the higher education terrain, there will be a need for more intersectional support systems on college campuses in the near future; such support systems will be needed for students, faculty, staff, and administrators alike. Unsurprisingly, some intersectional support groups have existed for quite some time but have not been fully analyzed or recognized for the intersectional support they offer (e.g., Black, Latina, and Asian sororities). In addition, newer intersectional support systems have emerged in recent years, such as minority male initiatives like the Huntley House for African American Men at the University of Minnesota-Twin Cities. While these intersectional spaces are worthy of full support, it is unlikely these support systems and practices will improve higher education as siloed spaces. The interconnectedness or "bordering" of these intersectional supports and the members who inhabit them also warrant attention (Yuval-Davis, 2013).

Ropers-Huilman and Winters (2010) wrote, "Context and the negotiation of lived experiences may take shape and be interpreted differently because of uniquely intersecting experiences….Intersectionality urges researchers to consider how individual and social constructions of 'difference' and 'commonality' matter in ways that are intertwined" (p. 38). Ropers-Huilman and Winters might agree that higher education researchers and practitioners need to understand and foster intersections and the interactions of different groups. Research and practices are needed that highlight and acknowledge intersectionality and accompanying interactions for meaningful paradigm shifts to occur in higher education. While scholars of intersectionality have "mapped the margins" (Crenshaw, 1991), what about the "spaces in between" (Ropers-Huilman & Winters, 2010)?

Another aspect of intersectionality that is undertheorized—and perhaps rightfully so given its original definition—is the intersections of privileged identities and how members of these groups influence marginalized groups. Intersectionality scholarship has focused on populations that are double or multiple minorities, as the intersections of their marginalized statuses amplify their oppressions and highlight their unique experiences (Crenshaw, 1991; Hancock, 2007). However, intersectionally marginalized groups are not oppressed in a vacuum in society. They are oppressed and marginalized by groups who possess power and privilege (e.g., male, White, heterosexual, Christian, and able-bodied privileges;

Yuval-Davis, 2013). Thus, explorations of (a) privileged and oppressed identities and their intersections (Nash, 2008), (b) multiple privileged identities and their intersections, and (c) the bordering, power dynamics, or interrelatedness of privileged and marginalized groups (Yuval-Davis, 2013) are needed to further intersectional praxis specifically within higher education.

The purpose of this text is to document and expand upon the foundational tenets of Crenshaw's (1991) articulation of intersectionality within the context of U.S. higher education. To do this, the volume is organized in three sections: theory, research, and praxis. And within this collection of individual works, the contributors display the ways in which scholars are using and advancing intersectionality in higher education theory, research, and praxis.

Intersectionality is valuable as framework because it is not meant to be solely theoretical; it is a critique that fosters conversations for real-world change and progress. By utilizing the present collection of works, scholars and practitioners may be able to incorporate or enhance the uses of intersectionality in their work so we can begin to move further towards social justice within U.S. higher education contexts. By doing this, we can strengthen the uses of intersectionality and ultimately change higher education as we know it.

REFERENCES

Branch, T. (1989). *Parting the waters: America in the King years 1954–63*. New York, NY: Simon & Schuster.

Crenshaw, K. (1989). Demarginalizing the intersection of race and sex: A Black feminist critique of antidiscrimination doctrine, feminist theory, and antiracist politics. *University of Chicago Legal Forum, 139*, 139–167.

Crenshaw, K. (1991). Mapping the margins: Intersectionality, identity politics, and violence against women of color. *Stanford Law Review, 43*, 1241–1299.

Du Bois, W. E. B. (2010). *The souls of Black folk*. Salem, OR: Bookbyte Digital. (Original work published 1903)

Friedman, T. L. (2005). *The world is flat: A brief history of the twenty-first century*. New York, NY: Farrar, Straus and Giroux.

Ginther, D. K., & Hayes, K. (2003). Gender differences in salary and promotion for faculty in the humanities 1977–95. *Journal of Human Resources, 38*, 34–73.

Glazer-Raymo, J. (2003). Women faculty and part-time employment: The impact of public policy. In B. Ropers-Huilman (Ed.), *Gendered futures in higher education: Critical perspectives for change* (pp. 97–109). Albany: State University of New York Press.

Griffin, K. A., & Museus, S. D. (Eds.). (2011). *Using mixed methods to study intersectionality in higher education: New directions in institutional research* (No. 151). San Francisco, CA: Jossey-Bass.

Hancock, A. (2007). When multiplication doesn't equal quick addition: Examining intersectionality as a research paradigm. *Perspectives on Politics, 5*, 63–79.

Jones, S. R., & Abes, E. S. (2013). *Identity development of college students: Advancing frameworks for multiple dimensions of identity*. San Francisco, CA: Jossey-Bass.

Malcolm, L. E., Dowd, A. C., & Yu, T. (2010). *Tapping HSI-STEM funds to improve Latina and Latino access to the STEM professions.* Los Angeles: University of Southern California.

Nash, J. C. (2008). Re-thinking intersectionality. *Feminist Review, 89,* 1–15.

Pascarella, E. T., & Terenzini, P. (2005). *How college affects students: A third decade of research* (Vol. 2). San Francisco, CA: Jossey-Bass.

Renn, K. A. (2011). Mixed race millennials in college: Multiracial students in the age of Obama. In F. A. Bonner, II, A. F. Marbley, & M. F. Howard-Hamilton (Eds.), *Diverse millennial students in college: Implications for faculty and student affairs* (pp. 227–242). Sterling, VA: Stylus.

Ropers-Huilman, R. A., & Winters, K. T. (2010). Imagining intersectionalities and the spaces in between: Theories and processes of socially transformative knowing. In M. Savin-Baden & C. M. Howell (Eds.), *New approaches to qualitative research: Wisdom and uncertainty* (pp. 37–47). New York, NY: Routledge.

Sax, L. J. (2008). *The gender gap in college: Maximizing the developmental potential of women and men.* San Francisco, CA: Jossey-Bass.

Solow, B. (2004, March 31). Academia under siege. *Independent Online.* Retrieved from http://www.aaup.org/our-work/government-relations/past-campaigns-academic-bill-rights/academia-under-siege

Strayhorn, T. (2012, October 16). *Inalienable rights: Life, liberty and the pursuit of belonging* [video file]. Retrieved from http://tedxcolumbus.com/speakers-performers/2012-the-future-revealed-speakers-performers/dr-terrell-strayhorn/

Strayhorn, T. (Ed.). (2013). *Living at the intersections: Social identities and Black collegians.* Charlotte, NC: Information Age.

Yuval-Davis, Y. (2013, April). *Intersectionality, complexity, and situated bordering.* Paper presented at the Thinking Intersectionality Symposium, Michigan State University, Lansing.

PART ONE

Theory

CHAPTER ONE

Intersectionality, Identity, and Systems of Power and Inequality

CHARMAINE L. WIJEYESINGHE AND SUSAN R. JONES

The concept of identity has received attention in many facets of higher education, including teaching (Adams, Bell, & Griffin, 2007; Goodman & Jackson, 2012; Jones & Wijeyesinghe 2011), research (Cross, 1991; Helms, 1990/1993; Torres, Jones, & Renn, 2009) and student affairs practice (Jones & Abes, 2013; Renn, 2004). Knefelkamp, Widick, and Parker (1978) noted that the developmental orientation of the college student personnel field, in particular, emphasized "the importance of responding to the whole person, attending to individual differences, and working with the student at his or her developmental level" (p. viii). Over the years, the ways in which the "whole person" has been conceptualized has shifted, with varying emphases on the parts and the whole (Torres, Jones, & Renn, 2009), and although the social world and its contexts have always been considered in identity theories, exactly what constitutes context has evolved to also include larger structures of inequality.

In this chapter, we focus on two areas increasingly linked in theory, research, and practice in higher education: models of social identity development (the parts) and the framework of intersectionality (the whole). We begin by exploring how intersectionality addresses themes often seen in the study and representations of identity. Next, we focus more specifically on the implications of applying an intersectional lens to models grounded in individual identity narratives. We conclude the chapter by identifying several issues and questions, referred to as tension points, that have arisen in our work and teaching related to identity and intersectionality.

INTERSECTIONALITY AND PSYCHOSOCIAL PERSPECTIVES ON IDENTITY

The question of "Who Am I?" has been the bedrock of identity research and models for decades. The study of identity in higher education emerged primarily from the psychological tradition of Erik Erikson (1959/1994), who described the psychosocial nature of identity development. From this perspective, identity evolves through a complex pattern of interaction between internal stages of growth and external social forces. Reflecting the sociocultural norms of his time, Erikson's conceptualization of these social forces or contexts led to very narrow views of individuals from nondominant groups. This realization led subsequent scholars in student development, racial identity development, and other fields to investigate social identities as significant contributors to understanding the whole person.

The term *social identity* has its roots in social psychology and the work of Tajfel (1982), who highlighted the role of intergroup dynamics and perceptions of group membership in understanding identity. Tajfel defined social identity as "that part of the individual's self-concept which derives from their knowledge of their membership in a social group (or groups) together with the value and emotional significance attached to that membership" (p. 2). Understanding identities as socially constructed means that "their significance stems not from some 'natural' state, but from what they have become as the result of social and historical processes" (Andersen & Collins, 2007, p. 62). Contemporary understandings of psychosocial identity, or how individuals see and understand their experiences in relation to various groups or roles they inhabit, incorporate specific attention to socially constructed groups that are tied to larger systems of power, privilege, and inequality. As Weber (2010) noted, "[A]t the individual level, race, class, gender, and sexuality are fundamental sources of identity for all of us: how we see ourselves, who we think we are. They are, in fact, so fundamental that to be without them would be like being without an identity at all" (p. 119).

Intersectionality is gaining currency among higher education scholars and practitioners because it acknowledges an individual's multiple social identities, thus creating a more complete portrayal of the whole person. While Dill, McLaughlin, and Nieves (2007) noted that "to a large extent, intersectional work is about identity" (p. 630), it is not *only* about identity (Jones & Abes, 2013). Although Nash (2008) referred to "intersectionality's theoretical dominance as a way of conceptualizing identity" (p. 3), the framework does not seek to unveil how each person within a marginalized group or many groups develops his or her sense of self under systems of oppression. It also does not foreground individual identity narratives (Collins, 2009). Instead, intersectionality highlights how people—as members of multiple groups of individuals—experience marginalization and inequality, even in movements designed to further social justice and institutional change. Clearly, individual voices inform the understanding and analysis of how inequality as well as privilege are experienced. Honoring the day-to-day experiences of *each person*, however, is not a core function of intersectionality.

Intersectionality attends to identity by placing it within a macrolevel analysis that ties individual experience to a person's membership in social groups, during a particular social and historical period, and within larger, interlocking systems of advantage and access. This complex view of identity more fully describes how individuals, as members of social groups constructed and affected by larger systems, experience their lives, interactions, and various contexts (Dill & Zambrana, 2009; Holvino, 2012). In describing her model of *simultaneity*, Holvino (2012) indicated that such an orientation toward identity

> attends to the ways in which race, gender, class, sexuality, and nation are not just about a personal and individual identity, but about the social and institutional processes that determine opportunities, which also produce and reproduce racial, gender, class, and other social differences. (p. 172)

An intersectional perspective also forms a foundation for understanding the interconnections between systems of power and privilege in which personal narratives related to identity develop, evolve, and are understood. Therefore, not only are the experiences of social groups complex and mutually constituted, so are the systems of power and privilege, such as classism, ageism, Christian hegemony, and racism, that so strongly shape personal and group experience. Extending the perspective that identity at the individual level embodies multiple social locations that interact and influence each other to larger social systems allows us to see how forms of oppression interface, support, and reinforce each other, as well as the experience of individual people based on their respective identities (Holvino, 2012). For example, Suzanne Pharr's (1988) classic book, *Homophobia: A Weapon of Sexism*, provides compelling analysis of how the interconnectedness of two systems of oppression, homophobia and sexism, combine with economic issues to create institutional heterosexism. In terms of interventions, Matsuda suggested a technique of "ask[ing] the other question. She wrote "When I see something that looks racist, I ask, 'where is the patriarchy in this?' When I see something that looks sexist, I ask, 'Where is the heterosexism in this?'" (Matsuda, as cited in Nash, 2008, p. 12). This strategy forces an analysis of how these systems reinforce one another and connects privilege and oppression in more complex ways.

INTERSECTIONALITY AND MODELS OF IDENTITY DEVELOPMENT

Several insights are revealed when psychosocial approaches to identity development are examined in the context of intersectionality. First, psychosocial theories often focus on experiences and developmental tasks facing a person or the experience of a person based on one social axis, such as race. Intersectionality complicates identity (Dill & Zambrana, 2009), because it highlights the intricacies of individuals' experiences when they embody multiple identities simultaneously. In addition, intersectionality acknowledges the diversity within social groups, often overlooked in earlier identity theories that described experiences based on a single social identity. Given this complexity and diversity, the question arises as to whether new identity models can legitimately attend to one "Black experience," or a single experience of gay or Lesbian students, since individuals who share one common social identity (such as race, or gender, or faith identity) may differ across several others. Those differences often include multiple locations of privilege and subordination (Collins, 1991; Weber, 2010) that must be acknowledged and integrated into interventions that promote equity and social justice. For example, if a campus organization sponsors a program on the lives of Latino/a students on campus, the event and the chosen speakers should address a range of experiences in addition to those attributed to race, ethnicity, and nationality.

Second, several identity models link an individual's multiple social group memberships and the salience that he or she attaches to each social identity at different life stages or in different contexts (Cross & Fhagen-Smith, 2001; Goodman, this volume; Jones & Abes, 2013; Wijeyesinghe 2001, 2012). While context and salience are reflected in how each person experiences identity in his or her daily life, intersectionality does not directly and purposefully address the concept of salience at the level of each individual's experiences. As opposed to understanding social identities as discrete parts of an individual, each with its own level of personal significance, intersectionality encourages the consideration of multiple identities, notwithstanding the salience individuals attach to them personally. A core tenet of intersectionality addressing the unveiling of power, recognizing interconnected structures of inequality, and promoting social justice, may be helpful in expanding how we view the concept of salience. People may feel drawn to various movements for social change—such as women working to address sexism in the work place—based on the salience they attach to their various social identities. If such actions do not also recognize the interconnection among race, class, and other social memberships, interventions may address the needs of only some of the people within that entire social group, such as White women in the aforementioned example.

Last, linking personal identity narratives to larger systems of domination helps individuals understand the connection between the social groups they inhabit and their day-to-day experiences within society, as well as concepts of privileged and marginalized positions. People working in social justice education often encounter individuals who deny that they receive any social benefit from being, for example, White, male, heterosexual, or economically advantaged. Intersectionality is useful as an awareness-building tool, in that through it, peoples' experiences transcend the lens of individual and personal, to that of a socially constructed group, differentially influenced by access to power and privilege. Increased recognition of the connection between personal identities and social systems that either support or confront oppression is an essential component in engaging people in social justice work (Bell, 1997; Goodman, 2011). Understanding how these systems shape opportunity and experience at the individual level is a cornerstone of anti-oppression work (Adams et al., 2007; Goodman, 2011) and can serve to motivate individuals to engage in actions toward a more just and equitable society, another cornerstone of intersectionality.

In light of the analysis thus far, one may begin to wonder: can models of psychosocial identity development capture core tenets of intersectionality, and are these models examples of intersectional practice? We believe that identity development models can integrate several themes drawn from intersectionality. Jones and Abes (2013) noted that "identity models *informed* [emphasis added] by intersectionality offer better ways of capturing the complexity of identity and portraying the full range of factors, contextual influences, social identities, lived experiences, and structures of power that contribute to a holistic interpretation of identity" (p. 154). Examples of such models include the Intersectional Model of Multiple Dimensions of Identity (Jones & Abes, 2013), the Intersectional Model of Multiracial Identity (Wijeyesinghe, 2012), and Simultaneity (Holvino 2012). To varying degrees, these models acknowledge the interplay among multiple social group memberships (such as race, gender, class, age, sexual orientation) and the fluid nature of identity. In addition, they all specifically reference the impact of larger social, political, institutional, and historical contexts on how individuals develop and experience their identities. Authors of new models exploring individual narratives from an intersectional framework should continue to investigate several areas: how various social group memberships and identities interface and mutually constitute others, how a more universal and omnipresent conception of salience can exist alongside a sense of personal connection to various identities, and how to represent the influence and confluence of all identities in models that primarily focus on one (such as gender, sexual orientation, or race).

TENSION POINTS: ISSUES AND QUESTIONS RELATED TO THE INTERPLAY BETWEEN IDENTITY AND INTERSECTIONALITY

A number of questions emerged as we considered the relationship between identity and intersectionality, how each informs the other, and the issues that arise when we attend to individual narratives, identity, and larger structures of inequality. We use the term *tension points* to describe these questions and issues, and we explore some of the more pressing ones in this section of the chapter. Fundamentally, these tension points reflect, or are informed by such questions as the following: how can evolving conceptualization and application of intersectionality assist in understanding, mapping, researching, and teaching about social identity? Is intersectionality experienced at the individual as well as the social group level? And what, if anything, do psychosocial models that highlight the experiences of individuals offer intersectionality, and how can they inform the development of intersectional interventions in higher education practice?

Identity

As we noted throughout the chapter, an intersectional perspective of identity requires the connecting of individual lived experience to larger structures of privilege and oppression. Therefore, there may be limits to the extent and the ways that intersectionality can be applied to the experience of individuals, even when psychosocial models of identity development include references to larger social systems, power, and privilege. As theorists and practitioners, we are faced with the following question: can identity truly be an individual experience when people embody social identities that carry meaning in society and result in differential access to resources and control of various domains that fundamentally influence a person's life, regardless of whether he or she acknowledges the existence or influence of those identities?

Psychosocial identity models that incorporate intersectional themes, like those examples mentioned in the previous section, can enhance our understanding of key concepts such as social group memberships and social location, institutional power and privilege, and oppression and liberation. This knowledge lays the groundwork for discussions that move beyond individual experiences to how systems of power and privilege support and intersect and the need to create interventions that reflect multiple social locations and concerns.

Tensions between managing the individual experience of identity and further reaching aspects of intersectionality should be considered when planning and implementing actions for social change. Dill et al. (2007) noted that "in the discussion surrounding identity, it is the tension between intersectionality as a tool for illuminating group identities that are not essentialist, and individual identities that are not so fragmented as to be meaningless" (p. 631). Attending to the mutually constituting nature of forms of oppression is not the same as treating them as the same or as so intertwined that the ways in which they differ become unrecognizable or disappear. Therefore, theories and change efforts must acknowledge common aspects and interconnections, while also attending to areas where experiences of identity and forms of inequality differ. Intersectionality, with its emphasis on individual and social location within multiple groups, pushes researchers, faculty, and practitioners to acknowledge the diversity within socially constructed groups, while avoiding the obscuring of real differences between manifestations of oppression by applying intersectionality uniformly (Luft, 2009).

Salience

In relation to identity, intersectionality illustrates how we embody all of our social identities and experience the world based on larger, interconnected systems that respond to these identities, at all times and in all circumstances. Weber (1998) pointed out the following:

> Race, class, gender, and sexuality simultaneously operate in every social situation. At the societal level, these systems of social hierarchies are connected to each other and are embedded in all social institutions. At the individual level, we each experience our lives and develop our identities based on our location along all dimensions, whether we are in dominant groups, subordinate groups, or both. (p. 24)

Tension may arise when individuals feel that their lived experience reflects one, or only some of their social identities, as when a gay, White man who is economically privileged feels that his identity is grounded primarily in his sexual orientation and resists considering how his race, economic position, and gender afford him social power and privilege. Intersectionality frames all identities as being mutually constituted, meaning that social identities are not discrete entities that are isolated from the influences of all others. Therefore, while the man described here may define himself and view the world primarily through the lens of sexual orientation, his class, race, emotional and physical ability, faith background, and other social groups also influence his particular experiences as a gay man. Thus, his experiences of being gay would be different if one or more of his other identities changed, for example, if he were Asian or economically disadvantaged. Scholars and practitioners may encounter challenges to operationalizing core tenets of intersectionality when there are perceived gaps between the lived experience of identity salience by the individuals with whom they are working and the perspective that all identities are at play at all times.

Tension related to salience also occurs at the systems levels of analysis. At a broader social level, intersectionality highlights that it is not possible to grasp an understanding of the complex interplay of power, privilege, and social structures if we view forms of oppression as singular and separate units (like racism, ableism, sexism, classism), or if the focus is only on those forms of oppression that feel most salient to an individual, in a specific setting, or at a certain point in life. A more intersectional level of awareness recognizes

> that each of us simultaneously experiences all of these dimensions, even if one is foregrounded in a particular situation, and can help us see the often obscured ways in which we benefit from existing race, class, gender, sexuality social arrangements, as well as the ways which we're disadvantaged. Such an awareness can be key in working together across different groups to achieve a more equitable distribution of society's valued resources. (Weber, 1998, p. 25)

Decades after Lorde (1983) so aptly highlighted that there is no hierarchy of oppressions, individuals may still feel that there is, based on how they live and experience their range of social identities.

Privileged and Oppressed Identities

Intersectionality centers the voices of people and groups previously overlooked or excluded, especially in the analysis of inequality and efforts to remedy specific social problems. An ongoing debate among intersectional scholars and observers of the popularity of the framework foregrounds the question of definition—what exactly is intersectionality and who is intersectional (Nash, 2008; Warner & Shields, 2013)? Stated another way, is intersectionality a general theory of identities or a theory focused only on those people from multiple marginalized social groups? Nash (2008) argued, "In its emphasis on black women's experiences of subjectivity and oppression, intersectional theory has obscured the question of whether all identities are intersectional, or whether only multiply marginalized subjects have an intersectional identity" (p. 9). If intersectionality is applied as a general theory of identity, all people may locate themselves within its purview. However, if intersectionality is primarily grounded in the experiences of individuals with multiple marginalized identities, those people with privileged identities are outside of the framework. Of course, many individuals inhabit both privileged and oppressed identities, so these boundaries may not be so clearly drawn.

What seems critical to us is what Nash (2008) advocated for as "a nuanced conception of identity that recognizes the ways in which positions of dominance and subordination work in complex and intersecting ways to constitute subjects' experience of personhood" (p. 10). The question of whether intersectionality applies to everyone reinforces a point made earlier, that intersectionality is not simply about multiple identities, which we all have, but multiple identities connected to groups and structures of power, thus, paving the way for a "both/and" approach. Considering the application and relevance of intersectionality to people and groups who receive social advantages begins to draw some boundaries related to privileged and oppressed identities.

The purpose of intersectionality is not simply to locate individuals within a matrix of domination and privilege. Instead, intersectionality sheds light on the ways that some people within social groups receive benefit while others are disproportionately targeted and constrained by certain social-structural situations (this was Crenshaw's [1991] initial analysis of the inutility of a gender-only lens when investigating domestic violence against women). Yet, individuals who hold multiple privileged identities can use an intersectional analysis in ways that are productive and contribute to a more socially just society. The task then becomes less about locating oneself within an intersectional framework and more so about using intersectionality to understand the experiences of others and the social structures that perpetuate privilege and oppression.

From discussion, research, and application of intersectionality in various settings, we may develop a greater awareness of how intersectionality captures the lived experiences of people who hold multiple privileged identities or how experiences related to these identities are mediated by any targeted groups to which these individuals belong. Caution is advised, however, so that the core tenet of intersectionality related to foregrounding the experience of marginalized groups remains central to its understanding and application and to prevent it from becoming a lens that is co-opted to reinforce and re-center the experience of those people and groups with privileged identities.

CONCLUSION

In closing this chapter, we reaffirm that identity and intersectionality are relevant to each other and can be used to explore questions and areas unanswered by foundational theories within the fields of student, racial, and social identity development. As authors of two models that are informed by intersectionality, we see psychosocial models that incorporate aspects of the framework as tools to enhance our understanding of the experiences of individuals and groups on campus. Yet, as new theories and approaches evolve, we also pay homage to the context, goals, and contributions of existing theories, especially those models that paved the way in the early years and formed the foundation for research and theory building related to identity.

Intersectionality is a powerful tool for understanding, constructing, and deconstructing: the experience of identity, the complex and mutually constituting nature of social identities, the relationships between identity and larger social systems, and the interwoven nature of manifestations of social oppression. While centering the interconnections inherent in intersectional analysis, we also must honor the unique aspects of various social identities, systems of inequality, and efforts to enact social justice. The journey of writing this chapter has led us to see that in relation to identity and intersectionality, the situation is not one of "either/or" when it comes to the exploration of individual narratives or narratives of larger group experiences influenced by social systems. Instead, we appreciate how these two levels of analysis inform each other, contribute to our understanding of identity, stretch our thinking, drive model building, and guide our work. Thus, our efforts as theorists, researchers, and practitioners becomes less about "capturing" intersectionality via models and more about using the complexity and connections in the framework to more fully understand the lived experience of individuals within the context of their social groups, oppression and inequality, and interventions for social change.

REFERENCES

Adams, M., Bell, L. A., & Griffin, P. (2007). *Teaching for diversity and social justice* (2nd ed.). New York, NY: Routledge.

Andersen, M. L., & Collins, P. H. (Eds.) (2007). *Race, class, & gender: An anthology* (7th ed., pp. 61–86). Belmont, CA: Thomson/Wadsworth.

Bell, L. A. (1997). Theoretical foundations for social justice education. In M. Adams, L. A. Bell, & P. Griffin (Eds.), *Teaching for diversity and social justice: A sourcebook* (pp. 3–15). New York, NY: Routledge.

Collins, P. H. (1991). *Black feminist thought: Knowledge, consciousness, and the politics of empowerment.* New York, NY: Routledge.

Collins, P. H. (2007). Pushing the boundaries or business as usual? Race, class, and gender studies and sociological inquiry. In C. J. Calhoun (Ed.), *Sociology in America: A history* (pp. 572–604). Chicago, IL: University of Chicago.

Collins, P. H. (2009). Foreword: Emerging intersections—Building knowledge and transforming institutions. In B. T. Dill & R. E. Zambrana (Eds.), *Emerging intersections: Race, class, and gender in theory, policy, and practice* (pp. vii–xiii). New Brunswick, NJ: Rutgers University Press.

Crenshaw, K. (1991). Mapping the margins: Intersectionality, identity politics, and violence against women of color. *Stanford Law Review, 43,* 1241–1299.

Cross, W. E. (1991). *Shades of black: Diversity in African-American identity.* Philadelphia, PA: Temple University Press.

Cross, W. E., & Fhagen-Smith, P. (2001). Patterns of African-American identity development: A life span perspective. In C. L. Wijeyesinghe & B. W. Jackson (Eds.), *New perspectives on racial identity development: A theoretical and practical anthology* (pp. 243–270). New York: New York University Press.

Dill, B. T., McLaughlin, A. E., & Nieves, A. D. (2007). Future directions of feminist research: Intersectionality. In S. N. Hesse-Biber (Ed.), *Handbook of feminist research* (pp. 629–637). Thousand Oaks, CA: Sage.

Dill, B. T., & Zambrana, R. E. (2009). Critical thinking about inequality: An emerging lens. In B. T. Dill & R. E. Zambrana (Eds.), *Emerging intersections: Race, class, and gender in theory, policy, and practice* (pp. 1–21). New Brunswick, NJ: Rutgers University Press.

Erikson, E. H. (1959/1994). *Identity and the life cycle.* New York, NY: W. W. Norton.

Goodman, D. J. (2011). *Promoting diversity and social justice: Educating people from privileged groups* (2nd ed.). New York, NY: Routledge.

Goodman, D. J., & Jackson, B. W. III (2012). Pedagogical approaches to teaching about racial identity from an intersectional perspective. In C. L. Wijeyesinghe & B. W. Jackson III (Eds.), *New perspectives on racial identity development* (2nd ed., pp. 216–239). New York: New York University Press.

Helms, J. E. (1990/1993). *Black and white racial identity theory, research, and practice.* Westport, CT: Praeger.

Holvino, E. (2012). The "simultaneity" of identities: Models and skills. In C. L. Wijeyesinghe & B. W. Jackson III (Eds.), *New perspectives on racial identity development* (2nd ed., pp. 161–191). New York: New York University Press.

Jones, S. R., & Abes, E. S. (2013). *Identity development of college students.* San Francisco, CA: Jossey-Bass.

Jones, S. R., & Wijeyesinghe, C. L. (2011). The promise and challenge of teaching from an intersectional perspective: Core components and applied strategies. In M. L. Ouellett (Ed.), *An integrative analysis approach to diversity in the college classroom: New directions for teaching and learning* (No. 125, pp. 11–20). San Francisco, CA: Jossey-Bass.

Knefelkamp, L., Widick, C., & Parker, C. (Eds.) (1978). *Applying new developmental findings: New directions for student services* (No. 4). San Francisco, CA: Jossey-Bass.

Lorde, A. (1983). *There is no hierarchy of oppressions.* New York, NY: Council on Interracial Books for Children.

Luft, R. E. (2009). Intersectionality and the risk of flattening difference: Gender and race logics, and the strategic use of antiracist singularity. In M. T. Berger & K. Guidroz (Eds.), *The intersectional approach: Transforming the academy through race, class, & gender* (pp. 100–1117). Chapel Hill: The University of North Carolina Press.

Nash, J. C. (2008). Re-thinking intersectionality. *Feminist Review, 89,* 1–15.

Pharr, S. (1988). *Homophobia: A weapon of sexism.* Inverness, CA: Chardon.

Renn, K. A. (2004). *Mixed race students in college: The ecology of race, identity, and community.* Albany: State University of New York Press.

Tajfel, H. (Ed.). (1982). *Social identity and intergroup relations.* Cambridge, UK: Cambridge University Press.

Torres, V., Jones, S. R., & Renn, K. A. (2009). Identity development theories in student affairs: Origins, current status, and new approaches. *Journal of College Student Development, 50,* 577–596.

Warner, L. R., & Shields, S. A. (2013). The intersections of sexuality, gender, and race: Identity research at the crossroads. *Sex Roles, 68,* 803–810.

Weber, L. (1998). A conceptual framework for understanding race, class, gender, and sexuality. *Psychology of Women Quarterly, 22,* 13–22.

Weber, L. (2010). *Understanding race, class, gender, and sexuality* (2nd ed.). New York, NY: Oxford University Press.

Wijeyesinghe, C. L. (2001). Racial identity in multiracial people an alternative paradigm. In C. L. Wijeyesinghe & B. W. Jackson III (Eds.), *New perspectives on racial identity development: A theoretical and practical anthology* (pp. 129–152). New York: New York University Press.

Wijeyesinghe, C. L. (2012). The intersectional model of multiracial identity: Integrating multiracial identity theories and intersectional perspectives on social identity. In C. L. Wijeyesinghe & B. W. Jackson III (Eds.), *New perspectives on racial identity development* (2nd ed., pp. 81–107). New York: New York University Press.

CHAPTER TWO

Racial Privilege, Gender Oppression, and Intersectionality

CLAIRE KATHLEEN ROBBINS AND STEPHEN JOHN QUAYE

In higher education, student affairs professionals work with college students in multiple settings to promote student learning, engagement, and development. Although students of color represent a growing proportion of the contemporary college-going population, the majority of the student affairs profession remains White and female (Olson, 2010; Renn & Jessup-Anger, 2008; Taub & McEwen, 2006; Tull, 2006). Practitioners and scholars have been right to insist on the need to recruit and retain more people of color and members of other historically underrepresented groups in the profession (Olson, 2010; Renn & Jessup-Anger, 2008). Still, educators too rarely scrutinize the structures of power and privilege (Brookfield, 2005; Johnson, 2006), especially White privilege, that undergird the historical underrepresentation of people of color in student affairs (Bondi, 2012). Remaining silent about White privilege in student affairs "may unwittingly contribute to the universalization of Whiteness, and consequently, the marginalization of non-White racial identities" (Ortiz & Rhoads, 2000, p. 81) in the profession.

One way to disrupt the universalization of Whiteness in student affairs is to facilitate racial consciousness among White professionals in general, and White women in particular, given their overrepresentation in the field. Ortiz and Rhoads (2000) found that for White student affairs professionals, developing racial consciousness requires coming to terms with one's White identity. Students in higher education and student affairs (HESA) graduate preparation programs may study theories of White racial consciousness and identity (e.g., Hardiman, 2001; Helms,

1995; McIntosh, 1988/2004; Tatum, 2003), particularly in student development theory courses (Evans, Forney, Guido, Patton, & Renn, 2010). Yet, as one of many topics in a single course, White racial consciousness and identity may receive limited attention. Further, HESA graduate preparation programs are uneven in their degree of focus on diversity and multiculturalism, and students report inadequate opportunities to apply these topics in their work settings (Gayles & Kelly, 2007). Even among those who study the topic in depth, traditional theories of White racial consciousness and identity development address only one dimension of identity, despite growing evidence that individuals experience multiple, intersecting dimensions of social identity simultaneously (Jones & Abes, 2013).

Among White women, theories of White racial consciousness and identity may not resonate due to a combination of resistance (Gillespie, Ashbaugh, & DeFiore, 2002; Watt, 2007) and the invisibility of gender and other salient dimensions of identity (Jones & Abes, 2013). As Accapadi (2007) astutely observed, White women have a "one up/one down identity" (p. 210) and thus "can be both helpless without the helplessness being a reflection of all White people and powerful by occupying a position of power as any White person" (p. 210). This phenomenon reflects the realities of intersectionality: "[T]he processes through which multiple social identities converge and ultimately shape individual and group experiences" (Museus & Griffin, 2011, p. 7). Based on the latter definition, an intersectional perspective on White women in higher education and student affairs "necessarily situates identity within larger structures of power and privilege" (Jones, 2009, p. 289) and recognizes that the convergence of racial privilege and gender oppression is more than the sum of its parts. Yet, HESA graduate students encounter few theories reflecting an intersectional perspective.

Taken together, the relatively unexamined nature of White privilege in student affairs, limitations of existing White identity theories, uneven focus on diversity and multiculturalism, and overrepresentation of White women in the profession highlight an important gap in the theoretical literature guiding the work of student affairs professionals. The absence of a theory of racial identity that resonates with White women's identity intersections may impede the process of understanding one's racial identity, and thus, the formation of White racial consciousness (Ortiz & Rhoads, 2000) among a significant, if not majority, population in the profession.

To address this gap, Robbins (2012) investigated racial consciousness, identity, and dissonance among White women in student affairs graduate preparation programs. The outcome of this study was a grounded theory that illustrated the interconnected nature of racial consciousness, identity, and dissonance among White women as they confronted the complex realities of racism and White privilege. Participants in Robbins's study displayed many examples of defensiveness and resistance, a hallmark of privileged identity exploration (Gillespie et al., 2002; Watt, 2007), especially among those who are not developmentally ready to encounter the concept of White privilege (Ortiz & Rhoads, 2000). Yet, multiple participants in Robbins's study struggled to confront racism in family, work, and educational settings in which they were directly targeted by sexism. Acknowledging the struggle to integrate multiple identities need not be counterproductive to the struggle to dismantle racism; yet, White women and U.S. feminist movements have repeatedly marginalized women of color and anti-racist movements (Lippin, 2007; Lugones, 1990; Sandoval, 1982/1990). Accapadi (2007) has written about how these same dynamics have led White women to do harm to women of color in student affairs.

How, then, can an intersectional perspective help us explore the relatively unexamined topic of identity among White women in higher education and student affairs? The purpose of this chapter is to engage this question by exploring findings from Robbins's (2012) study using a pedagogical approach grounded in principles of intergroup dialogue (Nagda & Maxwell, 2011; Quaye, 2012). Specifically, we use intergroup dialogue principles to consider selected findings from Robbins's study from three different perspectives: gender oppression, racial privilege, and the intersection of gender oppression and racial privilege. Through this approach, we illuminate the value of intersectionality for understanding racial consciousness and identity, as well as the complex intersections of racial privilege and gender oppression, among White women in student affairs. We conclude with implications for theory and practice in student affairs and higher education.

OVERVIEW OF ROBBINS'S STUDY

The methodological approach to this study was constructivist grounded theory for social justice (Charmaz, 2005, 2006). Participants were 11 White women, ages 23 to 28, enrolled full-time in their third of four semesters in a HESA master's degree program (with no two participants in the same program). Recruited nationally, participants were selected from a pool of 135 individuals who completed an initial interest form. Maximum variation sampling (Creswell, 2007) facilitated the construction of an inclusive sample in terms of social identities (e.g., gender expression, sexual orientation, dis/ability, religion), educational experiences (e.g., being a first-generation college or graduate student, studying abroad), and other life experiences (e.g., growing up in a military family, surviving interpersonal violence, having a gay parent).

Data sources included two intensive interviews (Charmaz, 2006) with each participant. Initial face-to-face interviews focused on participants' race-related experiences during childhood, high school, and college. Follow-up phone interviews explored racial identity, Whiteness, and White privilege within participants' postcollege, professional, and HESA graduate school experiences. Both interviews were digitally recorded and transcribed verbatim. Consistent with constructivist grounded theory for social justice, data analysis procedures included initial, focused, axial, and theoretical coding (Charmaz, 2006) to "locate subjective and collective experience in larger structures" (Charmaz, 2005, p. 508), such as racism and White privilege. Memo writing and the constant comparative approach facilitated the development, explication, and saturation of theoretical categories (Charmaz, 2006) related to White racial consciousness and identity. As a means of establishing trustworthiness (Jones, Torres, & Arminio, 2014), the researcher shared a short summary of the emerging theory and a one-page participant profile with each participant. Seven out of 11 participants responded, each expressing that she saw herself in the emerging theory.

EXPLORING SELECTED FINDINGS WITH AN INTERGROUP DIALOGUE FRAMEWORK

Intergroup dialogues bring together two groups of people that have a history of conflict to explore the sources of conflict, reflect on their intersected identities, and bridge differences and build alliances (Zúñiga, 2003). A critical component of these dialogues is that they are co-facilitated by members representing the identity group at the center of the dialogue. For example, a dialogue on gender might be co-facilitated by two individuals with different gender identities, and these identities would ideally be balanced in the group of 12–15 participants. According to Nagda and Maxwell (2011), these dialogues have a critical-dialogic framework, which works to engage participants in examining their individual roles in maintaining systems of oppression and how they might work to actively resist and transform these structures.

In Quaye's (2012) research on White educators facilitating racial dialogues, he found that a key strategy these educators employed was reflecting on their White racial identities and the privileges afforded by this racial identity. Consequently, a key advantage of utilizing intergroup dialogues to engage intersectionality is the acknowledgment of one's privileged and marginalized identities in the reflection that ensues from these dialogues. This reflection is necessary for considering ways to make meaning of one's role in addressing interlocking systems of oppression even as one might be marginalized and privileged simultaneously along the spectrum of their identities.

Having laid the groundwork for intergroup dialogues, we shift beyond the normal usage of these dialogues, which involves students exploring topics like race, class, gender, and sexual orientation in open and honest ways, to engage a dialogue, of sorts, between different theoretical frameworks that help us address the complexities of racial privilege and gender oppression colliding. In so doing, we borrow language from Abes (2009), who articulated the value of situating students' experiences in "theoretical borderlands" (p. 143) as a way to foreground "the messiness and complexity" (p. 150) of identity development. This theoretical dialogue illustrates the value of an intersectional perspective for understanding how racial privilege and gender oppression influence White women who are preparing to become higher education and student affairs professionals.

DIALOGUE BETWEEN THEORIES

In this section, we engage in a dialogue between theoretical perspectives highlighting gender oppression, racial privilege, and the intersection of these two realities to illustrate the value of an intersectional approach. In each section, we introduce selected findings from Robbins's (2012) study. Next, we introduce the work of one or more theorists to draw connections between participants' experiences and the arguments advanced by the theorists.

"I Hate Saying That Out Loud, but It's an Issue": A Gender Oppression Perspective

One participant in Robbins's (2012) study who highlighted gender oppression was Stacy (all names from Robbins's study are pseudonyms), a graduate assistant in student activities at a mid-Atlantic university. Stacy struggled to translate her knowledge about racism and White privilege into action because her work environment was dominated by White male cultural norms, which suggested to her that diversity was "not our responsibility" and difficult conversations should be avoided. When she overheard a student's racist comment during a leadership retreat, Stacy almost spoke up but thought better of it when she remembered her office environment. Recalling this decision to remain silent, Stacy acknowledged that she had missed an opportunity to challenge racism but had done so because of fear of repercussions for speaking out as a Woman: "Part of that battle is dealing with that power. And I think it is an issue for women.... I hate saying that out loud, but it's an issue."

Stacy's experience echoes the argument of Pasque and Nicholson (2011) that "the lived and systemic nature of sexism continues to prevail" in higher education and student affairs (p. xvi). Defined as oppression based on gender, sexism continues to emerge in research about policy, practice, and the lived experiences of students, staff, faculty, and administrators across multiple institutional types, within-college environments, and geographical locations (Pasque & Nicholson, 2011). Pasque and Nicholson's description and Stacy's lived experience both evoke words from Gilligan's "Letter to Readers" in the 1993 edition of *In a Different*

Voice, the groundbreaking book on moral and ethical development among women: "Choices not to speak are often well-intentioned and psychologically protective.... And yet by restricting their voices, many women are wittingly or unwittingly perpetuating a male-voiced civilization" (pp. x–xi). Stacy's decision reflects this tension between protecting oneself and reinforcing sexism, illuminating the challenges of individual oppression and systemic change. Still, Stacy's story also raises a troubling question: Even though they experience sexism, don't White women still have a responsibility to speak out against racism? To explore this question, we now shift the theoretical dialogue to a consideration of racial privilege.

"My Heritage Is Part of That Problem": A Racial Privilege Perspective

Becky, another participant in Robbins's (2012) study, credited her college coursework in sociology with teaching her about structural inequality, racism, and White privilege. Learning about racial privilege pushed Becky to move beyond White guilt, a form of cognitive dissonance, to a more complex understanding of racism: "This is a societal problem and my heritage is part of that problem, and I need to be aware that created problems for People [of Color] and that created privilege for me." This newfound awareness led Becky to work through White guilt and form a "vision for her life" as an educator; at the time of Robbins's study, Becky's vision was "to make things better for everybody, especially people who have had it really rough."

Becky's story echoes Watt's (2007) model of Privileged Identity Exploration (PIE), which emerged from research with helping professionals who took a dialogue-based course on multiculturalism. The model includes three layers, the first of which identifies "Dissonance Provoking Stimuli" on a continuum from "New Awareness About Self or Other" to "Social Justice Action Based on New Awareness" (Watt, 2007, p. 126). In the second and third layers, the model includes eight defense mechanisms employed by those with privileged identities when experiencing cognitive dissonance as a result of classroom dialogues about race, class, gender, and sexual orientation. These mechanisms correspond to three phases of development: "Recognizing Privileged Identity," "Contemplating Privileged Identity," and "Addressing Privileged Identity" (Watt, 2007, p. 126).

Watt's (2007) model is illustrated by Becky's developmental process of making meaning of racial privilege. Becky's sociology coursework constituted a dissonance-provoking stimulus that created a new level of awareness about the role of racism in shaping her experiences, as well as the experiences of people of color. Prior to this coursework, Becky's interpretation of racial privilege was consistent with the "Recognizing Privileged Identity" phase and one of its associated defense mechanisms, *denial* (i.e., denying that her heritage is part of the "societal problem" of racism). Through coursework, Becky recognized her privileged racial identity and sought out opportunities to contemplate it more deeply. After additional coursework and co-curricular experiences, Becky offered an explanation of racial privilege (i.e., "this is a societal problem") consistent with *intellectualization,* a defense mechanism associated with the "Contemplating Privileged Identity" phase. At the time of the study, Becky's understanding of racial privilege reflected the defense mechanism of *benevolence* (i.e., the desire "to make things better for everybody, especially people who have had it really rough"), which aligns with the "Addressing Privileged Identity" phase.

Importantly, Watt's (2007) PIE model and Becky's story suggest that making meaning of racial privilege is a complex process in which individuals display multiple defense mechanisms. Yet, Stacy's story (Robbins, 2012) raises a concern not fully addressed by a "Privileged Identity" perspective: gender oppression may influence the way White women make meaning of racial privilege. How might intersections of racial privilege and gender oppression complicate the identities and experiences of White women who are preparing to become higher education and student affairs professionals? Engaging this question exposes what Gorski (2011) called the "most heavy-handedly enforced rule" of conversations about White privilege: "*Nobody shall, during a conversation about white privilege, mention any identity that is not a racial identity or any oppression that is not racism*" (para. 8). We break this rule in the following section, which shifts the theoretical dialogue about White women to an intersectional perspective.

"There's Privilege and Oppression": An Intersectionality Perspective

Although several participants in Robbins's (2012) study openly discussed the complex intersection between racial privilege and gender oppression that White women occupy, Sally's reflection captured this phenomenon succinctly, beginning with these words: "At that intersectionality of White and female, there's privilege and oppression. And at that intersectionality of White and male, there's privilege and privilege." Sally's use of the word *intersectionality* mirrors both the foundational definition offered by Crenshaw (1991; see Preface) and the more recent one by higher education scholars Museus and Griffin (2011): "[T]he processes through which multiple social identities converge and ultimately shape individual and group experiences" (p. 7). Based on the latter definition, an intersectional perspective on White women in higher education and student affairs "necessarily situates identity within larger structures of power and privilege" (Jones, 2009, p. 289) and recognizes that the convergence of racial privilege and gender oppression is more than the sum of its parts.

Much of the intersectional scholarship in higher education has examined intragroup differences, particularly in historically marginalized groups (Jones, 2009; Museus & Griffin, 2011; Strayhorn, 2013). These contributions illuminate the shortcomings of an additive approach, as echoed in Sally's observations about gender differences among White individuals and racial differences among women. Recalling her process of learning about race and gender in a graduate school course about diversity, Sally mused, "I think it was easier maybe for me to understand oppression than it was for me to understand privilege, because I do feel oppressed as a Woman. But a man would not understand what that feels like." However, Sally also realized there might be experiences she as a White person could not understand:

> We had conversations about what it means to be a Black Woman and what it means to be a White Woman.... One girl made a specific comment about how we may both be women but people don't change sides of the street when you walk down.

Sally's observations elucidate what another participant, Michelle, called the "double-edged sword" of being a White Woman. The image of a sword evokes a conflict and, therefore, possibilities for dialogue (Zúñiga, 2003) among racial privilege, gender oppression, and intersectional perspectives.

IMPLICATIONS FOR STUDENT AFFAIRS

Findings from Robbins's (2012) study suggest that racial privilege protects White women from racism, and thus, from a racialized form of gender oppression that targets Black women as people to be feared when walking down the street. Other forms of sexism, however, still appear to shape White women's realities in higher education and student affairs. Stacy's hesitation to speak up about racism illuminates the consequences of the collision between racial privilege and gender oppression. Racial privilege offers White women the freedom of "choices not to speak" (Gilligan, 1993, p. x) about racism *or* sexism, and thus, to perpetuate multiple silences that may do harm to all historically marginalized groups in higher education and student affairs. Can an intersectional perspective provide new promise?

Addressing aspiring White anti-racist allies, Kivel (2002) argued compellingly that "[w]e must notice when we try to slip into another identity and escape being white" (p. 9). Some anti-racist scholars and activists have described such slippages as, at least in part, resistance or a rationalization (e.g., Watt, 2007) that White individuals employ to avoid acknowledging their complicity in racist power structures. Still, other scholars have argued that "slipping into another identity" is not solely a form of resistance; rather, acknowledging identity intersections can advance one's understanding of privilege and oppression (e.g., Gorski, 2011). In fact, Gorski (2011) argued that silencing dialogue about intersecting identities may pit race and class against each other, thus excluding working-class and poor White individuals while also diminishing the capacity of racial justice movements.

We, too, contend that participants' struggle to integrate their racial and other social identities is not solely resistant; rather, it reflects the complexities of identity development at the intersections (Jones, 2009). To dismiss this struggle would be to contribute to a discourse of whiteness that leaves other identities unmarked, and thus, reinforces compulsory masculinity, heterosexuality, and economic privilege—which, in turn, reinforce White supremacy (Collins, 2009). Further, acknowledging the struggle to integrate multiple identities need not be counterproductive to the struggle to dismantle racism, and it is not intended as a rationalization (Watt, 2007) that fails to hold White people accountable. Rather, honoring identity at the intersections (Jones, 2009) reflects our desire to foreground White privilege without excluding those who experience oppression associated with other identities.

The theoretical dialogue we have engaged in this chapter is intended to promote practical forms of dialogue in student affairs as well. Through an intersectional perspective, White women can reflect both individually and collectively on racial privilege without ignoring the realities of gender oppression. HESA graduate preparation programs offer many opportunities for such reflection to occur. Participating in intergroup dialogues might enable White women in higher education and student affairs to recognize when they may be placing too much emphasis on their oppressed gender identity while ignoring the ways in which gender works with race to offer advantages often unseen. Graduate preparation faculty could invite students to read Robbins's (2012) study and write reflection papers about their own experiences or observations about the intersections between gender and race.

Above all, we encourage those who educate HESA graduate students to heed the advice implied by Gorski's (2000) poignant reflection: "I found that it was not the experience of studying whiteness, but the process of examining my whiteness, that became vital to my development as an educator" (para. 1). For White women in student affairs, such development should include taking responsibility for racial privilege and the challenges associated with their overrepresentation in the field. This challenge, like many others in contemporary higher education, requires us to engage in difficult dialogues, recognize complex identity intersections, and explore theoretical borderlands (Abes, 2009). As we and the other authors of this volume have conveyed, the messiness of the work ahead need not derail us, as the emergent possibilities for student learning, engagement, and development offer new promise that is sure to be worth the struggle.

REFERENCES

Abes, E. S. (2009). Theoretical borderlands: Using multiple theoretical perspectives to challenge inequitable power structures in student development theory. *Journal of College Student Development, 50*, 141–156.

Accapadi, M. M. (2007). When white women cry: How white women's tears oppress women of color. *The College Student Affairs Journal, 26*, 208–215.

Bondi, S. (2012). Students and institutions protecting whiteness as property: A critical race theory analysis of student affairs preparation. *Journal of Student Affairs Research and Practice, 49*, 397–414.

Brookfield, S. D. (2005). *The power of critical theory: Liberating adult learning and teaching.* San Francisco, CA: Jossey-Bass.

Charmaz, K. (2005). Grounded theory in the 21st century: A qualitative method for advancing social justice research. In N. K. Denzin & Y. S. Lincoln (Eds.), *Handbook of qualitative research* (3rd ed., pp. 507–535). Thousand Oaks, CA: Sage.

Charmaz, K. (2006). *Constructing grounded theory: A practical guide through qualitative analysis.* Thousand Oaks, CA: Sage.

Collins, P. H. (2009). *Black Feminist Thought: Knowledge, consciousness, and the politics of empowerment* (2nd ed.). New York, NY: Routledge.

Crenshaw, K. (1991). Mapping the margins: Intersectionality, identity politics, and violence against women of color. *Stanford Law Review, 43,* 1241–1299.

Creswell, J. W. (2007). *Qualitative inquiry and research design.* Thousand Oaks, CA: Sage.

Evans, N. J., Forney, D. S., Guido, F. M., Patton, L. D., & Renn, K. A. (2010). *Student development in college: Theory, research, and practice* (2nd ed.). San Francisco, CA: Jossey-Bass.

Gayles, J. G., & Kelly, B. T. (2007). Experiences with diversity in the curriculum: Implications for graduate programs and student affairs practice. *NASPA Journal, 44,* 193–208.

Gillespie, D., Ashbaugh, L., & DeFiore, J. (2002). White women teaching white women about white privilege, race cognizance and social action: Toward a pedagogical pragmatics. *Race, Ethnicity and Education, 5,* 237–253.

Gilligan, C. (1993). *In a different voice: Psychological theory and women's development* (2nd ed.). Cambridge, MA: Harvard University Press.

Gorski, P. (2000). Narrative of whiteness and multicultural education. *Electronic Magazine of Multicultural Education, 21,* 43 paragraphs. Retrieved from http://www.eastern.edu/publications/emme/2000spring/gorski.html

Gorski, P. (2011, December). Complicating "white privilege." *Counterpunch.* Retrieved from http://www.counterpunch.org/2011/12/30/complicating-white-privilege/

Hardiman, R. (2001). Reflections on white identity development theory. In C. L. Wijeyesinghe & B. W. Jackson, III (Eds.), *New perspectives on racial identity development: A theoretical and practical anthology* (pp. 108–128). New York, NY: New York University Press.

Helms, J. E. (1995). An update of Helms's white and People of Color racial identity models. In J. G. Ponterotto, L. Casas, A. Suzuki & C. M. Alexander (Eds.), *Handbook of multicultural counseling* (pp. 181–198). Thousand Oaks, CA: SAGE.

Johnson, A. G. (2006). *Privilege, power, and difference.* New York, NY: McGraw-Hill.

Jones, S. R. (2009). Constructing identities at the intersections: An autoethnographic exploration of multiple dimensions of identity. *Journal of College Student Development, 50,* 287–304.

Jones, S. R., & Abes, E. S. (2013). *Identity development of college students: Advancing frameworks for multiple dimensions of identity.* San Francisco, CA: Jossey-Bass.

Jones, S. R., Torres, V., & Arminio, J. (2014). *Negotiating the complexities of qualitative research in higher education: Fundamental elements and issues* (2nd ed.) New York, NY: Routledge.

Kivel, P. (2002). *Uprooting racism: How white people can work for racial justice* (2nd ed.). Gabriola Island, British Columbia, Canada: New Society.

Lippin, L. B. (2007). Making whiteness visible in the classroom. In V. Lea & J. Helfand (Eds.), *Identifying race and transforming whiteness in the classroom* (pp. 109–131). New York, NY: Peter Lang.

Lugones, M. (1990). Hablando cara a cara/speaking face to face: An exploration of ethnocentric racism. In G. Anzaldúa (Ed.), *Making face, making soul/haciendo caras: Creative and critical perspectives by women of color* (pp. 46–54). San Francisco, CA: Aunt Lute.

McIntosh, P. (1988/2004). White privilege and male privilege: A personal account of coming to see correspondences through work in women's studies. In M. L. Anderson & P. H. Collins (Eds.), *Race, class and gender: An anthology* (pp. 70–81). Belmont, CA: Wadsworth Publishing Company.

Museus, S. D., & Griffin, K. A. (2011). Mapping the margins in higher education: On the promise of intersectionality frameworks in research and discourse. In S. D. Museus & K. A. Griffin (Eds.), *Using mixed-method approaches to study intersectionality in higher education: New directions for institutional research* (No. 151, pp. 5–13). San Francisco, CA: Jossey-Bass.

Nagda, B. A., & Maxwell, K. E. (2011). Deepening the layers of understanding and connection: A critical-dialogic approach to facilitating intergroup dialogues. In K. E. Maxwell, B. A. Nagda, & M. C. Thompson (Eds.), *Facilitating intergroup dialogues: Bridging differences, catalyzing change* (pp. 1–22). Sterling, VA: Stylus.

Olson, B. A. (2010). *Difficult dialogues: How white male graduate students in student affairs preparation programs make meaning of their whiteness, white privilege, and multiculturalism* (Doctoral dissertation). Available from ProQuest Dissertations and Theses database. (UMI No. 3425924)

Ortiz, A. M., & Rhoads, R. A. (2000). Deconstructing whiteness as part of a multicultural educational framework: From theory to practice. *Journal of College Student Development, 41,* 81–93.

Pasque, P. A., & Nicholson, S. E. (2011). Preface. In P. A. Pasque & S. E. Nicholson (Eds.), *Empowering women in higher education and student affairs: Theory, research, narratives, and practice from feminist perspectives* (pp. xv–xxi). Sterling, VA: Stylus and the American College Personnel Association.

Quaye, S. J. (2012). White educators facilitating discussions about racial realities. *Equity & Excellence in Education, 45,* 100–119.

Renn, K. A., & Jessup-Anger, E. R. (2008). Preparing new professionals: Lessons for graduate preparation programs from the National Study of New Professionals in Student Affairs. *Journal of College Student Development, 49,* 319–335.

Robbins, C. K. (2012). *Racial consciousness, identity, and dissonance among white women in student affairs graduate programs* (Doctoral dissertation). Available from ProQuest Dissertations and Theses database. (UMI No. 3543628)

Sandoval, C. (1990). Feminism and racism: A report on the 1981 National Women's Studies Association conference. In G. Anzaldúa (Ed.), *Making face, making soul/haciendo caras: Creative and critical perspectives by women of color* (pp. 55–71). San Francisco, CA: Aunt Lute. (Original work published in 1982)

Strayhorn, T. L. (Ed.). (2013). *Living at the intersections: Social identities and black collegians.* Charlotte, NC: Information Age.

Tatum, B. D. (2003). *"Why are all the Black kids sitting together in the cafeteria?" and other conversations about race.* New York, NY: Basic.

Taub, D. J., & McEwen, M. K. (2006). Decision to enter the field of student affairs. *Journal of College Student Development, 47,* 206–217.

Tull, A. (2006). Synergistic supervision, job satisfaction, and intention to turnover of new professionals in student affairs. *Journal of College Student Development, 47,* 465–480.

Watt, S. K. (2007). Difficult dialogues, privilege and social justice: Uses of the Privileged Identity Exploration (PIE) model in student affairs practice. *The College Student Affairs Journal, 26,* 114–126.

Zúñiga, X. (2003). Bridging differences through dialogue. *About Campus, 7,* 8–16.

CHAPTER THREE

Intersectionality

A Legacy from Critical Legal Studies and Critical Race Theory

ALLISON DANIEL ANDERS AND JAMES M. DEVITA

Activists, scholars, and researchers in education studies (Bettie, 2003; Patel, 2013), higher education (Abes, Jones, & McEwen, 2007; Mitchell & Means, 2014; Strayhorn, Blakewood, & DeVita, 2008, 2010), human rights (Raj, Bunch, & Nazombe, 2002), political science (Berger, 2004), and women's studies (Collins, 2008; Davis, 1983; Lorde, 1984) have studied experience at the intersection of multiple identities and have argued for understandings and practices that acknowledge them. In this chapter, we argue that studying the legacies of critical legal studies, critical race theory, and, in particular, *intersectionality* (Crenshaw, 1991a, p. 58), a term first used by Kimberlé Crenshaw, can guide research about multiple targeted identities in productive ways. Crenshaw (1991b), an African American Woman, legal scholar, and critical race theorist, argued that dominant social patterns and systemic inequities affect the lived experience of groups and individuals who embody multiple targeted identities and that such patterns and inequities often produce "intersectional disempowerment" (p. 1245). Crenshaw's conceptions of intersectionality deepen opportunities for activists, scholars, and researchers in higher education who are committed to studying racial and social justice, to theorize about experience at the intersection of multiple targeted identities and to strategize against dominant social patterns and systemic inequity.

Not only because Crenshaw (1991a) emphasized the importance of "the experiences and concerns of Black women" (p. 58), but also because too often White scholars committed to racial and social justice "tokenize" (Thompson, 2003, p. 13) the work produced by scholars of color, we trace intersectionality to its first use by Crenshaw and her applications.[1] Our aims are to situate the relevancy of intersectionality racially, historically, and politically, and to encourage White activists, scholars, and researchers interested in ideas produced by scholars of color to study the context of the work produced by scholars of color before applying it to their own. Thompson (2003) warned that, "taking the work of people of color seriously requires studying their projects, not just quoting the occasional point that coincides with what we were going to say anyway" (p. 13). Personally, as White scholars, applying Crenshaw's ideas means, too, representing the historical and political context from which she worked and celebrating the lived experiences she and her colleagues endured as they confronted predominantly White law schools, White colleagues, and White, conventional legal scholarship.

This chapter begins with introductions to the history, politics, and context of critical legal studies (CLS). Specifically, we address Crenshaw's critique of neoconservative influence on antidiscrimination law and the ways her critique informed her ideas about intersectionality and the field of critical race theory (CRT). We follow these sections with Crenshaw's (1991b) work on structural, political, and representational intersectionality. Lastly, we offer as example our application of Crenshaw's ideas to DeVita's (2010) study of Black, gay men in higher education. Ultimately, we argue that the application of Crenshaw's concept of intersectionality requires understandings of its historical and political context and offers activists, scholars, and researchers ways to critique the reproduction of power in the everyday subjugation of multiple targeted identities (Anders, DeVita, & Oliver, 2012; DeVita & Anders, 2014). In doing so, we invite readers to discern between scholarship that reflects Crenshaw's conception of intersectionality and scholarship that represents intersections of identity.

The privilege that Whiteness provides in "white supremacist capitalist patriarchy" (hooks, 1992), precludes any claim we (Anders & DeVita) might make about intersectionality and our own identities. Although Crenshaw did not exclude the possible application of intersectionality to analyze intersections of targeted and privileged identities (for example, the lived experiences of White women in higher education or White gay men in higher education), we argue that multiple targeted identities must remain prominent and centered in applications of intersectionality. As White folks, using intersectionality to theorize about our own lives would mean altering Crenshaw's arguments about multiple subordinations in order to fit our own needs. Other language and concepts exist for us to refer to our experiences. For example, "intersections of identity" reflects the general concept without misappropriating or co-opting the history and politics of Crenshaw's conceptions or applications of her term. Our approach is not prescriptive, as we believe each individual scholar must face the burden of application (DeVita & Anders, 2014). For us, keeping multiple targeted identities prominent and centered in empirical studies that utilize Crenshaw's work is what is important. We do not suggest that scholars count the number of multiple targeted identities to evaluate the applicability of Crenshaw's work but instead clarify the ways that multiple targeted identities remain prominent and centered in their analyses.

CRITICAL LEGAL STUDIES

According to Crenshaw, Gotanda, Peller, and Thomas (1995), in the 1970s civil rights lawyers faced "attacks on the limited victories they had only just achieved in the prior decade, particularly with respect to affirmative action and legal requirements for the kinds of evidence required to prove illicit discrimination" (p. xvii). During the same time, in law schools across the United States, groups of predominantly White, neo-Marxist scholars began to organize with colleagues, teachers, and practitioners to challenge presuppositions of legal doctrine and critique the ways it legitimated and reproduced systemic inequities. Critical legal studies scholars argued that dominant ideologies affect the construction of legal doctrine. Specifically, critical legal studies scholars analyzed legal doctrine "to reveal both its internal inconsistencies (generally by exposing the incoherence of legal arguments) and its external consistencies (often by laying bare the inherently paradoxical and political worldviews embedded within legal doctrine)" (Crenshaw, 1995, p. 108). CLS scholars explicated the ideology and politics of court decisions rendered in the name of legal doctrine. Together with a network of "New Left activists, ex-counterculturalists and other varieties of oppositionists in law schools" (Crenshaw et al., 1995, p. xvii), critical legal studies scholars encouraged students and left-leaning faculty to produce scholarship that confronted the myths of apolitical legal doctrine and a neutral legal system. Such analyses provided opportunities for scholars to identify ways that the practice of law creates, legitimates, and reproduces "an unjust social order" (Crenshaw et al., 1995, p. xviii).

For many CLS scholars, Antonio Gramsci's (1992) work on hegemony elucidated the enduring power of the law, the limits of rights-based approaches in reform movements, and the dominance of an economic system that continued to exploit laborers. As do other institutions of the state, the legal system legitimates and reproduces hegemonic relationships of power. Belief in the myth of an apolitical and neutral system of law contributes to the system's reproduction (Crenshaw, 1995; Kairys, 1998). Both the dominant and the dominated reify the law's centrality and the order of the state by consenting to the power of the law and to their own subjugation to it. Critical legal scholars criticized "mainstream legal ideology for its tendency to portray American society as basically fair, and thereby to legitimate the oppressive policies that have been directed toward racial minorities" (Crenshaw, 1995, p. 110). They established the Conference on Critical

Legal Studies and challenged the rising neoconservative rhetoric of equal opportunity in the 1970s.

Neoconservative agendas touted equal process and equality of opportunity arguments. Then and now, neoconservatives and many neoliberals argue that equal process, or access to equal protection under the law, addresses the axis of economic and racial inequity in the United States. Neoconservatives maintain that equal process is a sufficient doctrine; moreover, they contend that, "equal process is completely unrelated to equal results" (Crenshaw, 1995, p. 105). Decoupling equal process from equal process outcomes allows neoconservatives to ignore evidence of disparity along economic and racial axes, to reproduce the myth of color blindness, and to de-legitimate claims of discrimination based on race.

Crenshaw (1995) confronted the neoconservative rhetoric and argued that if color-blind policies were "the only legitimate and effective means of ensuring a racially equitable society, one would have to assume not only that there is only one 'proper role' for law but also that such a racially equitable society already exists" (p. 105). As the United States fails to reflect such histories, Crenshaw critiqued both the de-coupling of equal process from equal process outcomes and the myth of color blindness:

> Society's adoption of the ambivalent rhetoric of equal opportunity law has made it that much more difficult for black people to name their reality. There is no longer a perpetrator, a clearly identifiable discriminator. Company Z can be an equal opportunity employer even though Company Z has no blacks or any other minorities in its employ. Practically speaking, all companies can now be equal opportunity employers by proclamation alone. Society has embraced the rhetoric of equal opportunity without fulfilling its promise. (pp. 106–107)

According to Crenshaw "only in such a society, where all other social functions operate in a nondiscriminatory way, would equality of process constitute equality of opportunity" (p. 106). In a society where groups of people have been treated differently, as is the case of the United States, advocates for the idea of color blindness deny the histories of exploitation, oppression, and disenfranchisement and their effects. Moreover, they silence interpretations of the world that center the relationship of ontology to epistemology. That is to say, the ways one is located and positioned in the world and the ways one is classed, gendered, and raced, affect one's way of experiencing and knowing the world (Butler, 1999; Crenshaw, 1991b; Collins, 2008; Freire, 2000; hooks, 1992; Noblit, 1999; Noddings, 1992; Scott, 1999). Crenshaw signified Black experience as a meaningful and tactical response to neoconservative strategies designed to disrupt advocacy for economic and racial justice:

> The lasting harm must be measured by the extent to which limited gains hamper efforts of African-Americans to name their reality and to remain capable of engaging in collective action in the future…If the civil rights constituency allows its own political consciousness to

be completely replaced by the ambiguous discourse of antidiscrimination law, it will be difficult for this constituency to defend its genuine interests against those whose interests are supported by opposing visions that also employ the same discourse. The struggle, it seems, is to maintain a contextualized, specified worldview that reflects the experience of blacks. The question remains whether engaging in legal reform precludes this possibility. (p. 107)

Crenshaw urged African Americans to name their own realities in order to remain "capable of engaging in collective action" (p. 107). The challenge, she wrote, would be "to maintain a contextualized, specified worldview that reflects the experience of blacks" (p. 107). Crenshaw's critiques of neoconservative influence on interpretations of antidiscrimination law and her advocacy for the centrality of Black experiences in political action historicize her work on intersectionality. Ultimately, both the critiques she provides and the emphasis she places on experiences and identities in African American communities inform the development of CRT.

CRITICAL RACE THEORY

According to Crenshaw et al. (1995), although CLS scholars disrupted conventional thought and teaching in many law schools through analyses of hegemony in legal doctrine, questions of racial power were not part of the dominant discourse in CLS. The absence of analysis regarding institutionalized racism and experiences of coercion and threat by targeted groups and individuals remained unexamined (Crenshaw, 1995; Delgado & Stefancic, 2001). In the 1970s, "race crits" (Crenshaw et al., 1995, p. xxii) began discussing racial power within CLS and the historic dismissal of rights-based arguments in CLS. Although race crits agreed that rights discourse was indeterminate, many believed that a "rights discourse held a social and transformative value in the context of racial subordination that transcended the narrower question of whether reliance on rights could alone bring about any determinate results" (Crenshaw et al., 1995, p. xxiii). As analyses of racial power expanded in CLS the differences between CLS and analyses emphasizing contexts of race and racism eventually produced a body of scholarship that reflected what scholars think of now as critical race theory.

CRT was named such in order to specifically locate it at the intersection of critical theory, race, racism, and the law. Activists and scholars in the CRT movement sought

> to understand how a regime of white supremacy and its subordination of people of color have been created and maintained in America, and, in particular, to examine the relationship between that social structure and the professed ideals such as "the rule of law" and "equal protection." (Crenshaw et al., 1995, p. xiii)

They sought not merely to "understand the vexed bond between law and racial power but to *change* it" (Crenshaw et al., 1995, p. xiii). In contrast to positions in the civil rights movement, many of which embraced incrementalism, critical race theorists questioned "the very foundations of the liberal order, including equality theory, legal reasoning, Enlightenment rationalism, and neutral principles of constitutional law" (Delgado & Stefancic, 2001, p. 3).

According to Delgado and Stefancic (2001), CRT scholars argue that, "racism is ordinary, not aberrational" (p. 7) and the history of White supremacy and White dominance in the United States creates a racial hierarchy that serves the social and material purposes of Whites. CRT scholars argue that White elites acquiesce to change for racial justice only when the change produces benefit for them. CRT scholars studying this process named the response of White elites to targeted groups: interest convergence.

In an ongoing debate among CRT scholars, racial realists argue that racism is permanent; racial idealists do not. Many racial realists analyze issues of structural determinism. Some study the reproduction of legal precedent, others the diversity and at times conflict of Black interests in civil rights cases. Others analyze relationships of power always already present in everyday and judiciary contexts and critique the notion that empathy will generate equity amongst competing narratives of reality. Still others study the relationship between court decisions and the maintenance of the racial hierarchy in the status quo. Many CRT scholars critique liberalism, because neoconservative and neoliberal agendas that perpetuate the rhetoric of color blindness limit redress, and therefore, allow condemnation of only the most "egregious racial harms" (Delgado & Stefancic, 2001, p. 22). Relatedly, CRT scholars critique the ways rights-based tactics failed to produce substantive change. Other CRT scholars analyze the way "society invents, manipulates, or retires when convenient" (Delgado & Stefancic, 2001, p. 7) particular constructions of race. Many CRT scholars study ways race is socially constructed and deployed and differential racialization, or the ways "dominant society racializes different minority groups at different times in response to shifting needs such as the labor market" (Delgado & Stefancic, 2001, p. 8).

Related to differential racialization is Crenshaw's (1991a, 1991b) concept of intersectionality. Crenshaw's commitment to strategies for collective action amidst neoconservative and often neoliberal policymaking underscores the importance of analyses at the intersections of lived experience, identity politics, and context. The analysis and representation of lived experience of targeted groups and individuals generate evidence against a majoritarian history of the United States. CRT scholars, many of whom are racial realists, reexamine "America's historical record," in order to confront and replace "comforting majoritarian interpretations of events with ones that square more accurately with minorities' experiences" (Delgado and Stefancic, 2001, p. 30). Celebrating and encouraging ontological and epistemological understandings of race and racism from the perspectives of targeted people, many CRT scholars pursue the production of counternarratives and legal storytelling. Analyzing the ways dominant groups, in this case elite Whites in the United States, position groups of people racially, culturally, and economically for their own purposes allows targeted groups to build collective action and deploy tactics against the prevailing economic and social order.

INTERSECTIONALITY

Kimberlé Crenshaw (1991a, 1991b) is recognized as the first scholar to name and theorize the term *intersectionality*. She used intersectionality to conceptualize the intersections of race and gender in her analyses of antidiscrimination in legal cases, for example, cases where Black women and non-English-speaking immigrant women of color were plaintiffs. Crenshaw criticized the courts for forcing Black women and non-English-speaking immigrant women of color to articulate discrimination along only one category of identity. Crenshaw argued that "the intersectional experience is greater than the sum of racism and sexism" and that "any analysis that does not take intersectionality into account cannot sufficiently address the particular manner in which Black women are subordinated" (p. 58). The experience of racism and sexism is neither discrete nor summative for women of color. Women of color do not experience racism in the same ways that men of color do, nor do they experience sexism in the same ways that White women do. Procedurally, the courts denied the existence of everyday lived experience at the intersection of multiple targeted identities. Antidiscrimination law failed to account for the experiences of women of color.

In *Mapping the Margins*, Crenshaw (1991b) conceptualized structural intersectionality, political intersectionality, and representational intersectionality. To illustrate structural intersectionality, Crenshaw represented the issue of domestic violence and analyzed the issues of gender and race at the intersections of employment and housing, access and relationships to court advocates, and English as the language of the court in domestic violence cases. She examined the qualitative differences between women who have racial, economic, and linguistic privilege, and those who do not.

Crenshaw's (1991b) work on political intersectionality assessed the ways identity politics affect experiences of and participation by women of color in collective action. Crenshaw demonstrated political intersectionality by analyzing the ways dominant political agendas and social movements separate the politics of women of color into two (minimally) different subordinated groups: people of color in pursuit of racial equity and women in pursuit of gender equity. Because collective action for antiracist practice and policy is central to Crenshaw's work, finding ways to analyze and navigate productively identity politics across multiple targeted identities is paramount.

As an analytical tool, representational intersectionality demands the inclusion of multiple targeted identities and the discourses produced around and through them when the representation occurs of a single targeted identity. Crenshaw (1991b) warned: "when one discourse fails to acknowledge the significance of the other, the power relations each attempts to challenge are strengthened" (p. 1282). Representational intersectionality offers scholars a way to analyze the absences between the everyday experience of multiple targeted identities and the ways media produce representations of women of color for consumption.

Structural Intersectionality and LGBTQ Populations in Higher Education

Crenshaw's (1991b) structural intersectionality emphasized the ways that the everyday discourses, policies, and practices of an institution target the experiences of women of color and immigrant women differently than those of a dominant group, in this case, White women. In higher education, ideally LGBTQ (Lesbian, gay, bisexual, transgender, and queer) individuals of color will encounter systems of support that celebrate their identities. However, too often these institutions fail to support students holistically. For example, according to Strayhorn, Blakewood, and DeVita (2008, 2010), many college campuses develop cultural centers to provide support for targeted students. Typically, these centers reflect only one axis of identity (e.g., Black cultural centers and LGBTQ centers). Even on campuses where collaboration is encouraged, supported, and realized, these centers represent the ways campuses have been structured to recognize the issues faced by students from specific targeted groups at the expense of individuals who must navigate multiple targeted identities (see Chapter 23, this volume). The resources, though important, are inadequate when students who embody and enact multiple targeted identities must negotiate everyday campus politics and potential discrimination.

Indeed, research on the experiences of Black gay males at predominantly White institutions (PWI) conducted by Strayhorn et al. (2008, 2010) found that Black gay males seldom felt comfortable in either of the spaces established to support their identity affiliations: a Black cultural center and a LGBTQ center. Black gay male undergraduates at PWIs frequently experienced homophobia in the Black cultural center and racism in the LGBTQ center. Experiences with discrimination in both places forced them to choose the least oppressive space. The development of separate resource centers is directly linked to tensions associated with a lack of systemic support for a particular group (i.e., Black or LGBTQ), thus it should not be surprising that the distance established between physical spaces produced equally disparate social and political climates (Bentley Historical Society, 2007). Individuals who identify as non-White and LGBTQ are forced to endure targeting of their identities by institutional structures in ways individuals who identify as White and LGBTQ or non-White and straight do not.

On many campuses, it is not feasible to alter the physical spaces (i.e., distinct cultural centers) that have been established. Thus, programming and other initiatives must provide support to address structural intersectionality. Educational programming focused on LGBTQ topics (e.g., safe zones, safe spaces) should be inclusive of discussions that examine the intersections of LGBTQ identities with other targeted identities (e.g., race/ethnicity, socioeconomic status). The failure to include other axes of identity reifies the whitewashing of LGBTQ identities and further marginalizes racial identities.

Additionally, a common feature of educational programs is the issuance of a card or sign, which indicates that the individual has completed the training and is a "safe resource" for LGBTQ people (Consortium, 2013). This sign becomes a public proclamation that an individual is an LGBTQ ally, presumably with the ability to support all LGBTQ individuals, including those with multiple targeted identities. However, programs that reflect the neoconservative myth of color blindness ignore the explicit experiences and needs of non-White LGBTQ individuals and affirm a White normative view of LGBTQ topics on campus. Such programs re-center White privilege and limit the potential support for LGBTQ individuals of color.

Political Intersectionality and LGBTQ Populations in Higher Education

Paying close attention to political intersectionality may improve communication and resources in higher education and open new spaces for collective action. For example, the policies and initiatives supported by LGBTQ groups are whitewashed often by a lack of attention to the experiences and needs of non-White LGBTQ individuals (Teunis, 2007; Ward, 2008). Ward's (2008) research on an LGBTQ community center revealed numerous practices that aligned with White normative culture. The center "was sustained by its mainstream and corporate approach to diversity" (p. 582). Similarly, Teunis (2007) characterized various LGBTQ organizations' foci on marriage equality and military service as political agenda items that primarily privileged White, gay individuals. Teunis described the absence of attention to the intersections of identity in the pursuit of marriage equality this way:

> In the struggle for marriage equality, spokespersons are very generally white women and men who display little or no concern for critical political issues that face gays and Lesbians of colour. That these struggles promote whiteness is not due to the inherent nature of the issues, but rather due to the manner in which they are promoted and in which they usurp all other concerns that drive the community. (p. 268)

Similar tensions face LGBTQ cultural centers on college campuses. First, although centers exist on over 200 campuses across the United States and Canada

(Consortium, 2013), only three such centers exist at Historically Black Colleges and Universities (HBCUs; Human Rights Campaign, 2013). The prevalence of centers at PWIs suggests that services and support for LGBTQ individuals, educational programming for heterosexual individuals, and LGBTQ-inclusive programs for all individuals are more likely to be present at PWIs, and therefore, more likely to reflect policy and practice generated in and reproduced by White normative culture.

While a meaningful campus resource, the creation of a center based along a single axis of identity at a PWI likely primes White potential L, G, B, T, or Q identified-students for leadership roles. As Teunis' (2007) and Ward's (2008) findings suggest, White LGBTQ leadership must actively center experiences of LGBTQ people of color in order to produce an inclusive platform in agenda setting. Institutional inclusion and inclusive organizing are paramount as Crenshaw (1995) wrote:

> The struggle for blacks, like that of all subordinated groups, is a struggle for inclusion, an attempt to manipulate the elements of the dominant ideology in order to transform the experience of domination. It is a struggle to create a new status quo through the ideological and political tools that are available. (p. 119)

An intersectional approach to support individuals with multiple, targeted identities would include an examination of the ways in which different identity groups could align resources and energies to benefit from a common goal. "Alliance means action" is one theme that we (Anders & DeVita) have produced from in vivo coding and pattern coding (Saldaña, 2011) from an interview study with LGTQ-identified faculty, staff, and students in higher education. Participants articulated a distinction between heterosexual individuals, who only identify as an "ally" through the posting of a safe zone or safe space placard, and those who engage in activities, events, and policy changes that support LGBTQ communities. One participant, a White male faculty member who identified as gay, discussed his frustration with passive "allies," arguing that shared ideology and active political engagement was the tactic LGBTQ communities and their allies needed to use. As he explained: "We need to join in what is called ideology politics. Joining with people of like minds, of like visions of the world, from different identity groups." He and other participants discussed the need to work toward equal rights that demonstrate support for LGBTQ individuals on campus, such as partner benefits, gender neutral bathrooms, and inclusive policies and practices across all parts of higher education.

Relatedly, racial inequity persists on college campuses (Liptak, 2013). One such initiative is the development of an "anti-racism" working group as part of the Consortium of Higher Education LGBT Resource Professionals (Consortium, 2013). The consortium is an international organization comprised of administrators who work at institutions of higher education. The inclusion of an "anti-racism" working group centered issues of antiracism within the consortium. Such inclusion is one example of how individuals and professional entities can begin to diversify political agendas and collective action.

Representational Intersectionality and LGBTQ Populations in Higher Education

Often in higher education, faculty and staff fraction into separate spaces in acknowledgement of LGBTQ individuals of color. Consider the following examples: (a) end of year recognition ceremonies that honor students of color (e.g., Black graduation ceremony) and LGBTQ students (e.g., Lavender graduation); (b) separate commissions or committees that give voice to faculty, staff, and students of color, and LGBTQ faculty, staff; and (c) educational programming and events (e.g., film series, speaker series) that invite individuals to discuss issues of race/ethnicity *or* LGBTQ topics—and that may or may not be cosponsored by multiple offices or student organizations. In each of these examples, the representation of a single axis of identity is reified. Institutional structure, campus organization, and professional practice reinforce monolithic conceptions of identity. Unfortunately, everyday practice rarely includes critical consideration of individuals. Often targeted individuals are supported partially but never holistically.

Consider the additional example of center hiring practices and the diverse populations of individuals that center directors and staff must represent. At LGBTQ centers, student affairs professionals and students assume that the leadership must identify as Lesbian, gay, bisexual, transgender, or queer. Often the LGBTQ center leadership then becomes *the* people who represent all LGBTQ issues for the campus. Similarly, student affairs professionals and students assume that the leadership at a Black cultural center must identify as Black or African American. The Black leadership becomes, too, *the* people who represent all Black issues for the campus. Certainly, targeted group experiences inform practice in campus centers. Here we are not arguing that the recruitment and retention of LGBTQ-identified staff and staff members of color is not important; it is important. Rather, we are emphasizing Crenshaw's (1991a, 1991b) point that individuals with multiple targeted identities must work against multiple systems of oppression. Critiquing contemporary analyses of representation, Crenshaw (1991b) argued that

> [D]ebates over representation continually elide the intersection of race and gender in the popular culture's construction of images of women of color. Accordingly, an analysis of what may be termed "representational intersectionality" would include both the ways in which these images are produced through a confluence of prevalent narratives of race and gender, as well as a recognition of how contemporary critiques of racist and sexist representation marginalize women of color. (p. 1283)

Administrators and student affairs professionals need to work against monolithic representations of targeted groups and complicate their understandings of how multiple systems of oppression affect students, faculty, and staff who embody multiple targeted identities.

CONCLUDING THOUGHTS ON CRENSHAW'S INTERSECTIONALITY

In this chapter, we introduced brief histories of critical legal studies and critical race theory. Crenshaw's (1991a, 1991b) work on intersectionality stemmed from a rich history of neo-Marxist work on hegemony and the law, oppositional debate between neoconservatives and critical scholars on antidiscrimination law and equal process, the subsequent creation of color blindness by neoconservatives as a political tool, and the CLS critique of it as a myth. Centering the importance of ontology and its relationship to epistemology and in particular African American experience in her own work in CRT, Crenshaw reminded us to theorize carefully as well as tactically when we engage in racial justice work. Applying her concept of "intersectionality" means working with not only the legacies of CLS and CRT and the theoretical sophistication of political, structural, and representational intersectionality but also with the lived experiences Crenshaw and her colleagues endured as they confronted predominantly White law schools, White colleagues, and White, conventional legal scholarship. We invite readers to work with memory and care as they apply Crenshaw's work to their own.

NOTE

1. For a different interpretation of Crenshaw's emphasis on the lived experiences of women living at the intersection of multiple targeted identities see McCall (2005) and Nash (2008). For a conceptual critique of the binary position between poststructuralism and essentialism, as represented in McCall (2005) and Nash (2008), see Moi (1999).

REFERENCES

Abes, E. S., Jones, S. R., & McEwen, M. K. (2007). Reconceptualizing the model of multiple dimensions of identity: The role of meaning-making capacity in the construction of multiple identities. *Journal of College Student Development, 48,* 1–22.

Anders, A. D., DeVita, J. M., & Oliver, S. T. (2012). Southern predominantly White institutions, targeted students, and the intersectionality of identity: Two case studies. In C. Clark, K. J. Fasching-Varner, & M. Brimhall-Vargas (Eds.), *Occupying the academy: Just how important is diversity work in higher education?* (pp. 71–82). Lanham, MD: Rowman & Littlefield.

Bentley Historical Library, University of Michigan. (2007, October 17). *Gay, Lesbian, bisexual, and transgender collections.* Retrieved from http://bentley.umich.edu/research/guides/gaylesbian/

Bettie, J. (2003). *Women without class: Girls, race, and identity.* Berkeley: University of California Press.

Berger, M. (2004). *Workable sisterhood: The political journey of stigmatized women with HIV/AIDS.* Princeton, NJ: Princeton University Press.

Butler, J. (1999). *Gender trouble: Feminism and the subversion of identity.* New York, NY: Routledge.

Collins, P. H. (2008). *Black feminist thought: Knowledge, consciousness, and the politics of empowerment.* New York, NY: Routledge.

Consortium of Higher Education LGBT Resource Professionals. (2013). Retrieved from http://www.lgbtcampus.org

Crenshaw, K. (1991a). De-marginalizing the intersection of race and sex: A black feminist critique of antidiscrimination doctrine, feminist theory, and antiracist politics. In K. Bartlett & R. Kennedy (Eds.), *Feminist legal theory: Readings in law and gender* (pp. 57–80). Boulder, CO: Westview.

Crenshaw, K. (1991b). Mapping the margins: Intersectionality, identity politics, and violence against women of color. *Stanford Law Review, 43,* 1241–1299.

Crenshaw, K. (1995). Race, reform, and retrenchment: Transformation, and legitimation in anti-discrimination law. In K. Crenshaw, N. Gotanda, G. Peller, & K. Thomas (Eds.), *Critical race theory: The key writings that formed the movement* (pp. 103–122). New York, NY: The New Press.

Crenshaw, K., Gotanda, N., Peller, G., & Thomas, K. (1995). Introduction. In K. Crenshaw, N. Gotanda, G. Peller, & K. Thomas (Eds.), *Critical race theory: The key writings that formed the movement* (pp. xiii–xxxii). New York, NY: The New Press.

Davis, A. Y. (1983). *Women, race and class.* New York, NY: Vintage Books.

Delgado, R., & Stefancic, J. (2001). *Critical race theory: An introduction.* New York: New York University Press.

DeVita, J. M. (2010). *Gay male identity in the context of college: Implications for development, support, and campus climate* (Unpublished doctoral dissertation). University of Tennessee, Knoxville.

DeVita, J. M., & Anders, A. D. (2014). Intersectionality and the performances of identities: Experiences of Black gay male undergraduates at predominantly White institutions. In E. Meyer & D. Carlson (Eds.), *Gender and sexuality in education: A reader* (pp. 464–478). New York, NY: Peter Lang.

Freire, P. (2000). *Pedagogy of the oppressed.* New York, NY: Bloomsbury.

Gramsci, A. (1992). *Prison notebooks.* New York, NY: Columbia University Press.

hooks, b. (1992). *Black looks: Race and representation.* Boston, MA: South End.

Human Rights Campaign Staff. (2013, October 3). Fayetteville State University becomes third historically black college to open LGBT resource center. *HRC Blog.* Retrieved from http://www.hrc.org/blog/entry/fayetteville-state-university-becomes-third-historically-black-college-to-o

Kairys, D. (1998). Introduction. In D. Kairys (3rd ed.). *The politics of law: a progressive critique* (pp. 1–20). New York, NY: Basic.

Liptak, A. (2013, October 15). Justices weigh Michigan law and race in college admissions. *The New York Times.* Retrieved from http://www.nytimes.com/2013/10/16/us/justices-weigh-michigan-law-and-race-in-college-admissions.html?pagewanted=all&_r=0

Lorde, A. (1984). *Sister outsider: Essays and speeches by Audre Lorde.* Berkeley, CA: The Crossing Press.

McCall, L. (2005). The complexity of intersectionality. *Signs, 30,* 1771–1800.

Mitchell, D., Jr., & Means, D. R. (2014). "Quadruple consciousness": A literature review and new theoretical consideration for understanding the experiences of Black gay and bisexual college men at predominantly white institutions. *Journal of African American Males in Education, 5,* 1–13.

Moi, T. (1999). *What is a Woman? And other essays.* Oxford, UK: Oxford University Press.

Nash, J. C. (2008). Re-thinking intersectionality. *Feminist Review, 89,* 1–15.

Noblit, G. W. (1999). *Particularities: Collected essays on ethnography and education.* New York, NY: Peter Lang.

Noddings, N. (1992). *The challenge to care in schools: An alternative approach to education.* New York, NY: Teacher's College Press.

Patel, L. (2013). *Youth held at the border: Immigration, education, and the politics of inclusion.* New York, NY: Teacher's College Press.

Raj, R. Bunch, C. & Nazombe, E. (2002). *Women at the intersection: Indivisible rights, identities, and oppressions.* New Brunswick, NJ: Rutgers, the State University of New Jersey, Center for Women's Global Leadership.

Saldaña, J. (2011). *The coding manual for qualitative researchers* (2nd ed.). Los Angeles, CA: Sage.

Scott, J. (1999). *Seeing like a state: How certain schemes to improve the human condition have failed.* New Haven, CT: Yale University Press.

Strayhorn, T. L., Blakewood, A. M., & DeVita, J. M. (2008). Factors affecting the college choice of African American gay male undergraduates: Implications for retention. *NASAP Journal, 11,* 88–108.

Strayhorn, T. L., Blakewood, A. M., & DeVita, J. M. (2010). Triple threat: Challenges and supports of black gay men at predominantly white campuses. In T. L. Strayhorn & M. C. Terrell (Eds.), *The experiences of black college students: Enduring challenges, necessary supports* (pp. 111–134). Herndon, VA: Stylus.

Teunis, N. (2007). Sexual objectification and the construction of whiteness in the gay male community. *Culture, Health, & Sexuality, 9,* 263–275.

Thompson, A. (2003). Tiffany, friend of people of color: White investments in antiracism. *Qualitative Studies in Education, 16,* 7–29.

Ward, J. (2008). White normativity: The cultural dimensions of whiteness in a racially diverse LGBT organization. *Sociological Perspectives, 51,* 563–586.

CHAPTER FOUR

The Multiplicity and Intersectionality of Indigenous Identities

NICOLE ALIA SALIS REYES

According to the 2000 U.S. Census, American Indians and Alaska Natives along with Native Hawaiians and other Pacific Islanders comprise 1.5% and 0.3% of the U.S. population, respectively (Grieco, 2001; Ogunwole, 2002). When they comprise such a small portion of the nation's total population, it seems of little surprise that these groups are not broadly well understood. The misunderstanding of Native (referred to interchangeably as Indigenous) peoples in the United States is further compounded by a dominant grand narrative of Native peoples as vanishing into the distant past (Deloria, 1988; Smith, 2010).

Unfortunately, Native peoples are also not well represented or well understood within the context of higher education. Despite reporting high college aspirations, American Indian and Alaska Native students enroll in and graduate from college at lower rates than most other racial and ethnic groups nationally (Brayboy, Fann, Castagno, & Solyom, 2012). Similarly, Native Hawaiians enroll in and complete college at lower rates than all other major ethnic groups within Hawai'i (Kana'iaupuni, Malone, & Ishibashi, 2005). This is problematic since, through participation in postsecondary education, Indigenous peoples might equip themselves with Western academic tools, including skills and social capital, which might be bent toward meeting Indigenous community needs (Brayboy, 2005a; Brayboy et al., 2012).

If the academy is to better serve the needs of its Native students, it must begin with a better understanding of who Native peoples are. In this chapter, I apply an intersectional lens to reviewing bodies of Native feminist literature, other Indigenous literature, and higher education literature in order to highlight the complex nature of Native identities. Intersectionality may be considered a useful paradigm in this exercise because it calls attention to the coexistence of multiple, overlapping systems of oppression and privilege within society as well as to the coexistence of multiple, layered identities that become differently salient to individuals within different contexts (Collins, 2007; Griffin & Museus, 2011; D. G. Smith, 2012). Starting from a better understanding of the multiplicity and intersectionality of Indigenous identities, I suggest how higher education institutions might better serve their Indigenous students.

INDIGENOUS IDENTITIES AND THE CONTEXT OF HIGHER EDUCATION

There is often a tendency to consider Indigenous peoples as forming only a racial group. However, their identities have also been shaped by other experiences and entities, such as colonization, cultural connectivity, and nationhood. I expand on some of these identities and how they impact the college experiences of Indigenous students in this section.

Native Peoples as Colonized

Though they differ by culture and are separated by place, Indigenous peoples share common histories and contemporary experiences of colonization (L. T. Smith, 1999). This colonization has been accomplished in part through processes of racialization and the inculcation of patriarchy. Scholars point to how the literal and figurative deaths of Native peoples have been essential to the progress of Western colonial projects. With regard to the U.S. context, for example, Andrea Smith (2008) argued that the dominant national origin story, which claims that the country has been founded on principles of democracy, is nothing but a liberal myth. Instead, the United States only exists in its current form as a result of capitalism and colonialism, both of which have relied on the racialization of people of color for their fortification (Hall, 2009; A. Smith, 2008, 2010).

Through a racial logic of genocide, Native peoples have been posed as obstacles to non-Natives' land and resource acquisition (A. Smith, 2010). Only as Native peoples vanish may non-Natives lay claim to the commodities of Native nations, including land, natural resources, spirituality, and culture (A. Smith, 2010). The logic of genocide has driven the mass killing of many Indigenous peoples and continues to exist at the core of blood quantum policies, which determine Indigenous community membership according to arbitrarily designated percentages of Indigenous blood (Jaimes, 1992; Kauanui, 2008a; A. Smith, 2010). Although many Indigenous societies, such as that of Kānaka Maoli (Native Hawaiians), traditionally define community identity according to familial relationships and genealogies (Hall, 2009; Kauanui, 2008a), blood quantum policies suggest that individuals who do not have "enough" Indigenous blood cannot be counted as Indigenous. In this way, these policies limit the proliferation of Native populations and, as such, Native peoples become destined for extinction.

Unfortunately, Native populations remain largely invisible within the context of higher education. They are often considered statistically insignificant and excluded from higher education data reporting and research (Shotton, Lowe, & Waterman, 2012). And, though Native mascots might on the surface seem to glorify Native imagery in a hypervisible way, they often only contribute to the felt invisibility and marginalization of real Native students. Universities often do not fully acknowledge Native students' objections that the use of such mascots perpetuates stereotypes of Native peoples and does little to honor them (Castagno & Lee, 2007). Furthermore, some Native students themselves may strategically choose to reduce their visibility on campus in order to avoid unwanted scrutiny and to preserve their sense of personal and cultural integrity (Brayboy, 2004).

While the racialization of Native peoples has been essential to the furthering of colonialism, so too has been their regenderization. Many Native communities had more egalitarian gender structures prior to colonization. In traditional Diné (Navajo) society, for example, Denetdale (2006) noted that Diné women were frequently consulted on governance matters and sometimes held positions as headmen or chiefs. Kauanui (2008b) echoed that, in precolonial Hawaiian society, women were afforded similar positions of power. Hawaiian female gods were revered and considered directly related to Hawaiian women, Hawaiian women held chiefly positions alongside men, and both maternal and paternal lines determined individuals' lineage and kinship (Kauanui, 2008b). Yet, following Western contact, patriarchy was instilled in Native communities in order to provide a precursor for the acceptance of social hierarchy and subsequent colonial domination (A. Smith, 2008; Smith & Kauanui, 2008). As Native women were expected to emulate the behaviors and values of White women, they became relegated to life in the domestic sphere and have largely become silenced (Denetdale, 2006; Kauanui, 2008b; Million, 2009; Ross, 2009). Native women have been marginalized by both feminist discourses that speak only of the concerns of White women and Native sovereignty discourses that prioritize race and sovereignty over gender equality (Million, 2009).

Indeed, the gendered experiences of Native people in higher education are complicated. Native men have enrolled in and graduated from college at lower rates than their female counterparts (Brayboy et al., 2012). And, though female Native college students have reported the need to balance their responsibilities as students with their responsibilities to their families and communities, they have also reported their Womanhood to be a source of strength in life, including in college (Shield, 2009). More research must be conducted to explore how gender interacts with other identities and systems of oppression to impact the postsecondary experiences of Native students.

Native Peoples as Cultural Communities

According to Deloria and Wildcat (2001), "Indigenous" means "to be of a place" (p. 31). From this, it follows that Indigenous communities across the nation find meaning in their connections to particular places and these connections are based not only on human relationships but also on relationships with land, animals, natural forces, and spiritual entities (Meyer, 2001; Waterman, 2012). These connections permeate every aspect of the cultures of Native communities. Yet, while they may share some similarities, the cultural beliefs and practices of Native communities are distinct from one another (Waterman, 2012). They are intricately and inextricably related to particular epistemologies, languages, genealogies, and histories (Cannon, 2011; McCarty, Borgoiakova, Gilmore, Lomawaima, & Romero, 2005; Meyer, 2008). Indigenous people act as both keepers of cultural traditions and as producers of cultural adaptations that make the continued survival of the communities with which they identify possible within the contemporary world.

Such commitment to cultural perpetuation does not fade as Indigenous students enter the academy. Still, upon enrolling in college, many Indigenous students unfortunately experience cultural dissonance, where the cultural expectations of their postsecondary environment conflict with the cultural beliefs of their home communities (Brayboy, 2004; Brayboy et al., 2012; Huffman, 2001). Huffman (2001) explained that, due to this cultural dissonance, many Native students experience feelings of alienation, marginalization, and loneliness upon entering the academy. For some, this alienation can be so painful as to lead to disillusionment with, emotional rejection of, and eventual disengagement with higher education. Those Native students who do persist despite initial alienation sometimes face the challenge of not being understood by institutional officials and peers, who inappropriately judge Native students according to mainstream norms (Brayboy, 2004), or even by family members, who are not familiar with the benefits or responsibilities of college attendance (Guillory & Wolverton, 2008).

For many Native students, academic success cannot come at the cost of losing a sense of cultural identity. Some who feel overwhelming pressure to assimilate while in college may choose to leave college altogether in an act of self-preservation (Huffman, 2001). Others may remain enrolled but become silent and invisible on campus in an effort to keep their sense of Native "self" intact (Brayboy, 2004). Still, some others may return home frequently in order to fulfill family and community obligations and stay connected to cultural and spiritual traditions (Waterman, 2012). Though these actions might lead some Native students to spend less time participating in on-campus activities or to stop out of college temporarily in order to tend to family and community needs, they might be considered strategies for success in that they allow students to maintain a sense of who they are as Native peoples and thus provide them with the strength they need to persist through graduation. Literature indicates that Native students who are able to maintain a sense of cultural integrity while effectively functioning within mainstream culture feel empowered to walk in two worlds and are more likely to believe that a college education will be of practical benefit in their lives (Huffman, 2001; Okagaki, Helling, & Bingham, 2009).

Native Peoples as Sovereign Nations

As they did at the time of Western contact, Indigenous peoples continue to comprise sovereign nations. A. Smith (2008) suggested that Native nation-building should follow a two-pronged approach of taking power, which involves opposing the colonizing powers of corporations and nation states, and making power, which involves creating models of governance that fulfill community interests. Native peoples may begin to take power through breaking silences regarding their oppression and subsequently refusing to vanish (Million, 2009). Cooperation and sharing across communities can also be essential to the continued survival of Native nations (Goeman, 2009; Hall, 2009; Ramirez, 2008). Though federal policies to relocate Native communities to urban centers were designed to weaken community bonds and to accelerate their assimilation, Indigenous peoples, through oral tradition, have maintained connections to the lands of their ancestors while also recognizing their contemporary survivance on the lands of other nations (Goeman, 2009). Despite their differing tribal affiliations, they have also reached out to one another in order to create fictive kin relationships and new communities of support (Goeman, 2009).

Native college students continue to see themselves as tied to their Native nations. Having been given valuable support and resources from their families and communities throughout their lives, Native students often hope to succeed in college as a means both of making people at home proud and of gaining knowledge, skills, and social networks that they will need to do work that improves their home communities (Brayboy, 2005b; T. S. Lee, 2006, 2009; Salis Reyes, 2014; Shield, 2009; Shotton, Oosahwe, & Cintrón, 2007). Through completing their college educations while maintaining a strong sense of Native identity, Native students envision themselves as doing their parts in ensuring the continuity of their nations' future generations (Bosse, Duncan, Gapp, & Newland, 2011; Salis Reyes, 2014; Waterman, 2012).

PROMISING PRACTICES CONTRIBUTING TO NATIVE COLLEGE
STUDENT SUCCESS

It seems, then, that the racial, gendered, cultural, and political identities of Native peoples all play roles in forming Native students' college experiences. As the concept of intersectionality suggests, these multiple identities are inextricably linked and together impact Native people's experiences within social and power systems, such as that of higher education (Collins, 2007; Smith, 2012). Therefore, if institutions of higher education are to serve their Native students adequately, they must acknowledge these identities as they develop resources for Native students' postsecondary success.

L. Lee (2010) and T. S. Lee (2006) suggested transformative scholarship and Indigenous educational philosophy as critical components to higher education that can benefit Indigenous students. Both types of scholarship and educational philosophy involve honoring Native ways of learning and knowing for the purpose of achieving social justice and sovereignty. Thus, they encourage Native students to maintain and cultivate their Native identities, which in turn may be relied on as sources of strength and resilience (Huffman, 2001; Shield, 2009). They also cultivate in Native students a desire to use their educations in ways that will one day benefit their families and home communities (T. S. Lee, 2006, 2009). Some strategies that build on transformative scholarship and Indigenous educational philosophy may include discussion of decolonizing Indigenous histories; community-, cultural-, and place-based activities; as well as opportunities for self-reflection (T. S. Lee, 2006, 2009). Tribal Colleges and Universities, Native American Studies (NAS) programs, and other special programs designed to meet the needs of Native students already demonstrate the capacity to serve Native students well through their focus on culturally relevant and decolonizing curricula and programming (Brayboy et al., 2012; T. S. Lee, 2006, 2009). Still, more systemic fostering of transformative scholarship and Indigenous educational philosophy could perhaps further encourage Native students' maintenance of cultural identity and commitment to community.

Another important strategy for serving Native students involves helping them to maintain relationships with their families and home communities as well as to develop new relationships with others on their college campuses. Although family and community can sometimes be construed as factors pulling Native students away from their studies (Guillory & Wolverton, 2008), family and community are also frequently cited as providing Native students with their primary source of support and motivation to succeed in school (Bosse et al., 2011; Guillory & Wolverton, 2008; HeavyRunner & DeCelles, 2002; Salis Reyes, 2014; Shield, 2009; Waterman, 2012). Native students often note that their families and communities provide them with direct educational encouragement as well as with support for other needs through their enrollment in school (Guillory & Wolverton, 2008; Okagaki et al., 2009; Waterman, 2012). Through involving Native families in college-choice and college-going processes, institutions of higher education can help to provide them with important college knowledge and, in this way, help to bolster a crucial source of support for Native students (Bosse et al., 2011; Brayboy et al., 2012; HeavyRunner & DeCelles, 2002). Models that empower Native families to build on their strengths and to act as partners in their loved ones' higher education experiences also enhance Native students' sense of belonging in the academy (HeavyRunner & DeCelles, 2002).

Faculty, staff, and peers within higher education can also provide Indigenous students with vital support networks. Native student centers, NAS programs, and Native student groups all can provide Native students with validation and important fictive kin relationships (Bosse et al., 2011; Guillory & Wolverton, 2008; T. S. Lee, 2009). Native student peer mentors, having had to navigate their ways through the academy themselves, can provide peer protégés with emotional support and guidance on strategies for being "good students" and "good Natives" simultaneously (Brayboy, 2004; Shotton et al., 2007). While making connections with other Natives within higher education can be important for Native students, support from non-Native faculty, staff, and students, such as in the form of mentorship and validation, can also contribute to Native students' sense of belonging and bolster their resolve to finish college (Guillory & Wolverton, 2008). Thus, institutional support for programs that involve Indigenous families and encourage on-campus community building is essential to contributing to Indigenous student success.

CONCLUSION

Indigenous peoples form distinct cultural communities that are bound to specific places. They form sovereign nations that bear rights to exercising self-determination. And, despite hailing from unique cultural communities and nations, they come together to form pan-ethnic and transnational alliances due to their shared histories and experiences with colonialism, racism, and sexism. These multiple, layered identities are the results both of Native peoples' own interests and prerogatives as well as of Native peoples' resistance to the intersecting systems of oppression in which they find themselves. These identities simultaneously coexist and can become differently salient to Native peoples within different contexts. Thus, no singular identity can fully capture the complexity of who Native peoples are.

When Indigenous students enroll in institutions of higher education, they do not leave their multiple Indigenous identities behind. They carry these identities and others along with them into the academy. This being the case, intersectionality, in its attention to the coexistence of multiple identities and oppressions, proves an essential paradigm for better understanding the experiences of Native peoples in higher education. This review of the literature shows that, because of their unique, multiple identities, Native college students sometimes conceptualize their educational expectations, goals, and successes differently than has traditionally been done in mainstream higher education research. If institutions of higher education are to better serve their Native students, they must first recognize their own role in creating a system of oppression or empowerment and attempt to meet the academic, cultural, social, and political needs of Native students on these students' own terms. As more Native students are empowered to participate in higher education, they can assert their contemporary survivance and destroy the myth of Native extinction.

ACKNOWLEDGMENT

The author would like to thank Dr. Anne-Marie Núñez for her feedback on earlier versions of this manuscript.

REFERENCES

Bosse, S. A., Duncan, K., Gapp, S. C., & Newland, L. A. (2011). Supporting American Indian students in the transition to postsecondary education. *Journal of the First-Year Experience & Students in Transition, 23*, 33–51.

Brayboy, B. M. J. (2004). Hiding in the ivy: American Indian students and visibility in elite educational settings. *Harvard Educational Review, 74*, 125–152.

Brayboy, B. M. J. (2005a). Toward a tribal critical race theory in education. *The Urban Review, 37*, 425–446.

Brayboy, B. M. J. (2005b). Transformational resistance and social justice: American Indians in Ivy League universities. *Anthropology and Education Quarterly, 36*, 193–211.

Brayboy, B. M. J., Fann, A. J., Castagno, A. E., & Solyom, J. A. (2012). *Postsecondary education for American Indian and Alaska Natives: Higher education for nation building and self-determination.* San Francisco, CA: Wiley.

Cannon, M. (2011). Ruminations on red revitalization: Exploring complexities of identity, difference and nationhood in Indigenous education. In G. J. Sefa Dei (Ed.), *Indigenous philosophies and critical education: A reader* (pp. 125–141). New York, NY: Peter Lang.

Castagno, A. E., & Lee, S. J. (2007). Native mascots and ethnic fraud in higher education: Using tribal critical race theory and the interest convergence principle as an analytic tool. *Equity & Excellence, 40*, 3–13.

Collins, P. H. (2007). Pushing the boundaries or business as usual? Race, class, and gender studies in sociological inquiry. In C. J. Calhoun (Ed.), *Sociology in America: A history* (pp. 572–604). Chicago, IL: University of Chicago Press.

Deloria, V. (1988). *Custer died for your sins: An Indian manifesto.* Norman: University of Oklahoma Press.

Deloria, Jr., V., & Wildcat, D. R. (2001). *Power and place: Indian education in America.* Golden, CO: Fulcrum.

Denetdale, J. (2006). Chairmen, presidents, and princesses: The Navajo Nation, gender, and the politics of tradition. *Wicazo Sa Review, 21,* 9–28.

Goeman, M. R. (2009). Notes toward a Native feminism's spatial practice. *Wicazo Sa Review, 24,* 169–187.

Grieco, E. M. (2001, December). *The Native Hawaiian and other Pacific Islander population: 2000* (2000 Census Briefs C2KBR/01–14). Washington, DC: United States Census Bureau.

Griffin, K. A., & Museus, S. D. (2011). Application of mixed-methods approaches to higher education and intersectional analyses. In S. D. Museus & K. A. Griffin (Eds.), *Using mixed-method approaches to study intersectionality in higher education: New directions for institutional research* (No. 151, pp. 5–13). San Francisco, CA: Jossey-Bass.

Guillory, R. M., & Wolverton, M. (2008). It's about family: Native American student persistence in higher education. *The Journal of Higher Education, 79,* 58–87.

Hall, L. K. (2009). Navigating our own "sea of islands": Remapping a theoretical space for Hawaiian women and Indigenous feminism. *Wicazo Sa Review, 24,* 15–38.

HeavyRunner, I., & DeCelles, R. (2002). Family education model: Meeting the student retention challenge. *Journal of American Indian Education, 41,* 29–37.

Huffman, T. (2001). Resistance theory and the transculturation hypothesis as explanations of college attrition and persistence among culturally traditional American Indian students. *Journal of American Indian Education, 40,* 1–23.

Jaimes, M. A. (1992). *The state of Native America: Genocide, colonization, and resistance.* Boston, MA: South End.

Kanaʻiaupuni, S. M., Malone, N., & Ishibashi, K. (2005). *Ka Huakaʻi: 2005 Native Hawaiian Educational Assessment.* Honolulu, HI: Kamehameha Schools, Pauahi Publications.

Kauanui, J. K. (2008a). *Hawaiian blood: Colonialism and the politics of sovereignty and indigeneity.* Durham, NC: Duke University Press.

Kauanui, J. K. (2008b). Native Hawaiian decolonization and the politics of gender. *American Quarterly, 60,* 281–287.

Lee, L. L. (2010). Navajo transformative scholarship in the twenty-first century. *Wicazo Sa Review, 25,* 33–45.

Lee, T. S. (2006). "I came here to learn how to be a leader": An intersection of critical pedagogy and Indigenous education. *InterActions: UCLA Journal of Education and Information Studies, 2,* 1–23.

Lee, T. S. (2009). Building Native nations through Native students' commitment to their communities. *Journal of American Indian Education, 48,* 19–36.

McCarty, T. L., Borgoiakova, T., Gilmore, P., Lomawaima, K. T., & Romero, M. E. (2005). Editors' introduction: Indigenous epistemologies and education: Self-determination, anthropology, and human rights. *Anthropology & Education Quarterly, 36,* 1–7.

Meyer, M. A. (2001). Our own liberation: Reflections on Hawaiian epistemology. *Contemporary Pacific, 13,* 124–148.

Meyer, M. A. (2008). Indigenous and authentic: Hawaiian epistemology and the triangulation of meaning. In N. K. Denzin, Y. S. Lincoln, & L. T. Smith (Eds.), *Handbook of critical and indigenous methodologies* (pp. 217–232). Los Angeles, CA: Sage.

Million, D. (2009). Felt theory: An Indigenous feminist approach to affect and history. *Wicazo Sa Review, 24,* 53–76.

Ogunwole, S. U. (2002, February). *The American Indian and Alaska Native population: 2000* (2000 Census Briefs C2KBR/01–15). Washington, DC: United States Census Bureau.

Okagaki, L., Helling, M. K., & Bingham, G. E. (2009). American Indian college students' ethnic identity and beliefs about education. *Journal of College Student Development, 50,* 157–176.

Ramirez, R. K. (2008). Learning across differences: Native and ethnic studies feminisms. *American Quarterly, 60,* 303–307.

Ross, L. (2009). From the "F" word to Indigenous/Feminisms. *Wicazo Sa Review, 24,* 39–52.

Salis Reyes, N. A. (2014, April). *Higher education and Native nation-building: Native Woman college graduates and goals to give back.* Paper session presented at the meeting of the American Educational Research Association, Philadelphia, PA.

Shield, R. W. (2009). Identifying and understanding Indigenous cultural and spiritual strengths in the higher education experiences of Indigenous women. *Wicazo Sa Review, 24,* 47–63.

Shotton, H. J., Lowe, S. C., & Waterman, S. J. (Eds.). (2012). *Beyond the asterisk: Understanding Native students in higher education.* Herndon, VA: Stylus.

Shotton, H. J., Oosahwe, E. S. L., & Cintrón, R. (2007). Stories of success: Experiences of American Indian students in a peer-mentoring retention program. *The Review of Higher Education, 31,* 81–107.

Smith, A. (2008). American studies without America: Native feminisms and the nation-state. *American Quarterly, 60,* 309–315.

Smith, A. (2010). Heteropatriarchy and the three pillars of White supremacy: Rethinking women of color organizing. In M. Adams, W. J. Blumenfeld, C. R. Castañeda, H. W. Hackman, M. L. Peters, & X. Zúñiga (Eds.), *Readings for diversity and social justice* (2nd ed., pp. 88–93). New York, NY: Routledge.

Smith, A., & Kauanui, J. K. (2008). Native feminisms engage American studies. *American Quarterly, 60,* 241–249.

Smith, D. G. (2012). Diversity: A bridge to the future? In M. N. Bastedo (Ed.), *The organization of higher education: Managing colleges for a new era* (pp. 225–255). Baltimore, MD: The Johns Hopkins University Press.

Smith, L. T. (1999). *Decolonizing methodologies: Research and Indigenous peoples.* New York, NY: Zed.

Waterman, S. J. (2012). Home-going as a strategy for success among Haudenosaunee college and university students. *Journal of Student Affairs Research and Practice, 49,* 193–209.

CHAPTER FIVE

Contextualizing the Higher Education Pathways of Undocumented Students

HEIDI WHITFORD AND CARMEN L. MCCRINK

Undocumented immigrants, as well as their U.S.-born offspring, are experiencing uncertain futures due to the contentious and uneven development of laws and policies affecting their access to higher education (Abrego & Gonzales, 2010). Similarly, undocumented children who were brought to the United States by their parents at a young age are also affected by these laws and policies that relate to access to higher education and financial aid resources (Flores, 2010b). This chapter examines higher education policy and practice with a focus on contextualizing the educational experience of undocumented students as they navigate the higher education landscape. Higher education institutions have long incorporated notions of diversity, inclusiveness, and equity within their organizational missions (Locks, Hurtado, Bowman, & Oseguera, 2008). Still, the place of undocumented students within this framework is at a nebulous point, and further exploration is necessary. Are the higher education organizational structures, policies, practices, and campus climates congruous with inclusivity in relation to the educational experiences of undocumented students? This chapter explores the concept of the intersecting identities of undocumented students, as well as the question of what still needs to be accomplished from an organizational learning standpoint with respect to higher education institutional transformation.

Undocumented students must navigate many layers of identity that illustrate their intersectionalities. Their multifaceted identities may include college student, family member, national identities, regional identities, and multi-ethnic identities; these are in addition to other identities such as class, race, gender, and sexual orientation. As described by Cole (2008), coalitions can be formed among those who share certain parts of identities. Within the framework of intersectionality, higher education presents a setting in which such coalitions can be observed as social, economic, and national borders are crossed. Hancock (2007) argued that intersectionality should be incorporated into research as a methodological framework, which is appropriate for the topic of undocumented students because of the many layers of their identities. As a theoretical framework, intersectionality has had a somewhat fluid definition (Nash, 2008). Still, intersectionality has provided researchers who advocate for antiracist and anti-oppression positions with a framework that aligns with principles of social justice (McCall, 2005).

The questions that this chapter pursues are twofold: First, what is the experience of undocumented students as they navigate the higher education environment? Second, how have various laws and policies impacted the access to higher education opportunity for undocumented students? These questions will be used to contribute to a conceptual framework of organizational learning underpinned by principles of social justice, diversity, and intersecting identities; such a framework was described by Smith and Parker (2005) to facilitate social change in organizations.

LITERATURE REVIEW

For the purposes of this chapter, it is necessary to clarify the term *undocumented*. Within the body of literature, there are many variations of terminology that describe people who have different legal statuses related to citizenship or residency within the United States, and two of these overlapping definitions, which are utilized in this chapter, are illustrated by Gildersleeve and Ranero (2010) and Seo (2010). Gildersleeve and Ranero used the term undocumented to describe both those immigrants who arrived in the United States and have no legally documented status and their children who may have been born in the United States but who also do not have legally documented status. Therefore, the use of the term *undocumented* may include both immigrants and U.S.-born people. A review of the literature resulted in many overlaps and inconsistencies in the use of terms. For consistency, this chapter uses the term *undocumented students* to mean both undocumented immigrants and U.S.-born children of undocumented immigrants who do not have legal residency or citizenship documentation. Seo (2010) provided a definition of undocumented as someone who does not have legal citizenship or residency status in the United States. The term *student*, for the purposes of this chapter, is defined as both college-going and precollege students, as described by Gildersleeve and Ranero. While there are many variations among these terms throughout the literature, the use of the term *undocumented student* will allow a consistency of description. Where appropriate, more detailed descriptors are utilized and explained more fully.

Garcia and Tierney (2011) provided an overview of the current state of the research of undocumented students' experiences within the U.S. higher education system and argued that this group is in great need of further research. Undocumented students also have been studied from a sociological perspective. Glenn (2011) explored how citizenship is constructed through the lens of sociology and examined issues relating to the social exclusion of undocumented immigrants. Similarly, Gonzales (2010) examined the role that social capital plays in the lives of undocumented students, particularly as they navigate the structures of educational institutions. Research also has been undertaken that examines the impact of various laws and policies on undocumented students, particularly as it pertains to barriers to higher education opportunity. For example, several research studies have examined how undocumented students have both legal and financial barriers to higher education due to laws that impact college admission, tuition rates, and financial aid (Bozik & Miller, 2013; Gonzales, 2010; McLendon, Mokher, & Flores, 2011; Olivas, 2009). Nevertheless, little research has been done that examines how higher education institutions have adapted to the needs of undocumented students. Thus, the way that the higher education institutions have responded to shape the context of these students' experiences is a central theme of this chapter.

Experiences and Perspectives of Undocumented Students

A number of researchers have delved into the personal histories and life experiences of undocumented students relating to their educational experiences. Some, for example, examined the resilience of undocumented students within the higher education setting (Pérez, Espinoza, Ramos, Coronado, & Cortes, 2009). Other studies examined the educational experiences of undocumented students that related to social and academic capital (Gonzales, 2010). Such research is important to discuss, because understanding students' experiences is an essential component of constructing an overall framework for investigating key aspects of how higher education institutions have adapted and responded to the undocumented student population as those students pursue higher education.

Using critical race theory as well as an intersectionality lens, Pérez Huber (2010) explored the higher education experiences of undocumented Chicano/a students, revealing the complexities of overlapping identities within the context of higher education. Using the term *LatCrit* to denote the strand of critical race theory that incorporates Latino/a perspectives, Pérez Huber explored the views of undocumented students at a California research university. She explained that using a critical race theory lens in research is crucial to challenge the institutional response toward the emergence of the undocumented student demographic within higher education.

According to Pérez Huber (2010), higher education institutions often take on stances of neutrality or color blindness when faced with problems of ethnic or racial marginalization or inequality on their campuses. Institutions must face these issues, rather than obscuring them behind of veil of neutrality or color blindness, as illustrated by her findings, which revealed that the academic success stories ascribed to undocumented students often become part of a misleadingly romanticized narrative. Pérez Huber further argued that this romanticized success story narrative needs to be replaced with a more nuanced, local, and specific investigation. Her research showed that undocumented college students experienced both racism and nativism as they undertook the process of completing high school and gaining access to higher education. The participants described how these experiences erased their family's histories and accomplishments and instead placed them in a preconceived position of inferiority. The undocumented students further discussed how they were viewed as contributing to the demise of the United States by taking away jobs from U.S. citizens.

Although the study of undocumented students in higher education is still an emerging field of research, other researchers have also delved into this sector to contribute further understanding to this phenomenon. For example, Enriquez (2011) discussed the personal histories of undocumented students and described the ways they utilized social capital to achieve their higher education goals. Enriquez's findings pointed toward the often fragmented information and financial resources that undocumented students faced as they attempted to navigate the higher education system. Such fragmentation leads to further marginalization and obstacles to pursuing higher education for a large number of undocumented students. Similarly, Gonzales (2011) researched how being undocumented affects the political and social capital of youth as they transition into adulthood and specifically examined the transition from being quasilegally protected within the K-12 education system, to moving into the legally unprotected status of adulthood. Hernandez et al. (2010) explored the lives of undocumented students and investigated the source of their motivation to survive in the face of fear and marginalization. Hernandez et al. found that undocumented students in college tend to live with two identities simultaneously: their college identity, where they limit the information they provide about their legal status due to fear of deportation, is compartmentalized from the identity that they share with close family and friends. The researchers also found that undocumented students encountered difficulties paying back higher-education-related debts after graduating due to employment barriers resulting from their legal status.

Pérez, Cortés, Ramos, and Coronado (2010) further explored the academic experiences of Latino/a undocumented students as they encountered many barriers and challenges to success. Researchers also explored the resiliency of undocumented students as they persisted through higher education pathways despite the many challenges they encountered (Muñoz & Maldonado, 2012; Pérez et al., 2009). As the aforementioned literature illustrates, the research of undocumented students should not be limited to a single identity; their circumstances are much more complex and require the consideration of multiple overlapping identities such as family, ethnicity, legal status, and academics. Moreover, the variety of literature that explores undocumented student experiences suggests that it is necessary to investigate how higher education institutions have addressed the changing needs of undocumented students.

Legal and Financial Implications

Undocumented children in the United States have the right to free public education at the K-12 level due to the outcome of a court case in 1982, *Plyler v. Doe* (Gildersleeve, Rumann, & Mondragón, 2010). Yet, access to postsecondary education is less clear for undocumented students. Some states, such as South Carolina, have instituted laws barring undocumented students from attending public higher education institutions (Olivas, 2009). Beyond the question of admissions, undocumented students must also consider the financial implications of their college choice, as it pertains to their eligibility to receive in-state tuition rates and state and federal financial aid. For undocumented students, their unauthorized status often leads to additional barriers to higher education opportunity, because in most cases, they are legally ineligible for many state and federal higher education benefits. For instance, Bozik and Miller (2013), McClendon et al. (2011), and Olivas (2009) have investigated the legal and financial implications that are specific to undocumented students in higher education, while Flores (2010a, 2010b) also investigated states that did have some version of a DREAM Act in place. The DREAM Act, a bill first introduced by the U.S. Senate in 2001, stands for the Development, Relief, and Education for Alien Minors Act and is one of several similar bills that also have been introduced at the state level (State Impact, n.d.). If passed, this bill and similar state-level bills would provide a pathway to citizenship for minors who immigrated to the United States at a young age and who meet certain eligibility requirements. By being granted citizenship, these residents would then be able to receive federal and state financial aid and other higher education benefits (Schmid, 2013).

Still, this bill (and others like it at the state and federal level) has had a tumultuous history and its widespread implementation is far from clear. Thus, the legal implications faced by both the children of undocumented immigrants as well as children who immigrated to the United States at a young age remain unclear as they relate to the children's higher education prospects. Seo (2010) addressed the unresolved issue of the citizenship status of U.S.-born children of undocumented immigrants, who also are excluded from the financial benefits of higher education opportunity that they would be eligible for if they had legal citizenship status. Some states, such as Texas, have already passed versions of the DREAM Act (Flores, 2010a). Texas and New Mexico currently are the only states that allow undocumented students to be eligible for state-based financial aid programs; as many as 10 states currently allow undocumented students to have access to in-state tuition rates (Gildersleeve et al., 2010). Additional research has explored the topic of undocumented students in higher education from the perspective of whether they are eligible for in-state tuition (Flores, 2010b; McClendon et al., 2011; Olivas, 2009; Reich & Barth, 2010). Given the current financial conditions of higher education, being ineligible to receive in-state tuition rates or state and federal financial aid could impose a significant barrier for undocumented students' access to higher education. The impact of this barrier is described in further detail by Bozick and Miller (2013), who found that undocumented students who lived in states that had policies that made them eligible for in-state tuition benefits were 65% more likely to go to college compared with their peers in other states; conversely, undocumented students who lived in states in which they were ineligible for in-state tuition rates were 49% less likely to pursue higher education. Their findings pointed toward the scenario in which undocumented students acted in accordance with their perceptions of the availability of higher education opportunity. Further complicating the college access context for undocumented students is their future ability to obtain employment after graduating from college. As described by Ellis and Chen (2013), their future legal status and work eligibility had an impact on their choice of whether to attend college.

As the aforementioned literature illustrates, undocumented students face a plethora of financial challenges as they navigate the higher education system. Some states bar their admission entirely from public higher education institutions (Olivas, 2009), while other states have policies in place that eliminate their ability to access in-state tuition rates or other financial aid benefits. Few undocumented students are eligible for the federal financial aid that the rest of the population has access to, such as Pell Grants, federal loans, and work-study funds (Gildersleeve et al., 2010). Because undocumented students are often from lower socioeconomic backgrounds, financial obstacles may be one of the most significant barriers to pursuing higher education (Gildersleeve et al., 2010). Thus, an exploration of the financial and legal policies that impact undocumented students reveals areas for further research that focus on the intersecting issues of socioeconomic status, college admissions, financial aid policy, and legal status.

Organizational Learning

Intersectionality as a lens is a relatively new phenomenon across colleges and universities, albeit under the umbrella of diversity, given the interdependence between the crossing of national borders and ethnic identities. As such, an organizational learning framework appears to be "particularly well suited to colleges and universities that are dealing with demographic and other changes" (Smith & Parker, 2005, p. 115). In spite of the need for what sometimes may be considered immediate change, academic institutions are not programmed to implement radical change based on a top-down mandate unless collaboration, opportunities for dialogue, and organizational climate are taken into account (Kezar, 2005a; Smith & Parker, 2005).

The literature across higher education is replete with the question as to what colleges and universities need to do in order to succeed in their lofty efforts of educating a diversified student population and, specifically, how these institutions may become actively engaged in a process that is systemic, yet fluid, in its capacity to adapt to internal and external forces of change. One of these changes is the emerging demographic of undocumented students. Organizational learning theory aims at the degree to which institutions can actually learn given the threats and/or limitations that may exist (Kezar, 2005a). Further, one of the issues that has surrounded the implementation of organizational learning theory is the preponderance of discussing the theory in isolation in lieu of relating or aligning it to a specific institutional issue or problem (Kezar, 2005a). Indeed, one of the most salient issues of concern for colleges and universities in this second decade of the 21st century is how to respond to the critical needs of undocumented students and, even more emphatically, how to pose this question within politically charged institutional cultures.

For the most part, colleges and universities are and will continue to be regarded as unique organizations given their mission statements, those who they serve, and how internal constituencies interact to inform institutional agendas. In his seminal work, Birnbaum (1988) discussed how certain management theories, which are usually attributed to business and industry, are not applicable to higher education. Within this context, Birnbaum posited that there are four models that frame the governance or management of colleges and universities; these are referred to as the bureaucratic, collegial, political, and anarchical models. Clearly, each of these models contributes to the functioning of the institution from a different stance. Nevertheless, it is only through the integration and interdependence of positive elements within each of these models that a college or university may develop a system of self-regulation that Birnbaum referred to as the cybernetic model (Birnbaum, 1988). The ability to self-regulate or make changes aligns with organizational learning tenets that focus on performance and learning of those individuals within the institutional setting (Kezar, 2005a).

Indeed, regardless of which model of governance is more pronounced at a given institution, the fact remains that the world of academia is one of power and privilege where ideologies have permeated and created distinct cultures. Organizational cultures manifest themselves through a series of norms and practices that catapult into different forms of privilege such as those granted to nonminority students (Smith, 2012). Thus, the stronger the culture in terms of institutionalized values, processes, and goals (Tierney, 1988), the more difficult it becomes to implement change and a sense of collaborative learning in the organization. Clearly, in order for a new paradigm to emerge—one that would be receptive to the inclusiveness of all student populations, and in the presented case, undocumented students—institutional transformation needs to occur across all units of student affairs, academic departments, and administration.

Institutional transformation is a gradual process and one that may only develop through collaboration. Kezar (2005b) discussed the three stages of a collaboration model within higher education institutions. The first stage aims at building commitment of all constituencies through specific elements including the integration of structures, values, learning, and campus networks. Stage two is where commitment is anchored within the culture of the institution and priorities are established, whereas stage three is focused on sustainability through the integration of structures or divisions. A major component or prerequisite of this collaborative effort is providing all institutional players with the historiography of diversity within the academy and what that means in today's political environment.

In recent decades, diversity initiatives have taken the form of affirmative action policies as a means to promote access for all students in addition to the implementation of multicultural initiatives, as well as the development of institutionalized educational programs to foster intergroup relations across different racial groups (Engberg, 2004). These actions have centered on the context of race and its place in higher education specifically, as it relates to the study of segregation and what scholars such as Minor (2008) referred to as "segregation residual" (p. 862). Thus, the focus of critical race theory has been on those issues surrounding students of color (e.g., Blacks, Latinos, and Asians) as the minority and disenfranchised groups in colleges and universities. At present, however, a discussion of bias and/or prejudice necessarily goes beyond race and ought to include the implications of national borders and the undocumented student. In her seminal work, *Borderlands/La Frontera: The New Mestiza,* Anzaldua (1987) discussed the idea of living in an "interdependent cosmos" (p. 103) as a Chicana trying to gain acceptance by the dominant culture. Clearly, this premise of multiple identities aligns with intersectionality as a framework toward understanding the plight faced by undocumented students and the need to educate all constituents by providing institutional data on this new population of students and creating opportunities for collaborative group learning through open dialogue.

Organizational learning is by no means the panacea for institutionalizing a diversity agenda that will forge pathways for undocumented students as they attempt to cross the myriad "borders" in colleges and universities. Nonetheless, it may provide higher education institutions with a blueprint for developing a culture that is open to dialogue, regardless of politics, in an attempt to uphold the legacy of access to higher education.

CONCLUSION

As discussed by Garcia and Tierney (2011), undocumented students comprise a segment of the overall undocumented population that is in great need of additional research. These students are in a particularly vulnerable state due to the many obstacles they face as they navigate the higher education landscape; these obstacles are further complicated by the students' legal status. As Suárez-Orozco, Yoshikawa, Teranishi, and Suárez-Orozco (2011) found, undocumented students navigate through many challenges that have profound effects on their development as they transition from young adults to college students and beyond.

This chapter provided an analysis of the existing higher education environment through which undocumented students must navigate, by examining the policies, practices, and contexts that impact their higher education experience. Through this analysis, it became clear that undocumented students face a myriad of intersecting identities and obstacles that impact their lives. Many higher education institutions have already worked toward widening access to marginalized groups of students, by providing access to financial aid to make college more affordable and implementing campus initiatives aimed at inclusivity and diversity. Still, undocumented students remain in the shadows and are often not able to access such support systems. Even for students who do not have problems related to their legal status, financial aid support has been eroded by budget cuts and rising tuition costs; income and educational inequality is continuing to grow despite efforts by higher education institutions to mitigate these problems (Smith & Parker, 2005).

Undocumented students face similar financial barriers that are made even more acute by their limited ability to receive institutional support for these issues. As Gildersleeve et al. (2010) pointed out, higher education institutions are slowly forming a response to the undocumented student population. Future research in this vein will lend support to the efforts of higher education institutions to respond to the needs of these students. Further complicating matters is the still unresolved patchwork of various state and federal laws and higher education policies that affect the ability of undocumented students to gain access to higher education. Ultimately, undocumented students who do manage to successfully navigate the higher education system to earn a diploma will still be faced with the issue of obtaining work with their unresolved legal status.

Through the use of intersectionality as a lens, this chapter began a process of deconstructing the overlapping identities of these students so as to shed light on how higher education institutions can adapt to these intersecting identities. Higher education remains an important pathway to growth and development for young adults, as well as essential to economic success and civic engagement; thus, the higher education context of undocumented students should have greater access to higher education opportunity. The benefits of higher education are further elaborated in a study by Perez, Espinoza, Ramos, Coronado and Cortes (2010), which indicated the high level of civic engagement by undocumented Latino college students. Indeed, research suggests that civic involvement during college years "predicts membership and leadership in community organizations into adulthood" (Ladewig & Thomas as cited in Perez et al., 2010, p. 258). The results of this study align with Latinos' definition of social justice, which is focused on "equality of opportunity and rights" (Torres-Harding, Steele, Schulz, Taha & Pico, 2014, p. 64). Clearly, however, in order to promote this "equality of opportunity," college and university administrators must recognize the existence of these students as part of their demographics and develop an understanding of the issues that surround this population through professional development training opportunities (Nienhusser, 2014).

Undocumented students face many of the same problems gaining access to college as low-income students, minority students, or first-generation students; yet the barriers faced by undocumented students are made additionally problematic by their undetermined legal status. Thus, as undocumented students attempt to navigate the complex higher education system, their ability to utilize support systems that are intended to assist students having difficulties is limited.

Organizational learning, as described previously, is a broad-based, collaborative way in which higher education institutions can examine and transform existing structures and support systems that can help improve the higher education prospects of undocumented students (Kezar, 2005a). As an example, Smith and Parker's (2005) work could provide guidance for the inclusion of undocumented students in the implementation of diversity initiatives at higher education institutions. Using Smith and Parker's model, organizational learning can be used to frame the multilayered institutional response to the intersecting identities of undocumented students. In the researchers' analysis of diversity initiatives, they included identities such as race, ethnicity, gender, sexuality, and socioeconomic status. Yet a discussion of diversity within academia cannot be considered complete without including the multifaceted reality and experiences of undocumented students, who face further complications and barriers to higher education opportunity. This chapter sheds light on the importance of this growing portion of the student population so that higher education policymakers, gatekeepers, and stakeholders can examine the context of undocumented students and formulate a response that is in congruence with the mission of higher education that is inclusive, diverse, attuned to social justice, and serves the public good. In addition, as illustrated earlier, further research on the phenomenon of undocumented students is needed, particularly as it pertains to their experiences gaining access to higher education, completing higher education, and then transitioning into the workforce.

REFERENCES

Abrego, L. J., & Gonzales, R. G. (2010). Blocked paths, uncertain futures: The postsecondary education and labor market prospects of undocumented Latino youth. *Journal of Education for Students Placed at Risk, 15,* 144–157.

Anzaldua, G. (1987). *Borderlands/La frontera: The new mestiza.* San Francisco, CA: Aunt Lute.

Birnbaum, R. (1988). *How colleges work: The cybernetics of academic organization and leadership.* San Francisco, CA: Jossey-Bass.

Bozick, R., & Miller, T. (2013). In-state college tuition policies for undocumented immigrants: Implications for high school enrollment among non-citizen Mexican youth. *Population Research and Policy Review, 33,* 1–18.

Cole, E. R. (2008). Coalitions as a model for intersectionality: From practice to theory. *Sex Roles, 59,* 443–453.

Ellis, L. M., & Chen, E. C. (2013). Negotiating identity development among undocumented immigrant college students: A grounded theory study. *Journal of Counseling Psychology, 60,* 251–264.

Engberg, M. E. (2004). Improving intergroup relations in higher education: A critical examination of the influence of educational interventions on racial bias. *Review of Educational Research, 74,* 473–524.

Enriquez, L. E. (2011). "Because we feel the pressure and we also feel the support": Examining the educational success of undocumented immigrant Latina/o students. *Harvard Educational Review, 81,* 476–500.

Flores, S. M. (2010a). The first state Dream Act: In-state resident tuition and immigration in Texas. *Educational Evaluation and Policy Analysis, 32,* 435–455.

Flores, S. M. (2010b). State DREAM acts: The effect of in-state resident tuition policies and undocumented Latino students. *The Review of Higher Education, 33,* 239–283.

Garcia, L. D., & Tierney, W. G. (2011). Undocumented immigrants in higher education: A preliminary analysis. *Teachers College Record, 113,* 2739–2776.

Gildersleeve, R. E., & Ranero, J. J. (2010). Precollege contexts of undocumented students: Implications for student affairs professionals. In J. Price (Ed.), *Understanding and supporting undocumented students: New directions for student services* (No. 131, pp. 19–33). San Francisco, CA: Jossey-Bass.

Gildersleeve, R. E., Rumann, C., & Mondragón, R. (2010). Serving undocumented students: Current law and policy. In J. Price (Ed.), *Understanding and supporting undocumented students: New directions for student services* (No. 131, pp. 5–18). San Francisco, CA: Jossey-Bass.

Glenn, E. N. (2011). Constructing citizenship exclusion, subordination, and resistance. *American Sociological Review, 76,* 1–24.

Gonzales, R. G. (2010). On the wrong side of the tracks: Understanding the effects of school structure and social capital in the educational pursuits of undocumented immigrant students. *Peabody Journal of Education, 85*, 469–485.

Gonzales, R. G. (2011). Learning to be illegal: Undocumented youth and shifting legal contexts in the transition to adulthood. *American Sociological Review, 76*, 602–619.

Hancock, A. M. (2007). When multiplication doesn't equal quick addition: Examining intersectionality as a research paradigm. *Perspectives on Politics, 5*, 63–79.

Hernandez, S., Hernandez, I., Gadson, R., Huftalin, D., Ortiz, A. M., White, M. C., & Yocum-Gaffney, D. (2010). Sharing their secrets: Undocumented students' personal stories of fear, drive, and survival. *New directions for student services, 2010*, 67–84.

Kezar, A. (2005a). What campuses need to know about organizational learning and the learning organization. In A. Kezar (Ed.), *Organizational learning in higher education: New directions for higher education* (No. 131, pp. 7–22). San Francisco, CA: Jossey-Bass.

Kezar, A. (2005b). Redesigning for collaboration within higher education institutions: An exploration into the development process. *Research in Higher Education, 46*, 831–860.

Locks, A. M., Hurtado, S., Bowman, N. A., & Oseguera, L. (2008). Extending notions of campus climate and diversity to students' transition to college. *The Review of Higher Education, 31*, 257–285.

McCall, L. (2005). The complexity of intersectionality. *Signs, 30*, 1771–1800.

McLendon, M. K., Mokher, C. G., & Flores, S. M. (2011). Legislative agenda setting for in-state resident tuition policies: Immigration, representation, and educational access. *American Journal of Education, 117*, 563–602.

Minor, J. T. (2008). Segregation residual in higher education: A tale of two states. *American Education Research Journal, 45*, 861–885.

Muñoz, S. M., & Maldonado, M. M. (2012). Counterstories of college persistence by undocumented Mexicana students: Navigating race, class, gender, and legal status. *International Journal of Qualitative Studies in Education, 25*, 293–315.

Nash, J. C. (2008). Re-thinking intersectionality. *Feminist Review, 89*, 1–15.

Nienhusser, H. K. (2014). Role of community colleges in the implementation of postsecondary education enrollment policies for undocumented students. *Community College Review, 42*(1), 3–22.

Olivas, M. A. (2009). Undocumented college students, taxation, and financial aid: A technical note. *The Review of Higher Education, 32*, 407–416.

Pérez Huber, L. (2010). Using Latina/o critical race theory (LatCrit) and racist nativism to explore intersectionality in the educational experiences of undocumented Chicana college students. *Educational Foundations, 24*, 77–96.

Pérez, W., Cortés, R. D., Ramos, K., & Coronado, H. (2010). "Cursed and blessed": Examining the socioemotional and academic experiences of undocumented Latina and Latino college students. In J. Price (Ed.), *Understanding and supporting undocumented students: New directions for student services* (No. 131, pp. 35–51). San Francisco, CA: Jossey-Bass.

Pérez, W., Espinoza, R., Ramos, K., Coronado, H. M., & Cortes, R. (2009). Academic resilience among undocumented Latino students. *Hispanic Journal of Behavioral Sciences, 31*, 149–181.

Perez, W., Espinoza, R., Ramos, K., Coronado, H., & Cortes, R. (2010). Civic engagement patterns of undocumented Mexican students. *Journal of Hispanic Higher Education, 9*(3), 245–265.

Reich, G., & Barth, J. (2010). Educating citizens or defying federal authority? A comparative study of in-state tuition for undocumented students. *Policy Studies Journal, 38*, 419–445.

Schmid, C. L. (2013). Undocumented childhood immigrants, the Dream Act and deferred action for childhood arrivals in the USA. *International Journal of Sociology and Social Policy, 33,* 693–707.

Seo, M. J. (2010). Uncertainty of access: US citizen children of undocumented immigrant parents and in-state tuition for higher education. *Columbia Journal of Law and Social Problems, 44,* 311–352.

Smith, D. G. (2012). Diversity: A bridge to the future? In M. N. Bastedo (Ed.), *The organization of higher education: Managing colleges for a new era* (pp. 225–255). Baltimore, MD: The Johns Hopkins University Press.

Smith, D. G., & Parker, S. (2005). Organizational learning: A tool for diversity and institutional effectiveness. In A. Kezar (Ed.), *Organizational learning in higher education: New directions for higher education* (No. 131, pp. 113–125). San Francisco, CA: Jossey-Bass.

State Impact (n.d.). *Your guide to the Florida DREAM Act.* Retrieved from http://stateimpact.npr.org/florida/tag/dream-act/

Suárez-Orozco, C., Yoshikawa, H., Teranishi, R. T., & Suárez-Orozco, M. M. (2011). Growing up in the shadows: The developmental implications of unauthorized status. *Harvard Educational Review, 81,* 438–473.

Tierney, W. G. (1988). Organizational culture in higher education: Defining the essentials. *The Journal of Higher Education, 59,* 2–21.

Torres-Harding, S. R., Steele, C., Schulz, E., Taha, F., & Pico, C. (2014). Student perceptions of social justice and social justice activities. *Education, Citizenship and Social Justice, 9*(1), 55–66.

CHAPTER SIX

Realizing the Power of Intersectionality Research in Higher Education

SAMUEL D. MUSEUS AND NATASHA A. SAELUA

As postsecondary institutions have become more diverse, higher education scholarship has increasingly focused on diversity-related topics. For example, higher education research on the benefits of diversity, campus racial climates, and racialized campus cultures has become more common (e.g., Harper & Hurtado, 2007; Museus & Jayakumar, 2012). It is important to acknowledge, however, that this research can simultaneously contribute to a common diversity and equity agenda, while rendering particular identity groups voiceless within that narrative. If higher education research aims to increase understanding of all students in higher education and inform ways to maximize the likelihood that they will thrive, it is important for postsecondary education scholars to seek to excavate the voices of all marginalized populations and generate authentic understandings of these groups. In this chapter, we highlight intersectionality as a valuable conceptual lens and analytical tool for achieving these ends (Museus & Griffin, 2011).

Intersectionality has been described as an "analytic sensibility...a way of thinking about the problem of sameness and difference and its relation to power" (Cho, Crenshaw, & McCall, 2013, p. 795). Intersectionality was first introduced in the legal field but has been adopted and has informed discourse in multiple disciplines—including gender studies, ethnic studies, sociology, and education— allowing researchers to excavate many voices and experiences marginalized by dominant narratives (e.g., Cole, 2009; Museus & Griffin, 2011). As a concept, intersectionality suggests that the confluence of systems of subordination shape individual experiences in distinct ways (Crenshaw, 1993). As a method, intersectionality allows researchers to move beyond simplistic one-dimensional analyses to ensure that particular groups are not excluded or marginalized from discussions of diversity and equity in higher education and ensures that the voices of these populations are integrated into this discourse (Museus & Griffin, 2011). Therefore, intersectionality constitutes both a valuable tool for deconstructing complex dominant systems of oppression while also serving as a salient theoretical lens for pursuing new lines of inquiry and illuminating new voices in higher education research.

Still, while scholars have employed intersectionality in higher education research, many of those studies examine the intersections among identities without centering the role of systems of power and privilege in the discussion or providing in-depth analyses of the ways in which multiple systems of subordination shape experiences within higher education. Consequently, we believe that intersectionality, as both a concept and method, is an underutilized tool in higher education scholarship. In this chapter, we make an effort to advance higher education discourse by underscoring the importance of scholars applying intersectionality as a tool to gain deeper and more complex understandings of how systems of oppression intersect to shape the experiences of people within higher education. Specifically, we demonstrate the utility of intersectionality as an analytical tool for examining sexual violence targeted toward Asian American and Pacific Islander (AAPI) women in postsecondary education.

The experiences of AAPI women offer a valuable example of the ways in which intersectionality shapes experiences with sexual violence. AAPI women are stereotyped as model minorities who achieve universal academic and occupational success, but existing evidence suggests that this population faces significant challenges in higher education (Chen & Hune, 2011; Espiritu, 2007; Hune, 1998; Museus & Kiang, 2009; Museus & Truong, 2013; Yeung, 2013). First, the model minority stereotype fuels misconceptions that AAPI women do not encounter challenges or need support. Second, AAPI women are underrepresented in certain spheres of postsecondary education, such as in faculty and executive administrative ranks. Third, AAPI women are frequently ignored or marginalized in the academy, often rendering them voiceless and invisible in higher education. Finally, in addition to the model minority myth, several other racialized and gendered stereotypes plague the experiences of AAPI women. These stereotypes include assumptions that all AAPI women are passive, exotic, and hypersexual, which we discuss in more detail later.

First, we provide a brief discussion of the concept of intersectionality, paying particular attention to the advantages of using the framework in higher education research. Second, we analyze the experiences of AAPI women who have experienced sexual violence, including sexual harassment and sexual assault, to provide an example of how intersectionality can be employed to generate a deeper understanding of specific marginalized populations in higher education. Finally, we call on higher education researchers to utilize intersectionality to examine issues in a richer, more in-depth way to advance research and discourse.

OVERVIEW OF INTERSECTIONALITY

In her seminal work, *Mapping the Margins*, Crenshaw (1993) introduced the term *intersectionality* through an analysis of the ways in which social structures, politics, and identities converge to shape the lives of women of color. She emphasized three types of intersectionality. Representational intersectionality illuminates how the social production of images of individuals living at the intersections of systems of subordination can function to subordinate them while ignoring their interests. Structural intersectionality refers to ways in which the location of people at the intersections of systems of oppression makes their experiences qualitatively unique. And, political intersectionality illuminates how people can belong to multiple identity groups (e.g., women and communities of color) with different and sometimes conflicting political agendas, which can lead to the silencing of their voices. Through her analysis, Crenshaw called attention to the importance of looking at systemic intersections and how they shape and manifest in individual experiences.

Since Crenshaw (1993) introduced the concept of intersectionality, it has been used to combat overreliance on singular conceptions of identity in multiple disciplines. It also has been used to understand the multiplicity of social systems and how those systems intersect to create a unique experience for identity groups that occupy the corresponding intersections. Intersectionality is not employed as a method of arguing who is more or less oppressed but to illuminate the unique influence of intersecting identities.

Intersectionality also been critiqued as well. As a conceptual and analytical instrument, for example, intersectionality has been critiqued for its "excessive specificity" or "the complexity that arises when the subject of analysis expands to include multiple dimensions of social life and categories of analysis" (McCall, 2005, p. 1772). Intersectionality also has been critiqued because it multiplies lines of distinction among populations, creating boundaries that preclude generalization and diminish shared experiences within identity groups. Still, proponents of intersectionality have asserted that a truly intersectional analysis does not simply add variables (MacKinnon, 2013). That is, intersectionality is not an additive practice, whereby forms of subordination increase or decrease the amount of oppression experienced. Instead, intersectionality reveals and can create new possibilities for alliances across identity groups, because the specificity employed by intersectional researchers acknowledges, engages, validates, and empowers communities whose identities and experiences have otherwise been suppressed or ignored because of overreliance on a singular identity as the dominant analytical mode (Carastathis, 2013). Indeed, Crenshaw (1993) paid particular attention to the collaborative potential of intersectionality, pointing out how the framework can provide a basis for the building of coalitions against racism and other forms of oppression.

In the current discussion, we consider intersectional analysis a discursive exercise, allowing us to develop a discussion that magnifies intersections to develop a more nuanced understanding of social structures, politics, and individual experiences (Crenshaw 1989; MacKinnon 2013; Museus & Griffin, 2011). Employed in this way, intersectionality can enable higher education researchers to develop a more complex and multidimensional understanding of the confluence of race, gender, socioeconomic status, citizenship, and sexuality in the lives of administrators, faculty, staff, and students. In the following section, we present an example, specific to the AAPI community that disrupts dominant conversations about the community and generates new lines of inquiry and discourse.

RACIALIZED SEXUAL VIOLENCE AND ASSAULT IN THE ACADEMY

In this section, we utilize intersectionality as a conceptual lens to illuminate the ways in which it can be used to generate a more intricate understanding of higher education phenomena. More specifically, we employ Crenshaw's (1993) concepts of representational, structural, and political intersectionality to analyze sexual violence toward AAPI women in higher education.

Sexual harassment and assault is a persisting problem within the academy. For example, approximately 1 in 5 women in college will experience an attempted or completed rape (Centers for Disease Control and Prevention, 2012). Moreover, while all women can experience sexual harassment and assault in higher education, statistics suggest that women of color are both overrepresented among sexual harassment and assault victims and underreport such incidents compared to their White female counterparts (Hernandez, 2000). And, scholars have argued that the overrepresentation of women of color among victims and their underreporting can be better understood using intersectional lenses that help understand how the confluence of gender, race, and other factors shape the experiences of this population (e.g., Cho, 1997; Crenshaw, 1993).

Representational Intersectionality

For centuries, the dominant White majority in the West has racialized Asian and Asian American women as sexually desirable, submissive, hypersexual, and subordinate beings (Cho, 1997; Espiritu, 2007; Museus & Truong, 2013; Prasso, 2005). Congruent with this stereotype, a plethora of objectifying stereotypical images of Asian American women as prostitutes and sexual commodities have pervaded the Western media throughout history. For example, in the 1987 film *Full Metal Jacket,* which depicts the experiences of American soldiers during the Vietnam War, a Vietnamese prostitute approaches a group of soldiers and repeats the phrases "Me so horny" and "Me love you long time" in broken English, which have endured as phrases that are still used to subordinate and objectify Asian American women in the present day. Similarly, in a 2005 episode of the sitcom *Two and a Half Men,* Charlie Sheen's character is watching his brother's chiropractic office when an Asian American Woman comes in looking for work, is hired by Sheen, and is shown charging a customer for implied sex acts. Shortly thereafter, Sheen's character turns the office into a brothel. And, in 2013, the band *Day Above Ground* released a video called *Asian Girlz.* The video portrayed an Asian American model undressing for the band members, who were standing in a cage, and included lyrics filled with comments about engaging in sex acts, slanted eyes, private body parts, and other stereotypical words and phrases. These are just a few examples of images that permeate the media and reflect the exoticization of women of Asian descent.

Similarly, for centuries, the White majority in Western nations has historically racialiezd and currently racializes Pacific Islander women as flower-adorned, exotic, and lacking in sexual inhibitions (Johnston, 2003; Tiffany, 2005). Indeed, while many people in the continental United States are exposed to very few images of Pacific Islander women, the representations that they do encounter frequently take on the form of uninhibited dancing hula girls who exist for the pleasure of (often White) men. A simple Google images search for *women in Hawaii,* for instance, generates a plethora of provocative pictures depicting half-dressed women in Hawaii lying in sand, wearing coconut bras, and sporting grass skirts. This objecti-fication is different than, but parallel to, the hypersexual and submissive portrayals of Asian American women.

Such constructions of AAPI women as prostitutes or sexual commodities both inform the dominant majority's views of this population and contribute to the frequency with which these women might experience sexual harassment and assault in higher education specifically (Cho, 1997; Hernandez, 2000; Museus & Truong, 2013). Museus and Truong (2013), for example, demonstrated how Internet discussion boards illuminate college students' racialized and sexually objectifying views of Asian American women, and race-themed parties of White students dressed as geishas periodically illuminate these perspectives on college and university campuses around the country. Moreover, evidence suggests that these stereotypes shape the environmental conditions that AAPIs in postsecond-ary education must navigate. Cho (1997), for instance, detailed how the impact of race and gender converged to generate stereotypes of Asian American female faculty members and contributed to the sexist, hostile, and demeaning work environments that they were forced to negotiate within the academy.

Structural Intersectionality

As mentioned, structural intersectionality refers to the ways in which the location of women of color at the intersection of racism, sexism, and other systems of oppression shape the experiences of these women in unique ways (Crenshaw, 1993). In the case of sexual harassment and assault in higher education, structural intersectionality can shed light on the challenges that AAPI women face in their efforts to report and fight these encounters. Indeed, both societal structures and structures within higher education might contribute to challenges that AAPI women face in reporting and challenging their encounters with sexual harassment and assault.

Regarding societal structures, it is important to note that racism and sexism can intersect with other systems of subordination, such as classism and heterosexism, to shape the experiences of women of color in higher education (Crenshaw, 1993). For example, women who are burdened by poverty—including female students and pre-tenured faculty members—often must risk being put in vulnerable financial positions in order to report sexual harassment or assault from administrators and faculty. Specifically, they might risk jeopardizing their academic standing, employment prospects, or reputations at their institutions (which could influence promotion and tenure decisions for women faculty). In addition, international and undocumented AAPI women might not report incidents of sexual harassment or assault because of fear of deportation (Ontiveros, 2010).

Within institutions of higher education, there are environmental conditions that also pose challenges for female victims of sexual harassment and assault. For example, both women and AAPIs are underrepresented in leadership positions in institutions of higher education (Cobb-Roberts & Agosto, 2011–2012; Neilson & Suyemoto, 2010). While it is not impossible for men and non-AAPIs to be sympathetic or empathetic to the situation of victims, it is reasonable to suspect that they are less likely to fully understand the AAPI women's situations and support them. At the programmatic level, there is often an absence of racially, culturally, and linguistically relevant support services for AAPIs on college campuses (e.g., Suzuki, 2002), making it a challenge for AAPI women to locate such supports.

Political Intersectionality

In the previous section, we noted that political intersectionality underscores the reality that individuals can be situated within multiple subordinated groups that have incongruent and sometimes conflicting political agendas and that this intersection can work to silence their voices. In the case of AAPI women who experience sexual harassment and assault on college campuses, political intersectionality can also manifest in barriers to navigating these experiences. We highlight two of these barriers, including how political agendas can function to protect AAPI men and the adverse impact of cultural norms that work against disclosure.

AAPI women who experience sexual harassment or assault can encounter pressures not to report such experiences from within their own communities. Indeed, scholars have written about how women of color can face pressures to suppress such experiences because disclosure could reflect poorly on their racial or ethnic community (e.g., Crenshaw, 1993; Donovan & Williams, 2002). Thus, AAPI women in higher education can feel pressures to conceal their experiences with sexual harassment and assault in higher education. Moreover, systems of racism and sexism also function to emasculate and subordinate Asian American men in the United States through the construction of polarized images that frame these individuals as asexual and socially awkward or threatening hypersexual deviants (Eng, 2001; Museus & Truong, 2013; Shek, 2006), while those same systems racialize Pacific Islander men as savages (Jolly, 1997; Thomas, 1987). Therefore, when AAPI women pursue reporting of sexual harassment and assault incidents *within* the AAPI community, they run the risk of divulging information that can reinforce these racial stereotypes of their male counterparts of color as deviant. In this way, politics of race and gender can intersect to oppress Asian Americans in general but further subordinate the perspectives and needs of AAPI women.

Finally, researchers have written that racism and sexism intersect to silence women of color through patriarchal norms (Ontiveros, 2010). Culture is often multidimensional, intersecting, complex, and changing. Thus, it is difficult to make culture-based generalizations. However, some have asserted that many AAPI cultures are more often based on collectivism, familial interest, self-control, shame, and interpersonal harmony than Western cultures (McEwen Kodama, Alvarez, Lee, & Liang, 2002; Ontiveros, 2010). While AAPIs come from communities that differ along all of these dimensions and adopt these characteristics to varying degrees, conceptualization of AAPI cultures in this way has led to White men racializing AAPI women as people who will not report sexual crimes because they do not want to shame their families and targeting them in sexual assault activities (Museus, 2013). In addition, while the aforementioned traits might not characterize all AAPI cultures uniformly, it is possible that some of these communities do perpetuate such norms in ways that make it more difficult for AAPI women to report incidents of sexual harassment and assault (Olive, 2012).

The analysis of sexual harassment and assault experienced by AAPI women in higher education through the analytic lenses of representational, structural, and political intersectionality yields valuable insights. The preceding analysis provides one salient example of how intersectionality can be used to shed light on AAPIs in higher education. It can also inform policymakers and practitioners about how they can construct and revise policies to better support AAPIs, especially AAPI women, in their efforts to navigate university policies and procedures around sexual harassment and assault. For example, the racially specific experiences illuminated in the preceding analysis underscore the reality that postsecondary educators should ensure that their AAPI students are educated about the ways in which racism and sexism can contribute to the incidents of sexual harassment and assault on their campuses. It demonstrates the value of educators creating space to deconstruct racialized sexual constructions of AAPI men and women. The examination also highlights the importance of increasing the representation of women and AAPIs in leadership positions in postsecondary education institutions and having culturally and linguistically relevant support services for AAPI women on college and university campuses.

CONCLUSION

We conclude this chapter by calling on higher education researchers to engage in intersectional analyses that complicate and deepen existing understandings of the issues and experiences faced by marginalized populations in higher education. Intersectionality offers the potential of a paradigm shift in higher education— the centering of systems of oppression and marginalized identities in discourse around postsecondary systems and institutions. The framework also offers a way for researchers to be critical of what they bring to the table, intellectually, when they conduct higher education research. It behooves researchers employing intersectionality as an analytical tool to ask whether their work advances efforts to shed light on intersecting systems of oppression and power and informs efforts that might be aimed at dismantling these organizations. Thus, herein, we argue that researchers should pursue intersectional analyses in higher education that are embedded in a critique of systemic power.

While intersectionality is about research, it is also about the researcher. Therefore, it is valuable to underscore the communal aspect of intersectionality (Cho et al., 2013). As researchers, intersectionality can be about generating a community of higher education scholars who are concerned with knowledge production, as well as the struggle against systems of oppression and power. If one chooses this path, the community becomes a vital source of courage, constructive dialogue, and critical hope for the deconstruction of systems of oppression.

REFERENCES

Carastathis, A. (2013). Identity categories as potential coalitions. *Signs: Journal of Women in Culture and Society, 38*, 941–965.

Centers for Disease Control and Prevention. (2012). *Sexual violence: Facts at a glance.* Washington, DC: Author.

Chen, E. W., & Hune, S. (2011). Asian American Pacific Islander women from Ph.D. to campus president: Gains and leaks in the pipeline. In G. Jean-Marie & B. Lloyd-Jones (Eds.), *Women of color in higher education: Changing directions and new perspectives* (pp. 163–190). Bingley, England: Emerald.

Cho, S. (1997). Converging stereotypes in racialized sexual harassment: Where the model minority meets Suzie Wong. *Gender Race & Just, 7*, 177–185.

Cho, S., Crenshaw, K., & McCall, L. (2013). Toward a field of intersectionality studies: Theory, application, and praxis. *Signs: Journal of Women in Culture and Society, 38*, 785–810.

Cobb-Roberts, D., & Agosto, V. (2011–2012). Underrepresented women in higher education: An overview. *Negro Educational Review, 62–63*(1–4), 7–11

Cole, E. (2009). Intersectionality and research in psychology. *American Psychologist, 64*, 170–180.

Crenshaw, K. (1989). Demarginalizing the intersection of race and sex: A Black feminist critique of antidiscrimination doctrine, feminist theory, and antiracist politics. *University of Chicago Legal Forum, 139*, 139–167.

Crenshaw, K. (1993). Mapping the margins: Intersectionality, identity politics, and the violence against women of color. *Stanford Law Review, 43*, 1241–1299.

Donovan, R., & Williams, M. (2002). Living at the intersection: The effects of racism and sexism on Black rape survivors. *Women and Therapy, 25*, 95–105.

Eng, D. L. (2001). *Racial castration: Managing masculinity in Asian America.* Durham, NC: Duke University Press.

Espiritu, Y. L. (2007). *Asian American women and men: Labor, laws, and love* (2nd ed.). Lanham, MD: Rowman & Littlefield.

Harper, S. R., & Hurtado, S. (2007). Nine themes in campus racial climates and implications for institutional transformation. In S. R. Harper & L. D. Patton (Eds.), *Responding to the realities of race on campus: New directions for student services* (No. 120, pp. 7–24). San Francisco, CA: Jossey-Bass.

Hernandez, T. K. (2000). Sexual harassment and racial disparity: The mutual construction of gender and race. *Gender, Race, and Justice, 4*, 183–224.

Hune, S. (1998). *Asian Pacific American women in higher education: Claiming visibility and voice.* New York, NY: Association of American Colleges and Universities.

Johnston, A. (2003). *Missionary writing and empire, 1800–1860.* Cambridge, UK: Cambridge University Press.

Jolly, M. (1997). From Point Venus to Bali Hai: Eroticism and exoticism in representations of the Pacific. In L. Manderson & M. Jolly (Eds.), *Sites of desire, economics of pleasure: Sexualities in Asian and the Pacific* (pp. 99–122). Chicago, IL: University of Chicago Press.

MacKinnon, C. (2013). Intersectionality as a method: A note. *Signs: Journal of Women in Culture and Society, 38*, 1019–1039.

McCall, L. (2005). The complexity of intersectionality. *Journal of Women in Culture and Society, 30*, 1771–1800.

McEwen, M. K., Kodama, C. M., Alvarez, A. N., Lee, S., & Liang, C. T. H. (Eds.). (2002). *Working with Asian American college students: New directions for student services* (No. 97). San Francisco, CA: Jossey-Bass.

Museus, S. D. (2013). *Asian American students in higher education.* New York, NY: Routledge.

Museus, S. D., & Griffin, K. A. (2011). Mapping the margins in higher education: On the promise of intersectionality frameworks in research and discourse. In K. A. Griffin & S. D. Museus (Eds.), *Using mixed-methods approaches to study intersectionality in higher education: New directions for institutional research* (No. 151, pp. 15–26). San Francisco, CA: Jossey-Bass.

Museus, S. D., & Kiang, P. N. (2009). The model minority myth and how it contributes to the invisible minority reality in higher education research. In S. D. Museus (Ed.), *Conducting research on Asian Americans in higher education: New directions for institutional research* (No. 142, pp. 5–15). San Francisco, CA: Jossey-Bass.

Museus, S. D., & Jayakumar, U. M. (2012). *Creating campus cultures: Fostering success among racially diverse student populations.* New York, NY: Routledge.

Museus, S. D., & Truong, K. A. (2013). Racism and sexism in cyberspace: Engaging stereotypes of Asian American women and men to facilitate student learning and development. *About Campus, 18,* 14–21.

Neilson, P. A., & Suyemoto, K. L. (2010). Using culturally sensitive frameworks to study Asian American leaders in higher education. In S. D. Museus (Ed.), *Conducting research on Asian Americans in higher education* (pp. 83–94). San Francisco, CA: Jossey-Bass.

Olive, V. C. (2012). Sexual assault against women of color. *Journal of Student Research, 1,* 1–9.

Ontiveros, L. (2010). Three perspectives on workplace harassment of women of color. *Women's Law Forum, 23,* 817–828.

Prasso, S. (2005). *The Asian mystique: Dragon ladies, geisha girls, and our fantasies of the exotic orient.* New York, NY: Perseus.

Shek, Y. L. (2006). Asian American masculinity: A review of literature. *The Journal of Men's Studies, 14,* 379–391.

Suzuki, B. H. (2002). Revisiting the model minority stereotype: Implications for student affairs practice and higher education. In M. K. McEwen, C. M. Kodama, A. N. Alvarez, S. Lee, & C. T. H. Liang (Eds.), *Working with Asian American college students: New directions for student services* (No. 97, pp. 21–32). San Francisco, CA: Jossey-Bass.

Tiffany, S. W. (2005). Contesting the erotic zone: Margaret Mead's fieldwork photographs of Samoa. *Pacific Studies, 28,* 19–45.

Thomas, N. (1987). Complementary and history: Misrecognizing gender in the Pacific. *Oceania, 57,* 261–270.

Yeung, F. P. F. (2013). Struggles for professional and intellectual legitimacy: Experiences of Asian and Asian American female faculty. In S. D. Museus, D. C. Maramba, & R. T. Teranishi (Eds.), *The misrepresented minority: New insights on Asian Americans and Pacific Islanders, and their implications for higher education* (pp. 281–293). Sterling, VA: Stylus.

CHAPTER SEVEN

Heteronormativity Fractured and Fused

Exploring the College Experiences of Multiple Marginalized LGBT Students

TRACI THOMAS-CARD AND REBECCA ROPERS-HUILMAN

The college years provide a rich environment in which many students are exposed to new ideas and perspectives differing from their own. Friedman and Leaper (2010) acknowledged that "college especially can provide opportunities for identity exploration" and that "social support may also increase during college" (p. 153). Students often experience development in interpersonal, intrapersonal, and epistemological ways, the processes of which depend on both identity and context (Baxter Magolda, 2004). Yet, for Lesbian, gay, bisexual, and transgender or transsexual (LGBT) students, the college system may be more complex to navigate than it is for students who identify as heterosexual because of heteronormativity that shapes those environments. LGBT students who are also underrepresented because of their race or ethnicity, gender, socioeconomic status, age, religion, or ability may struggle to find reinforcement for their academic and social growth. Previous research about the LGBT population has established a need to address the ways in which sexual orientation and gender identity intersect with other aspects of one's identity (D'Augelli, 1994; Pascarella & Terenzini, 2005; Renn & Bilodeau, 2005). This chapter explores the experiences of college students who are marginalized because they identify as LGBT and with another identity that is marginalized in the United States. Specifically, it foregrounds research on how sexual orientation and gender identity intersect with race, ethnicity, religion, socioeconomic status, age, and ability.

This chapter will both assist higher education practitioners in helping to create meaningful and positive experiences for students and build on current research that examines the intersections of students' identities and college student development. The analysis draws on queer theory and intersectionality to elucidate how the multiple dimensions of LGBT students' identities affect their college experiences in a heteronormative culture. Heteronormativity calls attention to the assumption that identifying as heterosexual and cisgender is the norm in a given environment and is embedded in the foundation of the traditional college campus, from the physical space to the overarching organizational structure of higher education institutions (Burgess, 2005; Montgomery & Stewart, 2012). Considering how LGBT college students with multiple marginalized identities may be impacted by this heteronormative environment is significant to understanding how their identity impacts their development as students.

QUEER THEORY

Queer theory rejects the notion of a gender binary system and heterosexism and examines how societal constructs have contributed to the marginalization of individuals based on their sexual orientations and gender identities (Abes, 2009; Abes, Jones, & McEwen, 2007; Talburt, 2009). Teich (2012) defined sexual orientation as an individual's romantic or physical attraction to another and gender identity as an individual's internal sense of identifying along the gender continuum of man or Woman. Wilchins (2004) argued that queer theory was developed from feminist and postmodern thought to understand the inequities faced by those who identified as LGBT as well as the societal power that may marginalize individuals based on their sexual orientations and gender identities, while Talburt (2009) believed that queer theory was developed as a way of comprehending "the idea of a discrete, stable (sexual) identity, arguing that the homo/hetero division is constituted by a power/knowledge regime that organizes the normal and the abnormal and orders social and institutional relations" (p. 120). Abes (2009) explained that queer theory provides useful perspectives on the heteronormative nature of student development theory and the inequities faced by students who identify as LGBT. Using a queer theory perspective can enhance research on the ways in which college students may be influenced by the development of their sexual orientation or gender identity by examining the heteronormativity that shapes the college student environment. Still, Abes noted that because queer theory does not consider individual development, it "does not offer an interpretation of development that necessarily resonates with how many college students describe themselves" (p. 144). The use of LGBT identity development models in conjunction with queer theory offers one way of addressing this limitation. In this section of the chapter, we include a brief review of frequently cited models of identity development to foreground approaches to understanding student development that do not rely on a single, heteronormative way of experiencing development. Models by Cass (1979, 1984), D'Augelli (1994), and McCarn and Fassinger (1996) offer explanations of the various stages individuals who identify as LGBT may experience as they come to understand their sexual orientations or gender identities.

The model originally developed by Cass (1979, 1984) is a psychosocial model and features six stages of homosexual identity development. The first stage identified by Cass is known as identity confusion and explains reactions by individuals first beginning to question their previously held sexual identities. The second stage, identity comparison, describes the point when an individual has "accepted the *potentiality* of a homosexual identity" (Cass, 1984, p. 151). The third stage, identity tolerance, occurs when an individual seeks out others who identify as LGBT. The fourth stage, identity acceptance, happens when an individual has a more positive view of LGBT identity but still maintains a heterosexual act when perceived as necessary. The fifth stage, identity pride, occurs when "homosexuals as a group…are seen as important and creditable while heterosexuals have become discredited and devalued" (Cass, 1984, p. 152). The sixth and final stage in Cass's model, identity synthesis, happens when an individual acknowledges sexual identity as only one aspect of her or his character.

Like the model developed by Cass (1979, 1984), D'Augelli's (1994) model is also comprised of stages. The six identity processes are "exiting heterosexual identity, developing a personal Lesbian-gay-bisexual identity status, developing a Lesbian-gay-bisexual social identity, becoming a Lesbian-gay-bisexual offspring, developing a Lesbian-gay intimacy status, and entering a Lesbian-gay-bisexual community" (D'Augelli, 1994, p. 319). Both Cass and D'Augelli's models of identity development are linear in nature; individuals progress through various stages of acceptance in understanding their sexual orientation, assuming the completion of one stage of identity formation before moving to the next.

In an attempt to address limitations of previous identity development models, McCarn and Fassinger (1996) developed a model of Lesbian identity development that simultaneously examines individual sexual identity and group membership identity. McCarn and Fassinger's model has four phases. The first is awareness, which assumes an individual will experience a feeling of being different from the heterosexual norm. The second phase is exploration, which includes feelings about or relationships with other women, and the third phase is deepening/commitment, in which a Woman gains self-knowledge about her sexual orientation and makes choices about her sexuality. The fourth phase is internalization/synthesis, which occurs when a Woman "experiences fuller self-acceptance of desire/love for women as a part of her overall identity" (p. 523) and implies that reaching this stage may take many years. McCarn and Fassinger noted that a key difference between their model and others is that they do "not assume disclosure behaviors as evidence of developmental advancement, except, to some extent, at the last phase of group identity" (p. 522).

The models created by Cass (1979, 1984), D'Augelli (1994), and McCarn and Fassinger (1996) tend to be frequently referenced in literature focusing on the LGBT population and suggest an understanding that the experience of LGBT identity formation happens in stages. Some disagreement exists about whether this development occurs in a linear nature or is more fluid. Certain scholars view existing LGBT identity models as problematic because they study only sexual orientation while excluding consideration of other variables of identity (Eliason, 1996; McCarn & Fassinger, 1996; Pena-Talamantes, 2013). Existing identity models are also limited in that they tend to focus on Lesbian and gay identity formation. Currently, there is only a small amount of research on those who identify as bisexual, pansexual, queer/questioning, transgender and transsexual, intersex, and so forth; scholars and practitioners would benefit from further exploration of the development of identity within these populations. Because identity models typically address individual development but do not consider the influence of external factors, using queer theory in conjunction with existing identity models may broaden scholars' and practitioners' understanding of the way in which development for LGBT students occurs both on an individual (micro) level and a societal (macro) level.

In addition to a review of LGBT identity models, we call attention to research that uses a queer theory lens to study the transgender college student population as well as research on LGBT college student development. The term *transgender* can include a wide range of identities along the gender continuum (Beemyn, Curtis, Davis, & Tubbs, 2005; Effrig, Bieschke, & Locke, 2011). Research on transgender students in higher education is significant because "colleges have been slow to recognize, much less provide support to, transgender people" (Beemyn, 2003, p. 34). Perhaps in part because of this lack of support, research on the transgender or transsexual college student community often explores experiences of discrimination and violence. Name changes on official documentation, navigating appearance changes if students are in transition, and fear of identity disclosure are challenges frequently faced by transgender or transsexual students, and the existing research indicates that these students regularly experience both institutional discrimination as well as personal victimization.

Talburt's (2009) work points out the limitations in research that focuses solely around the negative experiences of LGBT youth. Talburt noted that, while this research is "well-intentioned, such practices rely on narrow ideas of who LGBT youth are and what they need" (p. 113). One way to address this concern is to focus on leadership in the LGBT community. In their study on LGBT college student leaders and allies, Renn and Bilodeau (2005) used D'Augelli's (1994) model to explore "the relationship between involvement in leadership of an LGBT student organization and student outcomes related to LGBT identity" (p. 50). Renn and Bilodeau applied D'Augelli's model against the narratives provided by participants regarding their development and found that it was able to accurately reflect the experiences of LGBT student leaders. Renn and Bilodeau argued for "conceiving student leadership itself as a way to develop identity" (p. 68). Engaging with students who may be marginalized because they identify as LGBT by creating leadership opportunities offers one way for practitioners to support students in their identity development while fracturing the heteronormative structure of leadership positions in higher education. However, if those opportunities do not also incorporate an understanding of the multiple identities of LGBT students, they risk reifying other normative and oppressive relations. Important to note is that the majority of the participants in the studies reviewed in this section identified as White or Caucasian. In the next section, we review studies on LGBT college students who are also marginalized based on another component of their identity.

INTERSECTIONALITY

While using queer theory in conjunction with identity models is one method of understanding more about the development of LGBT college students, the construct of intersectionality offers a means of comprehending how the multiple dimensions of college students' identities may contribute to their development. Intersectionality examines how various identities intersect to shape the structural, political, and representational experiences of an individual (Crenshaw, 1991; Davis, 2008). Not only do the dimensions of students' identities impact their social development and collegiate experiences, but they also have an impact on the way LGBT students experience the political, social, and economic power of an institution. For example, a student who identifies as first-generation, Latina, and transgender is likely to have very different experiences than a student for whom both parents attended college, who identifies as White and straight. As a result, the ways in which students' identities intersect and are influenced by power and privilege must be taken into consideration when attempting to understand how they experience higher education.

Research conducted on LGBT college students that use intersectionality as a framework examines the lack of power and privilege for certain LGBT populations in higher education. The studies reviewed in this chapter focus on the intersection of various dimensions of identity such as ability, race, gender identity, and sexual orientation within the college student population. These are significant studies because they examine within-group populations who also are marginalized based on at least one, but often multiple components of their identity. Harley, Nowak, Gassaway, and Savage (2002) used an intersectional approach in their study on LGBT students with disabilities by examining race and ethnicity as well as immigrant status in addition to identification as an LGBT student with a disability. They found that these students are often "confronted by a trilogy of discrimination because of their disability, sexual orientation and for some, racial and ethnic identity" (p. 534). Issues of concern include not only accessibility but academic retention, confidentiality, and risk of suicide. Friedman and Leaper (2010) discussed the discrimination, social identity, and collective action of sexual-minority women. The results of their study indicate that sexual-minority women experience discrimination that is "simultaneously sexist and heterosexist" (p. 162). Henry, Fuerth, and Richards (2011) sought to reveal issues of concern for Black sexual minority college students "that may impede the positive outcome of their experiences and identity development" (p. 64). They found that "at the intersection of these issues, students with multiple marginalized identities may be left feeling alone, isolated, alienated and ultimately, unable to persist and complete college" (p. 68). Henry, Fuerth, and Richards offered recommendations for both student and staff-based initiatives to better engage students of color who also identify as LGBT, for instance, discussing identity development in first-year experience and orientation programming, and argued that higher education institutions have both a moral and ethical obligation to do so. In another study on the intersection of sexual orientation and race, Worthen (2013) also found a significant relationship between stigma and LGBT people of color and advocated for further research on prejudice to consider not only the intersection of sexual orientation with other dimensions of identity but also the need to consider how dimensions of identity intersect for specific populations within the LGBT community. Worthen believed that considering these intersections of identity in relation to experience may generate ideas that encourage positivity toward these groups.

The existing research on the LGBT college student population indicates that discrimination occurs for these populations on a variety of levels, and the construct of intersectionality offers a way for scholars and practitioners to examine how individuals experience these layers of discrimination based on their identities. Crenshaw (1991) noted that through "an awareness of intersectionality, we can better acknowledge and ground the differences among us" (p. 1299). Examining the intersections of identity also furthers scholars' and practitioners' understanding of institutionalized privilege (Crenshaw, 1991; Grant & Zwier, 2011; Iverson, 2007; Montgomery & Stewart, 2012). Additionally, Museus (2011) argued that "intersectional analyses can help higher education researchers identify disparities within social groups, in addition to inequities across those groupings" (p. 66). Parent, DeBlaere, and Moradi (2013) pointed out that gender identity, sexual orientation, and racial or ethnic status may each contribute to levels of stigma experienced by an individual and argued the value in research that considers how the intersections of these identities aid in "conceptualizations of the experiential and contextual manifestations of these constructs as nuanced and continuous variables" (p. 643). Existing research using intersectional analyses often explores the connection between race and gender or sexual orientation or socioeconomic status but rarely explores additional dimensions such as age, ability, or religious affiliations. Considering how all components of students' identities intersect to shape their experiences is useful in that it reduces the risk that students will be categorized based on only one component of their identity and allows higher education scholars and practitioners to gain a more complete picture of how institutional policies and practices may impact student development.

FRACTURING HETERONORMATIVITY ON CAMPUS

Research on student development and the LGBT college student population has the potential to aid staff and faculty from multiple areas within higher education as they attempt to positively impact student development. For instance, research on the LGBT college student population can increase awareness of LGBT needs and provide further support for already existing LGBT centers and their staff. Academic advisors and those in teaching positions would benefit from studies on the ways in which LGBT students' identities impact areas such as development of verbal, quantitative, and subject matter competence or cognitive skills and growth. Understanding of how the law impacts this population of students is useful to those in admissions and financial aid. Research on the way that identity influences leadership development and career opportunities is an advantage to those in career counseling, and studies on the quality of life after college for LGBT alumni would benefit those who work in university foundations and alumni relations. Studies on students who identify as LGBT are of value to many stakeholders in higher education; thus, it is imperative that higher education scholars better understand this population of college students.

Other important reasons to study LGBT students include the challenges they encounter in colleges and universities across the United States. Students who identify as LGBT have unique needs that must be addressed in order to create a safe and inclusive environment that fosters positive development experiences. For instance, LGBT college students may be concerned about safe-space environments on campus, such as residence halls, gender-neutral or all-gender bathrooms, and locker rooms. Policies and practices related to issues such as discrimination, harassment, and insurance coverage have only recently started to become inclusive of gender identity and sexual orientation. Non-LGBT inclusive curriculums also are stigmatizing and problematic. In addition, inadequate resources and education for LGBT health care needs as well as LGBT-friendly counseling and advising resources are cause for concern.

Unfortunately, many of these problems have yet to be resolved; "the concept of fluid gender expression or sexuality is frightening to a lot of people, especially in cultures that have maintained rigid gender roles and haven't experienced diversity" (Howard & Stevens, 2000, p. 14). On many campuses, an institutional commitment to ensuring the safety and success of those students who identify as LGBT is lacking. Though institutions of higher education have increasingly concerned themselves with projecting an image of inclusivity, students who identify as LGBT continue to face discrimination, harassment, and other forms of violence (Friedman & Leaper, 2010; Harley et al., 2002; Iverson, 2007; Rankin, 2003). Often, these injustices relate directly to the existing heteronormative culture that privileges students who identify as straight and either as a man or a Woman (Swank & Fahs, 2013). Experiencing discrimination, harassment, and other forms of violence has the potential to negatively impact not only an individual student's experience but also the overall campus climate (Rankin, 2003; Rankin, Weber, Blumenfeld, & Frazer, 2010).

CONCLUSION

The combined use of queer theory and intersectionality is a more comprehensive approach to examining how the multiple dimensions of LGBT college students' identities intersect to influence their development while in college. Swank and Fahs (2013) noted that "responses to heteronormativity and heterosexism are multiple, depending on situational, contextual, political, and individual factors" (p. 660). Therefore, educators need research that will challenge heteronormative understandings and practices to create meaningful experiences that will positively impact the development of LGBT students. Scholars have proffered many recommendations for practitioners to undertake that will benefit higher education institutions in creating a safe and more equitable climate as they consider the multiple dimensions of LGBT students' identities (Abes, 2009; Beemyn, 2003; Harley et al., 2002; Henry et al., 2011; Sorgen, 2011). The literature reviewed in this chapter emphasizes the visibility and celebration of LGBT identity on campus and argues that tolerance of different identities and the inclusion of sexual orientation and gender identity in policy are not enough. Hiring staff and faculty who openly identify as LGBT and integrating LGBT support services into existing offices as well as providing campus trainings on the intersections of identity and its implications on retention, safety, health care, and many other areas of the college experience also are frequently discussed in the literature on best practices for higher education institutions. Yet there is something missing from the recommendations they offer, and that is students' perspectives of their own complex and multifaceted lives. As higher education scholars and practitioners, it is equally important that we give attention not only to what we perceive as areas of concern but also to what our students perceive as areas of concern and how they perceive their identities to intersect, especially in how they perceive that intersection of identities to influence their development as college students.

REFERENCES

Abes, E. S. (2009). Theoretical borderlands: Using multiple theoretical perspectives to challenge inequitable power structures in student development theory. *Journal of College Student Development*, *50*, 141–156.

Abes, E. S., Jones, S. R., & McEwen, M. K. (2007). Reconceptualizing the model of multiple dimensions of identity: The role of meaning-making capacity in the construction of multiple identities. *Journal of College Student Development, 48*, 1–22.

Baxter Magolda, M. B. (2004). *Making their own way: Narratives for transforming higher education to promote self-development.* Sterling, VA: Stylus.

Beemyn, B. (2003). Serving the needs of transgender college students. *Journal of Gay & Lesbian Issues in Education, 1*, 33–50.

Beemyn, B., Curtis, B., Davis, M., & Tubbs, N. J. (2005). Transgender issues on college campuses. In R. Sanlo (Ed.), *Gender identity and sexual orientation: Research, policy, and personal: New directions for student services* (No. 111, pp. 49–60). San Francisco, CA: Jossey-Bass.

Burgess, A. (2005). Queering heterosexual spaces: Positive space campaigns disrupting campus heteronormativity. *Canadian Woman Studies, 24*, 27–30.

Cass, V. C. (1979). Homosexual identity formation: Testing a theoretical model. *The Journal of Sex Research, 20*, 143–167.

Cass, V. C. (1984). Homosexual identity: A concept in need of definition. *Journal of Homosexuality, 9*, 105–126.

Crenshaw, K. (1991). Mapping the margins: Intersectionality, identity politics, and violence against women of color. *Stanford Law Review, 43*, 1241–1299.

D'Augelli, A. (1994). Identity development and sexual orientation: Toward a model of Lesbian, gay, and bisexual development. In E. Trickett, R. Watts, & D. Birman (Eds.), *Human diversity: Perspectives on people in context* (pp. 312–333). San Francisco, CA: Jossey-Bass.

Davis, K. (2008). Intersectionality as buzzword: a sociology of science perspective on what makes a feminist theory successful. *Feminist Theory, 9*, 67–85.

Effrig, J. C., Bieschke, K. J., & Locke, B. D. (2011). Examining victimization and psychological distress in transgender college students. *Journal of College Counseling, 14*, 143–157.

Eliason, M. J. (1996). Identity formation for Lesbian, bisexual, and gay persons: Beyond a "minoritizing" view. *Journal of Homosexuality, 30*, 31–58.

Friedman, C., & Leaper, C. (2010). Sexual-minority college women's experiences with discrimination: Relations with identity and collective action. *Psychology of Women Quarterly, 3*, 152–164.

Grant, C. A., & Zwier, E. (2011). Intersectionality and student outcomes: Sharpening the struggle against racism, sexism, classism, ableism, heterosexism, nationalism, and linguistic, religious, and geographical discrimination in teaching and learning. *Multicultural Perspectives, 13*, 181–188.

Harley, D. A., Nowak, T. M., Gassaway, L. J., & Savage, T. A. (2002). Lesbian, gay, bisexual, and transgender college students with disabilities: A look at multiple cultural minorities. *Psychology in the Schools, 39*, 525–538.

Henry, W. J., Fuerth, K. M., & Richards, E. M. (2011). Black and gay in college: A review of the experiences of students in double jeopardy. *College Student Affairs Journal, 30*, 63–74.

Howard, K., & Stevens, A. (2000). *Out and about campus: Personal accounts by Lesbian, gay, bisexual and transgendered students.* Los Angeles, CA: Alyson.

Iverson, S. (2007). Camouflaging power and privilege: A critical race analysis of university diversity policies. *Educational Administration Quarterly, 43,* 586–611.

McCarn, S. R., & Fassinger, R. E. (1996). Revisioning sexual minority identity formation: A new model of Lesbian identity and its implications for counseling and research. *The Counseling Psychologist, 24,* 508–534.

Montgomery, S. A., & Stewart, A. J. (2012). Privileged allies in Lesbian and gay rights activism: Gender, generation, and resistance to heteronormativity. *Journal of Social Issues, 68,* 162–177.

Museus, S. D. (2011). An introductory mixed-methods intersectionality analysis of college access and equity: An examination of first-generation Asian Americans and Pacific Islanders. In S. D. Museus & K. A. Griffin (Eds.), *Using mixed-method approaches to study intersectionality in higher education: New directions for institutional research* (No. 151, pp. 63–75). San Francisco, CA: Jossey-Bass.

Pascarella, E. T., & Terenzini, P. T. (2005). *How college affects students: A third decade of research* (Vol. 2). San Francisco, CA: Jossey–Bass.

Parent, M. C., DeBlaere, C., & Moradi, B. (2013). Approaches to research on intersectionality: Perspectives on gender, LGBT, and racial/ethnic identities. *Sex Roles, 68,* 639–645.

Pena-Talamantes, A. E. (2013). Empowering the self, creating worlds: Lesbian and gay latina/o college students' identity negotiation in figured worlds. *Journal of College Student Development, 54,* 267–282.

Rankin, S. R. (2003). *Campus climate for gay, Lesbian, bisexual, and transgender people: A national perspective.* New York, NY: The National Gay and Lesbian Task Force Policy Institute. Retrieved from http://www.ngltf.org

Rankin, S. R., Weber, G., Blumenfeld, W., & Frazer, S. (2010). *State of higher education for Lesbian, gay, bisexual, and transgender people.* Charlotte, NC: Campus Pride. Retrieved from http://lgbtq.sdes.ucf.edu/docs/campuspride2010lgbtreportsummary.pdf

Renn, K., & Bilodeau, B. (2005). Queer student leaders: An exploratory case study of identity development and LGBT student involvement at a midwestern research university. *Journal of Gay & Lesbian Issues in Education, 2,* 49–71.

Sorgen, C. H., IV. (2011). *The influence of sexual identity on higher education outcomes* (Doctoral dissertation). Available from Dissertation Abstracts International. (UMI No. 3483739)

Swank, E., & Fahs, B. (2013). An intersectional analysis of gender and race for sexual minorities who engage in gay and Lesbian rights activism. *Sex Roles, 68,* 660–674.

Talburt, S. (2009). Developing students: Becoming someone but not anyone. In E. Allan, S. Iverson, & R. Ropers-Huilman (Eds.), *Re/constructing policy in higher education: Feminist poststructural perspectives and policy analysis* (pp. 111–128). New York, NY: Routledge.

Teich, N. (2012). *Transgender 101: A simple guide to a complex issue.* New York, NY: Columbia University Press.

Wilchins, R. (2004). *Queer theory, gender theory: An instant primer.* Los Angeles, CA: Alyson.

Worthen, M. G. F. (2013). An argument for separate analyses of attitudes toward Lesbian, gay, bisexual men, bisexual women, MtF and FtM transgender individuals. *Sex Roles, 68,* 703–723.

CHAPTER EIGHT

Living Intersectionality in the Academy

LEAH J. REINERT AND GABRIEL R. SERNA

From its establishment, higher education has operated within a patriarchal system. Institutions of higher education are still overwhelmingly led and run by White men (Bystydzienski & Bird, 2006). Indeed, the reward system in the academy is heavily influenced by a historical legacy that decidedly values Whiteness, maleness, and heterosexuality over other identities (Cress & Hart, 2009). The literature indicates that the academy continues to operate within a distinctly patriarchal and androcentric structure (e.g., Acker, 2006; Cress & Hart, 2009; Dill & Kohlman, 2012; Hirshfield & Joseph, 2011; Mason & Goulden, 2004). Encompassed in the patriarchal and androcentric structure is the assumption of the normative "straight, White, and male" that supports and sustains heteronormativity within the climate and culture of academia (Bilimoria & Stewart, 2009; Danby, 2007; Rankin, 2005). Within the academic culture and climate, identities socially marked as subordinate to the dominant norm are often pressured to exist on the periphery, to be within the culture but to make invisible certain identities in particular contexts, in order to enable achievement and success (Carbado, 2013; Dill, 2009). For those in academia who are already on the periphery, the academic environment can serve to further marginalize those multiple identities that inform their research and teaching. It also can mediate the way policies in the academy, especially around these two areas, are experienced and understood. Within academia, often, the more intersecting minority identities one experiences, the more opportunities for marginalization and exclusion exist.

Within some minority communities, specific hierarchies exist, causing further oppression of those who have minority identities that intersect (MacKinnon, 2013; Patil, 2013). It is safe to establish that White and male continues to hold dominance and affect policy and procedure within the dominant community as well as within certain minority communities (Carbado, 2013; Choo & Ferree, 2010; Crenshaw, 1989). To this end, intersectionality can aid in understanding why a White female who identifies as a Lesbian experiences marginalization within the LGBT community and why those experiences in the academy will differ from that of a Hispanic male who identifies as gay. The dynamics and interplay of intersecting identities within different contexts and communities—with specific reference to academia—are important to highlight in the discussion of intersectionality and higher education.

Acknowledging that established social hierarchy and norms create and determine the identity categories that are defined as oppressed or privileged (Crenshaw, 1989; MacKinnon, 2013), this chapter employs intersectionality to explore how we experience academia through our intersecting identities and discuss how higher education and institutional policy affect those experiences. Further, through multiple identities that intersect race, ethnicity, gender, sexual orientation, social class, ability, first-generation status, and experiencing academia as students, employees, and faculty, this chapter discusses the ways in which we experience academia in relation to our intersecting identities. Additionally, we outline how intersectionality informs and affects academic policy and structure and how policy and structure both can serve as a mechanism for continued oppression.

Our guiding mission in this chapter is to further the understanding of how intersecting identities affect experiences in academia and how policy often furthers marginalization of individuals with multiple intersecting minority identities through exclusion or overt notions of what constitutes "good policy, research, and teaching" in higher education. To this end, we begin by discussing our individual experiences in academia through the lens of our intersecting identities, representing both privilege and oppression. We follow this with an exploration of the ways in which policy in the academy attends to and is informed by notions of intersectionality and conclude with recommendations on how higher education can better attend to the multiple intersections of identity to provide the best culture and climate for all individuals.

INTERSECTIONALITY AND ACADEMIA

Crenshaw (1991) noted that failing to think in intersectional terms often furthers the continuation of oppression and discrimination against those with multiple intersecting marginalized identities. Acker (2006) further noted that focusing on just one category of identity prohibits understanding of the complexity of the inequalities and realities facing those with oppressed or marginalized identities. For both Crenshaw and Acker, thinking about intersectionality is vital to understanding the experiences of those within academia with intersecting identities. Still, it is often difficult for those within academia to operate within an intersectional perspective, because society operates heavily within a binary system (e.g., male or female, man or Woman, Black or White, heterosexual or nonheterosexual).

Lived experiences frame our individual understandings of identity, context, opportunities, and perceptions (Cole, 2009; Ropers-Huilman & Winters, 2010), and how we experience life within the complexities of identity provides the lens within which we operate in the larger social world (Dill & Kohlman, 2012). Therefore, it is important to understand how our own intersecting identities shape our experiences and how we operate within academia. In the following sections, we each discuss how we have experienced and continue to experience academia within the lens of our intersecting identities.

Leah

The majority of my (LR) experiences in higher education have been as a student, both in the classroom and as a student leader. While I also have held the roles of employee and teacher, my role as a college student is the lens from which I write in this section. The identities that I carry with me into the classroom include, but are not limited to, Lesbian, feminist, researcher, female, atheist, and White. These are the identities that most often intersect in my academic world, and some are easier than others to label and identify publicly. Yet, they all play a large role in the triumphs and struggles that I have encountered in academia. In my experience, academia struggles with intersectionality and approaching individuals as having multiple, layered, complex, and intersecting identities.

Navigating academia with multiple intersecting identities, many of which are "invisible," identities not easily visible or recognizable, has taught me many lessons. When considering my experiences within academia as a student in relation to my identities, I think of the following quote from Audre Lorde (1984):

> Those of us who stand outside the circle of this society's definition of acceptable women; those of us who have been forged in the crucibles of difference—those of us who are poor, who are Lesbians, who are Black, who are older—know that survival is not an academic skill. It is learning how to stand alone, unpopular and sometimes reviled, and how to make common cause with those others identified as outside the structures in order to define and seek a world in which we can all flourish. (p. 112)

In my student role, I have often found myself standing alone and feeling unpopular due to my minority or marginalized identities while seeking out that "common cause" or understanding to which Lorde refers. I have often encountered occasions

in which I become the representative educator for those "different" identity categories individually. These occasions have been numerous and not always unwelcome.
As anyone who has been that token voice in the classroom knows, being that voice
can become tiresome and can feel so repetitive that you feel that it is the only
identity you reveal or discuss within the classroom, and the obligation to be that
voice always remains.

While my minority or marginalized identities have been prominent in my
experiences within the classroom, it is important to note that my White identity
and growing up middle class afforded me the opportunity and privilege to be in
the classroom in the first place. Within the frame of those identities, my access
and ability to succeed in higher education are privileges that have afforded me
opportunity and mobility. It is easy to lose sight of the privileges and privileged
identities one holds, because as the identities pile up and the minority or marginalized identities grow in number, the dominant identities are easily lost or forgotten.
The few years in my adult life outside of academia taught me about the privilege
of not only access to higher education but also in growing up with the cultural
capital to know that I had the access at all. These experiences led me to be careful
in my graduate career, lest I forget those identities that afford me great privilege.
However, I acknowledge that this is often difficult, while also fighting on behalf of
the identities that bring forth bias, discrimination, and oppression.

As my classroom time as a student comes to a close, my researcher role grows.
Within my doctoral experience thus far, I have made very careful choices on the
topics I will research and those that I will stray from until I establish a career.
Gaining employment since graduating with my baccalaureate degree has been difficult, because the majority of my experiences in leadership and skill development
occurred within my role as student leader of the campus Lesbian, gay, bisexual, and
transgender (LGBT) student group. The skills I gained made me career ready,
but many, if not most, employers could not look beyond the LGBT heading. This
obstacle and the experience with my master's thesis, which focused on Lesbian
academics, led me to realize that doing any further work explicitly with LGBT
groups or entities or research on LGBT topics would likely label me as a queer/
Lesbian/gay academic. Career success in academia relies on my ability to showcase
all of my identities, not just my identity as a Lesbian. The inability of academia and
larger society to think in intersectional terms leads to this overshadowing of one
identity and presents a barrier to success and being able to exist within an always
evolving and intertwined list of identities.

Gabriel

As a relatively new faculty member, my (GS) experience in the academy also has
been primarily as a student. Yet, because the demands on a new professor quickly

require a realigning of one's identities, I will focus on my experiences with the job market and through my short time as a faculty member.

I grew up in a very poor, Hispanic, Catholic family in a small town in New Mexico. While I was unaware of our poverty until I was a bit older, I realized that it informed our family's day-to-day perspectives and choices. With regard to education, college was not presented as an option; indeed, finishing high school barely was. In a family of five siblings, only one (my brother) obtained a high school diploma. Those without a diploma in my family included both parents, who incidentally divorced before I could walk. Growing up poor, many would argue, is already sufficiently difficult, but add to this a burgeoning awareness of my sexuality and the religiosity of my family, and the situation becomes more complex. Still, for the most part, I was surrounded by others with similar cultural capital endowments, that is, other than being gay. Since I had also dropped out of high school, I earned a GED and went to work. When I decided to continue my education at the community college, and transfer to the main campus of the local four-year university, I became keenly aware of a difference between my classmates and me, although I would have been hard-pressed to identify it at that time.

Ten years later, I found myself at the end of my PhD program, searching the job market, and seeking to start my career as a full-fledged member of the academy. Because much of my graduate education heavily emphasized social justice, I was completing my degree with a broad set of ideas, theories, and vocabularies that allowed me to identify that which eluded me earlier in life—that race, class, ethnicity, gender, and sexual orientation mattered. While looking for a job, I became intensely aware of the ways in which others perceived my identities and how being gay, Hispanic, male, poor, first-generation, both all at once and individually (Warner & Shields, 2013), influenced what others thought I should be doing and how I interpreted my experiences. The education I received helped me to understand that, in a very fundamental way, my identities had shifted. There were now more of them, namely, researcher and scholar, and some were, as Parent, DeBlaere, and Moradi (2013) explained, endowed with greater relative power and privilege.

In the job market, it became resoundingly clear that if I was to succeed, many of my marginalized identities would have to be set aside, lost, or replaced. It also was clear that if this were to occur, it would require a sort of balancing act. For example, during an on-campus interview, I was presenting some of my dissertation research. The audience was composed of both search committee members and a large group from the college and around campus. As I reached my conclusions, a number of individuals asked pertinent questions around the things many scholars would expect when presenting research, questions like, "How did you choose your method?" or "What are some implications of your research for practice?" At the end of my presentation, one search committee member raised his hand. With a perplexed look on his face he asked, "So you've done a really good job here, but I just don't understand why you didn't take it further." Perplexed, I asked for clarification. His response was, "Well you didn't really talk about poor students, Hispanics, or first-generation students; isn't that your focus?"

Around the room there were many hushed glances, and a sense of unease had set in. I responded that while my identities certainly informed my interest in the subject, my research agenda was focused on the interplay of state fiscal policies and higher education finance. This experience, coupled with other similar occurrences over the next few months, suggested that at least two things were taking place with regard to my experience in the academy. First, I had to validate my positionality in terms of the appropriateness of asking questions that are typically within the domain of White, heterosexual men, many of whom had come from advantaged backgrounds. Second, if I did not confine myself to questions relating to the intersecting identities that were most visibly identifiable, my work in academia would have to stand up to the highest levels of academic rigor, whereas the work of some of my colleagues, who shared dominant identities, might simply be assumed to be of high quality.

Upon reflection, I came to the conclusion that questions like those posed while seeking a job were asked because the individual posing them felt they had a right, or rather the privilege, to ask me to validate the very right that I had to ask such questions or to even exist within the academy, for that matter. This is not to suggest that valid questions regarding research are not in order. Rather, these examples are intended to highlight the notion that intersecting identities, and intersectionality as a construct, indicate a need for those in the academy to reexamine their notions of who is allowed to ask questions that pertain to areas considered to be in the sphere of actors from the dominant culture. It also underscores the power differentials that remain among those from dominant and marginalized groups, even in a field whose values are ostensibly closely tied to social justice.

Now I wish to discuss living intersectionality in the academy from the perspective of a teaching faculty member. As a new faculty member, the whirlwind of duties and pressures can often seem overwhelming. Adding to the already stressful transition, I also was confronted with another reality of the academy—that students can exert an oppressive power over faculty with marginalized identities, especially when many of those identities are visible externally and the majority of students are from the dominant culture. As mentioned previously, I had formed new identities and was aware that some were seen as more valuable than others.

In the classroom, it became evident that my intersecting identities would play a role in both the way I taught and how students perceived my teaching. For example, during a class session, an individual asked me why I preferred to go by Dr. Serna, rather than Gabriel, or for that matter, Gabe. His sense was that I was disconnecting myself from the class because the rest of the faculty went by their first names. Incidentally, the other faculty at this time shared a similar sociocultural background, although they were not privy to this exchange until much later. I explained that my cultural upbringing requires a certain level of formality when speaking to teachers, clergy, and other individuals who are in a position of authority or at a social distance as a sign of respect. I had to explain that my cultural capital differed from his, and that as a result, two interlocking identities were at play. That is to say, I was navigating a system where at least one of my intersecting identities conformed to the norms of the dominant culture and was valued (being a scholar/academic) and the other went against it to some extent (Hispanic notions of respect and social distance). This experience created a sense of marginalization on my part, although it is necessary to say that my privileged position as a male in academia probably made it easier for me to have this conversation and be taken more seriously by this particular student. Still, I had to explain that my cultural capital was just as valid and that my identities intersected in ways that were foreign to this individual, which reminded me of the extra burden placed on marginalized groups in the academy. It also highlighted for me how a number of salient, intersecting identities can inform the teaching and research one undertakes based on these same notions.

As mentioned previously, the academy remains a largely White, male, heterosexual institution. Hence, the reflection of the sociocultural norms of this group in the academy is not unexpected. Nonetheless, by providing these two experiences as examples of living intersectionality in the academy, my hope is that as an institution, we become more aware of the ways in which we attend to marginalized voices and the marginalized experience. Finally, while many a respected colleague has suggested that these experiences could serve as teaching moments, let us again be reminded that these moments place both a psychic and in some cases material burden on those with intersecting, nondominant identities.

ACADEMIA, POLICY, AND INTERSECTIONALITY

Within the frame of the patriarchal and androcentric environment of higher education, those with intersecting minority or marginalized identities must engage in a complex navigation of social norms and academic policy, especially if policy is linked to norms that privilege certain identities over others in implicit ways. This navigation includes undercurrents and occasional blatant messages (Schaefer Riley, 2012) of what is acceptable or "valid" research or research topics. Identity-related research—research on gender, sexuality, and race—is often discounted in academia. We have both provided examples of our own navigation of research and research topics, but it is important to note that these undercurrents give rise to the idea that certain individuals do not have the "right" to question the dominant culture or even to ask questions that are considered within the purview of those from the dominant culture.

As pointed out in the narratives, focusing on academic policy and structure through an intersectional lens is more important than ever before, as the demographics within institutions of higher education change and become exceedingly more diverse. When considering policy, in higher education intersectionality is important because it "suggests that we are composite, whole individuals whose membership in group matters, but is not definitive. All individuals within a group do not have the same 'essence'" (Ropers-Huilman & Winters, 2010, p. 40). While commonalities exist between intergroup identities, due to every individual having multiple, intertwined, and complex identities, no two individuals can be treated exactly the same. Creating policy that attends to the complexity of identity is difficult, as can be seen in the increasingly long list of identity categories offered in antidiscrimination policies.

For example, in my (GS) experience, it was clear to me that the social distance that was called for based on my less dominant sociocultural capital might be seen as bad teaching. Or my research, as evidenced by the exchanges I had seeking a job, might be seen as less valid or rigorous based on implicit assumptions about my visible identities.

In my (LR) case, I became aware that my research agenda was being interpreted in specific ways based on the assumptions surrounding my topic as understood by an androcentric and primarily heterosexual structure.

Therefore, we argue, that as policy makers and decision makers in higher education begin to understand the complex layers of identity, conversations and attempts to attend to intersecting identities in policy and the very structure of the academy itself must increase.

Although it is the ideal for academia to approach policy in an intersectional frame, both academia and the broader society continue to operate in a highly stratified structure. Cole (2009) noted, "[I]ntersectionality makes plain that gender, race, class, and sexuality simultaneously affect the perceptions, experiences, and opportunities of everyone living in a society stratified along these dimensions" (p. 179). Attempts by higher education institutions to protect individual identity categories from discrimination through policy only provide a "Band-Aid" over the problems of bias and oppression that exist within institutions, because policy must be met with broader societal or institutional change to be most effective. Additionally, discrimination policies often very carefully state which identities have fallen within the "protected class" and by omission those that are not worthy of protection. This also exemplifies which identities are considered marginalized, highlighting for all those identities that lie outside of the "norm" the fact that they are clearly seen as less important or possibly simply undeserving of consideration.

An example of policy marginalizing identity includes the reality that many institutions can decide whether to recognize LGBT couples in their benefits policies. The lack of recognition sets LGBT faculty, staff, and students apart.

Policies that make explicit the division between identities often do more harm than good in furthering marginalization by perpetuating the stratification of identity. Scholars have underscored the important symbolism and framing that policy narratives and policies themselves can have (e.g., Baumgartner & Jones, 1993; Jones & Baumgartner, 2005; Rosen, 2009). The nature of policy as both a symbolic mechanism by which marginalization is first understood and then accentuated, and as a framing device to understand what marginal identities should be protected, create a space where intersectionality can add to the policy dialogue. Beyond policies, the unwritten rules within academic culture in relation to scholarship and faculty roles prove problematic in the often overwhelming focus on one marginalized identity over any other identity, characteristic, or skill.

CONCLUSIONS AND RECOMMENDATIONS

In this chapter, we have discussed our own paths and experiences in higher education with reference to our intersecting identities and how policy attends to, disrupts, and negotiates the complexity of identities that exist within higher education. Through our experiences, we have discovered how intertwined and evolving identities can be and how our continuous exploration of our identities within higher education sometimes requires strategic negotiation. We also have learned and note that our strategic negotiation cannot always rely on or be supported effectively by policy. Considering intersectionality when creating and implementing policy is highly difficult, but Dill and Kohlman (2012) highlighted the following:

> In the discourse surrounding identity, it is the tension between intersectionality as a tool for illuminating group identities that are not essentialist and individual identities that are not so fragmentary as to be meaningless that provides the energy to move the concept forward to the future. (p. 164)

Future development of policy should consider intersectionality and avoid leaning on normative or binary ideas of identities. Instead of identifying what identity categories are protected or served in specific policies, policy makers might consider leaving the categories open for interpretation. In family leave policies, for instance, consideration of the multiple ways that individuals form and make meaning of "family" could allow for individuals to utilize the policy more toward their specific needs. In antidiscrimination policies, making clear that any and all identities are included in being protected from oppression or bias might make those policies more applicable to the diversity of individuals that exist within higher education today. Policies cannot perfectly attend to the complexities of identity; they can, however, make a better effort at adapting or evolving to the current needs of the stakeholders within higher education.

REFERENCES

Acker, J. (2006). Inequality regimes: Gender, class, and race in organizations. *Gender & Society, 20,* 441–469.

Baumgartner, F., & Jones, B. (1993). *Agendas and instability in American politics.* Chicago, IL: University of Chicago Press.

Bilimoria, D., & Stewart, A. J. (2009). "Don't ask, don't tell": The academic climate for Lesbian, gay, bisexual, and transgender faculty in science and engineering. *NWSA Journal, 21,* 85–104.

Bystydzienski, J. M., & Bird, S. R. (Eds.). (2006). *Removing barriers: Women in academic science, technology, engineering, and mathematics.* Bloomington: Indiana University Press.

Carbado, D. W. (2013). Colorblind intersectionality. *Signs, 38,* 811–845.

Choo, H. Y., & Ferree, M. M. (2010). Practicing intersectionality in sociological research: A critical analysis of inclusions, interactions, and institutions in the study of inequalities. *Sociological Theory, 28,* 129–149.

Cole, E. R. (2009). Intersectionality and research in psychology. *American Psychologist, 64,* 170–180.

Crenshaw, K. W. (1989). Demarginalizing the intersection of race and sex: A black feminist critique of antidiscrimination doctrine, feminist theory and antiracist politics. *University of Chicago Legal Forum, 139,* 139–167.

Crenshaw, K. (1991). Mapping the margins: Intersectionality, identity politics, and violence against women of color. *Stanford Law Review, 43,* 1241–1299.

Cress, C. M., & Hart, J. (2009). Playing soccer on the football field: The persistence of gender inequalities for women faculty. *Equity & Excellence in Education, 42,* 473–488.

Danby, C. (2007). Political economy and the closet: Heteronormativity in feminist economics. *Feminist Economics, 13,* 29–53.

Dill, B. T. (2009). Intersections, identities, and inequalities in higher education. In B. T. Dill & R. E. Zambrana (Eds.), *Emerging intersections: Race, class, and gender in theory, policy, and practice* (pp. 229–252). New Brunswick, NJ: Rutgers University Press.

Dill, B. T., & Kohlman, M. H. (2012). Intersectionality: A transformative paradigm in feminist theory and social justice. In S. N. Hesse-Biber (Ed.), *The handbook of feminist research: Theory and praxis* (pp. 154–174). Thousand Oaks, CA: Sage.

Hirshfield, L. E., & Joseph, T. D. (2011). "We need a Woman, we need a black Woman": Gender, race, and identity taxation in the academy. *Gender and Education, 24,* 213–227.

Jones, B., & Baumgartner, F. (2005). *The politics of attention: How government prioritizes problems.* Chicago, IL: The University of Chicago Press.

Lorde, A. (1984). *Sister outsider: Essays and speeches by Audre Lorde.* Berkeley, CA: The Crossing.

MacKinnon, C. A. (2013). Intersectionality as method: A note. *Signs, 38,* 1019–1030.

Mason, M. A., & Goulden, M. (2004). Marriage and baby blues: Redefining gender equity in the academy. *The Annals of the American Academy of Political and Social Science, 596,* 86–103.

Parent, M., DeBlaere, C., & Moradi, B. (2013). Approaches to research on intersectionality: Perspectives on gender, LGBT, and racial/ethnic identities. *Sex Roles: A Journal of Research, 68,* 639–645.

Patil, V. (2013). From Patriarchy to Intersectionality: A Transnational Feminist Assessment of How Far We've Really Come. *Signs, 38*(4), 847–867.

Rankin, S. (2005). Campus climate for sexual minorities. In R. Sanlo (Ed.), *Gender identity and sexual orientation: Research, policy, and personal: New directions for student services* (No. 111, 17–23). San Francisco, CA: Jossey-Bass.

Ropers-Huilman, R., & Winters, K. T. (2010). Imagining intersectionality and the spaces in between: Theories and processes of socially transformative knowing. In M. Savin-Baden & C. H. Major (Eds.), *New approaches to qualitative research: Wisdom and uncertainty* (pp. 37–48). New York, NY: Routledge.

Rosen, L. (2009). Rhetoric and symbolic action in the policy process. In G. Skyes, B. Schneider, & D. Plank (Eds.), *The AERA handbook of education policy research* (pp. 267–285). New York, NY: American Educational Research Association.

Schaefer Riley, N. (2012, April 30). The most persuasive case for eliminating black studies? Just read the dissertations. *The Chronicle of Higher Education.* Retrieved from http://chronicle. com/blogs/brainstorm/the-most-persuasive-case-for-eliminating-black-studies-just-read-the-dissertations/46346

Warner, L. R., & Shields, S. A. (2013). The intersections of sexuality, gender, and race: Identity research at the crossroads. *Sex Roles, 68*, 803–810.

CHAPTER NINE

The Tapestry Model

Exploring Social Identities, Privilege, and Oppression from an Intersectional Perspective

DIANE J. GOODMAN

An intersectional perspective requires a shift in how social identities and social oppression are often conceptualized. Instead of a multiple identities or additive approach, which treats different social identities and forms of inequality as separate and independent from each other, an intersectional approach focuses on understanding how different social categories simultaneously interact, shaping people's identities and lived experiences. I have found for myself and others that this shift in perspective is clearer on a theoretical level but more challenging to fully embody in practice. Even when there is an intention to examine situations with an intersectional lens, there is a tendency to default to a single identity/ oppression analysis.

As I have tried to fully grasp, apply, and teach about intersectionality. I have searched for ways to conceptualize key aspects of an intersectional approach and highlight its distinctiveness from a multiple identities/additive approach. To this end, I developed the Tapestry Model. The Tapestry Model (TM) uses the metaphor of weaving a tapestry to explicate some of the main tenets of an intersectional framework and other aspects of how people experience social identities within larger systems of structural inequality. In this chapter, I first provide background and context for the TM and then describe how it can be used to illustrate concepts of intersectionality. Next, I suggest additional ways the TM can be used to explore other issues related to identity, privilege, and oppression. The chapter concludes with some ideas for how the TM could be applied in higher education settings.

FROM A MULTIPLE IDENTITIES/ADDITIVE APPROACH
TO AN INTERSECTIONAL APPROACH

While intersectional lenses are becoming increasingly popular in exploring social identity, oppression, and social justice, multiple identities or additive perspectives have been most commonly used thus far (Adams, Bell, & Griffin, 2007; Johnson, 2006). In a multiple identities/additive approach, the primary focus is on examining social identities within various social identity categories (e.g., race, gender, sexual orientation, class, age, religion, nationality), the corresponding forms of oppression (e.g., racism, sexism, gender oppression, heterosexism) and social location being part of dominant and/or subordinated groups. Each social identity/inequality is examined independently without considering its interrelationship with other identities/inequalities. Using a metaphor of a striped cloth to illustrate this perspective, imagine that each stripe represents an individual's different social identity. A multiple identities or additive approach explores the significance of each of the colored stripes. Since the stripes are separate and parallel, this approach does not allow for analyzing how various social identities and experiences of advantage and disadvantage intersect and interact.

The paradigm of intersectionality grew out of the voices of women of color who asserted that their experiences could not be captured by considering sexism or racism alone or separately (Collins, 2000; Crenshaw, 1991; Moraga & Anzaldúa, 2002). As Bowleg (2008) aptly put it in the title of her article, *When Black + Lesbian + Woman ≠ Black Lesbian Woman*, individuals are not simply a sum of their identities. There is a more complex interplay among social identities and experiences of privilege and oppression. Intersectional theory initially focused on the intersection of multiple forms of subordination. It is evolving to also look at how privileged identities and the experiences of privilege intersect with one's other identities and experiences, both privileged and marginalized (Kimmel & Ferber, 2014; Pliner & Banks, 2012).

An intersectional framework can be used to explore social identities, social identity statuses, and/or manifestations of inequality (Anderson & Collins, 2010; Dill & Zambrana, 2009). At the microlevel, it can serve as a lens to analyze the interconnections among personal social identities; at the macrolevel, it can elucidate interconnections among systems of power (Wijeyesinghe & Jones, this volume). Even when an intersectional analysis is focused on the level of the individual, social identities cannot be adequately understood without recognizing that individuals are members of social groups within larger systems of social inequality. People's social locations or positions within these hierarchical oppressive structures affect their access to power, resources, and opportunities, which shapes how they see and experience themselves and the world. Collins (2000) reminded us of the importance of considering one's personal identity and social position within the matrix of domination or interlocking systems of oppression.

THE TAPESTRY MODEL

The TM explores the ways in which social identities and the experiences of domination and subordination interweave and interplay. The TM can help people examine the intersection of different identities and inequalities at different times and in different contexts. Just as tapestries are woven on the structure of a loom, which shapes what gets created, social identities and lived experiences are also shaped by and embedded in larger societal structures. As I describe the TM, using concepts from intersectional theory, it will be from the viewpoint of individuals weaving their own tapestries, how they reflect on their own identities and realities of being members of privileged and marginalized groups. Later I address when people weave the tapestry to represent others' lives. In developing and teaching about the TM, I use an actual tapestry or picture of one to help visualize these concepts. (See my website for colored pictures of tapestries that can be used for illustration: http://www.dianegoodman.com.)

Simultaneously Intersecting Identities

All people have many social identities that may have different social locations. Thus, one's tapestry is made up of different colored threads, each thread reflecting a different social identity and corresponding privilege or oppression. In my personal tapestry, I could choose red threads to represent my gender identity as a female and my experience of sexism, white threads for my racial identity as a White person and my experience of racial privilege, and yellow threads as my age thread as a middle-aged person and experience of age privilege, and so on. The whole tapestry is multicolored, since people always embody all their identities.

Even though theoretically individuals live all their identities simultaneously, intersectional theory focuses on the intersections of particular social categories at a given time (Weber, 2004). Certain identities are in the foreground, while others are in the background. In order to analyze different combinations of intersecting identities, people can consider what happens when certain threads are more closely interwoven in different parts of the tapestry. I refer to these as the *intersecting threads*. As these intersecting threads interweave, they form new colors and designs: *intersectional colors and designs*. If I wanted to examine my experience as a White Woman, I would interweave my red (gender) and White (race) threads. When we look at a tapestry where red and white threads are tightly interwoven, it looks pink. There are not actually pink threads in the tapestry; the pink appearance comes from the overlapping and intertwining red and white threads. The pink color that is formed reflects the intersection of my gender and race. I am simultaneously White and a Woman; these identities mutually affect each other, and subsequently, I am not just a stripe of red and a stripe of white (as in the striped cloth metaphor). For example, when I walk into a classroom to teach, students see me, make assumptions about me, and respond to me differently than if I were a White man or an Asian Woman. The intersectional colors and designs that would be formed by those individuals' intersectional threads would not look the same as mine. If I wanted to explore this further, I could add in other threads. To reflect the impact of age, or what it is like to be a middle-aged White Woman teaching, I could add my yellow age thread. This would change the pink into a more orange color reflecting the intersection of my gender, race, and age. It is critical to understand not just the significance of each individual social identity or thread but how they simultaneously affect each other or the new intersectional color that appears when they are interwoven. This concept is a central component of intersectionality and a key way the TM can be used to illustrate an intersectional perspective.

As people's identities intersect, so do their experiences of privilege and oppression. The degree of their privilege or marginalization in any given situation cannot be calculated by simply counting up how many identities are from subordinated groups and how many are from dominant groups—it is not additive. Privilege and oppression operate and interact simultaneously. The intersections of identities with different social statuses can increase or mitigate experiences of advantage and disadvantage. The intersectional color that gets created when intersectional threads are interwoven reflects not just the interplay of identities but the interaction among different positions within systems of power.

One of the challenges of capturing intersectionality conceptually is not simply having all of one's identities just blend into one indistinguishable conglomeration. Social identities are both distinct, people have individual social identities (a particular gender, race, age, etc.), *and* they simultaneously interact. Unlike mixing paints or ingredients in baking, intersectional threads retain their form and color as they interweave with other threads to create a new intersectional color.

For example, if a Black women's class identity and status change (going from working class to upper middle class), it does not change her race, being Black, but it does form a new dynamic between her class identity and racial identity; being an upper-middle-class Black Woman creates a different sense of self, life experience, and degree of privilege/oppression than being a working-class Black Woman. Similarly, if a man becomes disabled and now needs to use a wheelchair, it does not change the fact that he is still a man. Yet, it may change how he is treated and experiences himself as man and his male privilege. In his tapestry, the color of his ability thread will change to now reflect his new identity and lived reality as someone with a disability. This new disability thread when interwoven with his gender identity thread will create a different intersectional color than before—he is now a man with a disability, not an able-bodied man. Similarly, his other color threads, reflecting his other social identities, remain the same, but when combined with this new disability thread will create different intersectional colors than they did previously.

Salience

Context affects how people experience their identities. Salient identities are the ones that are predominant or foregrounded in a particular setting. They have the greatest impact on or relevance to an individual's sense of self and lived experience in a given situation. There also may be times when people are just more conscious of certain identities. Often, an intersectional analysis focuses on salient identities. The Woman in the following passage describes how context affects her experiences of her intersecting identities and forms of discrimination:

> As a disabled Lesbian Woman, I have experienced that it is seldom that all aspects discriminate at the same time. The most apparent are being a Woman and disabled, but in a female context the aspect of disability plays a more predominant role than the fact of being a Woman. The fact of being Lesbian plays a secondary role, except in very traditional, religious women's groups. (la Rivière-Zijdel, 2009, p. 33)

She goes on to explain how her experience is different in other contexts:

> When the surrounding society is basically white, male and heterosexual, the aspects of ethnicity, sexual orientation and sex intersect. In the disability movement I have experienced discrimination on the intersecting identities of sex and sexual orientation. The disability movement tends to be quite homophobic as disabled people desire to belong as much as possible to the majority norm (i.e. heterosexual)…the disability movement is mostly run by (disabled) men, which has put the women's agenda on a secondary and often tertiary place (i.e. impairment specific first and men second). I discovered a similar process within the LGBT movement that has difficulty with the aspects of being disabled, as the norm is beauty, virility, independence and so on. (la Rivière-Zijdel, 2009, p. 34)

In the tapestry, the colored threads representing the salient identities would be the intersectional threads, interweaving to create new intersectional colors and designs. Consider this story I heard from a low-income Latina at a predominantly White, elite private college about her experience in a sorority. This young Woman felt she could not fully participate in sorority life because of all the costs associated with the various activities. There was no understanding of or support for her financial situation. Moreover, she was derided for spending time with her Latina/o friends who were not in the sorority. She ultimately dropped out of the sorority. From her perspective, the intersection of her gender, ethnicity, and class threads were most salient, and those would be the intersectional threads interwoven in that part of her tapestry. This does not mean that her other identities (including privileged group identities) were not relevant, but they were not seen by her as having the most impact in this situation.

As the previous examples indicate, the identities that are most salient are often related to feeling oppressed or marginalized. Salience can also be related to simply feeling different, conspicuous, or aware of certain identities in a given context. People may feel conscious of that aspect of themselves even though they do not feel unfairly treated or believe that it makes much difference. For example, the only male in a class of women, or the only person of color in a staff of White people, may feel that their gender or racial identity are salient even though they may be comfortable and well-integrated into the class or department. This may be due to other shared identities such as age or professional status that are intersecting with their gender or race. As a Jew who grew up and lives near New York City with an appearance, cultural style, and lifestyle that reflects this identity (dark hair and complexion, direct and rapid communication style, and access to urban cultural activities), my New York Jewish identity becomes more salient when I do training at predominantly White, rural, Christian Midwestern colleges. I have very positive and constructive experiences there, but I become more conscious of my religious and ethnic identities and geographic location.

Even among salient intersecting identities, not all the salient identities exert the same degree of influence on how individuals experience a particular situation. For an even more nuanced illustration of salience and the interplay of various forms of identity and inequality, the number of threads of each salient identity can be varied to reflect each identity's relative weight. In the previous situation of the Latina in the sorority, the student may feel that her socioeconomic class status had the greatest impact on her experience compared to her gender or race/ethnicity, even though all three were relevant and interplayed. More class threads than race or gender threads could be included in the intersectional threads being interwoven in her tapestry. As a result, the color of her class threads would more strongly affect the intersectional color and design that gets created. Another way the degree of salience can be illustrated is by making the color of a thread more vibrant or increasing the thickness of the thread as its salience grows. Adjusting the number or thickness of the threads or the vibrancy of the color of threads to reflect which identities or forms of oppression have the most influence allows for a more complex consideration of how positions in societal power hierarchies interact and shape our reality in varying contexts.

There may be times when individuals intentionally want to explore the significance of nonsalient identities. Frequently, dominant group identities are less salient, since people fit into the societal norms and do not experience the barriers faced by subordinated groups. It can be valuable to consider how identities people may not often think about still impact how they see and experience the world and affect and are affected by other social identities. In these cases, people may choose to have nonsalient identity threads included in the combination of intersectional threads being interwoven in the tapestry.

Integration and Tension between Identities

Like a tapestry weaver, most people strive to integrate their social identities into a holistic sense of self with the ability to be resilient. When individuals experience this, the threads are evenly and solidly interwoven, creating a firm and strong tapestry. At times, however, certain identities may be unexplored, disassociated, or devalued. They are not well integrated into one's larger sense of self or with other identities. The part of the tapestry with those social identity threads may be woven very loosely, with gaps and spaces between the threads, and thus be more flimsy. For example, for White people who have not examined what it means to be White, they may not see clearly how their Whiteness is coloring their other identities, interactions, or experiences. Their race thread may not be firmly interwoven with the other colored threads. Or, people with a learning disability may be struggling to acknowledge and deal with their disability, so their disability thread may be more loosely interwoven in their tapestry. In other situations, there may be times when "identities collide" (Oslander, 2008). There can be tensions or conflicts with specific identities or between particular intersecting identities. For instance, some people experience tension between their sexual orientation and their religious identity. In those cases, the threads may be woven too tightly and there can be pulling and bunching. Other individuals with wealth may feel a conflict between their beliefs in equal opportunity and their unearned class privilege; thus, their class thread may pucker the tapestry as it runs through it.

Extending the Tapestry Metaphor

The aforementioned concepts and examples focused on facets of intersectionality and the interrelationship among different axes of identity. There are many other ways the TM can be used to examine aspects of social identities, privilege, and oppression. As I present this model in workshops and classes, people often suggest ways to extend the tapestry metaphor. One way the image of a tapestry can be used is to reflect on how the public expressions of people's identities and experiences may be different from their private ones. For some people, the front of the tapestry, what is shown to the world, might look nice and pretty with many beautiful colors and designs, while the back of the tapestry may be full of knots and loose threads. This side may reveal their internalized oppression and self-doubts, as well as the stresses of trying to exist in situations that are not equitable or inclusive. Even people who appear to "have it all"—upper-middle-class, straight, White males, may be experiencing the pressures of living up to others' expectations based on societal norms. In other cases, the back of the tapestry may reveal people's more authentic selves, which are not as visible on the front of the tapestry, their public face.

The TM also can help us compare individuals' own self-definitions and perceptions of their lives with how others see them. They can consider the similarities and differences in how they weave our own tapestry with how someone else might weave their tapestry. How people self-identify may be at odds with how they are identified by others. Discrepancies may also be due to different perspectives on the identities or experiences that are considered most salient or how identities intersect or to their own lack of awareness of how a particular identity or form of privilege/oppression manifests.

Another concept that can be explored using the tapestry is the notion of central versus salient identities. While salience varies due to particular contexts, centrality more broadly captures one's sense of self and experience that transcend specific situations. For identities that feel most fundamental to who one is, there would be more of those colored threads throughout that part of the tapestry. Central identities remain stable or people may think more about certain identities than others at different times throughout their lives. For example, people of color who experience race as a central identity may be highly conscious of their race and feel that it plays a major role in who they are and how they live their lives. Or, as individuals get older, becoming more aware of health issues and ageism, age may become more significant and central to their sense of identity and lived experiences, so their age threads may be more prevalent in their tapestries. Therefore, the number of colored threads of a particular social identity and the overall hue of the tapestry may also change over time.

Since individuals and society are always evolving, people are continually weaving their tapestries. Social identities are not static. The salience and centrality of our identities are ever-changing depending on who we are, where we are, and what we are doing. Moreover, societal changes also affect how we identify and experience our identities. People can add threads, alter the color of their threads, and weave different intersectional colors and designs to reflect the dynamic nature of their identities and lived experiences. Looking at individuals' entire tapestry can reveal the variations and changes in how they have experienced themselves and their lives over time.

APPLICATIONS

The TM can be used in various higher education settings. In educational or counseling contexts, the tapestry can be used as a way to help people learn about intersectionality and to better understand themselves and others. It can be very helpful to have an actual tapestry or pictures of one to assist people in visualizing the concepts. Individuals can weave their own tapestry (literally or figuratively) to reflect on how they simultaneously experience different intersectional identities (both salient and less salient, privileged and marginalized) in a variety of contexts at different times in their lives. These tapestries could be shared with others in order to discuss similarities and differences in experiences and how these experiences are connected to larger systems of inequality. Based on reading or hearing other's life stories, individuals can use the TM to represent and gain insight into other people's intersectional identities and lived realities. People can be asked to consider how one's sense of identity and experiences change as different threads are included in the mix of intersectional threads and the meaning of the new intersectional colors.

These ways of using the TM also could have implications for other areas of higher education. People could think in terms of intersectional threads, intersectional colors, and salient identities to develop policies, programming, or research projects that reveal, examine, and address experiences based on different intersectional identities (e.g., students' experiences in the classroom, feelings of safety on campus, factors that affect retention). Generally, this model can be a conceptual frame and tool to examine issues of social identity and inequality in more complex ways, recognizing the intersectionality of people's lived experiences and the impact of context. Asking people to think about the new intersectional colors and designs created refocuses their attention on the more challenging task of how identities and inequalities simultaneously interact rather than the impact of each identity separately.

CONCLUSION

The TM offers one way to conceptualize elements of an intersectional approach and issues related to social identities and social power. It has numerous implications for use in higher education. I encourage readers to consider how to expand, adapt, and utilize the tapestry metaphor. My hope is that the TM will help people grasp the ways social identities and experiences of oppression and privilege interact and interplay for ourselves and others, and thus, inform our ability to create greater equity and inclusion on our campuses and larger communities.

REFERENCES

Adams, M., Bell, L. A., & Griffin, P. (2007). *Teaching for diversity and social justice* (2nd ed.). New York, NY: Routledge.

Anderson, M., & Collins, P. (2010). Why race, class and gender still matter. In M. Anderson & P. Collins (Eds.), *Race, class and gender: An anthology* (8th ed., pp. 1–15). Belmont, CA: Wadsworth.

Bowleg, L. (2008). When black + Lesbian + Woman ≠ black Lesbian Woman: The methodological challenges of qualitative and quantitative intersectionality research. *Sex Roles, 59,* 312–325.

Collins, P. (2000). *Black feminist thought: Knowledge, consciousness and the politics of empowerment.* New York, NY: Routledge.

Crenshaw, K. (1991). Mapping the margins: Intersectionality, identity politics, and violence against women. *Stanford Law Review, 43,* 1241–1299.

Dill, B. T., & Zambrana, R. (2009). Critical thinking about inequality: An emerging lens. In B. T. Dill & R. Zambrana (Eds.), *Emerging intersections: Race, class and gender in theory, policy and practice* (pp. 1–21). New Brunswick, NJ: Rutgers University Press.

Johnson, A. (2006). *Privilege, power and difference* (2nd ed.). New York, NY: McGraw-Hill.

Kimmel, M., & Ferber, A. (2014). *Privilege: A reader* (3rd ed.). Boulder, CO: Westview.

la Rivière-Zijdel, Lydia (2009). The ignored aspects of intersectionality. In M. Franken, A. Woodward, A. Cabó, & B. Bagilhole (Eds.), *Teaching intersectionality: Putting gender at the centre* (pp. 31–44). Utrecht, the Netherlands: ATHENA3 Advanced Thematic Network in Women's Studies in Europe, Zuidam Uithof Drukkerijen. Retrieved from http://gallery.mailchimp.com/ b191e660f005d37f84a4e431d/files/Teaching_Intersectionality_FULL.pdf

Moraga, C., & Anzaldúa, G. (Eds.). (2002). *This bridge called my back: Writings by radical women of color* (3rd ed.). Berkeley, CA: Third Woman.

Oslander, R. N. (2008). When identities collide: Masculinity, disability and race. *Disability and Society, 23,* 585–597.

Pliner, S., & Banks, C. (2012). *Teaching, learning and intersecting identities in higher education.* New York, NY: Peter Lang.

Weber, L. (2004). A conceptual framework for understanding race, class, gender, and sexuality. In S. N. Hesse-Biber & M. Yaisier (Eds.), *Feminist perspectives on social research* (pp. 121–139). New York, NY: Oxford University Press.

PART TWO

Research

CHAPTER TEN

Backward Thinking

Exploring the Relationship among Intersectionality, Epistemology, and Research Design

DANIEL TILLAPAUGH AND Z NICOLAZZO

Scholarship on intersectionality, particularly in educational research, often focuses on the intersecting identities of participants (e.g., Jones & Abes, 2013; Tillapaugh, 2012). Despite this focus, Renn (2010) argued that some scholars' use of intersectionality inadvertently created "some slippage of the term among educational researchers" (p. 7). The lack of exploration regarding the interrogation of power implicit in intersectionality, how it influences one's multiple identities and how it mediates one's interactions with others, troubles us as scholars. We believe intersectional thinking that begins and ends with research participants' identities misses an important step, which is how intersectionality is implicated in, and thus influences, the research design. We argue that one's epistemological grounding, how one conceptualizes truth and power and the ways in which scholars influence each other's thinking about their research projects, has a direct impact on the fecundity of the research content. These are the topics around which we frame our analysis within this chapter. In doing so, we find it important to engage in *backward thinking*, or the idea that one not only needs to leverage intersectionality with participants and in data analysis but also prior to seeking participants, specifically in terms of one's epistemology, reflexivity, and overall research design.

In this chapter, we pose the following questions, which serve as a guide to our backward thinking:

1. What happens when one thinks about intersectionality as a concept influencing study design and the research process itself?

2. How might thinking about intersectionality as affecting what happens before data collection and analysis be an important lens for better addressing
   the multifaceted political aspects of research?
3. What could an investigation of intersectionality of researchers' epistemological groundings offer the field of educational research, particularly for
   higher education?

In asking these questions, we seek to expand our collective thinking about the concept of intersectionality by reflecting on how it impacts the design of research studies as well as how one thinks about the research one does. By doing so, we argue that not only do researchers and participants benefit, but the potential effect(s) of one's research may be positively influenced as well. In other words, by engaging in backward thinking regarding intersectional research, we allow for greater visibility for highly marginalized student populations, thus increasing our visibility of their (and our) lives.

EPISTEMOLOGY DEFINED

Epistemology, or the theory of knowledge, comprises "the relationship between what we know and what we see [and] the truths we seek and believe as researchers" (Lincoln, Lynham, & Guba, 2011, p. 103). Seen in this way, a researcher's epistemological grounding is always already embedded in a relationship between oneself (e.g., one's social identities) and something or someone else. Although concerns about truth, power, values, and knowledge are central to one's epistemology, these are understood not solely through internal thought but as a result of didactic interactions between an individual and others in one's social context, including between researcher(s) and participant(s). For higher education researchers, this means one comes to one's own epistemic beliefs as a result of interacting with research participants as well as other scholars.

Epistemes may range from positivism—the belief in absolute and objective truths that can be established through scientific inquiry—to poststructuralism—the belief that categories of identification are constantly in flux and do little to convey specific meaning about that which is being explained (Lincoln et al., 2011). Furthermore, some epistemologies foreground participants and their voices (e.g., constructivism), while others place primary emphasis on exposing and interrogating overarching systems of societal power, privilege, and oppression (e.g., criticalism; Lincoln et al., 2011). Although research studies have traditionally been rooted in one episteme (e.g., constructivism), some scholars (e.g., Abes, 2009; Kincheloe, 2001) have begun to recognize how epistemologies overlap, converge, and can work in collaboration to provide a more complete and complex understanding of data. Because how one thinks about knowledge is rooted in how our identities intersect with one another, we must reflect on and understand how our chosen epistemes inform our own worldview as researchers but also as people. For this theoretical analysis, we as authors discuss how researchers can work together across epistemological perspectives to enhance the research process and resulting analysis.

INTERSECTIONALITY DEFINED

Dill and Zambrana (2009) framed intersectionality "as an analytical strategy—a systematic approach to understanding human life and behavior that is rooted in the experiences and struggles of marginalized people" (p. 4). Citing the increasing emergence of studies on intersectionality in higher education, Jones and Abes (2013) maintained, "with an explicit focus on locating individuals within larger structures of privilege and oppression, intersectionality as an analytic framework for understanding identity insists on...a more holistic approach to identity" (p. 135). By centering the conversations of social identities in an intersectional view, scholars begin to interrogate the "interconnected structures of inequality" (Dill & Zambrana, 2009, p. 5) by which power and privilege are granted (or not granted) based on the intersections of one's social identities, as well as how these systems are maintained and replicated within society (Berger & Guidroz, 2009; Crenshaw, 1995). Elaborating on this point, Weber (1998) highlighted that one's own internalized understanding of one's identity (e.g., gender, race) "depends on one's *simultaneous* location in the race, class, gender, and sexuality hierarchies" (p. 26). As a result, power intrinsically plays a role in the identity politics at both an individual and collective/societal level (Crenshaw, 1995; Weber, 1998).

The Concept of Systemic Power

The notion of power is deeply implicated in intersectionality. Baca Zinn and Dill (1996) argued that intersections of identity create a confluence of privilege and oppression for individuals. Shields (2008) expanded on this idea, stating that the intersection of identities "instantiate social stratification" whereby identities "may be experienced as a feature of individual selves, but [they] also reflect...the operation of power relations among groups that comprise that identity category" (p. 302). In their work, Dill and Zambrana (2009) offered four domains by which power structures subordinate others based on dimensions of their identities and maintain systems of inequality. These included the following:

1. The structural domain, which consists of the institutional structures of the society including government, the legal system, housing patterns, economic traditions, and educational structure.
2. The disciplinary domain, which consists of the ideas and practices that characterize and sustain bureaucratic hierarchies.

3. The hegemonic domain, which consists of the images, symbols, ideas, and ideologies that shape social consciousness (Collins, 2000).
4. The interpersonal domain, which consists of patterns of interaction between individuals and groups. (p. 7)

Any discussion of intersectionality without due consideration given to the implications and effects of systemic power misses the proverbial mark. Rather than talking about intersectionality, which includes the ways in which power mediates the lived experiences of people based on dominant and/or subordinated identities, the lack of focus on the effects of systemic power often leads researchers to equate intersectionality with the notion of identity convergence (D. L. Stewart, personal communication, July 5, 2013) or the exploration of individuals' multiple identities without considering their social contexts and the influence of power on their experiences and, thus, the livability of their lives (Butler, 2004).

INTERSECTIONAL IDENTITIES ⟸⟹ INTERSECTIONAL RESEARCH

Who a researcher is—one's worldview, life experiences, and social identities—often influences the research one undertakes (Jones, Torres, & Arminio, 2006). Moreover, a researcher rarely if ever conducts data collection and analysis in isolation. Instead, researchers work within a community of scholars, examples of which include not only the conferences at which research results are disseminated but also the personal interactions researchers have with one another to discuss and work through the particularities of one's work. Therefore, not only is there a synergistic relationship between who one is as a researcher and one's work but also how one interacts with others in a community of scholars and one's work. In other words, while we are not suggesting every research project needs to have multiple researchers, we are suggesting that researchers' identities do influence the ways in which they make meaning and view their own research from a variety of epistemological foundations (e.g., those of our colleagues).

Dill (2009) stated, "Intersectional work is dependent upon collaborations, alliances, and networks among scholars with similar intellectual interests, visions, ideas, and values" (p. 234). Additionally, Kincheloe (2011) suggested researchers bring together multiple ways of thinking and collecting data as a way to engage in inquiry with emancipatory aims. Here, it becomes clear that who one is as a researcher and how one interacts with others in the community of scholars directly influences the way one thinks, constructs, and enacts research. As examples of how these intersectional relationships enhance one's research, we as authors will now reflect on how our own thinking has been altered as a result of our ongoing dialogue and collaboration with each other.

The Evolution of Dan's Research

As a qualitative researcher, I (DT) have come to understand the importance of reflexivity and its role within my work. Being a White, gay, cisgender male from a middle-class, rural farm family in upstate New York, I know that my own lived experiences and multiple social identities play a significant role in how I make meaning of myself and others. My research interests are really passion areas of mine that stem from my personal life. The feminist slogan of "the personal is political" (Hanisch, 2006, p. 1) resonates with me in that my research is informed by my personal life and vice versa. My interest in intersectionality in higher education stems from my interest in student development and my critique that much of the traditional theories used in practice in higher education subjugate and splinter aspects of one's identities into fragmented parts rather than encouraging one to take a holistic approach. To me, intersectionality provided an outlet for understanding one's multiple identities within the context of the larger systems of power in which one lives.

My line of research has been largely focused on how sexual minority males in college make meaning of their multiple identities, particularly their sense of masculinities and sexuality (see Tillapaugh, 2012). As a researcher who tends to identify as a constructivist, I embrace the notion of social construction of identities. Therefore, in my research, I place an emphasis on understanding data (e.g., students' personal narratives) in the social contexts in which they live as well as examine the construction of knowledge between the participants and myself (Charmaz, 2006). Exploring my own meaning making process of my social identities illuminated important aspects of my positionality, which certainly helped me check some biases and assumptions. At the same time, my peer review team—of which Z was a member—also played an important role in the evolution of my work.

Z's role within my research shifted my work forward tremendously, particularly in thinking critically about aspects of identity, especially the location of power and difference. As a critical researcher entrenched in critical trans politics—a critical theoretical perspective centered on increasing the life chances of trans*[1] individuals via broad-based coalitions and movements for social change (Spade, 2011)— I appreciate Z's interrogation of aspects of my work that I often take for granted or on which I did not push back. The tensions between our different theoretical paradigms may be present, but they have allowed for a blending—an epistemological bricolage (Kincheloe, 2001), of sorts—that has certainly helped my own thinking around intersectionality. As a constructivist, I appreciated the aspects of one's multiple identity development within the work but often would find myself bringing in aspects of Z's critical approaches to the systemic parts of my research. For example, in discussions of heteronormativity experienced by many of my participants in college, conversations with Z heightened my ability to dig into how heteronormativity tended to be replicated within the LGBT (Lesbian, gay, bisexual, transgender) community and its advocacy for same-sex marriage rather than issues that may take higher priorities for others within our community (e.g., employment nondiscrimination laws, immigration laws for same-sex partners, access to health care for trans* people). This epistemological bricolage has provided a more nuanced and complex examination into the ways in which intersectional approaches to research can provide significant implications for practice, policy, theory, and research in higher education, which we discuss further in this chapter.

The Evolution of Z's Research

When positioning myself (ZN) within my research, I often struggle to provide "something other than a list of attributes separated by those proverbial commas (gender, sexuality, race, class), that usually mean that we have not yet figured out how to think [about] the relations we seek to mark" (Butler, 2011, p. 123). Although I am a queer, trans*, temporarily able-bodied researcher who, due to my educational attainment, has transcended the lower middle-class background I was thrown into when my parents divorced, stating these identities does little to shed light on who I am. Similarly, stating that Dan, as a gay cisgender man, has influenced my work also seems devoid of meaning. I am not saying that social identities do not matter. Quite the opposite; I am suggesting that they matter too much to just string them together with commas and think one has explored fully one's positionality.

In reflecting on my work with Dan, what does seem important is that we simultaneously converge regarding some identities (e.g., we both identify as White) while diverging across other categories of difference (e.g., Dan identifies as cisgender and I as trans*). Additionally, we negotiate dominant and subordinate identities, both individually and between us. As such, my relationship with Dan, which has spanned more than a decade, has set the stage for us to support each other as our identities shift over time as well as challenge how our thinking, life experiences, and social identities mediate our worldviews and how we make meaning of our research. Specifically, Dan's commitment to constructivist grounded theory (Charmaz, 2006) has reminded me of the importance of listening to the voices of my participants and building strong, reciprocal relationships with them. Concurrently, in keeping with the tenets of critical trans politics (Spade, 2011), I also maintain a focus on interrogating the genderism in which the trans* students with whom I research are culturally embedded to increase the livability of our lives. Furthermore, Dan has impressed upon me the importance of focusing on my own feelings, reactions, and responses throughout the research process. As a result of this new affective orientation toward my research, I am continually drawn back to my participants and the process of working alongside of them rather than solely foregrounding the systemic forms of oppression on which my critical theoretical perspective centers.

Thinking Through Intersectionality Together

It is evident in reflecting on our own experiences as researchers that our work has been enhanced by recognizing not only the connections we have to our lines of inquiry but also to each other as scholars. Nevertheless, because we have different epistemological groundings (e.g., I [DT] am a constructivist and Z a criticalist), which tend to foreground different things (e.g., constructivism foregrounds participants' voices while criticalism foregrounds a thorough critique of social inequity), we have to negotiate what our working together means. For example, we want study participants to share their stories in whatever way they make meaning of them (a constructivist tenet), but we also realize that how they tell these stories, and the context in which these stories are placed, are often laced with elements of power, privilege, and oppression (a critical tenet). Put another way, participants' stories may be studded with elements of power, privilege, and oppression that they may not know how to articulate or make meaning of but may be highlighted by a critical analysis. As such, our working together in an intersectional way has mandated that we address questions regarding how each of us approaches research, the ways we structure research questions, and how we collect and analyze data. Furthermore, we were constantly cycling back to how our social identities, life experiences, and social contexts were mediating our responses both to each other and our work. For example, the salience of my (ZN) trans* identity allowed me to recognize a theme of gender policing grounded in transphobia that emerged from the data obtained in Dan's research (Tillapaugh & Nicolazzo, 2013). Our own vantage points as researchers have been informed by our multiple identities and the institutional and societal systems in which we are embedded, which is consistent with taking an intersectional approach to the research process. Although thinking through intersectionality requires consistent and intense reflection in all phases of the research process, we have found the resulting effects to be worthwhile.

Due to the lack of emphasis on power as a mediating force in educational research on intersectionality, we now turn to do some backward thinking on its influence on the research process prior to data collection and analysis. In doing so, it is important to recognize the way power has the potential to influence participants despite them not articulating the connection. In other words, the constellation of identities for any given researcher (see Chapter 12), along with one's epistemological and methodological choices for any given study, influence the following: which participants seek to join a study, which participants are selected, what experiences they share, how they share their experiences, and what meaning is made from their sharing on behalf of the researcher, participant(s), and for them as co-constructors of knowledge. For example, my (ZN) epistemological choice to use critical trans politics (Spade, 2011) likely had an influence in who I was able to recruit for my dissertation study as well as the meaning(s) my participants and I reached as a result of our collaboration. How one talks about one's work, the questions one uses to frame one's inquiry, and the places one seeks (and does not seek) participants not only impact what data one collects (and does not collect), but also are directly related to one's personal identities as an individual and researcher as well as one's interactions among one's scholarly community.

These are not idle decisions, and they are not without consequence. Power not only mediates the direction in which a study goes and how meaning making in the data analysis process occurs. Additionally, power also affects how the research is perceived, the extent to which it is welcomed, by whom it is welcomed, and the access one may or may not get to publish and/or present in certain venues. Scholars have pointed out that the complex intersections of personal identities and overarching social contexts (e.g., neoliberalism) may influence one's ability to be recognized as a knowledge producer in the academy (Elia & Yep, 2012; Pasque, Carducci, Kuntz, & Gildersleeve, 2012). Furthermore, although researchers on the margins certainly do gain access to publish their work, questions of in what venue, at what cost, and if such access acts as a form of "buffer zone" (Kivel, 2007; Spade, 2010) that occludes the continued pervasiveness of systemic oppression (e.g., sexism, genderism, heterosexism, ableism, classism) embedded within the institutions through which such knowledge is shared persist. As Dill (2009) reinforced, research on intersectionality should actively call for and maintain social justice and the disruption of these pervasive systems of oppression for the benefit of those marginalized within society. For example, Tierney's (1997) commentary on whether gay scholars should look to publish in mainstream journals or queer publications, and the effects of such decisions, shows how power mediates not only how one approaches research and the research process but the extent to which one's research is viewed as valid, appropriate, and useful by others in one's respective field of study.

IMPLICATIONS FOR EDUCATIONAL RESEARCH

What does all of this mean for those individuals interested in conducting research through the lens of intersectionality? We believe the process of backward thinking has several important implications for one's individual and collective work. Taking an intersectional perspective in one's work is deeply enriching and rewarding in that everyone has multiple competing identities and multiple ways of thinking. Thus, intersectional approaches seem natural as a means of engaging in and with research. At the same time, conducting research informed through the lens of intersectionality is extremely difficult to do (Jones & Abes, 2013).

As researchers and scholars, one needs to engage those aspects of oneself through reflexivity by considering one's positionality as well as one's work with collaborators, when possible, to help examine and illuminate potential biases. Additionally, one needs to also have a keen awareness of the contexts in which participants live and learn and become well-versed in considering those while engaged in data analysis. For example, one of my (DT) participants, a first-generation Cambodian American gay male from a working-class family, discussed his experiences of taking out additional student loans to provide money to his family back home for their expenses, working two part-time jobs, and thus not being connected to student organizations on campus. In the interviews, the student discussed this as being connected to his Buddhist upbringing, but I, from my positionality of being from a middle-class background, felt as though these behaviors were indicative of the student's social class. During the study's focus group, I asked the student directly about his social class and its potential impact on his college experience; the student once again pressed back and said his faith had more to do with his personal engagement with family and college and that his social class played very little into his identity. This experience was significant because ultimately the power I had as a researcher could easily have been used to manipulate the student's truth, that his faith was more salient than his social class. Instead, I had a transformative learning experience related to his own reflexivity and the ways in which he made meaning of the data needed to be in concert with thoughtful discourse with himself and others to limit his biases and suspend judgment.

This connects to Warner's (2008) discussion of master categories versus emergent categories in intersectional research. Warner stated, "Before researchers make the assumption that the master category validly represents all or most groups, the researcher must first establish the merit of that assumption" (p. 458). As with the aforementioned example, my (DT) positionality ultimately played into an incorrect assumption around the master category of the participant. The participant's religious beliefs combined with his racial identification as well as his status as a first-generation American played a much more significant role in his own master narrative than his socioeconomic status. Through the act of suspending my own judgment and engaging with my participant around his own meaning making of his intersectional identities, his truth was validated rather than my own incorrect assumptions. By engaging in reflexive work, I (DT) came to understand that it is essential that individuals become vigilant in understanding their own reflexivity as it relates to how they think about research, who they are, and how they approach their work.

Another implication of using intersectionality in educational research is to understand the political ramifications of that work on a micro and macro level. Truly intersectional research must address the micro and macro levels in concert with one another to frame one's multiple social identities in the larger context of systems of inequality in which one is a part (Dill & Zambrana, 2009; Jones & Abes, 2013). Jones and Abes (2013) highlighted this point when discussing the difficulty of completing research that adheres to the core tenets of intersectionality by stating, "Although some research focuses more closely on the micro analysis of individual narratives, this is not true to intersectional tenets, as macro considerations—variables and constructs in research terminology—must also be integrated" (pp. 155–156). Similarly, Choo and Ferree (2010) posited, "The complexity of multiple institutions that feed back into each other—both positively and negatively—can become obscured when the macrostructures of inequality are separated from the microstructures of social construction of meaning" (p. 146). When thinking backward, it becomes critical to situate one's work at both the micro and macro levels to allow for the visibility inherent at illuminating the phenomenon being studied. As Warner (2008) cautioned, "One of the central issues in the study of intersectionality is that of visibility—who is granted attention, who is not, and the consequences of these actions for the study of social issues" (p. 462). Therefore, care must be taken as one sets forth with one's research to ensure that questions of visibility are addressed in the name of research that interrogates social structures and attempts to forward human dignity and social equity.

CONCLUSION

In articulating the importance of intersectionality, Dill and Zambrana (2009) stated the following:

> We argue that intersectionality challenges traditional modes of knowledge production in the United States and illustrate how this theory provides an alternative model that combines advocacy, analysis, theorizing, and pedagogy—basic components essential to the production of knowledge as well as the pursuit of social justice and equality. (p. 1)

As researchers who are heavily invested in intersectional approaches to research, we agree with this statement. Yet, rather than just thinking about how intersectionality can be used as an analytical tool, we place emphasis on the notion of backward thinking, or identifying how intersectionality is essential to thinking through one's epistemological, axiological, and/or ontological groundings. These aspects of one's thinking are foundational for the ways in which research studies are framed and carried out. Whether one does research alongside other researchers, in collaboration with participants, or by oneself, backward thinking is one strategy to engage in deeper reflection about the research *process* rather than just using intersectionality as a lens for analyzing research *content*. In doing so, scholars are able to provide richer and more complex analyses of their research—both the process by which research was done and the data co-constructed with participants—and to promote equity and justice for those participants with whom one researches.

NOTES

1. The use of the asterisk in the word *trans** is used to symbolize the multiplicity of gender identities, expressions, and embodiments within the trans* community. For more information about the use of the asterisk in the term trans*, see Killermann (2012).

REFERENCES

Abes, E. S. (2009). Theoretical borderlands: Using multiple theoretical perspectives to challenge inequitable power structures in student development theory. *Journal of College Student Development, 50*, 141–156.

Baca Zinn, M., & Dill, B. T. (1996). Theorizing difference from multiracial feminism. *Feminist Studies, 22*, 321–331.

Berger, M. T., & Guidroz, K. (Eds.). (2009). *The intersectional approach: Transforming the academy through race, class, and gender.* Chapel Hill: University of North Carolina Press.

Butler, J. (2004). *Undoing gender.* New York, NY: Routledge.

Butler, J. (2011). *Bodies that matter: On the discursive limits of "sex."* New York, NY: Routledge.

Charmaz, K. (2006). *Constructing grounded theory: A practical guide through qualitative analysis.* Los Angeles, CA: Sage.

Choo, H. Y., & Ferree, M. M. (2010). Practicing intersectionality in sociological research: A critical analysis of inclusions, interactions, and institutions in the study of inequalities. *Sociological Theory, 28*, 129–149.

Collins, P. H. (2000). *Black feminist thought: Knowledge, consciousness, and the politics of empowerment* (2nd ed.). New York, NY: Routledge.

Crenshaw, K. W. (1995). Mapping the margins: Intersectionality, identity politics, and violence against women of color. In K. W. Crenshaw, N. Gotanda, G. Peller, & K. Thomas (Eds.), *Critical race theory: The key writings that formed the movement* (pp. 357–383). New York, NY: New Press.

Dill, B. T. (2009). Intersections, identities, and inequalities in higher education. In B. T. Dill & R. E. Zambrana (Eds.), *Emerging intersections: Race, class, and gender in theory, policy, and practice* (pp. 229–252). New Brunswick, NJ: Rutgers University Press.

Dill, B. T., & Zambrana, R. E. (2009). Critical thinking about inequality. In B. T. Dill & R. E. Zambrana (Eds.), *Emerging intersections: Race, class, and gender in theory, policy, and practice* (pp. 1–21). New Brunswick, NJ: Rutgers University Press.

Elia, J. P., & Yep, G. A. (2012). Sexualities and genders in an age of neo-terrorism. *Journal of Homosexuality, 59*, 879–889.

Hanisch, C. (2006). The personal is political. Retrieved from http://www.carolhanisch.org/CH writings/PersonalisPol.pdf

Jones, S. R., & Abes, E. S. (2013). *Identity development of college students: Advancing frameworks for multiple dimensions of identity.* San Francisco, CA: Jossey-Bass.

Jones, S. R., Torres, V., & Arminio, J. (2006). *Negotiating the complexities of qualitative research in higher education.* New York, NY: Routledge.

Killermann, S. (2012). What does the asterisk in "trans*" stand for? [Web log post]. Retrieved from http://itspronouncedmetrosexual.com/2012/05/what-does-the-asterisk-in-trans-stand-for/

Kincheloe, J. L. (2001). Describing bricolage: Conceptualizing a new rigor in qualitative research. *Qualitative Inquiry, 7*, 679–692.

Kincheloe, J. L. (2011). Critical ontology. In K. Hayes, S. R. Steinberg, & K. Tobin (Eds.), *Key works in critical pedagogy: Joe L. Kincheloe* (pp. 201–217). Rotterdam, the Netherlands: Sense.

Kivel, P. (2007). Social service or social change? In INCITE! Women of color against violence (Eds.), *The revolution will not be funded: Beyond the non-profit industrial complex* (pp. 129–149). Cambridge, MA: South End.

Lincoln, Y. S., Lynham, S. A., & Guba, E. G. (2011). Paradigmatic controversies, contradictions, and emerging confluences, revisited. In N. K. Denzin & Y. S. Lincoln (Eds.), *The Sage handbook of qualitative research* (4th ed., pp. 97–128). Thousand Oaks, CA: Sage.

Pasque, P. A., Carducci, R., Kuntz, A. K., & Gildersleeve, R. E. (2012). *Qualitative inquiry for equity in higher education: Methodological innovations, implications, and interventions* (ASHE Higher Education Report). San Francisco, CA: Jossey-Bass.

Renn, K. A. (2010). LGBT and queer research in higher education: State and status of the field. *Educational Researcher, 39,* 132–141.

Shields, S. A. (2008). Gender: An intersectionality perspective. *Sex Roles, 59,* 301–311. doi:10.1007/s11199-008-9501-8

Spade, D. (2010). Be professional! *Harvard Journal of Law & Gender, 33,* 71–84.

Spade, D. (2011). *Normal life: Administrative violence, critical trans politics, and the limitations of law.* Cambridge, MA: South End.

Tierney, W. G. (1997). *Academic outlaws: Queer theory and cultural studies in the academy.* Thousand Oaks, CA: Sage.

Tillapaugh, D., & Nicolazzo, Z. (2013). *"It's kind of apples and oranges": Gay college males' conceptions of gender transgression as poverty.* Manuscript submitted for publication.

Tillapaugh, D. W. (2012). *Toward an integrated self: Making meaning of the multiple identities of gay men in college* (Unpublished doctoral dissertation). University of San Diego, San Diego, CA.

Warner, L. R. (2008). A best practices guide to intersectionality in psychological research. *Sex Roles, 59,* 454–463. doi:10.1007/s11199-008-9504-5

Weber, L. (1998). A conceptual framework for understanding race, class, gender, and sexuality. *Psychology of Women Quarterly, 22,* 13–22.

CHAPTER ELEVEN

Raw Tongue

How Black Women and Latinas Bring Their Multiple Identities into Collegiate Classrooms

SHELLY A. PERDOMO

If one considers the intersecting identities of race, socioeconomic status, and gender in relation to verbal participation in classrooms, a number of feminist and educational scholars suggest that women of color employ voice and silence differently than White women (Anzaldúa, 1990; Blue, 2001; Collins, 2000; Fordham, 1993; Gilmore, 1997; hooks, 1989; Hurtado, 1996; Lorde; 1984; Luke, 1994). Unlike some White women, a number of women of color deliberately adopt voice and silence as methods of knowledge acquisition and/or resistance within classrooms (Hurtado, 1996). Although verbal participation and silence within a classroom have the potential to function as a process of knowledge acquisition and learning for women of color, women of color must constantly be aware of what they say and how they speak within classroom settings, because of the visible markers of race and gender (Hurtado, 1996; Luke, 1994; Winkle-Wagner, 2009). Because voice and silence have come to occupy vitally important places in U.S. educational systems (Kim & Markus, 2005), and voice is linked to effective learning in classrooms for women (Belenky, Clinchy, Goldberger, & Tarule, 1986; Hayes, 2000; Hurtado, 1996), this chapter explores how voice and silence, especially for Black women and Latinas, are never neutral or without meaning in collegiate classrooms.

The chapter focuses on undergraduate Black women and Latinas because racial and gender stereotypes, institutional climate, admissions criteria, socioeconomic issues, and financial need continue to be factors impacting their educational persistence (Allen, 1995; Collins, 2000; hooks, 1989; Howard-Vital, 1989; Hurtado,

1996; Vasquez, 1997). According to Kerby (2012), "in 2010, 30 percent of white women had a college degree or higher, compared to 21.4 percent of black women and a mere 14.9 percent of Hispanic women" (p. 5). Additionally, more than half of African American women students and Latina students are low income (Kerby, 2012). Although, Black women and Latinas are completing college at a higher rate and obtaining advanced degrees in higher numbers than their male counterparts, Black women and Latinas continue to lag behind White and Asian American women in academic enrollment and degree attainment (Kerby, 2012). With lower completion rates than White women and financial barriers that continue to hinder their full potential (Kerby, 2012), there have been relatively few empirical studies examining how Black women and Latinas experience and understand their learning. As such, in the larger study that informed this research, "Unpacking Voice and Silence: A Phenomenological Study of Black Women and Latinas in College Classrooms" (Perdomo, 2012), I explored how Black women and Latinas employed their intersectional identities to develop nuances of voice and silence that allowed them to navigate formal and informal structures of collegiate classrooms. This chapter focuses on the development of a raw tongue, a product of the intersectional identities of Black women and Latina participants and how collegiate classrooms of a traditional, single-sex, White institution can force Black women and Latinas to deny the expression of their multiple identities.

By placing the academic experiences of Black women and Latinas at the center of analysis, the intention of this chapter is to share relevant information that will help students, faculty, higher education administrators, and student affairs practitioners to understand how Black women and Latinas attempt to use their raw tongue to navigate institutional climate and cultural stereotypes that distort the ways they are perceived, evaluated, and treated by their student peers and professors. Moreover, this research is not an attempt to essentialize, minimize, or disregard the experiences of ethno-racial groups. Black women and Latinas are not a monolithic group, and there is no one size fits all. Nevertheless, this research is an effort to understand the intricacies of how diverse Black women and Latinas navigate the traditionally White collegiate classroom. As such, the concepts of linguistic habitus and oppositional/multiple consciousness (outsider-within) serve as theoretical tools for this study.

BOURDIEU'S THEORY OF LINGUISTIC HABITUS

Bourdieu's (1977) linguistic habitus forces one to examine how social institutions (family and schools, specifically) function to provide individuals with linguistic expressions/forms that influence individual dispositions and preferences, which in turn affect how individuals interact with their social world. Central to understanding linguistic variations/exchanges within and among groups is social class affiliation, as it has the ability to provide individuals with linguistic competency or linguistic deficiency. For Bourdieu, variations in the forms of linguistic expression and speech are based on class variations (Thompson, 1991). Lacking the means of legitimate expression, according to Bourdieu, led individuals to silence. Linguistic competence yields linguistic capital. Individuals not endowed with the dominant language or those lacking dominant modes of language use were at a distinct disadvantage.

Because Bourdieu's (1977) theory of linguistic habitus was based on the fairly rigid and class-based determinist framework, class variation cannot solely explain the difference or lack of linguistic/verbal expressions of Black women and Latinas. Historically, Black women (including women of African descent) have been seen as having nothing important to say (Davies, 1995). "When a black women gets up in a crowd to speak or present herself publicly, she has to battle all the cultural and historical meanings about her even to begin to speak and then the content of her speaking is already framed as non-speech or not important" (Davies, 1995, p. 5). The boundaries imposed to render Black women and Latinas incapable of full expression of their creativity and knowledge are based on a host of structural and ideological forms of oppression. As such, the denial of voice of Black women and Latinas is rooted in relationships of power and oppressive systems, more so than class variations, as Black and Latina feminists suggest.

BLACK AND LATINA FEMINIST THEORY OF OPPOSITIONAL AND MULTIPLE CONSCIOUSNESS

The writings of Black and Latina feminists (Anzaldúa, 1987; Davies, 1995; hooks, 1989; Lorde, 1984) have addressed the need for finding multiple ways that women of color can raise their own voices and locate sources of their power. Feminists of color, such as Anzaldúa (1987), wrote about a "home tongue" (p. 58), where women of color communicate the realities and values that are true to themselves. Lorde (1984) referred to the transformation of silence into words to find the source of women's power. hooks's (1989) concept of *transgressive speech* forces women to challenge situations of oppression and power by talking back to authority when necessary, regardless of the consequences. In one way or another, moving from silence to voice requires that Black women and Latinas engage in a process of (re)defining themselves and asserting their agency. As such, silence, muteness, and voicelessness for women of color must be understood in the context of a racist, sexist, and classist society that acts to suppress and marginalize their multiple identities. However, Black women and Latinas are in a unique position to challenge the negative images existing about their identities. Existing and living in an "outsider-within" (Collins, 2000, p. 11) status entails interacting and gaining knowledge of a dominant group without repudiating one's cultural experience but rather by building from this unique marginal position (Anzaldúa, 1987, 1990; Collins, 2000; hooks, 1989; Jackson, 2002). Anzaldúa (1987) best described the outsider-within/border crossing process as a state of reaching a *nueva concienca* (new consciousness). Anzaldúa explicitly argued that the outsider-within process of culturally navigating many worlds brings Latina and women of color to self-definition, self-reflection, and self-valuation. Hence, as Black women and Latinas become aware of their position within a racist, classist, sexist, oppressive environment, they enter a process of critical consciousness/new consciousness.

When a Woman of color develops a new consciousness, she transforms silence into voice. A Woman transgresses, she moves beyond, becoming empowered to express her personal creative power, personal passions, thus engaging in transformational politics (Anzaldúa, 1987, 1990; Collins, 2000; hooks, 1989; Lorde, 1984). Because of these factors, the full expression of Black women and Latinas voices is more complicated than simply lacking linguistic capital. Social structures and ideologies still exist that deny women of color their voice.

METHOD

Unlike previous studies on voice that have employed an ethnographic research genre (e.g., Belenky et al., 1986; Fordham, 1993; Luke 1994), hermeneutic phenomenology was the most suitable methodological approach for this study because it emphasizes the interpretation of the phenomenon of voice as experienced and understood by Black and Latina participants (Laverty, 2003). Following the structure of in-depth phenomenological interviewing, nine undergraduate women (four Black women, four Latinas, and one who identified as Afro-Latina) from various majors and class years underwent a series of three 90-minute intensive and iterative interviews to discuss and reflect on their lived experiences of using their voice in educational settings. The first set of 90-minute interviews focused on life history, which requires participants to reconstruct and share as much as possible about their early educational classroom experience with voice and silence. The second set of interviews allowed participants to reflect on their current academic collegiate experience, and the third set of questions required participants to reflect on the information provided to generate an overall impression of their academic experience.

Purposeful sampling was employed to identify a diverse group of working-class, poor, or middle-class women. None of the participants identified herself or her family as wealthy/rich. All the participants were in the process of completing their bachelor's degree at Noel College (a pseudonym for a highly selective, non-denominational, residential, liberal arts college for women). While "women at single-sex institutions reported being more engaged in effective educational practices and reported higher levels of feelings of support and greater gains in college" (Kinzie, Thomas, Palmer, Umbach, & Kuh, 2007, p. 145), the majority of the research on single-sex education focuses mostly on White women samples (Sax, Arms, Woodruff, Riggers, & Eagon, 2007). Thus, it is my hope that a deeper understanding of the academic experiences of Black women and Latinas attending traditionally White, single-sex institutions is reached.

Three research questions guided this study:

1. How do Black women and Latinas experience and understand their voice in collegiate classrooms?
2. What meanings do Black women and Latinas ascribe to their voice?
3. What do Black women and Latinas perceive to be the academic implications of engaging in a politics of voice?

Because the phenomenological structure of reflecting on the past and present experiences generated extensive data from the nine participants, analysis of interview transcripts was based on an inductive approach geared to identifying patterns in the data by means of thematic codes. Themes emerged from the participants' meanings and shared meaning that came from the variations on how each participant described her own understanding and experience of voice. Three distinguishing features of voice emerged for participants: *instrumental voice, raw tongue,* and *symbolic voice.* This chapter illustrates how Black women and Latina participants attempted to bring their whole selves (multiple identities) in collegiate classrooms through employing their raw tongue, but internal collegiate classroom dynamics, or what Weaver and Qi (2005) referred to as formal classroom structures (class size, faculty as the authority of knowledge, faculty-student interaction, student-student interaction, and fear or professor's criticism) and informal classroom structures (fear of peer disapproval, excessive student participation, and student attributes), prohibit this process.

RAW TONGUE

When participants entered the collegiate classrooms of Noel College, they had an established pattern of talk. In fact, like any student, Black women and Latina participants entered Noel College with a raw tongue. Whether they described themselves as outspoken or more reserved, these women expressed what one participant referred to as "rawness" or what I deem to be a "raw tongue," which builds from Anzaldúa's (1987) concept of "a home tongue."

Home tongue refers to a type of language/dialect spoken in the company of sisters, brothers, friends, and community. In this case, raw tongue is a mixed, fluid dialect. It is neither proper Spanish nor Standard English. Their raw tongues consist of an English slang, working-class English, Ebonics/Black English, or Spanglish. It is a language/dialect that is unrefined, untrained, honest, full of emotions, passion, and often filled with hostility/anger. It is a language/dialect that grounded these women in their families, social communities, and their multiple interlocking ethno-racial/social identities. As such, the raw tongue of participants was as much a product of their intersectional identities as it was a process of their linguistic habitus, a socialization rooted in family and community. Regardless of the socioeconomic background and cultural/ethno-racial makeup of their families and communities, each Woman was socialized to speak and interact with individuals (within their family, community members, and friends) utilizing a raw tongue. It is a voice that developed from the intersections of race, class, and gender in the lives of these women. Raw tongue is a synergy of cultures that is literally manifested in language. When Black women and Latinas used their raw tongue within the traditionally White collegiate classrooms of Noel College, their voice became a marker of their racial identity and economic status, which is seen in the following example:

> [Responding to a White student's comment] Who am I? You don't know who I am! I am sick and tired of always having to educate…. The girls in the classroom were like, "Wow!" We were talking about being poor and living in poor communities. And the term ghetto was being thrown around like nothing. By the second week of class, I said I was sick and tired of all you [White students] talking about the ghetto! Let me tell you about the ghetto! Let me tell you what fucking welfare is, and I just went off on them! In another situation I went off again on the teacher and the students. We were talking about poverty and privilege, and I said to [the] professor, "How dare you tell me that I was formerly poor? You don't know me! You don't know what it took for me to be here! You don't know how sad I am that my mom is in a small apartment, and I am here taking classes, not working and unable to assist her the way I would want to!" And my professor looked at me, and he said, "Tell us, Dalis," and I said, "No! I am not going to be your guinea pig right now!" (Dalis)

This example illustrates how classroom discussions and interactions with White peers and some professors forced participants to employ their raw tongue out of discomfort and frustration of not being understood, heard, and/or taken seriously within collegiate classrooms. As a result, their raw tongue created discomfort and tension amongst their White peers and even with some faculty. Their blunt, assertive responses toward their White peers' White privilege, entitlement, and lack of sensitivity and racial understanding, created situations where participants spoke with no inhibitions or filters. When Black women and Latina participants used their raw tongue in collegiate classrooms, their honest and heartfelt responses were often misunderstood by their White peers. Their White peers often perceived such interactions/responses as "hostile," "aggressive," "too firm," and/or "unfriendly." Instead of listening to the comments and questions posed by Black women and

Latina participants, White students and faculty were either intrigued and wanted to learn more about their lived experiences or they expressed discomfort through explicit verbal and nonverbal cues: "White students loved to hear what I had to say. Professors too, they saw me as an exotic contribution, an exotic addition. I brought validity to the Latina experience! Whatever that means" (Dalis). Another participant (Jada) shared the following: "I expected something different, but in class I do feel this overemphasis on what I say, especially when we are talking about race. The White students become very interested in my opinions."

When Black women and Latina participants used their raw tongue, they became visible/spotlighted/on display within the classroom, impacting their level of verbal participation/engagement. Participants believed that White peers judged them according to unconscious/conscious stereotypes and attitudes. This was the kind of prejudice that was not overt; instead, it was subconscious, subtle, and learned through early socialization. As a result, how White peers looked at and understood participants was connected to how they heard them within collegiate classrooms. The raw tongue of Black women and Latinas in this study was perceived as "too ghetto" by their White peers. "Too ghetto" usually refers to the experiences of people of a particular race or ethno-racial group who act or are perceived to behave improperly through fulfilling negative stereotypes. Being perceived as "too ghetto" by their White peers had serious implications for participants. One student candidly expressed how she felt after employing her raw tongue during a discussion: "People were looking at me and…what came out of my mouth, it wasn't really what I wanted to say or how I wanted it to come out.… I didn't sound intelligent, especially in an academic space. I sounded angry" (Dalis). Because the raw tongue of participants was juxtaposed to what was considered the "appropriate academic discourse," they were led to believe that their linguistic skills were deficient. Although some of the women in this study were monolingual and brought different linguistic backgrounds and forms of expressions to classrooms, their linguistic styles were not valued. Instead, through a number of encounters/ interactions with students and faculty, participants received explicit and implicit cues that their raw tongue was not only a risk but a responsibility that needed to be self-monitored to speak and be heard.

RISK AND RESPONSIBILITY: SELF-MONITORING BEHAVIOR

Prior to attending Noel College, participants did not perceive their raw tongue or linguistic skills as deficient; rather, they entered the collegiate environment with their diverse linguistic backgrounds, eager to be part of a learning community of intelligent women. Yet, for the first time in their academic experience, these women believed they were forced to learn a different language from the raw tongue they learned from their parents and social communities. They recognized that a particular type of voice was required for them to be heard in their classrooms.

The academic discourse that participants were forced to employ was not by their own choosing but was imposed by the institution, professors, and student peers; "They [White female] talk a language that is very elite. Sometimes, they will say things that, shit, I have never heard in my life! It's different, and it's something I am not used to, but I have had to learn how to talk like that!" (Yoli). Participants realized early in their educational trajectory that their raw tongue functioned as both a risk and a responsibility within collegiate classrooms. With their every utterance in class, participants were aware that they were at risk of fulfilling negative stereotypes held of their ethno-racial group:

> I think at first it [speaking] was risky. It felt like I was vulnerable because I didn't know what their [White peers'] response would be to my response.... I just felt alone in my contributions.... I felt scared to be confronted with not being intelligent or being looked down upon or fulfilling the stereotype of all my people, so it was a lot of responsibility...or at times I was so pissed off at their ignorant comments that I could not even blink 'cause that thing was going to come out! That rawness and that again I will fulfill a stereotype. (Dalis)

> It's even more pressure when you are at a high caliber institution, and, you know, there is that pressure that you are here and you're Latina. I think about it every day. As a Latina there is this fear that if I say something stupid or if I go off on a tangent that is going to be blamed on the fact that I am Latina. *Oh mira esa Latina tan Estupida* (oh look at the Latina, so stupid). She has no idea what she is talking about.... I don't want them to think I am stupid...so if I don't say something really smart, I prefer not to say anything. (Issy)

Speaking within the collegiate classroom was considered a risk because these women did not want to be perceived by their White peers and professors as unintelligent, incompetent women fulfilling negative stereotypes of their entire ethno-racial group. Because the way White students looked at and understood participants was so predicated on how they heard them speak in class, women in this study felt pressure and responsibility to speak and demonstrate that individuals in their ethno-racial group could successfully enter and complete college. The responsibility to speak and attempt to dispel/undo the negative stereotypes, that their peers and/or professors may have, also forced participants to modify their behavior within classrooms.

To speak and be heard, participants had the burden of self-monitoring their behavior in their classrooms. Because their communication patterns often determined how they were perceived in collegiate classrooms, participants became more conscious of what they said and how they expressed themselves. This self-monitoring took the form of modifying their voice and/or behavior in classrooms to refute the negative stereotypes of being "too ghetto," "too angry," and to prove they are serious students. Dalis and Yoli described the change in their behavior as follows: "I am not raw anymore, I was at the beginning, but I don't talk like that anymore" (Dalis). "There has been so many times, I can't even count, that we have been told to hush, that we are too loud...so I am very cautious of what I say and how I say things in the classrooms now" (Yoli). Thus, voice for participants, as expressed through their raw tongue, was not simply about expressing themselves, their thoughts, ideas, and feelings; their raw tongue became a negative marker of their racial, gendered, and economic status that required them to self-monitor their behavior and to modify their linguistic expressions to be viewed as academically serious.

IMPLICATIONS FOR FACULTY AND STUDENT AFFAIRS PRACTITIONERS

Much of the discomfort and alienation experienced by participants resulted from negative faculty-student interactions in classrooms, lack of diversity, and racial consciousness of peers and faculty, White privilege/entitlement of student peers and/or faculty, and stereotype threat existing in collegiate classrooms. Because much of the ways that participants experienced collegiate classrooms was determined by their interactions and academic engagement with faculty and student peers, having curricula and co-curricular programming that addresses diverse cultures, abilities, and experiences might provide all students with exposure to diverse perspectives. Incorporating scholarly works by people of color and other marginalized groups in the curriculum has the ability to heighten diversity awareness of White students enrolled in these courses and to empower students of color. White students who learn about diversity and engage in cross-cultural discussions have the potential to help create a climate where students of color and other marginalized groups feel more comfortable. At the same time, if faculty acknowledge and value the diverse linguistic forms of expression and communication that Black women and Latinas bring to the classroom, students of color will not feel the need to alter their behavior and/or to give up who they are in order to be heard within collegiate classrooms. However, where curricula fall short in addressing diversity or when institutions reflect cultural insensitivity, faculty and student affairs practitioners can become more supportive by creating educational spaces that allow for safe, meaningful exchanges among students. One way this might be accomplished is by employing pedagogies and programs that support and promote collaborative learning environments where students' ideas, voices, and contributions to knowledge are heard and acknowledged in creative ways. Nevertheless, it is not sufficient to confine multiculturalism, social justice, and diversity teaching to classrooms. Congruent messages from faculty and academic and student affairs practitioners could support a more diverse and supportive academic environment that promotes student development for students of color.

Campus communities that value and promote an understanding of diversity, multiculturalism, and inclusivity could become more supportive of students of color by providing workshops/forums to engage all students in transformative learning to empower them to become agents of social change. Inviting speakers of color to add diversity education to campus programs and speak of their lived experience as agents of effective social change could contribute to personal growth and inclusive and intentional learning for students. These processes can also benefit White students who would be better equipped to serve as allies to students of color, and students of color could develop strategies of empowerment where they learn to express themselves with no inhibitions. Creating and supporting co-curricular programs that acknowledge students' diverse experiences and cultures in a positive light could invite students to engage and participate without forcing them to change and alter who they are in classroom and co-curricular activities.

CONCLUSION

As someone who shares a Black and Latina ethno-racial identity, research on voice and silence was important to my work as an educator. Anzaldúa (1987) said it best when she stated, "ethnic identity becomes twin skin to linguistic identity" (p. 59). Because language is so intricately linked to ethno-racial identity and cultural expression of a people, honoring raw tongue is important for students who belong to marginalized groups. It validates their lived experience in collegiate classrooms and allows them to express their perspectives without having to modify their voice or feel as though they have assimilated and abandon their ethno-racial identities. As such, it is important for faculty and academic and student affairs practitioners to be aware that nuances of voice, like raw tongue, exist for Black women, Latinas, and targeted groups who share multiple marginalized identities.

REFERENCES

Allen, B. J. (1995, November). *Twice blessed, doubly oppressed: Women of color in the academe.* Paper presented at the annual meeting of the Speech Communications Association, San Antonio, TX.

Anzaldúa, G. (1987). *Borderlands: La frontera: The new mestiza.* San Francisco, CA: Aunt Lute.

Anzaldúa, G. (1990). *Making face, making soul:* Haciendo caras, *creative and critical perspectives by feminists of color.* San Francisco, CA: Aunt Lute.

Belenky, M., Clinchy, B., Goldberger, N., & Tarule, J. (1986). *Women's ways of knowing: The development of self, voice and mind.* New York, NY: Basic.

Blue, D. A. (2001). Breaking the silence: Racial identity development of post baccalaureate African American women. In R. Mabokela & A. Green (Eds.), *Sisters of the academy: Emergent black women scholars in higher education* (pp. 117–138). Sterling, VA: Stylus.

Bourdieu, P. (1977). *Reproduction in education, society and culture.* Beverly Hills CA: Sage.

Collins, P. H. (2000). *Black feminist thought: Knowledge, consciousness and the politics of empowerment.* New York, NY: Routledge.

Davies, C. B. (1995). Hearing black women's voices: Transgressing imposed boundaries. In C. B. Davies & M. Ogundipe-Leslie (Eds.), *Moving beyond boundaries: International dimensions of black women's writing* (pp. 3–14). New York: New York University Press.

Fordham, S. (1993). "Those loud black girls": (Black) women, silence, and gender "passing" in the academy. *Anthropology and Education Quarterly, 24,* 3–32.

Gilmore, A. D. (1997). It is better to speak. In A. K. Wing (Ed.), *Critical race feminism: A reader* (pp. 51–56). New York: New York University Press.

Hayes, E. (2000). Voice. In E. Hayes, D. D. Flannery, A. K. Brooks, E. J. Tisdell, & J. M. Hugo (Eds.), *Women as learners: The significance of gender in adult learning* (pp. 79–109). San Francisco, CA: Jossey-Bass.

hooks, b. (1989). *Talking back: Thinking feminist, thinking black.* Boston, MA: South End.

Howard-Vital, M. R. (1989). African-American women in higher education: Struggling to gain identity. *Journal of Black Studies, 20,* 180–191.

Hurtado, A. (1996). Strategic suspensions: Feminists of color theorize the production of knowledge. In N. Goldberger, J. Tarule, B. Clinchy, & M. Belenky (Eds.), *Knowledge, difference, and power: Essays inspired by women's ways of knowing* (pp. 372–392). New York, NY: Basic.

Jackson, V. (2002) In our own voice: African-American stories of oppression, survival and recovery in mental health systems. *International Journal of Narrative Therapy and Community Work, 2,* 11–31.

Kerby, S. (2012). *The state of women of color in the United States: Although they've made incredible strides many barriers remain for this group.* Retrieved from http://www.americanprogress.org/issues/race/report/2012/07/17/11923/the-state-of-women-of-color-in-the-united-states/

Kim, H. S., & Markus, H. R. (2005). Speech and silence: An analysis of the cultural practice of talking. In L. Weis & M. Fine (Eds.), *Beyond silenced voices: Class, race, and gender in United States schools* (pp. 181–196). Albany: State University of New York Press.

Kinzie, J., Thomas, A. D., Palmer, M. M., Umbach, P. D., & Kuh, G. D. (2007). Women students at coeducational and women's colleges: How do their experiences compare? *Journal of College Student Development, 48,* 145–165.

Laverty, S. M. (2003). Hermeneutic phenomenology and phenomenology: A comparison of historical and methodological considerations. *International Journal of Qualitative Methods, 2,* 1–29.

Lorde, A. (1984). *Sister outsider.* Trumansburg, NY: Crossing.

Luke, C. (1994). Women in the academy: The politics of speech and silence. *British Journal of Sociology of Education, 15,* 211–230.

Perdomo, S. A. (2012). *Unpacking voice and silence: A phenomenological study of black women and Latinas in college classrooms* (Unpublished doctoral dissertation). University of Massachusetts Amherst.

Sax, L., Arms, E., Woodruff, M., Riggers, T., & Eagon, K. (2007). *Women graduates of single sex and coeduational high schools: Differences in their characteristics and the transition to college.* Retrieved from http://sudikoff.gseis.ucla.edu//archive/pdfs/genderstudies/Summary_SingleSexEd_Sax.pdf

Thompson, J. B. (1991). *Language and symbolic power: Pierre Bourdieu.* Cambridge, MA: Harvard University Press.

Vasquez, M. J. (1997). Confronting barriers to the participation of Mexican American women in higher education. In A. Darder, R. D. Torres, & H. Gutierrez (Eds.), *Latinos and education: A critical reader* (pp. 454–467). New York, NY: Routledge.

Weaver, R. R., & Qi, J. (2005). Classroom organization and participation: College student's perceptions. *Journal of Higher Education, 76,* 570–602.

Winkler-Wagner, R. (2009). *The unchosen me: Race, gender and identity among black women in college.* Baltimore, MD: The John Hopkins University Press.

CHAPTER TWELVE

Identity Constellations

An Intersectional Analysis of Female Student Veterans

SUSAN V. IVERSON

Researchers are increasingly aware of the limitations of identity dimensions as singular analytic categories (Berger & Guidroz, 2009; Montoya, 1998; Reynolds & Pope, 1991). Many feminist researchers, by example, have critiqued the use of gender as a sole identity category for analysis, and scholars have sought a framework to describe and understand the interaction of different forms of oppression and disadvantage, including race, sexuality, and gender (Baca Zinn, Hondagneu-Sotolo, & Messner, 2000; Collins, 1998; Fine, 1994; McCall, 2005). While many scholars have grappled with conceptualizations to describe the complexity of interrelated forces acting on dimensions of identity (e.g., Andersen, 2005; Baca Zinn et al., 2000; Ken, 2008), Crenshaw's (1991) analogy of traffic through an intersection has become a dominant conceptualization of how individuals' experiences are "frequently the product of intersecting patterns of racism and sexism" (p. 1243), along with other oppressions. Yet, some (e.g., Baca Zinn et al., 2000; Ken, 2007, 2008), with whom I align, argue that the intersection is a limited conceptual image and instead theorize alternatives. This chapter advances the metaphor of a constellation to the intersectionality literature. More than a theoretical manuscript, this chapter illustrates this conceptualization with findings from a qualitative study of female student veterans (Iverson, Seher, DiRamio, Jarvis, & Anderson, 2013).

LITERATURE REVIEW

Intersectionality originally emerged to destabilize categories of identity, for example, exposing how the category of "women" excludes "others" within that category (McCall, 2005). For instance, research on student veterans, in its efforts to describe their transition to college (DiRamio & Jarvis, 2011; Rumann & Hamrick, 2010), has treated *veteran* as a one-dimensional category. This "elision of difference" (Crenshaw, 1991, p. 1242) opened the door for recent studies on women veterans (Burns Phillips, 2010; Iverson et al., 2013), but they too risk describing women as a monolithic group. An intersectional analysis provides "an antidote to this erasure" (Cole, 2009, p. 172).

An intersectional approach also illuminates how individual experiences reflect macrolevel inequalities and "how power and power relations are maintained and reproduced" (Hankivsky et al., 2010, p. 3). This tenet is perhaps most widely used as a theoretical approach for analyzing relations among different forms of oppression (Diamond & Butterworth, 2008). Yet, for all the power of using the analogy of traffic through an intersection to "disrupt the tendencies to see race and gender as exclusive or separable" (Crenshaw, 1991, p. 1244, n9), attention to "particular location" (Crenshaw, 1991, p. 1243) has led to a dominance of orthogonality in intersectional research: disproportionate attention has given to the intersection an image that implies linearity and stability.

Contemporary intersectionality theorists assert, instead, that social processes such as social interaction, context, and social-structural factors inform and create fluid, negotiated, social identities (Bowleg, 2013; Diamond & Butterworth, 2008; Warner, 2008; Warner & Shields, 2013). Further, several scholars have sought to establish alternatives to the metaphor of the traffic intersection to illuminate how "systems of inequality create qualitatively distinct experiences" (Warner & Shields, 2013, p. 804). For instance, Ken (2008) posited the metaphor of sugar: "[T]he production, use, experience, and digestion of sugar as a way...to focus on the structural and individual forces at work in their continual and mutual constitution" (p. 154). Baca Zinn et al. (2000) used the metaphor of a prism to explain how "gender is organized and experienced differently when refracted through the prism of sexual, racial/ethnic, social class, physical abilities, age, and national citizenship differences" (p. 1). I align with those who suggest we must further complicate what is meant by intersectionality to illuminate how social location changes the nature of experience (Bowleg, 2013; Singh, 2013).

CONSTELLATION OF IDENTITIES

Diamond and Butterworth (2008) called for a closer analysis of the processes and intersections "between different identities and social locations [that] give rise to altogether novel forms of subjective experience"; they add that these dynamic interactions yield "constellations of identity" (p. 367). While they were using a "turn of phrase," I advance *constellation* as a metaphor for thinking about the dilemma of identities as stable *and* fluid, as relational and in process, and for illustrating "how *all* subjective experiences of selfhood are continually transformed, reenacted, and renegotiated as a function of shifting landscapes of social context" (Diamond & Butterworth, 2008, p. 375).

A constellation is a pattern formed by prominent stars within proximity to one another. The stars that comprise a particular constellation have varying degrees of brightness or magnitude. The brightest stars are considered of the first magnitude, while the faintest stars are of the sixth magnitude (the limit of human visual perception, without the aid of a telescope; Comins & Kaufmann, 2003). Identity is much like a constellation. One's sense of self or self-awareness is formed through the *apparent magnitude* of particular dimensions of one's identity. For instance, being a Woman, and a mother, is of the first magnitude in my constellation; yet, being White and heterosexual are also stars within my constellation; and my religion, age, and able-bodiedness are fainter stars in my constellation. Notably, the rules for classifying the magnitude of stars can be as subjective as my preceding description of self (American Association of Variable Star Observers, 2013).

Any constellation is an arbitrary formation of stars as perceived by the stargazer. Our modern constellations, 88 of them, were officially designated by the International Astronomical Union (IAU) in the early 20th century (Comins & Kaufmann, 2003). However, it is important to note that before the IAU comprised an official list, anyone could (and anyone still can) arrange and group stars, in much the same way one might stare at clouds and see shapes. Further, stargazing is temporally, culturally, and geographically constituted, meaning that a different night sky is visible in the northern hemisphere than in the southern hemisphere, and different cultural stories exist for the same constellation. For instance, the Ursa Major constellation is likely associated by many U.S. readers with stories of a big bear; however, Chinese astronomers call this constellation the "Jade Balance of Fate," and an Arab myth associates this star pattern with a coffin and mourners (NF/Observatory, n.d.). Identity, too, is both socially constructed and personally defined and "embedded within specific contextual, interpersonal, and developmental circumstances" (Diamond & Butterworth, 2008, p. 369).

AN INTERSECTIONAL ANALYSIS OF FEMALE STUDENT VETERANS

This section illustrates this conceptualization with data from a qualitative study of female student veterans (Iverson et al., 2013). The data used in this intersectional analysis were from "responsive interviewing" (Rubin & Rubin, 2005) with 12 women from two public research universities. Transcripts from the interviews were analyzed independently, and then, in an effort to see how to subsume the "particulars into the general" (Miles & Huberman, 1994, p. 245), emerging patterns and themes were visually mapped. Findings from this analysis revealed that participants were grappling with identity shifts while in the military and in college. Participants were walking a gender tightrope as soldiers and women, and then in college, as undeserving veterans struggling with the social and cognitive dissonance experienced as students (for more on study design and findings, see Iverson et al., 2013).

The 12 participants included women from the Army, Navy, Air Force, and National Guard, with most (5) from the Army. [Of note, the term *veteran* is used to represent the very broad category of individuals who are serving and/or have previously served in the U.S. military.] Their length of service ranged from 2 to 38 years; half had served in the Iraq/Afghan wars, and one-third was still active military at the time of the interview. The women ranged in ages from mid-20s to mid-50s. Their racial composition was nine White and three African American participants. Most (9 of the 12) spoke of being married, divorced, or engaged in heterosexual relationships (the other 3 identified as single), and 7 of the 12 referred to having children.

Four women are featured here—Constance, Cathy, Anne, and Latesha—as a strategy to illuminate participants' "subjectivities, and their experiences" (Holley & Colyar, 2009, p. 685). Evident in their stories is the *apparent magnitude* of particular dimensions of identity, which is mapped in respective constellations.

Constance

Constance married her high school sweetheart at the age of 18. She completed her associate's degree while her husband enlisted in the military. Then she enlisted in the Army, only to have a training accident 6 months later, leaving her with a shattered hip, broken pelvis, and a medical discharge. She was told by the Army that she couldn't have children, but after two miscarriages and deep sadness, she gave birth to one son. Shortly thereafter, her husband was deployed again and she got divorced. She then completed her undergraduate degree and began working for the U.S. Department of Defense (DoD), teaching in Germany. She then transferred to the western United States, completed her master's degree, and started a new position with the DoD, teaching in a medical school. The high cost of living, including limited and expensive day care, led Constance to request a transfer to a new position: "They started the in-processing for the job and then…everything froze." With her relocation to the southeastern United States in motion, she applied for and was accepted to a PhD program. She stated that, for all the changes she has experienced, "the biggest transition…, hands down, was actually when [she] came to [her current university]."

Constance described many points in her constellation of identity (see Figure 1). Her status as an adult student is the brightest point in her identity right now. She noted that her age, coupled with being a single parent from a working-class background, has left her with "no one else to identify with" in college. She reflected that this was different while she was obtaining her master's degree, an executive cohort program in which all 13 adult professionals started and finished the program together in 18 months. Now, she observes, at 29 years old, and as a mom, that she doesn't identify with the undergrads. "It's also socio-economically very different.... I don't really fit in."

Her working-class (even low-income) background has magnitude now, while at college, but it has been prominent at other points in her life, such as when she qualified for WIC (Women Infant and Children) assistance in both Germany and while living in the western United States. Her disability is part of her identity, but it is less prominent today than it was when she was in the military, trying to have a child. Of note, her status as a veteran is nearly inconsequential, and her race (White) is noted in Figure 12.1, but it is the faintest star.

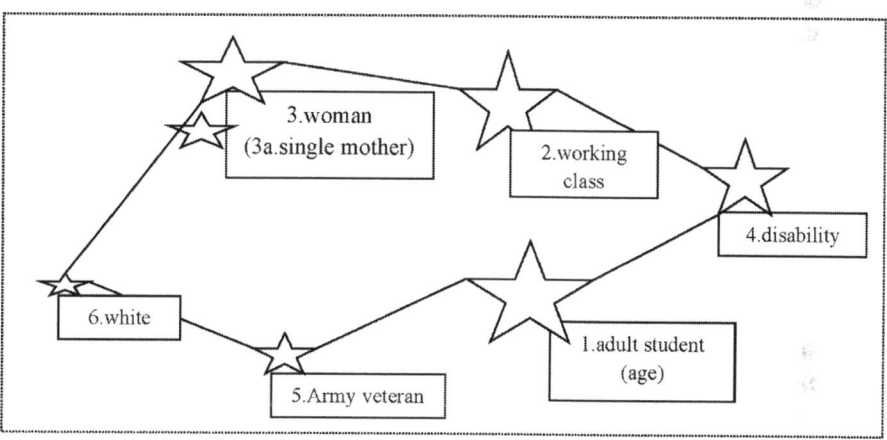

Fig 12.1. Constance's constellation.

Cathy

Cathy, an African American Woman, joined the Air Force in 1996. She had been attending college but dropped out because "I couldn't get money for college... [and] I wasn't sure about my major." In need of "something to do with [her] life," she joined the military: active duty Air Force for 4½ years, followed by active Reserves for 2½ years. Then after discharge, and seven years as a flight attendant, she reenlisted, this time with the Army. It was during this service duty that her daughter was born, and she was deployed to Afghanistan for 10 months when her daughter was 9 months old. As a single mother, her daughter was in the care of Cathy's mother, who herself was a single mom.

Cathy continued to take classes, on and off since the 1990s, both online and at a community college, but she had yet to earn her degree. She was now enrolled in college: "I definitely have to get my degree…. You can't do anything in this world without that piece of paper." And, returning to the same campus she attended nearly 25 years ago, she added, "it was a personal thing, full circle…. I started here. I want to finish here." But returning to college is hard; she felt her age on campus: "I'm old enough to be everybody's mother." She shares that when she is "sitting in class with someone, just to hear the conversations going on, and I think back 'was I like that 20 years ago?' Probably so… but now I'm older [and] I just came from Afghanistan and my mindset is on alert."

In addition to juggling classes, being a single mom, and feeling isolated on campus, Cathy struggled with post-traumatic stress disorder (PTSD); she described nightmares, depression, anxiety, difficulty sleeping, and a general feeling of "hyper alert." She also battled "feelings of guilt" for leaving her daughter when she was deployed. Still, she's been reluctant to use Veterans Affairs (VA) mental health services because she "wasn't on the front lines." Cathy's job consisted of "dignified transfers," meaning when "they [Army personnel] put the bodies on the plane to send them home, I just video tape, so they [can] send the video home to their mom, their families." She adds, "[I]t was like a funeral every day."

In Cathy's constellation of identity (see Figure 12.2), being a Woman, more specifically a single mother, is paramount. She describes her age—feeling so much older than her peers—as the next point of magnitude in her identity; yet, her struggles with PTSD were prominent. She did not claim a disability, as other participants did, but the effects of PTSD have magnitude in shaping and defining her sense of self. Notably, for her nearly 15 years of service in two branches of the U.S. military, she is slow to identify as a veteran. She views veteran identity as conflated with combat duty, and she—in her words—wasn't "on the front lines."

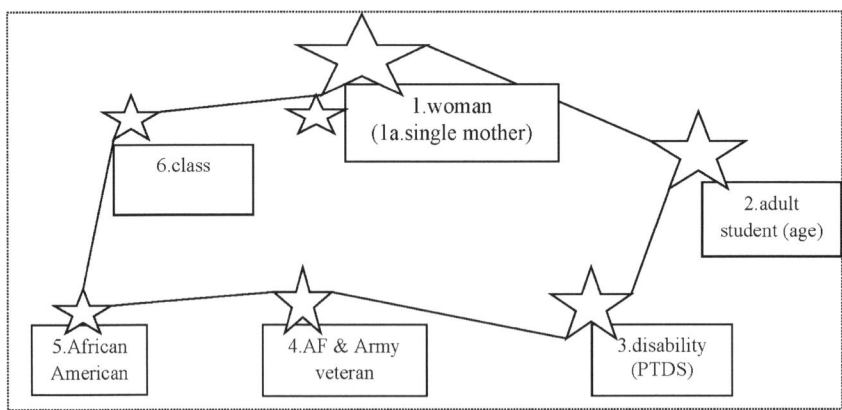

Fig 12.2. Cathy's constellation.

Anne

In contrast, for Anne, being a veteran is of the greatest magnitude in defining herself (see Figure 12.3). Anne enlisted in the Navy during her sophomore year in college. She qualified as a nuclear mechanic and was one of 15 women who started in the nuclear program. While in "power school," Anne met and married her husband, "also a Navy nuke." After she completed all the military schooling, she was assigned to a ship. Standing watches, during her seven months on board, "six on, six off, six on, six off…took a toll on [her] knees." She was transferred to shore duty and got pregnant. Married military couples must submit a "care plan" to indicate who will care for the child so the "two active duty parents" can continue their service. If "you can't comply," then the Navy will "pick who's the better person to keep." Her husband was deployed when the baby was born and a few months later, the Navy approved for Anne to remain on shore duty as an instructor (during which her second child was born). When the time came for her and her husband to reenlist, they opted for civilian life. Anne's veteran identity remained prominent, however; she worked for many years as a state veteran representative, and during the study, as a college student, while serving as president of the campus veterans club.

While Anne's identity as a married Woman (being a mother and a wife) was important to who she is, her rural working-class upbringing (on a Midwestern farm) was of the second magnitude, after being a veteran:

> Growing up on a farm…I was used to hanging out with guys…. So, I wasn't intimidated by guys. I may be little and petite but…I can look at a bolt and say "Let's get a 9/16th [wrench]."…My dad did maintenance for the farm machinery on the farm and I got to be on the ground and help out.

When asked about being a Woman in the military, or even about campus programming for (women) veterans, she was incongruent about her experience. She was at ease in male-dominated environments and was "used to hanging out with guys." She did express shock at being "the last female of the 15" in her initial nuclear program at the time of her discharge: "What? I'm the last?" But she added, "I don't push the male-female card; that seems to get the guys' dander up." She distanced herself from those women who she believes "use their feminine tricks to try to get their way." As president of the campus veterans club, she observed, "[W]e don't have a lot of females that actively come out to the meetings because the guys use that social downtime as theirs." Anne felt comfortable in that context and doesn't understand why other women aren't more at ease: maybe it's "women's brains… maybe it's hormones." She felt that support networks are built from those around you, and those "networks would include guys too…we talk and try to help each other…we'd become kinda brothers and sisters."

Other aspects of her identity have less magnitude. She had a disability while in the military, but it gives little definition now to her sense of self. Rather, her husband's struggles with PTSD dominated her story. Also, challenging economic times led her husband to take a job in another state, with Anne as the full-time parent: "I think my gray hairs have doubled."

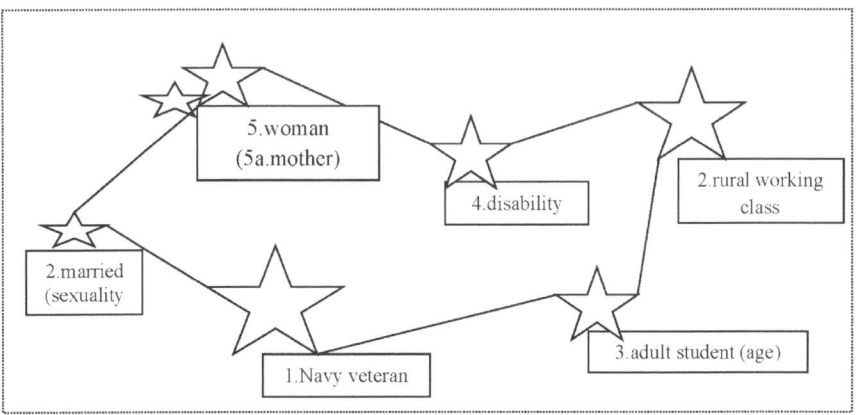

Fig 12.3. Anne's constellation.

Latesha

For Latesha, being a Woman had the greatest magnitude in her constellation (see Figure 12.4). She joined the Navy when she was 20, and like Anne, she was in a gender asymmetrical field: "I was a construction mechanic." But she quickly added that her male peers were not "really pleased about it because, not only was [she] joining the battalion, but [she] was not in the kitchen or the admin type… [She] was in the shop where there were no females." Referring to her male peers as "salty dogs," she said, "[E]verybody was really hard on me…. They did not want to work alongside a Woman." But as she showed that she "could pull [her] own weight…[she] was able to gain some respect." And then, "once [she] married [her] husband [also in the Navy], it was totally different…. A whole new level of respect."

Since that time, Latesha and her husband left the Navy and had two children. Her husband worked full-time as a police officer, and Latesha was the primary caregiver and was pursuing her undergraduate degree. But she noted that campus was a "very lonely place." She felt isolated—by her age, being a parent, and a veteran. She said, "I am a veteran and a mom." Referring to her young peers, she noted, "I know that at 20 years old, nobody wants to hear about somebody else's kids…. I am not really very relatable to anybody." She reflected that when she and her husband were in the Navy, they were "highly respected," but now, "nobody even knows that [she] served in the military."

Still, being a Woman—whether reflected in her role as a mother or her challenges as a female in the military—is orienting for her. When asked about how the university could better support veterans, and in particular women veterans, she said, "I think as female veterans, we're so used to multi-tasking.... We're not looking for…an easy pass.… I just have to figure it out, and I figure it out a little more each day."

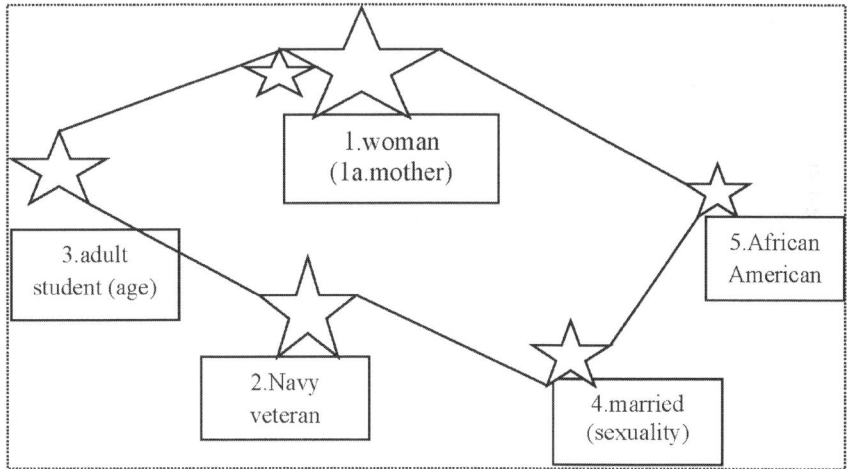

Fig 12.4. Latesha's constellation.

CONCLUSIONS

Traditional perspectives on (female) veteran students examine their experiences as transitions; yet, the women in this project described fluidity as they moved in and out of different social contexts: military, family, and college. They were not approaching an "intersection" in their life; rather, they were experiencing degrees of magnitude. The participants' experiences did not have a clear beginning, middle, or end. Rather they were, as Diamond and Butterworth (2008) articulated, "continually interacting…to produce multiple, dynamic senses of self over time" (p. 375).

In applying this metaphor (and adopting intersectional practice), practitioners should not focus on a point of time (a transition) or a monolithic identity (veteran status) but instead on the subjective, developmental, and contextual moments in students' lives. For the women in this study, their "stable identities" shifted and changed as did their contexts. Their gender identity, for instance, had greater magnitude when they were in the military context, but it held less magnitude on campus. Their age had faint magnitude in the military, but it gained in apparent magnitude on campus when surrounded by younger peers. Thus, practitioners are called to consider the overlapping, intersectional, and contextualized dimensions of individuals' identities. Understanding the magnitude of various dimensions of individuals' identities, and how these shift depending on context, can guide practitioners as they design programming and offer resources on campus.

Walby, Armstrong, and Strid (2012) argued that scholars must resolve the dilemma in intersectional research of "how to balance the stability and fluidity" (p. 236) of identity. Yet, seeking such "balance" may be futile: one dimension of self that has the greatest magnitude at one point in time may grow faint when context changes. By using the constellation metaphor, this chapter demonstrated that identities are both stable and fluid; dimensions of identity (e.g., race, gender, sexuality), like stars in a constellation, comprise selfhood but also gain and lose meaning through subjectivity and context. In this way, identity categories have "their meaning temporarily stabilized at the point of analysis, even while recognizing that their social construction is the outcome of changes and interactions over time" (Walby et al., 2012, p. 236). This analysis, and the use of the constellation metaphor, illuminate how "social identities wax or wane in prominence depending in part on environmental and contextual influences" (Rumann & Hamrick, 2010, p. 435).

REFERENCES

American Association of Variable Star Observers (AAVSO). (2013). *AAVSO manual for visual observing of variable stars.* Cambridge, MA: Author. Retrieved from http://www.aavso.org/sites/default/files/publications_files/manual/english_2013/Chapter3-2013.pdf

Andersen, M. L. (2005). Thinking about women: A quarter century's view. *Gender & Society, 19,* 437–455.

Baca Zinn, M., Hondagneu-Sotolo, P., & Messner, M. (Eds.). (2000). *Gender through the prism of difference* (2nd ed.). Boston, MA: Allyn & Bacon.

Berger, M. T., & Guidroz, K. (Eds.). (2009). *The intersectional approach: Transforming the academy through race, class, and gender.* Chapel Hill: The University of North Carolina Press.

Bowleg, L. (2013). "Once you've blended the cake, you can't take the parts back to the main ingredients": Black gay and bisexual men's descriptions and experiences of intersectionality. *Sex Roles, 68,* 754–767.

Burns Phillips, D. (2010, July). *The female veteran-friendly campus.* Washington, DC: American Council on Education's Office of Women in Higher Education. Retrieved from http://www.acenet.edu

Cole, E. R. (2009). Intersectionality and research in psychology. *American Psychologist, 64,* 170–180.

Collins, P. H. (1998). It's all in the family: Intersections of gender, race, and nation. *Hypatia, 13,* 62–82.

Comins, N. F., & Kaufmann III, W. J. (2003). *Discovering the universe* (6th ed.). New York, NY: W. H. Freeman & Company.

Crenshaw, K. (1991). Mapping the margins: Intersectionality, identity politics, and violence against women of color. *Stanford Law Review, 43,* 1241–1299.

Diamond, L. M., & Butterworth, M. (2008). Questioning gender and sexual identity: Dynamic links over time. *Sex Roles, 59,* 365–376.

DiRamio, D., & Jarvis, K. (2011). *Veterans in higher education: When Johnny and Jane come marching to campus: ASHE Higher Education Report, 37.* San Francisco, CA: Wiley.

Fine, M. (1994). Working the hyphens: Reinventing self and other in qualitative research. In N. Denzin & Y. Lincoln (Eds.), *Handbook of qualitative research* (pp. 130–155). Thousand Oaks, CA: Sage.

Hankivsky, O., Reid, C., Cormier, R., Varcoe, C., Clark, N., Benoit, C., & Brotman, S. (2010). Exploring the promises of intersectionality for advancing women's health research. *International Journal for Equity in Health, 9,* 1–15.

Holley, K. A., & Colyar, J. (2009). Rethinking texts narrative and the construction of qualitative research. *Educational Researcher, 38,* 680–686.

Iverson, S. V., Seher, C., DiRamio, D., Jarvis, K., & Anderson, R. (2013). *Figure it out: A qualitative study of female student veterans' experiences within military and campus cultures.* Manuscript submitted for review.

Ken, I. (2007). Race-class-gender theory: An image(ry) problem. *Gender Issues, 24,* 1–20.

Ken, I. (2008). Beyond the intersection: A new culinary metaphor for race-class-gender studies. *Sociological Theory, 26,* 152–172.

McCall, L. (2005). The complexity of intersectionality. *Signs: Journal of Women in Culture and Society, 30,* 1771–1800.

Miles, M., & Huberman, A. M. (1994). *Qualitative data analysis: An expanded sourcebook of new methods* (2nd ed.). Newbury Park, CA: Sage.

Montoya, M. E. (1998). Border/ed identities: Narrative and the social construction of legal and personal identities. In A. Sarat, M. Constable, D. Engel, V. Hans, & S. Lawrence (Eds.), *Crossing boundaries: Traditions and transformations in law and society research* (pp. 129–159). Evanston, IL: Northwestern University Press.

NF/Observatory (n.d.). *The myths of Ursa Major.* Retrieved from http://nfo.edu/astro/ursamj.htm

Reynolds, A. L., & Pope, R. L. (1991). The complexities of diversity: Exploring multiple oppressions. *Journal of Counseling and Development, 70,* 174–180.

Rubin, H. J., & Rubin, I. S. (2005). *Qualitative interviewing: The art of hearing data* (2nd ed.). Thousand Oaks, CA: Sage.

Rumann, C. B., & Hamrick, F. A. (2010). Student veterans in transition: Re-enrolling after war zone deployments. *The Journal of Higher Education, 81,* 431–458.

Singh, A. A. (2013). Transgender youth of color and resilience: Negotiating oppression and finding support. *Sex Roles, 68,* 690–702.

Walby, S., Armstrong, J., & Strid, S. (2012). Intersectionality: Multiple inequalities in social theory. *Sociology, 46,* 224–240.

Warner, L. R. (2008). A best practices guide to intersectional approaches in psychological research. *Sex Roles, 59,* 454–463.

Warner, L. R., & Shields, S. A. (2013). The intersections of sexuality, gender, and race: Identity at the crossroads. *Sex Roles, 68,* 803–810.

CHAPTER THIRTEEN

"Letting Us Be Ourselves"

Creating Spaces for Examining Intersectionality in Higher Education

SHERI C. HARDEE

Although postsecondary institutions typically pay lip service to diversity in mission and vision statements, many fail to embrace programs and approaches that change the dominant structure (d'Arlach, Sánchez, & Feuer, 2009; Goodwin, 2006; Tatum, 2007; Tinto, 2012). As a result, too many of our students live in the margins without mechanisms for supporting and understanding their multiple, simultaneous, and intersecting identities (Weber, 2009). Many scholars have written about the need for academic and financial support for underrepresented students (Carnevale & Rose, 2004; Timpane & Hauptman, 2004; Tinto, 2012), and while these are important, the culture of higher education institutions has to change to serve all students (Goodwin, 2006; hooks, 1989, 2003; Sidel, 1995; Tatum, 2007). For students who are not part of the dominant group, their experiences are too often ignored, and they can be made to feel as if they do not belong. hooks (2003) reminded us of the following:

> I have known many brilliant students who seek education, who dream of service in the cause of freedom, who despair or become fundamentally dismayed because colleges and universities are structured in ways that dehumanize, that lead them away from the spirit of community in which they long to live their lives. (p. 48)

The concerns, then, center on what types of support are needed and whether institutions can develop support networks that embrace intersectionality and create spaces where marginalized students are empowered through individual strength and communal solidarity.

This chapter highlights a three-year qualitative case study of one Student Support Services (SSS) program, a federal TRIO program seeking to increase college retention and completion rates for first-generation and low-income students (Student Support, 2014). In addition, students of color were in the majority in this particular program. My goal in studying this program, located at a predominantly White, flagship university in the South, was to explore institutional and systemic barriers that underrepresented students faced at the intersections of race, class, and gender as they journeyed through college and whether and/or how support programs such as SSS assisted students at the intersections without demanding assimilation to dominant ideologies. In writing about academic, financial, and social support systems, Tinto (2012) indicated that TRIO's success resulted from "an extra layer of support and guidance as well as membership in a community of students who are on a similar journey" (p. 50). The question centers on what makes up this "extra layer of support" and how institutions, not just TRIO programs, can actualize this support for their students.

Students who have been marginalized at higher education institutions need physical and theoretical spaces to explore their multiple, fluid, and intersecting identities and how these identities change and are changed by the world around them (Weber, 2009). Thus, this study examines the potential of SSS as a postcolonial borderland, "a vague and undetermined place created by the emotional residue of an unnatural boundary…. The prohibited and forbidden are its inhabitants" (Anzaldúa, 1999, p. 25). For the students in this study, the necessary support and guidance came in the form of a borderland to examine socially/historically constructed boundaries, a place to become border crossers who could take their knowledge beyond the margins and disrupt the dominant narrative.

METHOD

In terms of positionality, my interest in this program stemmed from my involvement as an undergraduate participant in SSS. While I knew early on that I would not have been successful without the support of SSS, it was after my experience with other postsecondary institutions that I realized that support for underrepresented students was not often holistic. While financial and academic supports are key, there are deeper measures of understanding that should be integrated into higher education support systems. Thus, my research questions included the following: (a) What barriers are marginalized students facing at the intersections of identities? (b) What types of support networks do students living in the margins need? and (c) How does intersectionality function in a postsecondary support network?

Data for this qualitative case study included participant observation (Spradley, 1980); 16 semistructured interviews with SSS students, faculty, and staff; anonymous open-ended surveys from a random sampling of SSS students; archival program information; and narratives from 19 SSS students enrolled in a course centered on the intersections of race, class, gender, and sexuality in American education and taught by the researcher. I coded data using in-vivo and process coding (Bogdan & Biklen, 2007; Charmaz, 2008; Saldaña, 2013; Strauss & Corbin, 1998), and I organized data into themes and code maps (Saldaña, 2013). Participants had access to all data, and I continued to work with participants as I wrote, asking follow-up questions and member checking for continuous feedback on accuracy of my analysis (Lincoln & Guba, 1985). Additionally, I used pseudonyms and removed any identifying information. For the purposes of this chapter, I use a small sample of "telling cases" (Mitchell, 1984, p. 239), highlighting the most commonly seen themes of individual and communal identity development.

FINDINGS

In their journey from high school to college, the participants in this study needed borderlands to explore their multiple, intersecting identities and wanted spaces where those identities were valued instead of pushed to the side or toward assimilation. Students in this particular TRIO program faced macrolevel, institutionalized stereotypes based on their labels as lower-income, first-generation students of color. Henrietta Stacks, the SSS academic counselor, shared the following about the institution's stereotypes of her students:

> I think they [the university] view it as a program where students may not be up to par academically and, and gosh, how many times have I had to say, "No. These students aren't transition year students. They're not academically short (laughs). They're smart." They just have, I think they see it as students who aren't academically on par with other students at the University. And they are wrong (laughs).

Regardless of students' prior academic success, the institution viewed TRIO students as academically deficient, a common misconception of underrepresented students (Goodwin, 2006). In this case, the institution was not interested in what they viewed as "problematic students" (Goodwin, 2006, p. 12) who might require changes in traditional approaches to support.

Moreover, professors outside of SSS did not appear to value their students' intersecting identities. When I interviewed Niesha, an SSS student working on her doctor of pharmacy degree, she stated, "I had a professor tell me from the get go I'd never make it. I'm not sure if that was 'cause of where I was coming from, but I wanted to prove him wrong. And I did." As an African American female from a lower income family in a field where she was the "exception," this was where she "was coming from." Although her professor never mentioned race, class, or gender, his comment caused Niesha to question whether he had stereotyped her based on her intersecting identities. While Niesha believed that her identities made her a target of a professor's negative stereotypes, Jackson saw his intersecting identities as making him a target for fulfilling a diversity quota. When asked about the university's approach to diversity, Jackson related the following:

> I don't think the regular university does a great deal. And I know engineering doesn't, 'cause I'm, like, the token Black guy (laughs). It's more so a thing where it's, like, it wasn't nothing like, it wasn't disrespectful or like that, in my classes it's always one Black person or two at the most. So, you know, it wasn't nothing, it was something that I guess we both could laugh at cause everybody knows differences that you can see. It wasn't nothing. Most Black males think money first, though, so there's a lot of opportunity for engineering to do things they don't.... Males don't usually do too good. They're more into the wrong side, like short-term money.

In this narrative, although Jackson stated three times, "it wasn't nothing" or it was something he "could laugh at," he had become "the token Black guy" in his engineering courses—courses with hundreds of students. Rather than develop a recruitment plan for students from diverse backgrounds, the institution viewed one "token" student as a sufficient representation of diversity. Jackson also highlighted a stereotype concerning Black males and the drive for money. Two interviewees were engineering majors, and each pinpointed the reason behind their choice as money over interest. Jackson further complicated this choice by explaining, "Most Black males think money first." This brings to the surface the complex history surrounding Black males, family structure, and socioeconomic status (Battle, Alderman-Swain, & Tyner, 2005), and behind this is the need to disprove the stereotype of Black males' involvement in illegal activities to gain short-term money. Even while the desire is to disprove the stereotype, there is a sense here that assimilation to dominant norms is the answer. hooks (1989) noted the following years ago:

> Within universities, there are few educational and social spaces where students who wish to affirm positive ties to ethnicity—to Blackness, to working-class backgrounds—can receive affirmation and support. Ideologically, the message is clear—assimilation is the way to gain acceptance and approval from those in power. (p. 80)

For Niesha, Jackson, and Benjamin, who we will hear from later in the chapter, they were struggling to navigate their multiple identities while simultaneously being pulled between stereotypes and dominant "norms" that did not represent them.

In such an unsupportive environment, SSS students needed places where these intersections could come together for individual and communal exploration. Tatum (2007) wrote that institutions should focus on "affirming identity, building community, and cultivating leadership, three critical dimensions of effective learning environments" (p. 114). Once students explore and affirm their identities and participate in communities where such examination is valued, they have the potential to share their knowledge of intersectionality outside these borderlands. And, indeed, one identity exploration theme that emerged in 100% of the interviews was the importance of having formal and informal spaces to dialogue about issues of race, class, gender, and self, not only with peers but also with professors and staff. In terms of formal spaces, SSS developed smaller classes (10–12 students), which not only allowed more one-on-one time but provided a space for discussions about issues that mattered to the students. As one student stated of her English professor, "You know, she made the class interactive. She made it fun, letting us be ourselves, stating whatever we felt we needed to state, regardless of whether it was crazy or didn't make sense to her." She specifically noted the importance of "letting us be ourselves" without judgment. In reference to the same instructor, another student remarked as follows:

> Well, I really think that all my talks with Dr. Barnes, inside of class and outside of class, has really changed me a lot and it has really opened me up, so I would have to say that that might be one of the best things because I always kind of felt like I questioned a lot of things that my family didn't and my friends didn't, and she kind of said, "Well, that's okay. That's what you're supposed to do."

The professor provided a space for the opportunity to question and go against the grain. This same student continued:

> I think that SSS, it just kind of lets you be yourself and so you get to the point where you're like, if they can accept me for me, then, I can too…. So it just gives you more confidence.

In her interview, she related this exploration and self-acceptance specifically to class discussions centered on race, class, and gender. Once students are provided an opportunity to explore their identities and share their stories, this process can result in increased confidence. As Tatum (2007) noted, "Most of us are more willing to engage in the often-taxing work of crossing social borders when we are operating from strength" (p. 115), but this strength first comes from within oneself.

Part of the reason behind the success of these classroom spaces was because professors knew students' backgrounds and thus could create spaces where students felt comfortable discussing and exploring identity. Professors met on a biweekly basis along with the academic counselor and program director to discuss students' strengths and areas for improvement, and their dedication was evident to the students. When I asked Benjamin what stood out to him the most from his experience with SSS, he stated the following:

> Individual communication. You know, they knew all students…and they knew the personality of all their students…the student usually don't get that a lot of times. And if you do get it in these larger classes, you have to fight for it.

While it may have been a battle for attention in classes outside of SSS, these professors made it a point to know each student. When I asked Steph what she liked best about SSS, she responded as follows:

> That they stay on you. That you're not just like a number or a last name and they actually know who you are, and if you don't do what you're told, then they're gonna tell Ms. Stacks [the counselor], who in turn is gonna tell your mother.

While some might see this as hand-holding, the academic counselor stated, "it's being able to relate to them and knowing that they can overcome whatever obstacles there are because I've done that too." As a first-generation student of color from a limited-income family, the counselor recognized the support systems they needed for success. This is not to say that faculty and staff from different backgrounds cannot relate, but this does demonstrate the importance of making a more concerted effort to diversify faculty and staff. Allies from the dominant group are important, but, as hooks (2003) wrote, to catalyze change, "We need to hear from the individuals who know" (p. 40).

Small classes, preplanned events, a mentoring program, and a space for "hanging out" resulted in a strong peer community as well. Rhianna stated the following in reference to her peer community at SSS:

> Having your classes with the same people and being able to talk to them and automatically have friends as soon as you get here I think is a really big benefit from the program. You kind of get the same high-school feeling but not as much, like you're not babied as much but you still kind of have, like, "Okay, I know I'm not in this alone because I'm not in a big classroom with hundreds of people that I don't know and I only see for that one hour in class." So I think that it really did help transition. It was a good transition phase from high school to college.

She explained the importance of having a "transitional" space or borderland to gain communal strength for use outside of these spaces. Even though Rhianna did not go so far as to connect this statement to her intersecting identities, she noted the importance of not feeling "alone," and this sense of isolation is magnified for students who do not fit into dominant "norms" (Tatum, 2007).

Within this particular program, students, faculty, and staff got to know one another so well that all but one interviewee described the program as a second family without being prompted. In his description of the program, for example, Benjamin stated the following:

> I mean it's basically like making you feel at home, you know, a lot of kids that go off to college away from home have a hard time transitioning from home to the college life. After SSS, it makes that an easy transition. That makes it pretty easy, like a family.

As hooks (1990) explained, once one creates borderland spaces for deconstruction of dominant ideologies, one develops new definitions of home: "home is no longer just one place. It is locations. Home is that place which enables and promotes varied and everchanging perspectives, a place where one discovers new ways of seeing reality" (p. 148). For many students, SSS is the space that supports new ways of thinking and allows for exploration of tension and fears. When discussing his roommate's decision to leave college, for instance, Benjamin stated, "Yeah. I had a family [SSS], and he was sort of in the wild by hisself." The general university, then, is an untamed space where the survival skills gained through a family-type community are necessary.

In expanding the definition of home, many students referred to SSS faculty and staff with kinship terms. In reference to the academic counselor, Ms. Stacks, Steph told the following story:

> I think if I had came to [this university] without being in SSS then I'm not so sure I would still be here. Ms. Stacks has been such a great support system.... Ms. Stacks watches [my daughter] when I need her to. Yeah, so when I need somebody to talk to, I call Ms. Stacks my mother.

SSS provided familial support to the point where several students referred to Ms. Stacks and other professors as their "college mothers." Here, Ms. Stacks ensured that Steph was set up with a peer mentor who, as a single mother, understood that university-wide offices failed to provide support for facing stereotypes and oppression based on their identities as single, teenage mothers (Adair, 2003). Ms. Stacks even took the time to watch students' children when they attended school-related events, a decision perhaps impacted by her identity as a single mother.

As with many familial relationships, the hope is that SSS students gain confidence before "leaving the nest," although family connections remain. In terms of maturity, Benjamin explained as follows:

> I've grown tremendously. I've grown from a boy to a man. I came here as a boy, even though they called me an adult. Actually, I was a MIT…a man in training. So I went from a boy, to a MIT, to a man. All in college. I went from being not focused like I should, to be focused like the sun focuses on the earth eight hours a day. That kind of focus, it be hot outside, so that's focus.

As they discover individual and communal strength, the students also gain confidence and learn to navigate the university-wide system outside of SSS and TRIO. Bernal (2002) wrote, "Because power and policies are at the center of all teaching and learning, the application of household knowledge to situations outside of the home becomes a creative process that challenges the transmission of 'official knowledge' and dominant ideologies" (p. 109). In this particular program, the sense of family helps students develop the strength to take these identities outside of the "home" without assimilating to dominant ideologies.

As with any family, though, students return to the source for continued strength and to give back as leaders, which Tatum (2007) highlighted as an important aspect of development for marginalized students. Rhianna related the following:

> I think that working for SSS, to me, is the best way to give back.... It's a really good way to give back to the program, to show them that you really appreciate having tutors for yourself when you were a freshman and everything that they do.

Dominique also mentioned that her decision to work as an SSS tutor stemmed from her desire to give back. Additionally, being a student at and working at SSS solidified her decision to become an African American studies major, which, she noted, "also helped me develop a love for community that I never realized before." Niesha, another SSS student and tutor, credited her desire to open a small pharmacy in her African American community as stemming, in part, from her time with TRIO. As she noted, "I truly learned what was important about having a strong and healthy community." McKay (2010) discussed how dominant culture can fragment historically underrepresented communities, and she pinpointed communal, dialogical spaces as keys to community revitalization.

While not every student viewed SSS as family or developed a desire to give back, most indicated an increased sense of strength in self and community through their participation in these intersectional spaces. Confidence to be themselves in the wild can carry students far, as Sierra summed up beautifully in the following journal entry:

> As a Black female, I understand that I will continuously have to prove myself. Each of my families [including TRIO] have taught me to never be ashamed of my heritage. They have taught me to embrace it, which is somewhat difficult—being that I do not know who my ancestors are three generations removed. I indicate African American on the US Census report; nonetheless, my great-grandmother was Native American and my great-grandparents were slaves. I speak Standard English, African-American Vernacular English, and some Spanish, and slang. Not because I want to…I must. It's an adaptive mechanism that some say ensures my survival. I am unapologetically a Woman of color. I discovered at an early age that race does matter and affects my daily life. I am a mature Woman of color. I am an articulate scholar, educator, and survivor. I am neither a lost cause nor a statistic. I am me.

Sierra's words illustrate confidence in herself, and she is not who society may want her to be, but she is someone better—a strong Woman of color and a change agent. She is someone "who can transform the world into a more just place" (Bernal, 2002, p. 108).

This does not mean that the program is without faults or that all students engage in intersectional work without difficulty. As Anzaldúa (1999) and hooks (1990) warned, borderlands are full of tension and are difficult to navigate. As Dominique wrote, "Once in college, everyone but me noticed that I had changed. I don't feel like I fit in. I can code switch, but it's not who I am anymore." Another student wrote, "Now that I am in college, it is like I live two lives. When I am at school, I talk to my friends and family at home, but they cannot relate to what I am doing." Scholars from DuBois (2007) to hooks (1989) have written about this tension, the push and pull between family and college and between dominant and nondominant cultures. No matter how much programs like SSS try to create spaces to affirm intersecting identities, there is still the constant battle outside these walls to have these identities recognized. The community and sense of family created within this borderland, though, make the journey easier. Ms. Stacks summed up the difficulty of college without the proper support networks when she stated the following:

> These students just energize me, and I see in all of them the potential to do great things, potential that probably wouldn't be tapped if they were just out there floundering. To have to find your own way through—oh, that can be hard.

CONCLUSIONS

Many TRIO programs promote assimilation by requiring cultural events and etiquette luncheons to increase the social and cultural capital valued by dominant culture. Rather than strengthening students' abilities to be successful within dominant culture, though, our goal should be deconstructing the boundaries created by this culture. While this program also included such events, it is in the creation of spaces for dialogue and reflection surrounding identity that real change occurred, change that did not necessitate assimilation but required reflection on society, culture, and the self in relation. Even in the case of this TRIO program, though, faculty and staff should make more concerted efforts to engage students in an examination of the intersections. While intersectionality emerged from data analysis as an important factor, it was not identified by faculty and staff as central to their work. Carefully constructed borderlands have the power to help students discover individual and communal strength at the intersections, thus allowing them to sidestep assimilation to dominant ideologies and move toward change. As seen through these students' words, intersectional studies are necessary to unpack how the multiple parts of our identities are created, viewed, and lived—not that all are equal at the same time or as impactful at the same time, but to view race, class, and gender in isolation is to create an incomplete picture (Belkhir & Barnett, 2001).

Additionally, while borderland support is vital for students experiencing oppression based on these multiple, simultaneous, and intersecting identities, it is equally important that one engage those living outside the borderlands in intersectionality studies. As Weber (2004) wrote, "These systems are simultaneously experienced. All operate to shape everyone's lives at all times" (p. 134), and thus this theoretical framing should be at the foundation of everything one does, from teaching to research (Belkhir & Barnett, 2001). The struggle to create spaces of individual and collective strength around the intersections of race, class, gender, and sexuality will be increasingly difficult if borderlands do not overflow into dominant spaces and if we fail to require those outside the margins to listen and respond (McKay, 2010). In failing to listen, "the entire national American identity is incomplete and fragmented. This fragmented identity lends itself to an impaired and repressed capacity for intelligence, competence and informed action of the American citizen" (McKay, 2010, pp. 32–33). Without the help of allies from both nondominant and dominant cultures, this places a great deal of pressure on students who have been marginalized. As Tatum (2007) noted, leadership development is important for marginalized students for this very purpose, yet underrepresented students cannot be expected to deconstruct these borders on their own.

The beauty of what we learn from the students in this study, though, is that it is not difficult to create borderlands—more than funds and physical space, it takes dedication and desire for change. It is not a matter of simply adding intersectional stories to the research (Collins, 2000), but we need examples of the power of personal experiences to alter institutional landscapes. As Anzaldúa (2002) reminded us, "The emerging narratives are multicultural. They not only insist on analyzing and combatting oppressive power systems, but advocate the need to collaborate and capacitar (empower) in realizing common goals" (p. 561). This work toward the common goal of creating inclusive environments can empower students at the intersections but can also answer a larger call to help *all* students become more critical and complex thinkers (Arum & Roksa, 2011), thus changing campus climates. As scholars have noted, higher education institutions, in particular, are in a prime position to explore and highlight intersectionality in ways that make one stronger (Cole, 2009; Tatum, 2007). This necessitates moving beyond surface-level approaches to diversity and creating support systems that include but expand on those traditionally utilized to improve access and retention. Intersectionality is not a one-size-fits-all approach, but its potential as a framework is exciting for the future of postsecondary education.

REFERENCES

Adair, V. C. (2003). Fulfilling the promise of higher education. In V. C. Adair & S. L. Dahlberg (Eds.), *Reclaiming class: Women, poverty, and the promise of higher education in America* (pp. 240–266). Philadelphia, PA: Temple University Press.

Anzaldúa, G. (1999). *Borderlands/la frontera: The new mestiza* (2nd ed.). San Francisco, CA: Aunt Lute.

Anzaldúa, G. E. (2002). Now let us shift…the path of conocimiento…inner work, public acts. In G. E. Anzaldúa & A. Keating (Eds.), *This bridge we call home: Radical visions for transformation* (pp. 540–578). New York, NY: Routledge.

Arum, R., & Roksa, J. (2011). *Academically adrift: Limited learning on college campuses*. Chicago, IL: The University of Chicago Press.

Battle, J., Alderman-Swain, W., & Tyner A. R. (2005). Using an intersectionality model to explain the educational outcomes for black students in a variety of family configurations. *Race, Gender, & Class, 12*, 126–151.

Belkhir, J. A., & Barnett, B. M. (2001). Race, gender and class intersectionality. *Race, Gender & Class, 8*, 157–174.

Bernal, D. D. (2002). Critical race theory, Latino critical theory, and critical raced-gendered epistemologies: Recognizing students of color as holders and creators of knowledge. *Qualitative Inquiry, 8*, 105–126.

Bogdan, R. C., & Biklen, S. K. (2007). *Qualitative research for education: An introduction to theories and methods* (5th ed.). Boston, MA: Pearson.

Carnevale, A. P., & Rose, S. J. (2004). Socioeconomic status, race/ethnicity, and selective college admissions. In R. D. Kahlenberg (Ed.), *America's untapped resource: Low-income students in higher education* (pp. 101–156). New York, NY: The Century Foundation.

Charmaz, K. (2008). Grounded theory. In J. A. Smith (Ed.), *Qualitative psychology: A practical guide to research methods* (2nd ed., pp. 81–110). Thousand Oaks, CA: Sage.

Cole, B. A. (2009). Gender, narratives and intersectionality: Can personal experience approaches to research contribute to "undoing gender"? *International Review of Education, 55*, 561–578.

Collins, P. H. (2000). Gender, black feminism, and black political economy. *Annals of the American Academy of Political and Social Science, 568*, 41–53.

d'Arlach, L., Sánchez, B., & Feuer, R. (2009). Voices from the community: A case for reciprocity in service-learning. *Michigan Journal of Community Service Learning, 16*, 5–16.

Du Bois, W. E. B. (2007). *The souls of black folk.* New York, NY: Cosimo.

Goodwin, L. (2006). *Graduating class: Disadvantaged students crossing the bridge of higher education.* Albany: State University of New York Press.

hooks, b. (1989). *Talking back: Thinking feminist, thinking black.* Boston, MA: South End.

hooks, b. (1990). *Yearning: Race, gender, and cultural politics.* Boston, MA: South End.

hooks, b. (2003). *Teaching community: A pedagogy of hope.* New York, NY: Routledge.

Lincoln, Y., & Guba, E. (1985). *Naturalistic inquiry.* Newbury Park, CA: Sage.

McKay, C. L. (2010). Community education and critical race praxis: The power of voice. *Educational Foundations, 24*, 25–38.

Mitchell, J. C. (1984). Typicality and the case study. In R. F. Ellen (Ed.), *Ethnographic research: A guide to general conduct* (pp. 238–241). New York, NY: Academic.

Saldaña, J. (2013). *The coding manual for qualitative researchers* (2nd ed.). Thousand Oaks, CA: Sage.

Sidel, R. (1995). *Battling bias: The struggle for identity and community on college campuses.* New York, NY: Penguin.

Spradley, J. P. (1980). *Participant observation.* Fort Worth, TX: Harcourt Brace Jovanovich.

Strauss, A., & Corbin, J. (1998). *Basics of qualitative research: Techniques and procedures for developing grounded theory* (2nd ed.). Thousand Oaks, CA: Sage.

Student Support Services Program. (2014). *U.S. Department of Education.* Retrieved from http://www2.ed.gov/programs/triostudsupp/index.html

Tatum, B. D. (2007). *Can we talk about race? And other conversations in an era of school resegregation.* Boston, MA: Beacon.

Timpane, P. M., & Hauptman, A. M. (2004). Improving the academic preparation and performance of low-income students in American higher education. In R. D. Kahlenberg (Ed.), *America's untapped resource: Low-income students in higher education* (pp. 59–100). New York, NY: The Century Foundation.

Tinto, V. (2012). *Completing college: Rethinking institutional action.* Chicago, IL: The University of Chicago Press.

Weber, L. (2004). A conceptual framework for understanding race, class, gender, and sexuality. In S. N. Hesse-Biber & M. L. Yaiser (Eds.), *Feminist perspectives on social research* (pp. 121–139). New York, NY: Oxford University Press.

Weber, L. (2009). *Understanding race, class, gender, and sexuality: A conceptual framework* (2nd ed.). New York, NY: McGraw-Hill.

CHAPTER FOURTEEN

Now You See Me, Now You Don't

Ignoring Intersections and Supporting Silence in Elite Liberal Arts College Classrooms

TARA L. AFFOLTER

The scene had become an all too common one. I slid the tissue box closer to Tabatha as she attempted to capture the frustration and exhaustion she felt at being one of a relatively few Black women on this campus. "I just realized that who I am here, in this body and where I'm from is not at all the 'normative' student here. No one seems academically or socially interested in listening to my understandings of things."

She gestures to herself and I take in her curvy figure, the rich red-brown tones of her skin, the magenta highlights of her hair twists, and listen to the slight Southern cadence that peppers her speech. She continues, "This body and what I learned from home doesn't fit here. I'm just really tired." On this New England campus, where the "normative" female student is more often a thin White Woman with long, straight brown, blond, or red hair, who hails from the East Coast, Tabatha doesn't fit. Instead, her brown skin, physical type, geographic home, and gender intersect in ways that simultaneously make her visible and invisible. In the weeks leading up to this meeting with Tabatha, our campus had been mired in the very issues that point out the urgency of enacting inclusive education: education that recognizes the complexity of identity and the interlocking systems of privilege and oppression that shape our lives and often deny students of color full access to an education.

As an advisee and current student Tabatha had come to my office to process campus events from the past week. It started when she and other women of color on campus received an e-mail from the theater department urging them to try out for a role in an upcoming play. The department needed a Woman of color to play the wet nurse for a White family. To "complicate the role," the casting call indicated that this Woman was the only one who had a satisfying sexual experience in the play and that the White husband in the play fell in love with this character. Perhaps a naïve reader could suggest that multiplicity of identities were at work in this call. After all, gender and race were named. However, given the limited ways that race and gender are involved here, this is hardly a move toward grappling with complicated historical intersections of identity. In this example, there are two problematic portrayals being called on. First is the "mammy" stereotype, which Collins (2000) defined as, "the faithful, obedient, domestic servant. Created to justify the economic exploitation of house slaves and the sustained to explain Black women's long-standing restriction to domestic service" (p. 72). The "mammy" character adores the White family whom she serves and is typically portrayed in film as a larger, darker-skinned Black Woman devoid of sexuality (Glenn & Cunningham, 2009). The second contrasting stereotype is the "Jezebel." This stereotype "conceptualizes Black Woman as sexually deviant and aggressive" (Glenn & Cunningham, 2009, p. 139). Merely combining these damaging stereotypes into one character does not engage intersectionality in any liberatory manner. Instead, this is another example of how women of color on campus might be made to feel marginalized and seen only for the stereotypical role they might fulfill. The weekend after the theater call went out, a Black male rapper sparked controversy after he performed a song containing lyrics lauding himself as "a happy faggot slapper." Some members of the queer community on campus (in this case, predominantly White students) had attempted to ban his visit and were quite upset at the joyous reaction of the crowd when he sang the song he had specifically been asked not to perform. Some students of color on campus were upset that the rapper was being unduly profiled with terms like "threatening" and "menacing," not because of any song, but because he was a Black male in a predominantly White space. Reflecting on the forum that was held to address the issues a few days after the concert, one student, who identifies as a Woman of color, stated the following: "It was really interesting listening to both sides. I just kept thinking though, God forbid you are both a person of color and queer. Where are you supposed to fit?"

In each of the earlier scenarios, racial identity and narrow constructions of race play a significant role in understanding the oppression and silencing felt by various stakeholders. In each example, race is noted only to indicate non-White racial identity, and White is left unnamed. In each example, race is not the only identity factor functioning, yet race is often treated as the sole identity by which students of color come to be seen or just as often ignored in predominantly White spaces such as this elite liberal arts campus. This becomes even more problematic when one considers that the same essentializing practices form much of the curricular and pedagogical choices made in many college classrooms (Davis et al., 2004; Solórzano, Ceja, & Yosso, 2000; Vaccaro, 2010). Critical race theorists assert that while one must center race in any analysis of systemic inequity experienced by people of color, one must do so in a manner that acknowledges the "inextricable layers of racialized subordination based on gender, class, immigration status, surname, phonotype, accent and sexuality" (Yosso, 2005, p. 73).

Drawing from a large qualitative study on classroom experiences of students of color at predominantly White and highly selective liberal arts colleges, this chapter explores how the multiple identities defining students in this study were often overlooked in the classroom. The narratives shared by the students indicate ways various intersections of identity were ignored in favor of monolithic racial categories that presumed not only race but narrowed the category such that ethnicity, class, family, geography, immigration status, and gender were assumed and encompassed *within* racial categories.

This chapter poses the following questions to college and university professors: What if professors took seriously the call to build inclusive classrooms instead of relying on monolithic categories and racialized assumptions to inform practice? What if classrooms and curricula were constructed to incorporate the intersecting identities of students while still understanding the continuing significance of race?

REVIEW OF LITERATURE

The research on students of color at predominantly White institutions has generally presented a troubling picture (Davis et al., 2004; Harper, 2009; Morrison, 2010). Researchers examining what is commonly called the "campus climate" at predominantly White institutions have found that students of color experience patterns of "exclusion, alienation and racism" (McClelland & Auster, 1990, p. 638). Some of these alienating practices include Eurocentric course offerings and exclusionary pedagogical practices (Mayhew, Grunwald, & Dey, 2005), continued instances of racial microaggressions (Solórzano, Ceja, & Yosso, 2000), and lack of access to high-impact academic activities (such as working with faculty on research) linked to student development and success (Kuh, 2008). Perhaps Vaccaro (2010) offered the most succinct summary of the research on campus climate: "No matter how one defines it, research has shown that negative, hostile, and unwelcoming campus climates have a detrimental impact on the success and retention of students of color" (p. 203).

Liberal arts colleges, like the one featured in this study, appear to hold a unique and often contradictory place in the literature on diversity, student engagement, and racial campus climate. For example, Umbach and Kuh (2006) found that students at liberal arts colleges were "significantly more likely than are their counterparts at other types of institutions to engage in diversity-related activities and to report greater gains in understanding people from diverse backgrounds" (p. 183). And yet, such promising news is complicated by other realties. Others have found a strong disconnect among the surface-level interactions between White students and students of color and more subtle "hidden tensions" that exist on liberal arts campuses (McClelland & Auster, 1990).

The research on diversity in higher education highlights the differing (and often inequitable) experiences between White students and students of color. While scholars such as Yosso (2005), and Donnor (2005, 2006) have engaged the complexity of student identity and equitable education, there remains limited research attempting to understand the continuing significance of race in higher education while grappling with the multiple intersections of student identity.

Morrison (2010) stressed the following crucial element in transforming the racial climate at colleges and universities: "The voices of students of color must be heard, validated, and utilized in shaping the nature of change that must take place if, indeed, colleges and universities are to become truly welcoming and integrated environments of positive change" (p. 1010). This current research heeds that challenge by focusing on students' experiences to better understand classroom climate and the impact of exclusive curriculum and pedagogy on students of color within an elite liberal arts college. The research seeks to further complicate the challenge by engaging an intersectional lens to understand the complexity of student experiences.

METHOD

For this qualitative study, semistructured interviews were conducted, utilizing an interview guide that aided in the development of a specific line of inquiry regarding students' classroom experiences at college (Weiss, 1994). Given the goal of centering student voice in this study, interviews were the most appropriate method.

Each interview lasted between 60 and 120 minutes. Initially, the interviews' examining phrases and words as well as themes that emerged from the interviews were coded. The repetition of words like "invisible," "token," and "silenced" were evident in every interview. Major patterns emerging from this work indicate themes of (a) silenced discourse around race, (b) the policing of classroom discourse such that only narrowly defined "academic" discussions are rewarded or truly acknowledged, (c) the presence of stereotype threat (Steele, 2003) and frequent microaggressions (Solórzano et al., 2000), and (d) the absence of race as a topic in classroom discussions and throughout the curriculum.

As the transcripts were coded, it was important to complicate essentialized notions of racial identity and consider a more complex picture of students struggling to be seen, heard, and understood. In many ways, the need to complicate essentialized notions of race came from participants themselves, as they frequently pushed me, a White heterosexual female professor from a working-class background, to consider what I might be neglecting in my analysis. Though all students in the study noted how race was a major identifying factor for them, they were also quick to point out how, in this predominantly White space, race came to take on heightened meaning. Thus, while my work to examine the racist and racializing practice on college campuses was important, it was not the only story. Dex, a 19-year-old student who identifies as multiracial, responded to a question I posed about her experience as a student of color:

> I don't feel comfortable calling myself a student of color; I don't think other students are called "students of White." I don't think that is fair. I don't feel like I need to identify myself or distinguish myself as a student on those terms. I can identify as a Woman of color, because that is part of my personal identity, but I don't think being of color plays into my role as a student on this campus. Or it should. But it definitely does. It totally does.

Part of Dex's resistance to this term and this classification can be understood in the very narrow light in which students of color were constructed and treated within classrooms at Rural College (a pseudonym for the college). Dex pushed me to remember that she is more than any non-White racial classification and helped me avoid replicating the same systems of dominance and essentializing that this study hopes to interrogate.

Setting

All of the interviewees attended Rural College, located in the northeastern United States. It has been recongnized as one of the top liberal arts schools in the country. Students at schools like Rural College go to class together but also live in close on-campus communities with only a small town nearby. In such settings, it is relatively rare to encounter and interact with fellow students only in classes. Students at Rural College attend class together and share dining halls and living and social spaces. It is important to note this because on a campus such as Rural College, being narrowly and only defined as a student of color (while the White students are viewed incorrectly as racially neutral and seen as individuals rather than solely members of a collective group) has heightened implications. Ignored in this false neutruality is the privilege that goes along with being White and the ways in which Whiteness is never named, yet always present as the normative standard. What does it mean to learn, work, eat, and socialize in an environment that has coded students of color into narrow socially constructed, racial categories while ignoring the power and privilege of Whiteness?

Participants

All participants were initially recruited for interviews with the help of an administrative assistant working in the equity and diversity office on Rural's campus. An initial e-mail invited students to partipate in a study "exploring classroom practices that resulted in [a] welcoming and inclusive environment." The e-mail emphasized that the study sought to uncover some of the "lived experiences of students of color inside Rural college classrooms" (T. Affolter, e-mail communication, 2010). Once interviews began, participants would frequently recommend friends or fellow students as interviewees. Of the 32 students interviewed, roughly 20 students responded to the initial e-mail invitation, and the remaining students were invited to participate due to participant reccommendations. All interviews discussed here took place with students that do not identify as White. All students were guarenteeed confidentiality and, as such, in the reporting data, students' names are represented by psuedonymns.

FINDINGS

Analysis of the transcripts revealed a number of themes that characterized the alienation and isolation experienced by students of color on Rural's campus. In each interview, race remained important. Nonetheless, utilizing a lens of intersectionality, which takes into account students' multiple identities, allows for a much more nuanced understanding of the troubling classroom experiences of these students while still grappling with the continuing significance of race.

Invisibility, Hyper-Visibility, and Race as a Single Story

Participants in this study frequently noted a feeling of being passed over either by being ignored or by having one's perceived racial identity stand in for all other identity markers and thus become the spokesperson for all topics that have been racialized. Morgan, a 21-year-old student who identifies as African American and a Black, Woman illustrated this tension at Rural College:

> It means being very visible and invisible. For the most part being very glossed over and people not paying very much attention to what you say. Sometimes I make a comment in class and there is silence. Then, two comments later they [other students] will be jumping on the same comment, but it was not made by a student of color.

At this point in the interview, Morgan stops talking, laughs uncomfortably, and tries to change the subject. It is as if in that moment, she is again not supposed to speak or her observation is not valid. She takes a deep breath and says the following:

> I make a comment and people don't respond in a very agreeable way or in any way that they understand. But then two comments later, a White student or White male usually will make the same type of comment and they will get that point more than they will get me.

Morgan's invisibility in this case is the denial of her White classmates and professors to hear or affirm her words or ideas.

Dex relays a story regarding an exchange in her First Year Seminar that illustrates the overlapping nature of visibility and invisibility:

> I remember there was a big heated debate on immigration and I did not participate. So as we were leaving I overheard people talking about who was very active in the discussion and my name came up. When I didn't say anything at all!
>
> That says to me that because I am not White I was expected to participate in that discussion because I should have and it didn't matter if I did or not because apparently I did and apparently I had a whole lot to say. So I guess I should have an opinion on immigration when in fact you don't know if anyone in my family has immigrated from anywhere.

In this case, in contrast to Morgan, Dex is seen, but her words are imagined and then given heightened meaning due to a preconceived idea that she *should* have an opinion on immigration. In the White normative classroom, she somehow visually represents a racialized definition of immigrant.

Deborah, a 21-year-old who racially identifies "most of the time as a student of color or Black," talked about the intersection of race and gender that function to simultaneously silence her voice in classrooms and spotlight her identity by narrowly defining what a Black Woman is and what she can be. She stated the following:

> I can't be angry…as a Black Woman? Please. Because first of all, people are going to be like, oh no, she is talking about race again. And then people are going to be like, "calm down and bring the tone down." "Why are you *all* angry?" "Just relax."

For the majority of men of color in this study, notions of hyper-visibility were most discussed. Here Nick, a 20-year-old student who identifies as Black, speaks of his frustration with the intense scrutiny he feels in classrooms at Rural College:

> There's a certain point, I feel, when you're talking about race events in the classroom when you're analyzing them where you're the lone Black student, you no longer become student in the classroom, you become the lab rat where people are analyzing your emotions and what not. That's when I say, "I'm not really comfortable with that situation." In many ways I won't let certain people have that.

Donald, a 21-year-old student, expanded on this notion of hyper-visibility by highlighting the narrowing of identity and the stereotypes that accompany being a Black man on this campus:

> Here you are Black. It is not like you just exist as a person. The first thing people realize about me is that I am Black. For me, being a Black male on campus, it is very hard to define your own identity because others define it for you. That is how I feel.... Being a Black male on Rural's campus means being aggressive, pretty much not doing as well as other people, people don't expect you to do as well. You can see it in various classrooms here. It doesn't really feel like you are included in the curriculum in many classes.

Nearly all of the participants challenged the ways they had been essentialized by their perceived racial categories on this predominantly White campus. This played out in multiple ways, including students' lack of ability to identify in ways they might choose and having aspects of their perceived racial identity projected onto them. Sandra, a 22-year-old Woman who identifies as Hispanic or Dominican, discussed a professor's narrowly defined notion of racial identity:

> It's the first day of the semester, and she wants to get to know everyone. So she says, "Say where you're from. Say something about yourself, what you do here." And so everyone went around, and I gave my spiel. I'm from New York. I do this on campus. I studied abroad; I want to go back...that's basically all I said. And she then asks, "Oh, so where are your ancestors from?" I was a little taken aback by it. I was the only one—you know there was [a] half-Lebanese kid in the class. She didn't ask him, where are your ancestors from? But he also looked White. I was the only—no, no, she asked another—she asked an Asian student, "Is your family from China?"

Sage, a 21-year-old student, explained the limits and expectations projected onto her perceived racial identity and how this plays out in the classroom:

> I am a Black Woman; an African American Woman and here comes the rub, everyone sees me and assumes that my ancestry lies in the American South. But my ancestry actually lies in the West Indies. I am a first generation American. I found that a whole host of associations came with me when I walked in a classroom. Whenever slavery or the Civil Rights Movement came up in the classroom everyone either looked at me or became quiet and I was like, you have got to be kidding me! My family didn't teach me American History. When people learn that I don't know the ins and outs of the Civil Rights movement, people are shocked. You can't expect me to know something I wasn't taught.

Deirdre, a 19-year-old Woman who identifies as Black, helped illustrate the narrowing of an individual student's education and agency when one is asked to be the spokesperson for an entire racial group:

> I don't know, before coming here it was more of...this is your history you know, this is a part of who you are...but you are also your own person. But here it is more I feel like I am more of a symbol, even though I don't claim I am, I feel like I am representing what "African-Americanness" means in every aspect and I don't know what that even means.

DISCUSSION

In each of these examples, one can see the ways in which race stands in to erase individual student identity while eliminating the nuances of any sort of group identity. Thus invisibility and hyper-visibility function in the same ways within a classroom community: they rob students of the multiplicity of identity, silence nondominant perspectives, and deny opportunities to explain the complexity of lived experiences.

Students in this study repeatedly reported being seen only in particular ways, and as a result, they were never fully seen or acknowledged. The silence and marginalization come at a significant cost to all. Continually silencing students by erasing their identity and simultaneously affixing a static racial category and thereby limiting the narrative of their lived experiences damages the classroom community for all students. Delgado (1989) asserted the following:

> Reality is not fixed, not a given. Rather, we construct it through our lives together. Racial and class-based isolation prevents the hearing of diverse stories and counter stories. It diminishes the conversations through which we create reality, construct our communal lives. Deliberately exposing oneself to counter stories can avoid that impoverishment, heighten "suspicion," and can enable the listener and the teller to build a world richer than either could make alone. (p. 2439)

Understanding experiences of invisibility and hyper-visibility as they relate to racial identity is crucial to move forward in creating more welcoming classrooms that engage all students. Yet, as this study points out, viewing students only through a stand-alone prescribed variable of race neglects the differing ways that students are silenced and marginalized because of the multiplicities of identities that mark them in the classroom. The goal in using intersectional analyses is not to rank oppression or to determine that having more marginalized identities equates to experiencing more oppression. Instead, "intersectionality suggests that the confluence of one's multiple marginalized identities is an interaction that creates unique experience distinctive from those with whom they may share some identities but not others" (Museus & Griffin, 2011, p. 8).

For example, consider how race and gender interact to render Morgan and Donald silent, but in very different ways. Morgan's comments were only heard after someone, "a White male student," makes a comment very similar to hers. Contrast this with Donald's assertion that Black men on campus are seen as aggressive and not "doing as well as others" academically. It is worth noting in both cases the ever-present concept of Whiteness and White privilege that works to enforce both students' marginalizations. Frankenberg (1993) stressed, "Whiteness is a location of structural advantage, of race privilege 'Whiteness' refers to a set of cultural practices that are usually unmarked and unnamed" (p. 1). McLaren (1991) clarified the notion of what it means to be White: "being White is an entitlement, not to preferred racial attitudes, but to a raceless subjectivity" (p. 167).

The ways in which Morgan and Donald are othered stem in part from the invisibility and power of "Whiteness" to name them as "other." In Morgan's example, she is not heard both because of gender and race. Her words are most amplified when a White male student echoes them or in some way affirms what she has said. However, it is not only gender that is functioning in this silencing; Morgan's non-White racial identity intersects with gender. Hurtado (1996) noted, "[E]ach oppressed group is positioned in a particular and distinct relationship to White men" (p. 2). Gender, in other words, is important to understanding systems of oppression, but to divorce gender from race is to miss a crucial intersection.

White privilege and White racial dominance are at work here. Part of White privilege is confidence; Whites believe that what they say will be heard and welcomed and is worth being said (Wise, 2005). Recall that when Morgan was relaying her experiences of being "highly visible and invisible," she stopped and had to be prompted and encouraged to continue, as if her own perceptions could not be trusted or were not worth noting. Being passed over or trivialized in class is a common experience shared by many students of color, but to only look at this through an antiracist agenda misses the duality of oppression Morgan is experiencing. Crenshaw (1995) highlighted this tension:

> Although racism and sexism readily intersect the lives of real people they seldom do in feminist and antiracist practices. Thus, when the practices expound identity as "Woman" *or* person of color as an either/or proposition, they relegate the identity of women of color to a location that resists telling. (p. 357)

> In Donald's case, his racial identity eclipses his sense of being authentically seen.

He stated, "it's not like you just exist as a person." This lack of "existing" is heightened by the exclusion of non-White people in the curriculum and in what is honored and listened to in class discussion. Donald and Morgan shared this exclusion as Black students on this predominantly White campus. Nevertheless, when applying an intersectional lens and considering gender in the analysis, Donald's silence is different. He is under intense scrutiny because as a Black male, he is not expected to do well. When he speaks, his words are heard, but only through a narrow and racist construction. Thus his racial identity is heightened but it cannot be removed from gender. Again, the unnamed presence of Whiteness works to label him as different and define his Blackness in narrow terms dictated by White dominant ideology. As Donald stated, his Black male identity means "being aggressive, pretty much not doing as well as other people, people don't expect you to do as well." The two identities intersect here to narrow and marginalize. In both cases, these students are silenced, and the different interaction of gender and race impacts the way invisibility is enforced.

A lack of nuance and intersectional understanding also works to silence the multiplicity of knowledge and ability to choose when and how a student engages in class discussion. For example, by assuming that Sage has roots in the South and requesting her expertise on the Civil Rights Movement, there is a lost opportunity to understand the complexity of Black experiences in the United States. Instead, Sage's racial identity becomes attached to geography and place. Her experience as a first-generation immigrant in the United States becomes irrelevant to the dominant narrative that if she is Black, her roots lie in the American South and thus her perspectives on the world are also rooted there. Cultural geographer Nayak (2011) reminded us that while race is a "floating signifier" and an unstable category, "we must ask under what conditions is it summoned-to-life and allowed to materialize within time and place" (p. 545). In this case, Sage's race is allowed to materialize only if her knowledge, sense of home, and sense of place align with the dominant narrative that geographically Black people come only from the southern United States. An intersectional approach to identity, one that includes place, cultural traditions and history, immigration status and family, could complicate monolithic notions of race and ease the marginalization and silencing that accompany such practices.

The role of race and perceived immigration status is an intersection that deserves special mention here. In multiple stories, students of color were perceived as permanent outsiders when their race was read in a manner that suggested "foreigner." Recall the warm-up activity Sandra explained, in which she identifies as a New Yorker only to have her professor ask her (and the only other student of color in the class) the true "origin" of her family. Or consider how Dex was assumed and expected to have opinions on immigration because her racial identity marked her as an immigrant. In each of these moments, fixed racial identity becomes a stand in for nationality and immigration status. Intersections of identity are ignored in favor of a narrow story that uses race as a proxy for citizenship status.

CONCLUSION

For some time, researchers have been suggesting strategies for improving campus racial climate. There appears to be no shortage of quality suggestions and proven strategies to help ease what is an ongoing problem within higher education In addition, I would posit that without expanding the lens to consider race as it intersects with other marginalized and privileged identities, and without naming the presence of Whiteness, it is unlikely real progress will be made in terms of making classrooms and pedagogy more inclusive. Educators must incorporate multiplicities of student identity into classroom communities and stop asking students to be spokespeople for the myth that people groups can be captured in a socially constructed racial category.

REFERENCES

Collins, P. H. (2000). *Black feminist thought: Knowledge, consciousness, and the politics of empowerment.* New York, NY: Routledge.

Crenshaw, K. (1995). Mapping the margins: Intersectionality, identity, politics, and violence against women of color. In K. Crenshaw, N. Gotanda, G. Peller, & K. Thomas (Eds.), *Critical race theory: The key writings that formed the movement* (pp. 276–290). New York, NY: The New Press.

Davis, M., Dias-Bowie, Y., Greenberg, K., Klukken, G., Pollio, H., Thomas, S., & Thompson, C. (2004). "A fly in the buttermilk": Descriptions of university life by successful black undergraduates at a predominantly white southeastern university. *The Journal of Higher Education, 63,* 539–569.

Delgado, R. (1989). Storytelling for oppositionists and others: A plea for narrative. *Michigan Law Review, 87,* 2411–2441.

Donnor, J. K. (2005). Towards an interest-convergence in the education of African American football student athletes in major college sports. *Race, Ethnicity and Education, 8,* 45–67.

Donnor, J. K. (2006). Parent(s): The biggest influence in the education of African American football student-athletes. In A. D. Dixson & C. K. Rousseau (Eds.), *Critical race theory in education: All God's children got a song* (pp. 153–166). New York, NY: Routledge.

Frankenberg, R. (1993). *White women: Race matters: The social construction of whiteness.* Minneapolis: University of Minnesota Press.

Glenn, C., & Cunningham, L. (2009). The power of black magic: The magical Negro and white salvation in film. *Journal of Black Studies, 40,* 135–152.

Harper, S. (2009). Race-conscious student engagement practices and the equitable distribution of enriching educational experiences. *Liberal Education, 95,* 38–45.

Hurtado, A. (1996). *The color of privilege: Three blasphemies on race and feminism.* Ann Arbor: University of Michigan Press.

Kuh, G. D. (2008). *High-impact educational practices: What they are, who has access to them, and why they matter.* Washington, DC: Association of American Colleges and Universities.

Mayhew, M., Grunwald, H., & Dey, E. (2005) Curriculum matters: Creating a positive climate for diversity from the student perspective. *Research in Higher Education, 46,* 389–412.

McClelland, K., & Auster, C. (1990). Public platitudes and hidden tensions: Racial climates at predominantly white liberal arts colleges. *The Journal of Higher Education, 16,* 607–642.

McLaren, P. (1991) Decentering culture: Postmodernism, resistance, and critical pedagogy. In N. B. Wyner (Ed.), *Current perspectives on the culture of schools* (pp. 232–257). Boston, MA: Brookline.

Morrison, G. Z. (2010). Two separate worlds: Students of color at a predominantly white university. *Journal of Black Studies, 49,* 987–1010.

Museus, S. D., & Griffin, K. A. (2011). Mapping the margins in higher education: On the promise of intersectionality frameworks in research and discourse. In S. D. Museus & K. A. Griffin (Eds.), *Using mixed-method approaches to study intersectionality in higher education: New directions for institutional research* (No. 151, pp. 5–13). San Francisco, CA: Jossey-Bass.

Nayak, A. (2011). Geography, race and emotions: Social and cultural intersections. *Social and Cultural Geography, 12,* 548–562.

Solórzano, D., Ceja, M., & Yosso, T. (2000). Critical race theory, racial microaggressions and campus racial climate: The experiences of African American college students. *Journal of Negro Education, 69,* 60–73.

Steele, C. (2003). Stereotype threat in African American student achievement. In T. Perry, C. Steele, & A. Hilliard III (Eds.), *Young gifted and black: Promoting high achievement among African American students* (pp. 109–130). Boston, MA: Beacon.

Umbach, P., & Kuh, G. (2006). Student experiences with diversity at liberal arts colleges: Another claim for distinctiveness. *The Journal of Higher Education, 77,* 169–192.

Vaccaro, A. (2010) What lies beneath seemingly positive campus climate results: Institutional sexism, racism, and male hostility toward equity initiatives and liberal bias. *Equity & Excellence in Education, 43,* 202–215.

Weiss, R. (1994). *Learning from strangers: The art and method of qualitative interview studies.* New York, NY: The Free Press.

Wise, T. (2005). *White like me: Reflections on race from a privileged son.* Brooklyn, NY: Soft Skull.

Yosso, T. (2005). Whose culture has capital? A critical race theory discussion of community cultural wealth. *Race Ethnicity and Education, 8,* 69–91.

CHAPTER FIFTEEN

Black ≠ Poor

Understanding the Influence of Class on Black Students' Educational Outcomes

MARJORIE L. DORIMÉ-WILLIAMS

The plight of poor or low-income minorities, particularly Black individuals, has received a great deal of attention from scholars (e.g., Boyington, Johnson, & Carter-Edwards, 2007; Engberg & Allen, 2011; King, 2010; Moynihan, 1965; Parks-Yancy, 2012; Peskin, Tortolero, Markham, Addy, & Baumler, 2007) in various fields of inquiry (e.g., education, sociology, health). Relatively little extant research focuses on the experiences of middle-income and upper-income Black individuals in the United States. This scarcity is particularly conspicuous in scholarship on higher education in the United States. Indeed, scholarship documenting the collegiate experiences and academic outcomes of Black students who are *not* classified as low income are all but nonexistent. This intersecting identity offers an important area for research. For many reasons, race and class have become interchangeable in discussions on the conditions of Black people in this country. One apparent reason for this is that there are a disproportionate number of Black indidviduals and families who are below the poverty line. In 2011, 28% of Black individuals were below the poverty line, in comparision to only 10% of White individuals. These statistics along with extensive literature on low-income Black families and individuals contribute to the term *low income* becoming synonymous with *Black*, although there is little scholarship on this popular trend (Boyington & Carter-Edwards, 2007; Engberg & Allen, 2011; King, 2010; Moynihan, 1965; Parks-Yancy, 2012; U.S. Census Bureau, 2012a). The problem with this notion is that although Black families are overrepresented among low-income families, there are still many whose experiences are not captured by this label.

According to census information from 2011, 45.1% of Black families were among the middle-income quintile or higher in the United Sates (U.S. Census, 2012b). While Black individuals disproportionately represent low-income or low socioeconomic status (SES) backgrounds, the Black middle class and upper class exist and continue to expand. Further, research suggests that the benefits of higher SES, that are usually accrued by White students, do not eliminate some of the negative impacts of race for Black students (Diel-Amen & Turley, 2007; Perry, Link, Boelter, & Leukefeld, 2012). For example, an increase in neighborhood median income is associated with a significant increase in test scores for White children but not for Black children (e.g., Diel-Amen & Turley, 2007). Other research shows that Black students from higher-income households and/or with more highly educated parents do somewhat better in school than Black students who lack these advantages, but not nearly as well as their White counterparts in similar family circumstances (Gosa & Alexander, 2007). The following section briefly discusses literature on Black middle-class and upper-class people in general and on Black students in postsecondary education.

LITERATURE REVIEW

Race, class, and gender as areas of study in intersectionality research can be examined in many ways. This section focuses on the literature on the Black middle and upper class as well as the experiences of these students in education.

Feagin (1991) defined discrimination as, "actions or practices carried out by members of dominant racial or ethnic groups that have a differential and negative impact on members of subordinate racial and ethnic groups. This differential treatment ranges from the blatant to the subtle." This definition of discrimination focuses on the the actions being carried out by the dominant racial group, White people. Feagin described several responses that he has observed among the Black middle class as a result of discriminatory experiences they encounter in public spaces. They include withdrawal, resigned acceptance, verbal responses, and physical counterattacks. Unfortunately and perhaps too often, Blacks respond to acts of discrimination with resigned acceptance. There is some relief, however, when Blacks are in settings where their class or occupation status is recognized. For example, a Black female professor at a major predominantly White institution (PWI) describes how her professorial status gives her some protection from discrimination. However, as she moves into public spaces such as gorcery stores there is no clear symbol of class status (Feagin, 1991). Although being in settings where middle-class status is recognized does not entirely eliminate discrimination against Blacks, it does serve to mediate some of the more blatant discrimination that lower- and working-class Blacks encounter. Having access to middle-class resources, such as occupational status, allows middle-class Blacks to protect themselves from more overt forms of discrimination (Feagin, 1991).

In educational settings, many Black students do not have the protection of recognized middle- and upper-class status symbols that can mediate overt discriminaroty behavior. Furthermore, in environments that are dominated by White teachers, administrators, and peers, there are structural and institutional barriers that can separate and alienate academically successful upper- and middle-class Black students from their less academically successful peers (Ainsworth-Darnell & Douglas, 1998).

Too often educators, administrators, policymakers, and researchers, focus on addressing the needs of Black students by associating SES with social, cultural, and academic need. Many institutional, state, and national programs designed to improve educational outcomes for Black students often include, implicitly and/or explicitly, "low-income" status as a requirement for participation. For example, the federal TRIO Student Support Services program serves to support persistence and retention of first-generation and low-income students, many of whom are Black. Black students from middle-class and upper-class backgrounds are often only referred to as a point of comparison to their low-income peers. This comparison is problematic because it ignores challenges Black students encouter across SES and fails to understand that Black students are more than a dichotomous group based on class status. Only recently have researchers begun to seriously address the disparities that exist between middle-class and upper-class Black students and White students (i.e., Attewell, Lavin, Domina, & Levey, 2004; Espenshade & Radford, 2009; Fhagen-Smith, Vandiver, Worrell, & Cross, 2010; Gillborn, Rollock, Vincent, & Ball, 2012; Gosa & Alexander, 2007; Ogbu, 2008).

In a study on racial identity, gender, class, and community conducted by Fhagen-Smith et al. (2010), analyses revealed "statistically significant differences in racial identity attitudes across gender and community type (i.e., suburban vs. urban), but not across socioeconomic status" (p. 164). For middle-class and upper-class Black students who do attend college, the intersection of race, class, and other identity aspects can significantly influence how they interact with both their White and less affluent Black peers. Black students who grew up in affluent or predominantly White suburban communities reported feeling isolated from other Black collegiates, "actively avoided other Black students on their campus" (Davis et al., 2004, p. 165), and experienced discomfort with their White peers. Alienation from both White and other Black peers can be a difficult experience for these students who may already be feeling isolated at PWIs. Each of these behaviors can have a negative impact on the academic and social well-being of Black middle-class and upper-class students, which in turn leads to poor retention rates and academic performance for this population.

A previous study examining SES, academic and nonacademic involvement, and educational expectations (Dorimé-Williams, 2013) found that students from different SES backgrounds have statistically significant differences in their involvement, volunteer activities, and educational expectations. High-middle-SES students also reported the highest rates of "never" being involved in academic activities, compared to their peers. Analysis from this study also found that students from all SES backgrounds were more likely to have high educational expectations if they were more involved, both academically and nonacademically.

RESEARCHER POSITIONALITY

My parents are Haitian immigrants who achieved the "American Dream." After moving to this country as young adults, they both attended community college, transferred to a four-year institution, and earned professional degrees in pharmacology. They worked hard to ensure that I had access to the best academic preparation they could afford. I attended private Catholic schools, took SAT and ACT prep courses, and participated in numerous academic and social enrichment activities. I always knew that I would go to college. By the time I was in the ninth grade, I wanted to be a "doctor" so that I could help others. As an honor roll student and a highly involved participant in numerous extracurricular activities, I had no doubt that I could make this goal a reality.

My collegiate experience proved different from what I had envisioned. During my first semester I received the lowest grades I had ever seen in my life, earning a 2.3 grade point average (GPA). I had never been so discouraged. My second semester was not much better and I seriously considered transferring to a college closer to home or taking a leave of absence. In addition to my academic struggles, I also found it difficult to adjust to a social atmosphere that was predominantly White and an institution that felt overtly hostile to minority students, especially Black students. I felt that there was no one I could turn to for help or support. So my solution, based on the worlview inherited from my parents, was to just work harder to figure out what I was doing wrong.

I offer this story as an example of the intersections of being upper middle class, Black, and a college student. There were no targeted resources to help Black upper- and middle-class students at my institution. I was expected to succeed on my own. Because I was not a low-income student, I could not participate in the summer bridge program or any of the other college outreach and academic support programs (COASP) designed to bolster student retention. For example, the summer bridge program allowed students to arrive at the university early, take summer courses, and get accustomed to college life. These students also were assigned a college couselor, in addition to an academic counselor, who worked with them to ensure that they maintained a balanced academic, social, and extracurricular life while at college. Everything from tutoring to selecting a manageable course schedule was provided. All I received was a T-shirt and a bumper sticker at orientation a month before classes started.

PURPOSE

The purpose of this chapter is to explore how the intersection of race and class influences Black collegians' experiences and educational outcomes. For the purposes of this discussion, the term *Black* will be used to reference individuals with African ancestral origins, who self-identify as Black, African or Afro-Caribbean (Bhopal, 2004). Based on previous research, this chapter explores the ways in which the intersection of race and social class can potentially create barriers for Black students in postsecondary education. Specifically, it addresses the following research question: Does class status influence the relationship between race and educational expectations?

THEORETICAL FRAMEWORKS

The following section provides a brief overview of the theoretical frameworks that help to guide this study. Understanding how the racial development of Black collegiates can shape how they choose to navigate the college setting is important for long-term outcomes. Building on this understanding of identity, acknowledging that students' come to postsecondary education with multiple identity dimensions is also significant for those who work to improve college outcomes, such as persistence and retention.

Cross's Nigrescence Theory–Expanded

The convergence of multiple identities contributes to the unique formation of each individual. Cross's (Cross & Vandiver, 2001) Nigrescence Theory is cited (see, e.g., Harrison, Harrison, & Moore, 2002; Howard-Hamilton, 1997; Kambon & Bowen-Reid, 2010; Tenney, 2008) in reference to Black racial identity development. Though limited to only one dimension of students' identity (i.e., race), Cross's theory is useful in developing a context for understanding Black students' experiences in education. An aspect central to explaining the experiences of Black middle-class and upper-class students is directly related to understanding the various stages of racial identity development and how they affect behavior in academic settings. In Cross's Nigrescence Theory, he provides stages that Black students may encounter in their process of identity development. The latest revision of Cross's theory is Nigrescence Theory–Expanded (NT–E; Cross & Vandiver, 2001). In NT–E, racial identity attitudes are grouped into three categories: pre-encounter, immersion/emersion, and internalization.

Various racial identity types can be found under these categories. NT–E provides classifications and descriptions of the most prevalent types of racial identity attitudes that exist among Black individuals. In the pre-encounter category, NT–E describes three types of racial attitudes: assimilation, miseducation, and self-hatred. Assimilation relates to pro-American attitudes, miseducation focuses on negative stereotypes about Black people as a collective group, and self-hatred refers to self-loathing on the basis of one's race (Cross & Vandiver, 2001). Immersion/emersion racial identity attitudes involve either anti-White or pro-Black attitudes. On one end of this spectrum are attitudes that exhibit a strong disdain for White people. On the other end are attitudes that show an "uncritical romanticization" of anything related to Black people and culture (Cross & Vandiver, 2001). The final category in NT–E is internalization. This involves accepting and embracing Blackness in addition to a more understanding appraoch to other cultures. This is revealed through four identity types: Afrocentric, bicultural, multiculturalist-racial, and multiculturalist-inclusive; these stages focus on a more positive, internalized, and accepting stance. While limited in their scope on identity development as a whole, these categories of Black racial identity provide an introductory understanding of the nuanced ways that Black students see themselves. These identity types reflect only one dimension of the intersecting identities that Black students may have. Factors such as class, gender, and sexual orientation also shape the myriad ways in which Black collegiates see themselves.

Abes, Jones, and McEwen's Model of Multiple Dimensions of Identity

Moving beyond Cross's model, Jones and McEwen (2000) developed a conceptual model of multiple dimensions of identity. Nigrescence Theory (Cross & Vandiver, 2001) only accounts for the progression and development of Black identity, and more specifically in a context of oppression. The use of multiple dimensions of identity takes into consideration other significant identity dimensions such as race, gender, and sexual orientation, as well as contextual factors such as family background. In 2007, this model was reconceptualized to incorporate how contextual influences impact identity development for individuals through a meaning-making filter and furthered the study of student identity with respect to intersectionality (Abes, Jones, McEwen, 2007). This filter functions in a way that either rejects or incorporates messages from an individual's outside world. An individual's identity is therefore partially shaped by the outside or contextual influences that pass through this filter.

The importance of this model stems from the fact that it is not static; identity development is an ongoing process and is influenced by changing contexts and life experiences (Jones & McEwen, 2000). This also is important because identity is complex and can be experienced differently at different points in time. What is relevant to this discussion of race and class is that these parts of students' identities are not isolated but instead function in concert with other aspects of students' experiences. To single out social class or SES as a way to identify a student as

"Black" denies the many other social and cultural influences that shape Black collegians as individuals. This approach also fails to recognize how intersectionality shapes Black college students' experiences. Using only characteristics such as race and class does not provide a meaningful understanding of the complexities that create students' inner identities. In their study, Jones and McEwen (2000) found that students felt terms that "conveyed external definitions and identity categories" (p. 409) failed to describe who they were as people and "lacked complexity, accuracy, and personal relevance" (p. 409).

METHOD

This study was conducted using data from a nationally representative sample of students who responded to the U.S. Department of Education's National Center on Education Statistics (NCES) Education Longitudinal Study (ELS), initiated in the spring of 2002 (ELS:2002). ELS:2002 is designed to monitor the transition of young students from 10th grade through postsecondary education and into the workforce. To that end, this longitudinal dataset follows a nationally representative cohort of students beginning with their sophomore year of high school (the base year survey), with follow-ups in 2004 (12th grade), 2006 (sophomore year of college), and 2012.

Sample

The sample in this analysis was restricted to full-time Black students at four-year public and private not-for-profit postsecondry institutions who participated in a 2006 follow-up survey. Based on this criteria, the study sample included 1,402 participants. The sample is almost evenly divided between male (50.6%) and female participants (49.4%). The average age of the students is 21 years. The mean high school GPA is between 2.01 and 2.50. Many of the students in the sample are first-generation college students (68%), meaning that both parents have less than a bachelor's degree. Approximately 63% of the students expected to earn a bachelor's degree or less. It is important to note here that the students who participated in this follow-up survey were all in their sophomore year of college at four-year institutions. Despite this, 29.6% indicated that they expected to earn less than a bachelor's degree.

Study Constructs

The dependent variable in this analysis is educational outcome. Because there are no variables presently available that directly measure students' academic achievement, like college GPA, student educational expectations were used to measure a positive educational outcome. This variable indicates the level of education students expected to complete. Higher educational aspirations were used to indicate a more positive educational outcome. For the purpose of this study, educational expectations were placed into two groups: expectation to "earn a bachelor's degree or less" and expectation to "earn a master's degree or higher."

The main independent variable in this study was SES. This variable was measured by students' SES quartile in 2002, when they were high school sophomores. This variable is provided by NCES and places students into quartiles based on five equally weighted, standardized components: father's education, mother's education, family income, father's occupation, and mother's occupation. In the full dataset (which includes all survey participants), 35.2% of the Black students were in the lowest quartile, 29.8% in the low-middle quartile, 21.8% in the high-middle quartile, and 13.1% in the highest quartile. In the analytic sample, Black students are distributed more evenly in the four quartiles, with 20.3% in the lowest quartile, 26.6% in the low-middle quartile, 29% in the high-middle quartile, and 24% in the highest quartile. Students in these groups also are referred to by SES quartile: low SES, low-middle SES, high-middle SES, and high SES.

Descriptive statistics were calculated to determine the mean and standard deviation for all variables included in the study. Crosstabs and chi-square tests were used to conduct bivariate analyses on the key variables.

Limitations of the Study

As with any research investigation, there are limitations that should be considered when interpreting the results of this study. First, a limitation of this study is related to the dataset chosen for analysis. The ELS:2002 from the NCES is available for public use; however, there are several variables throughout this dataset that have restricted access. Information variables such as institutional selectivity, SAT and ACT scores, grant and loan acceptance, and major are not available in the public dataset. Limited access to variables such as these also limits the analyses that can be conducted to answer the proposed research question. For example, there may be differences in Black students' involvement based on institutional selectivity, but this is a factor that cannot be considered in the current analysis. There also may be a correlation between students' choice of major and educational expectations; however, this also is an issue that cannot be addressed without access to additional data. Without the full dataset, there may be several significant background and institutional factors that simply cannot be accounted for, which could possibly provide a better model for analysis.

RESULTS

Recall the research question guiding this study: Does class status influence the relationship between race and educational expectations? This was addressed using crosstabs and chi-square tests to determine whether statistically significant differences existed between students in different SES quartiles and their educational expectations. Table 15.1 shows the percentage of students within each educational expectations grouping: those who expect to earn a bachelor's degree and those who expect to earn a master's degree or greater. The table also shows the percentage of students by SES quartile and educational expectations and the final percentage of students in each quartile for each educational expectation choice. Analysis shows that there is a significant difference between students in some SES groups and their educational expectations. In addition, results show that differences between students in SES quartiles is statistically significant at p < .001. (See Table 15.2).

Table 15.1. Crosstab of Educational Expectation and Socioeconomic Status (SES).

			SES Quartile				Total
			Lowest quartile	Second quartile	Third quartile	Highest quartile	
Graduate educational expectation	Earn a bachelor's degree or less	Count	283	225	150	61	719
		Percentage within educational expectation	39.4%	31.3%	20.9%	8.5%	100.0%
		Percentage within SES quartile	72.6%	66.4%	60.5%	37.4%	63.1%
		Percentage of Total	24.8%	19.7%	13.2%	5.4%	63.1%
	Earn a master's degree or higher	Count	107	114	98	102	421
		Percentage within graduate educational expectation	25.4%	27.1%	23.3%	24.2%	100.0%
		Percentage within SES quartile	27.4%	33.6%	39.5%	62.6%	36.9%
		Percentage of Total	9.4%	10.0%	8.6%	8.9%	36.9%
Total		Count	390	339	248	163	1140

Table 15.2. Chi-Square Analysis.

	Value	df	Asymp. Sig. (2-sided)
Pearson chi-square	63.422[a]	3	.000
Likelihood ratio	61.991	3	.000
Linear-by-Linear Association	54.940	1	.000
N of valid cases	1140		

Note. df – degrees of freedom; $p < .001$

[a]Zero cells (0.0%) have an expected count less than 5. The minimum expected count is 60.20.

There are significant differences between high-SES students and all other SES groups. Yet, the same is not necessarily true for differences between high-middle and low-middle SES students. Examining the first line of the table, one can see that of the students who expect to earn a bachelor's degree or less, 39.4% are low-SES students, while only 8.5% are high-SES students. The differences between low-, low-midde-, and high-middle-SES students are much less drastic. When observing differences within individual SES groups, there exists a similar pattern. Almost 73% of low-SES students expect to earn a bachelor's degree or less, and only 27.4% expect to earn a master's degree or higher. In comparision, among high-SES students, close to 63% expect to earn a master's degree or higher. Again, low-middle- and high-middle-SES students' expectations more closely mirror those of low-SES students than high-SES students. Further analysis also shows that the differences between high-SES students' educational expectations and their less affluent peers is significant ($p < .05$); however, the same is not true for the differences in educational expectations for low-, low-middle-, and high-middle-SES students.

DISCUSSION

So what do the current results mean for Black students from different SES backgrounds in higher education? First, these findings point to the need for a nuanced understanding of SES for Black students. Our current system of classifying students as either low income or not low income fails to account for the ways in which race and class intersect to influence educational outcomes. Analysis seems to suggest that a better dichotomy may be between high-SES Black students and their peers. These findings also indicate a need for greater research on Black middle-SES students. Many theories on the poor performance of Black students in postsecondary education are based on the premise that barriers due to low SES are what cause so many to struggle in postsecondary education. Often, researchers theorize that low-SES Black students do not have access to the social, academic, or cultural resources that many White students do. This premise is often confirmed in studies that focus on barriers for low-SES Black students. Yet, this theoretical framing is flawed. First, it ignores the heterogeneity among Black students in postsecondary education, particularly around issues of identity and class. This also ignores how intersecting identities influence student experiences and outcomes. Second, such theories fail to explain how and why more affluent Black students who have access to academic resources prior to college also continue to struggle. The findings in this study demonstrate the need for theory and research in education that accounts for differences among Black students that do not automatically link higher SES status with higher educational expectations and improved outcomes. Analysis from this study shows that low-middle- and high-middle-SES quartile students make up a substantial portion of students who expect to earn a bachelor's degree or less. It also shows that race as an identity intersection is salient to educational outcomes. Theories and research on Black student performance in higher education needs to expand to account for differences among Black students and not just between Black students and their other racial peers. This quantitative investigation used empirical data from a large national dataset that has longitudinal data on students beginning in 2002. Future studies on Black students in different SES groups and educational outcomes also could be qualitative in nature. Results from this study are an important start to better understand how SES affects Black students' educational expectations. Yet, qualitative studies on this topic have the potential to offer a more nuanced understanding of the experiences of Black students in high, high-middle, and low-middle SES groups and their choices surrounding academics. Longitudinal mixed-methods studies can provide future researchers with an improved understanding of how trends in Black students' outcomes may be influenced by other background characteristics, such as SES. Such a study would be an important contribution to the literature on intersectionality by using qualitative and quantitative data to offer a more comprehensive understanding of Black students' outcomes in higher education and the effects identity intersections have on these outcomes.

IMPLICATIONS

Findings from this study also are significant to the larger discussion in higher education for several reasons. First, one of the purposes of this study was to examine what differences, if any, exist among Black college students based on their SES. Black students come from various socioeconomic, cultural, ethnic, geographic, religious, and other backgrounds that shape their experiences prior to and during their time in college: they bring many intersections beyond race and class. This study provides empirical support for distinguishing Black students from one another based on more than just low-income status.

This chapter also holds importance for student affairs practitioners and administrators, particularly those who manage student support, extracurricular, and other involvement programs. One area of importance that can be shaped by this study relates to college outreach and academic support programs (COASPs). Student affairs personnel invest substantial time, energy, and resources into COASPs. The findings in this chapter provide information on a student population that has previously not been targeted by college educators and services: upper and middle-class Black students. Practitioners and educators need to understand that Black students are not a homogenous or a monolithic group. Social class, gender, sexuality, and many other factors help to shape students as individuals and their educational experiences. These intersecting identities should be recognized by those who work in higher education. This research also could contribute to a more nuanced delivery of services to support Black students in postsecondary education. Knowing that other identities are relevant to student success besides low-income status should encourage educators to offer services to Black students that focus more on need and less on a single status. Information from this study can help to better tailor efforts to get Black students involved, improve persistence rates, and better distribute resources. For example, as a way to recognize differences among students, an improved financial aid system would have a more nuanced categorization including "middle income" and "high-middle income."

Finally, this discussion on intersectionality with respect to middle-income Black students is significant for institutional, state, and federal policymakers in higher education. Many decisions about funding, programming, and efforts to improve educational outcomes for college students are made on a macrolevel. Initiatives to improve college achievement, particularly for Black students, are often tied to financial aid status. Federal programs such as the Ronald E. McNair Postbaccalaureate Achievement program or the Student Support Services program provide students with access to academic services, resources, networks, and knowledge that assist in promoting undergraduate and graduate school success. At institutions of higher education, "at least two-thirds of the participants must be low-income, potential first-generation college students. The remaining participants may be from groups that are underrepresented in graduate education" (U.S. Department of Education, 2006). While low-income status and being underrepresented in graduate education may overlap, there are many underrepresented Black students who are not low income but would benefit from programs such as these. This study can inform policymakers of the importance of these and other programs to Black students from various SES backgrounds, not just those who are classified as low income. By building on the concepts introduced by the model of multiple dimensions of identity, faculty, staff, and policymakers can become more aware of the multiple identities of Black students rather than trying to have students choose to identify with a single aspect of their identity. Using only one characteristic such as race or class does not provide a meaningful understanding of the complexities that create students' inner identities.

CONCLUSION

The importance of recognizing the racial struggles of Black middle-class and upper-class students is too often overlooked. Yet, the outcome of this study highlights the fact that regardless of SES, Black students encounter experiences and problems that contribute to similar educational expectations. Furthermore, because of higher expectations, Black students from the middle class and upper class can have an even more challenging time when it comes to academic achievement and positive educational outcomes due to a lack of targeted support. The needs of middle-class and high-middle-class Black students have, to this point, been ignored by policymakers at all levels. It is my hope that this information will help move policy in a direction that pays more attention to the fact that Black students in higher education are in fact a very diverse group. This diversity must be met with equally diverse forms of support.

REFERENCES

Abes, E. S., Jones, S. R., McEwen, M. K. (2007). Reconceptualizing the model of multiple dimensions of identity: The role of meaning-making capacity in the construction of multiple identities. *Journal of College Student Development, 48,* 1–22.

Ainsworth-Darnell, J., & Downey, D. B. (1998). Assessing the oppositional culture explanation for racial/ethnic differences in school performance. *American Sociological Review, 63,* 536–553.

Attewell, P., Lavin, D., Domina, T., & Levey, T. (2004). The black middle class: Progress, prospects, and puzzles. *Journal of African American Studies, 8,* 6–19.

Bhopal, R. (2004). Glossary of terms relating to ethnicity and race: For reflection and debate. *Journal of Epidemiology & Community Health, 58,* 441–445.

Boyington, J., Johnson, A., & Carter-Edwards, L. (2007). Dissatisfaction with body size among low-income, postpartum black women. *Journal of Obstetric, Gynecological & Neonatal Nursing, 36,* 144–151.

Cross, W. E., Jr., & Vandiver, B. J. (2001). Nigrescence theory and measurement: Introducing the Cross Racial Identity Scale (CRIS). In J. G. Ponterotto, J. M. Casas, L. A. Suzuki, & C. M. Alexander (Eds.), *Handbook of multicultural counseling* (pp. 371–393). Thousand Oaks, CA: Sage.

Davis, M., Dias-Bowie, Y., Greenberg, K., Klukken, G., Pollio, H. R., Thomas, S. P., & Thompson, C. L. (2004). A fly in the buttermilk: Descriptions of university life by successful black undergraduate students at a predominately white southeastern university. *Journal of Higher Education, 75,* 420–445.

Deil-Amen, R., & Turley, R. L. (2007). A review of the transition to college literature in sociology. *Teachers College Record, 109,* 2324–2366.

Dorimé-Williams, M. L. (2013). Understanding socioeconmic differences in the relationship between black college students' involvement and educational outcomes. (Unpublished doctoral dissertation). University of Illinois at Urbana-Champaign, Champaign.

Engberg, M. E., & Allen, D. J. (2011). Uncontrolled destinies: Improving opportunity for low-income students in American higher education. *Research in Higher Education, 52*, 786–807.

Espenshade, T. J., & Radford, A. W. (2009). *No longer separate, not yet equal: Race and class in elite college admission and campus life.* Princeton, NJ: Princeton University Press.

Feagin, J. R. (1991). The continuing significance of race: Antiblack discrimination in public places. *American Sociological Review, 56*, 101–116.

Fhagen-Smith, P., Vandiver, B. J., Worrell, F. C., & Cross, W. E. (2010). (Re)examining racial identity attitude differences across gender, community type, and socioeconomic status among African American college students. *Identity, 10*, 164–180.

Gillborn, D., Rollock, N., Vincent, C., & Ball, S. J. (2012). "You got a pass, so what more do you want?" Race, class and gender intersections in the educational experiences of the black middle class. *Race, Ethnicity And Education, 15*, 121–139.

Gosa, T. L., & Alexander, K. L. (2007). Family (dis)advantage and the educational prospects of better-off African American youth: How race still matters. *Teachers College Record, 109*, 285–321.

Harrison, L., Jr., Harrison, C., & Moore, L. N. (2002). African American racial identity and sport. *Sport, Education & Society, 7*, 121–133.

Howard-Hamilton, M. F. (1997). Theory to practice: Applying developmental theories relevant to African American men. *New Directions for Student Services, 80*, 17–30.

Jones, S. R., & McEwen, M. K. (2000). A conceptual model of multiple dimensions of identity. *Journal of College Student Development, 41*, 405–414.

Kambon, K. K. K., & Bowen-Reid, T. (2010). Theories of African American personality: Classification, basic constructs and empirical predictions/assessments. *Journal of Pan African Studies, 3*, 83–108.

King, M. P., Jr. (2010). The misrepresentation of the black poor. *Journal of Black Studies, 40*, 835–850.

Ogbu, J. U. (2008). History and framework. In J. U. Ogbu (Ed.), *Minority status, oppositional culture & schooling* (pp. 3–11). New York, NY: Routledge.

Moynihan, D. P. (1965). *The negro family: The case for national action.* Washington, DC: Department of Labor, Office of Policy Planning and Research.

Parks-Yancy, R. (2012). Interactions into opportunities: Career management for low-income, first-generation African American college students. *Journal of College Student Development, 53*, 510–523.

Perry, B. L., Link, T., Boelter, C., & Leukefeld, C. (2012). Blinded to science: Gender differences in the effects of race, ethnicity, and socioeconomic status on academic and science attitudes among sixth graders. *Gender and Education, 24*, 725–743.

Peskin, M. F., Tortolero, S. R, Markham, C. M., Addy, R. C., & Baumler, E. R. (2007). Bullying and victimization and internalizing symptoms among low-income black and Hispanic students. *Journal of Adolescent Health, 40*, 372–375.

Tenney, L. J. (2008). Parallels to a black liberation psychology. *Radical Psychology: A Journal of Psychology, Politics & Radicalism, 7*, 7.

U.S. Census Bureau. (2012a). *People in poverty by selected characteristics: 2011 and 2012.* Retrieved from http://www.census.gov/hhes/www/poverty/data/incpovhlth/2012/table3.pdf

U.S. Census Bureau. (2012b). *Percent distribution of households, by selected characteristics within income quintile and top 5 percent in 2011.* Retreived from http://www.census.gov/hhes/www/cpstables/032011/hhinc/new05_000.htm

U.S. Department of Education. (2006). *Ronald E. McNair Postbaccalaureate Achievement Program: Eligibility.* Retrieved from http://www2.ed.gov/programs/triomcnair/eligibility.html

CHAPTER SIXTEEN

Hidden Populations and Intersectionality

When Race and Sexual Orientation Collide

MITSU NARUI

Asian/Americans are one of the fastest-growing groups of students within U.S. higher education. From 1996 to 2003, Asian/American (as defined by the U.S. Census and including noncitizens of Asian descent) student enrollment increased 31.6% or by 282,000 students (Ryu, 2009). As of 2004, nearly 950,000 undergraduate Asian/American students were enrolled in higher education (KewalRamani, Gilbertson, Fox, & Provasnik, 2007). Also, nearly 60% of all 18- to 24-year-old Asian/American students were enrolled in higher education, making their participation rate the highest among any racial or ethnic minority group (KewalRamani et al., 2007). These numbers do not include international students studying in the United States. During the 2012–2013 academic year, over 819,000 students from foreign countries were studying in the United States, of which a majority were Asian countries, as defined by the U.S. Census (Institute of International Education, 2013).

Participation rates for nonracial minority groups, such as gay, Lesbian, and bisexual (GLB) students, are more difficult to obtain; the demographic characteristics on admissions applications do not ask about sexual orientation. As a result, statistics regarding GLB student enrollment are more anecdotal. Nonetheless, with the average coming out age now between 14 and 16 years (down from 21 years in 1979; Marklein, 2004; Ryan, 2003; Tamashiro, 2007), many more young adults are starting higher education aware of their sexual orientation (Marklein, 2004). These statistics reflect the increased likelihood that GLB students of all backgrounds, and highlighting Asian/Americans within this chapter, are enrolling into colleges and universities nationwide.

Given the growth in these two populations, it is important to consider how ethnic minority college students who also identify as GLB are affected by their double marginalized status. For Asian/American GLB students, their double marginalized status means that they face challenges adapting to a dominant pervasive paradigm (i.e., White, Asian, heterosexual). The purpose of this study was to explore the impact that Asian/American GLB students' decisions about revealing or concealing their sexual orientation had on their college experience while providing a groundbreaking perspective on the identity formation process of Asian/American GLB students. By understanding the lived experiences of these individuals, one can gain insight into the complex ways in which sexual orientation and ethnic identity intersect; in turn, this information can help improve their college experience and create a more supportive environment for all.

LITERATURE REVIEW

Equity and Language

Of note, the participants in this study were both Asian American and Asian international students. They are referred to collectively as *Asian/American;* sub-populations are defined when necessary. The reason for the use of the solidus is best summarized by Palumbo-Liu (1999):

> As in the construction "and/or" where the solidus at once instantiates a choice between two terms, their simultaneous and equal status, and an element of indecidability, that is, as it at once implies both exclusion and inclusion, "Asian/American" makes *both* the distinction between "Asian" and "American" *and* a dynamic, unsettled, and inclusive movement. (p. 1)

The use of the solidus helps to maintain the distinction between the Asian international and Asian American students, while also maintaining the similarity between the two groups.

Historical Context

To fully understand the complexity of the Asian/American GLB experience, one must first have an understanding of the context by which Asian/American and GLB oppression developed. While Asian/American history goes back many years, the roots of contemporary Asian/American college student oppression focuses on the model minority myth and figure of yellow peril or perpetual foreigner. The model minority myth has been sustained by aggregate numbers, which suggest that Asian/Americans have been more successful in completing higher education (e.g., see Cook & Cordova, 2006; Ryu, 2009). Yet, when these numbers are disaggregated, many subpopulations within the Asian/American community are at a socioeconomic and educational disadvantage when compared to their White counterparts (Museus & Kiang, 2009; Teranishi et al, 2010). This myth, along with the idea of Asian/Americans, as a yellow peril that could threaten the dominant culture, contributes to creating an environment that favors the White college student experience, and racializes the experiences of Asian/American individuals, as many assume that Asian/American students do not need support through their education.

When considering the oppression of GLB college students, Wolf (2009) presented a perspective centered on capitalism. She contended that modern Western capitalist society, one that privileges heterosexual marriage and relationships, has led to the current heterosexist and homophobic climate. In this climate, heterosexual behavior and traditional gender roles are rewarded and nonnormative behavior is often oppressed or punished. This heterosexist and homophobic climate is also evident in higher education, where sexual minorities feel that they must conceal their orientation to others for fear of retribution by their peers, faculty, or staff (Rankin, 2003, 2005). Thus, the college environment can be hostile for GLB students, and this environment can negatively impact their perceptions of themselves and their sexual orientation.

For Asian/American GLB students, both ethnicity and sexual orientation intersect and create challenges for them. For example, behind this model minority myth is an expectation that Asian/American students be "good" children, "save face," and maintain a specific public persona (Kimmel & Huso, 2004). This expectation that they must be ideal children is particularly difficult when they are attracted to those of the same sex or gender. Often parents project these model minority expectations onto their children; they expect them to be in heterosexual relationships and start a family (Kimmel & Huso, 2004). These expectations and challenges create a unique situation that Asian/American GLB students have to manage. The ways in which these factors influence Asian/American GLB students' decision to reveal or conceal their sexual orientation is explored further in this study.

Contemporary Research

Research on GLB students' coming out experience has largely focused on the White population (e.g., Clark, 2005; Grov, Bimbi, Nanin, & Parsons, 2006) and has either focused on "coming out" (e.g., Cain, 1991; Evans & Broido, 1999; Rasmussen, 2004) or on the campus climate for GLB students (e.g., Evans, 2000, 2001; Evans & Broido, 1999; Rankin, 2003). While these studies have increased our understanding of the impact of disclosing one's sexual orientation and the environmental challenges GLB students may face, ethnic minority GLB students have many additional factors to consider when deciding to reveal their sexual orientation to others.

Additionally, much of the research on the Asian/American college student experience centers on how these students form opinions about themselves, others, and their environment (e.g, Alvarez & Helms, 2001; Kawaguchi, 2003). In general, Asian/American student research has been limited in focus and does not consider the impact of having multiple marginalized identity traits on the college experience (Kawaguchi, 2003; Ying et al., 2001). Therefore, when considering the identity formation process and coming-out experience for Asian/American GLB students, a deeper understanding, one that goes beyond studying single identity traits, is needed. This study explored how multiple marginalized identity traits, in this case ethnicity and sexual orientation, influenced the educational experience and the identity formation of Asian/American GLB college students.

THEORETICAL PERSPECTIVE

The findings for this study are explained using the works and concepts of Michel Foucault (1970, 1977a, 1977b, 1978). More specifically, Foucault's concepts of discourse, power/knowledge, the subject, and agency are used. Understanding the Asian/American GLB student experience from a Foucauldian perspective is a departure from previous research on the identity formation process, which has utilized a developmental, psychosocial approach (e.g., see Cass, 1979; D'Augelli, 1994; Kim, 1981; Phinney, 1989). These psychosocial approaches (a) essentialize and universalize student identity development, (b) fail to acknowledge the possibility of identity beyond what is being studied at the moment, and (c) do not fully consider the impact of multiple identities on identity formation (Jones, Kim, & Skendall, 2012). Foucault's concepts are constructed to allow for multiple possibilities and multiple forms of reality. As a result, employing Foucault's work facilitates creating a new perspective about how Asian/American GLB students come to develop and form their self-identity.

METHOD

Participants and Setting

The participants for this study were Asian international and Asian American GLB students at a large Midwestern university, with a total enrollment of 45,000 students. Approximately 10% of the population were made up of international students, with a majority of those international students from countries in Asia.

Overall, Asian/American students comprised 5.2% of the student body. Finally, the institution has developed a reputation for being GLB friendly. Table 16.1 describes the nine participants of this study.

Hidden Populations and Recruitment

After initial difficulty recruiting participants through flyers, social media, and e-mail, I recruited nine students by contacting several Asian/American and GLBT student organizations and their leaders. All GLB students who consented and participated received a $25 bookstore gift card for their participation.

A challenge to this study was the fact that Asian/American GLB individuals are considered a hidden population. Heckathorn (1997) defined the hidden population as having

> Two characteristics: first, no sampling frame exists, so the size and boundaries of the population are unknown; and second, there exist strong privacy concerns, because membership involves stigmatized or illegal behavior, leading individuals to refuse to cooperate, or give unreliable answers to protect their privacy. (p. 174)

Asian/American GLB college students are considered a hidden population because no solid set of data exists as to their prevalence. In addition, privacy concerns existed because these students' sexual orientations were central to this study. The disclosure process has shown that publicly disclosing one's sexual orientation could lead to discrimination and experiences with homophobia and heterosexism (Evans & Broido, 1999; Rasmussen, 2004). Fear of the general population knowing their sexual orientation and the potential for prejudicial behavior may have been a reason why it was difficult to identify willing participants who met the criteria for the study.

Table 16.1. Summary of Characteristics of Study Participants.

Name	Education level	Country of origin or background	Gender	Self-Identified sexual orientation	International student
Beth	Freshman	Korean–adoptee	Female	Lesbian	No
Carrie	Freshman	Korean	Female	Pansexual	No
Java	Junior	Malaysia	Female	Lesbian	Yes
Kangsik	Sophomore	South Korea	Male	Gay	Yes
Dan	1st year Masters	Taiwanese/ Biracial	Male	Gay	No
Han	1st year Masters	Taiwanese	Male	Bisexual	No

Name	Education level	Country of origin or background	Gender	Self-Identified sexual orientation	International student
Ian	1st year Masters	Vietnamese/ Biracial	Male	Gay	No
Ling	Masters– exchange program	China	Female	Bisexual	Yes
Chen	PhD candidate	China	Male	Gay	Yes

Note. Pseudonyms were assigned based on the country of origin.

Data Collection and Analysis

All of the participants participated in a 1.5- to 2-hour semistructured interview. The data were analyzed utilizing Clarke's (2005) situational analysis method. Situational analysis seeks to "regenerate" the "very popular and epistemologically sound approach" (Clarke, 2005, p. xxi) of grounded theory by incorporating aspects of poststructural, deconstructive research design. Grounded theory works on the assumption that the applicability of theory "cannot be divorced from the process by which it is generated" (Glaser & Strauss, 1967, p. 5). The advantage of using situational analysis is that it allowed for the study of Asian/American GLB identity from a Foucauldian perspective. While traditional grounded theory examines single social issues, situational analysis takes the complexity of the social circumstances into consideration (Clarke, 2005), and thus lends itself toward understanding the complexity of the university environment. Therefore, situational analysis allowed for a better understanding of the subjects (in this case Asian/American GLB students) and the decisions they make within a specific environmental context.

FINDINGS

From this study, three major themes emerged: (a) management of multiple discourses, (b) discourse of higher education, and (c) Foucauldian subjects and agency. These themes are discussed in more detail later.

Management of Multiple Discourses

For Foucault, discourse can be defined as "a body of ideas, concepts and beliefs that have become established as knowledge or as an accepted way of looking at the world" (as cited in Doherty, 2007, p. 193). People view their world through a particular discursive lens. The data obtained from the Asian/American GLB students in this study demonstrated that they were managing multiple discourses (e.g., home life, country of origin, religion, higher education, and social networking sites) within their lives. Table 16.2 describes these discourses in greater detail, including the discursive norms regarding sexual orientation and key relationships within each.

These discursive norms regarding sexual orientation created conflict and anxiety for the students in the study. In addition, the students' Asian/American ethnicity impacted the expectations others had of them within the discourses. For example, within home life, some of the students had parents who wanted them to have children, with the unspoken expectation that they be in heterosexual relationships in order to create that family. This expectation made them hesitant to reveal their sexual orientation to their family members. Chen explained as follows:

> I want to settle down but I don't know how to deal with my parents though. So I mean everyone in my extended family was questioning me why I don't have a girlfriend, and I don't know, it's going to be tough. Sometimes, I think maybe I just get married to a girl, maybe I should try it, maybe I'll like it, getting married to a girl. But that's a huge step.... Even if I do that, I'd know I'll be more attracted to guys than girls because I don't know how to deal with that after I get married. I don't know.

Chen knew gay Chinese men who married women yet continued to be sexually active with men. He therefore contemplated doing the same. For Chen, his parents created a discursive norm that made it difficult for him to reveal his sexual orientation to them.

While the discursive norms within home life created conflict for students like Chen, all of the students with social networking site (SNS) profiles used the discursive norms and associated power as a way to control how knowledge about their sexual orientation was communicated. Some saw SNS as an easy and liberating way of communicating their sexual orientation. For them, SNS fell outside of the constraints of other discourses and therefore was a way to tell others about their orientation. Others saw SNS as too open, with potential negative consequences if too many people found out about their sexual orientation. As Beth stated, "Randomly, it's just, I don't really need it out there yet." In either scenario, the students' point of view and opinions about SNS influenced their decisions about revealing their sexual orientation. In turn, they used Foucauldian power to control exactly how that information (or lack thereof) was communicated through the SNS.

Table 16.2. Explanation of Participants' Major Discourses/Environments.

Discourse/ Environment	Discursive norms/expectations	Key relationships
Home life	-Start a family (presumably in a heterosexual relationship) -GLB orientation unacceptable due to cultural, familial, or religious values	-Parents -Siblings -Grandparents
Religion	-Homosexuality not accepted within the religion (mostly had to deal with Christianity, but also other religions)	-Friends -Family members who observed that religion
Higher education: Professors/ Classroom	-Homosexuality often not discussed in classes	-Professors -Classmates
Higher education: Residence halls	-GLB orientation accepted or not accepted depending on students' perception of hall	-Hallmates -Resident assistant (RA)
Higher education: Student organizations	-Asian American organizations: Homosexuality not discussed or culturally known to be not accepted -GLBT organizations: Advocacy promoted; free to express GLBT orientation	-Advisor -Student leaders -Other organization members
Higher education: Campus events	-GLBT related events: Free to express GLBT orientation	-Other event participants
Country of origin	-GLB orientation not accepted within the society	-Family -International students from related Asian countries
Social networking sites	-Many people can view the profile -Control over the information people can view	-General online community

The relationships within these discourses impacted the formation of their ethnic and sexual identities. Their relationships with certain individuals often resulted in them exploring their sexual identity over their ethnic one or vice versa. For students such as Dan, the change from home life to higher education was the impetus needed for him to prioritize the exploration of his ethnic identity:

> Finding that sense of self, dealing with coming out issues, dealing with the racial identity piece, which really didn't integrate until I was 18 because I grew up in a town of 1,000

people where it was where your *family* mattered, not what you look like, and I had a good family, so people just treated me as [Dan].

So it took me a long time to realize that when I'm in a crowd, especially in [a Midwest university], which is only, what? 9.4 percent minority. I look different than most people around me. And that was a shocking realization, and…so I joined Asian-American Student Union, and I was actually a student senator for a semester, and tried on the role of seeing how that fit. And for me it just really didn't fit because it wasn't how I was raised.

For Dan, his familial relationships impacted how he explored his identities. Once he was in college and no longer around his family, he used it as an opportunity to further explore his ethnicity.

Overall, the students in the study had multiple discourses to consider and manage. Doing so often made students feel conflicted or anxious. Many times, moving within these discourses gave them different opportunities to explore their ethnic identity and/or sexual orientation. In turn, managing these different discourses impacted their overall educational experience.

Discourse of Higher Education

The impact that the discourse of higher education had on the students warrants further explanation because of its multiple facets and many nuances. The college environment is its own "system," with a set of rules, language, and people (i.e., students, faculty, staff, and administrators). For many of the students, the reputation for being a GLBT-friendly campus translated into their actual experience. As Kangsik stated, "I mean I really like the atmosphere on campus. I mean most people are accepting" [when speaking about sexual orientation]. Beth appreciated the relative diversity on campus. She believed that the diversity meant that the campus community would be more open and accepting of self-identified GLB persons. Dan, being in graduate school and with more life experience, understood the safety being in higher education provided him and also recognized the liberal attitudes of the campus community, which was why he continued his education. However, in spite of the relative comfort afforded to them within the environment, the students had to manage different aspects of higher education and within those aspects decide if and when to reveal their sexual orientation to others. These included the residence halls, the classrooms and professors, student organizations, and campus events. Within each of these settings, the students had to evaluate and assess the norms regarding their sexual orientation and make informed decisions about revealing or concealing their sexual orientation based on those norms.

For example, Carrie concealed her sexual orientation from those in her residence hall. As she said, "They don't agree with gay issues and gay rights and stuff like that so I just keep it quiet." Java also kept her orientation hidden during her freshman year in the residence hall. As an international student, she felt that she could not relate to those in her hall:

> I find it like hard at first to like adjust to American people in general. Somehow I couldn't click with them as much. It's easier with like international students. So back in the dorm, I was just keeping to myself, doing my own stuff.

Because she was an international student, Java had a difficult time forming supportive relationships with other students. She felt that she could not connect with them because of their cultural differences. This lack of cultural acceptance made her hesitant to reveal her sexual orientation to others in her hall, as she was concerned that revealing her sexual orientation would further inhibit her from forming supportive relationships. Overall, while the students may have felt comfortable on campus because of the GLBT-friendly reputation, they still had to manage multiple aspects of the college environment and make their decisions based on each area's discursive norms.

Foucauldian Subjects and Agency

Foucault (1977, 1978, as cited in Bevir, 1999) believed that individuals could not obtain true autonomy and that only agency was possible. As resistance within any discourse is inevitable (at least according to Foucault), agency is also inherent within discourses; individuals need the constraints associated with discursive expectations to enact any degree of agency. For these students, agency meant that they had to learn to define themselves and their ethnic/sexual identities within various discourses.

Asian/American GLB students, by virtue of their social group memberships, are part of a dominant discourse that considers them marginalized. This struggle to behave as agents and be empowered within any discourse was further complicated by having to manage stereotypes associated with the students' Asian/American race/ethnicity. Kangsik described his keen awareness of this issue:

> I thought about it for long time and I didn't know that it was disadvantage for me to think about, but I just realized that if I were straight and White I would never ever think about that.... I don't have to worry about being Asian in Europe because they don't like immigrants. I don't have to worry about being in South Korea because I would perfectly fit in the social norm. I don't really have to worry about being here because I will be White and will not be gay. I will just hang out with other people. But today I realized that it is something that I have to take care of throughout my life and straight people and White people would never ever seriously think about. I never thought that it was really a bad thing and I don't still.

While Kangsik struggled with different emotions associated with his identity as gay and Asian/American, he ended with this statement: "I never thought that it was really a bad thing." Thus, in spite of his struggle to define himself and enact agency within any discourse, he still retained a sense of pride about his identity. For Kangsik, the relationship between his gay and Asian/American identities leads him to find agency within various discourses in order to find agency for the other. He elaborated:

> I try to be openly gay because I was Asian.... There are a lot of international students like from Korea and from China and most Korean people don't think that there is any gay guys any place in the country or something. That's why I was like okay here I am. There's gay guy from South Korea so I hope you guys please understand that there is some who is gay no matter what their nationalities are.... I am concerned about what [they] will think of me because I'm gay and what [they] will think because I'm Asian.

Kangsik's ethnic identity informed his ability to enact his agency as a gay male. In turn, his gay identity helped to enact his ethnic/racial identity. He wanted to create awareness among others, and particularly among other Asian international students, that the gay Asian/American identity did exist and that he was one of them. Because of that intersection between his Asian/American and gay identity, he also wanted to downplay and minimize any stereotypes of Asian/Americans. As he said, "I try not to use chopsticks as much as I could." His desire to be openly gay because of his ethnicity can be considered an act of Foucauldian resistance. As Foucault states, resistance by subjects is inevitable within any discourse. By proclaiming his gay identity and outwardly disclosing it to others, he was outwardly resisting the hegemonic discourse's vision of gay, Asian/American men (or in some cases, creating the vision and making the hegemony realize his existence).

IMPLICATIONS

When considering higher education as a dominant discourse, the focus should be on initiatives that can work toward changing the dominant ideology and enhance people's understanding about the experiences of the Asian/American GLB population and the intersection of their race/ethnicity and sexual orientation in particular. Doing so would allow these students to establish relationships where they would feel comfortable revealing their sexual orientations. Potentially, the decision and act of revealing their sexual orientation can positively affect the students' emerging sense of agency and positively impact their educational outcomes.

When considering the experiences of Asian/American GLB students, this study has shown that their relationships with others within the discourses are important for them to be able to feel safe revealing their sexual orientation, safely enact their given agency, and help them to achieve educational outcomes. Therefore, instead of a single-minded approach to addressing the climate for these students, administrators need to ask in what ways they can affect the norms and expectations associated with GLB identity, especially when also considering its intersection with ethnicity. In doing so, they can help change people's perceptions about the population and eventually work toward changing their understanding and beliefs about this group of students. For example, the students in this study felt that GBT topics were not often discussed in their classes. In addition, because of the large classes they often took, they felt that they could not approach their professors and thus could not establish relationships where they might feel comfortable revealing their sexual orientation. Administrators could address these issues in a variety of ways.

While many would consider it unreasonable to require that homosexuality be a required topic within a mechanical engineering class, educating instructors on the issues facing Asian/American GLB students and giving the instructors concrete ways to create a welcoming and open classroom can help create an environment where students might feel comfortable establishing positive relationships, which in turn makes them feel comfortable revealing their sexual orientation to others. Besides educating the classroom instructors, administrators can also look at their academic structure, for example, offering classes on intersectionality as a way to promote and educate the greater community. Creating these types of academic initiatives can also communicate to Asian/American GLB students that the university administration supports them and is actively seeking to educate others about them as a group.

LIMITATIONS AND DIRECTIONS FOR FUTURE RESEARCH

This study was conducted at a large, public research institution in the Midwest. This area of the country is known to be politically conservative (Coleman, 2010). While the university studied had been cited as being a GLBT-friendly campus, the politically conservative nature within the geographical area likely affected the students' perceptions about their sexual orientation and their willingness to disclose to others outside of the university. Conducting this study on another GLBT-friendly campus in a more politically liberal geographical area could yield different results and would also allow for comparison across institutions.

Finally, another approach to studying this group is to conduct a longitudinal, qualitative assessment of students' experiences. For the younger students in this study, their understanding of their sexual orientation and their overall self-identity was evolving and changing to a greater degree than some of the older graduate students in the study. For the younger students, their lack of life experiences meant that they were still learning about themselves and their place within society. An extension of this study would be to interview these students at various points in their college career to see how their understanding about their self-identity or how their decision making about revealing their sexual orientation changed over time. A longitudinal assessment would also allow for future study on additional effects of revealing or concealing their sexual orientation, such as its effects on stress levels, overall psychological health, and their perceptions of new and previously established relationships.

CONCLUSION

For these students, their experience as Asian/American and GLB was a challenging and complex one. Because they were Asian/American, those within the majority considered them to be the model minority. With that stereotype also came the assumption that they did not have any trouble adjusting to the college experience. The reality of their lived experience is that as Asian/American GLB individuals, they were far from being a model group without any challenges. The intersections between their GLB and Asian/American identities placed them outside of the margins of the White, heterosexual, and Asian/American communities.

The students in this study came from a variety of ethnic, social, and familial backgrounds, and because they did not self-identify as heterosexual, they also had to co-manage and balance an emerging sexual identity with their ethnic ones. The intersectionality between ethnic identity and sexual orientation for these students was what compelled me to study this understudied population.

Previous studies on college student development and the impact of the college experience on student's self-identity assume that identity development occurs in the ways that Erikson (1968) intended (i.e., a stepwise, linear fashion). The manner in which Foucault (1970, 1977a) explained the interrelationship among power, truth, knowledge, and discourse is a useful and meaningful framework that contradicts these essentialist assumptions. The results of this study demonstrate that the Asian/American GLB students in this study came to learn about themselves and their self-identity in far more complicated ways. They navigated multiple discourses and managed different discursive expectations to discover how to "be" an Asian/American GLB individual within society. Within this study, I focused specifically on one way to enact their sexual identity (i.e., revealing one's sexual orientation). Through repeatedly making decisions about revealing their sexual orientation within various discourses, the students would eventually make their Asian/American GLB identity a "reality." In doing so, they also worked toward achieving agency and defined themselves both within and beyond the dominant discourse.

Reconceptualizing the Asian/American GLB student experience in this way has numerous implications for campus administrators and community members. Administrators should think about more than just governing and regulating the masses and focus on multifaceted approaches to creating mutual understanding about the involved nature of the Asian/American GLB experience. As even the most remote college campuses become increasingly diverse, this perspective and approach to policy and practice will become increasingly important, as one approach will not meet the needs of all students. Also, this reconceptualization through a Foucauldian framework reveals that the students were looking for role models and to form positive relationships with others. Proper education and training on the issues facing Asian/American GLB students and on the complexities of deciding on revealing their sexual orientation are crucial to establishing those positive relationships. Addressing these issues and implementing such changes would enhance the college experience for these students and make them more likely to be successful in pursing their education.

REFERENCES

Alvarez, A. N., & Helms, J. E. (2001). Racial identity and reflected appraisals as influences on Asian Americans' racial adjustment. *Cultural Diversity & Ethnic Minority Psychology, 7*, 217–231.

Bevir, M. (1999). Foucault and Critique: Deploying Agency against Autonomy. *Political Theory, 27*(1), 65–84. doi: 10.2307/192161

Cain, R. (1991). Stigma management and gay identity development. *Social Work, 36*, 67–73.

Cass, V. C. (1979). Homosexual identity formation: A theoretical model. *Journal of Homosexuality, 4*, 219–235.

Clark, C. (2005). Diversity initiatives in higher education: Deconstructing "the down low"—People of color "coming out" and "being out" on campus: A conversation with Mark Brimhall-Vargas, Sivagami Subbaraman, and Robert Waters. *Multicultural Education, 13*, 45–59.

Clarke, A. E. (2005). *Situational analysis: Grounded theory after the postmodern turn.* Thousand Oaks, CA: Sage.

Coleman, J. (2010). Conservatives outnumber liberals in 49 states. Retrieved from http://www.examiner.com/x-14820-Gallup-Polls-Examiner~y2010m8d9-Conservatives-Outnumber-Liberals-in-49-States

Cook, B. J., & Cordova, D. I. (2006). *Minorities in higher education: Twenty-second annual status report.* Washington, DC: American Council on Education.

D'Augelli, A. R. (1994). Identity development and sexual orientation toward a model of Lesbian, gay, and bisexual development. In E. J. Trickett, R. J. Watts, & D. Birman (Eds.), *Human diversity: Perspectives on people in context* (pp. 312–333). San Francisco, CA: Jossey-Bass.

Doherty, R. (2007). Critically framing education policy: Foucault, discourse, and governmentality. In M. A. Peters & T. Beasley (Eds.), *Why Foucault? New directions in educational research* (pp. 193–204). New York, NY: Peter Lang.

Erikson, E. H. (1968). *Identity: Youth and crisis.* New York: W. W. Norton & Company.

Evans, N. J. (2000). Creating a Positive Learning Environment for Gay, Lesbian, and Bisexual Students. *New Directions for Teaching and Learning, 2000*(82), 81–87. doi: 10.1002/tl.8208

Evans, N. J. (2001). The experiences of Lesbian, gay, and bisexual youth in university communities. In A. R. D'Augelli & C. J. Patterson (Eds.), *Lesbian, gay, and bisexual identities and youth: Psychological perspectives* (pp. 181–198). New York, NY: Oxford University Press.

Evans, N. J., & Broido, E. M. (1999). Coming out in college residence halls: Negotiation, meaning making, challenges, supports. *Journal of College Student Development, 40,* 658–668.

Foucault, M. (1970). *The order of things: An archaeology of the human sciences.* New York, NY: Vintage.

Foucault, M. (1977a). *Discipline and punish: The birth of the prison* (A. Sheridan, Trans.). New York, NY: Vintage.

Foucault, M. (1977b). Nietzsche, genealogy, history. In D. F. Bouchard (Ed.), *Language, counter-memory, practice: Selected essays and interviews* (pp. 139–164). Ithaca, NY: Cornell University Press.

Foucault, M. (1978). *The history of sexuality: An introduction, volume 1.* New York, NY: Vintage.

Glaser, B. G., & Strauss, A. L. (1967). *The discovery of grounded theory: Strategies for qualitative research.* Chicago, IL: Aldine.

Grov, C., Bimbi, D. S., Nanin, J. E., & Parsons, J. T. (2006). Race, ethnicity, gender, and generational factors associated with the coming-out process among gay, Lesbian, and bisexual individuals. *Journal of Sex Research, 43,* 115–121.

Heckathorn, D. D. (1997). Respondent-driven sampling: A new approach to the study of hidden populations. *Social Problems, 44,* 174–199.

Institute of International Education. (2013). Open doors 2013: International students in the United States and study abroad by American students are at all-time high. Retrieved from http://www.iie.org/Who-We-Are/News-and-Events/Press-Center/Press-Releases/2013/2013-11-11-Open-Doors-Data

Jones, S. R., Kim, Y. C., & Skendall, K. C. (2012). (Re-) framing authenticity: Considering multiple social identities using autoethnographic and intersectional approaches. *Journal of Higher Education, 83,* 698–723.

Kawaguchi, S. (2003). Ethnic identity development and collegiate experience of Asian Pacific American students: Implications for practice. *NASPA Journal, 40,* 13–29.

KewalRamani, A., Gilbertson, L., Fox, M. A., & Provasnik, S. (2007). *Statistics and trends in education for racial and ethnic minorities.* Washington, DC: U.S. Department of Education.

Kim, J. (1981). *Development of Asian American identity: An exploratory study of Japanese American women.* Springfield, MA: Western New England College.

Kimmel, D. C., & Huso, Y. (2004). Characteristics of gay, Lesbian, and bisexual Asians, Asian Americans, and immigrants from Asia to the USA. *Journal of Homosexuality, 47,* 143–172.

Marklein, M. B. (2004, June 21). Colleges grow gay-friendlier. *USA Today.* Retrieved from http://www.usatoday.com/news/education/2004-06-21-lgbt-main_x.htm

Museus, S. D., & Kiang, P. N. (2009). Deconstructing the model minority myth and how it contributes to the invisible minority reality in higher education research. In S. Museus (Ed.), *Conducting research on Asian Americans in higher education: New directions for institutional research* (No. 142, pp. 5–15). San Francisco, CA: Jossey-Bass.

Palumbo-Liu, D. (1999). *Asian/American: Historical crossing of a racial frontier.* Stanford, CA: Stanford University Press.

Phinney, J. S. (1989). Stages of ethnic identity development in minority group adolescents. *The Journal of Early Adolescence, 9,* 34–49.

Rankin, S. R. (2003). *Campus climate for gay, Lesbian, bisexual and transgender people: A national perspective.* Washington, DC: National Gay and Lesbian Task Force.

Rankin, S. R. (2005). Campus climates for sexual minorities. In R. Sanlo (Ed.), *Gender identity and sexual orientation: Research, policy, and personal: New directions for student services* (No. 111, 17–23). San Francisco, CA: Jossey-Bass.

Rasmussen, M. L. (2004). The problem of coming out. *Theory Into Practice, 43,* 144–150.

Ryan, C. (2003). LGBT youth: Health concerns, services and care. *Clinical Research and Regulatory Affairs, 20,* 137–158.

Ryu, M. (2009). *Twenty-third status report: Minorities in higher education 2009 supplement.* Washington, DC: American Council on Education.

Tamashiro, D. (2007). Coming out. *GLBTQ Social Sciences, X,* 1–5.

Teranishi, R., Briscoe, K., Behringer, L., Pineda, D., Goldman, E., & Carolino, M. A (2010). *Federal higher education policy priorities and the Asian American and Pacific Islander community.* Washington, DC: National Commission on Asian American and Pacific Islander in Education.

Wolf, S. (2009). *Sexuality and socialism: History, politics, and theory of LGBT liberation.* Chicago, IL: Haymarket Books.

Ying, Y. W., Lee, P. A., Tsai, J. L., Hung, Y., Lin, M., & Wan, C. T. (2001). Asian American college students as model minorities: An examination of their overall competence. *Cultural Diversity & Ethnic Minority Psychology, 7,* 59–74.

CHAPTER SEVENTEEN

Demographic Information Collection in Higher Education and Student Affairs Survey Instruments

Developing a National Landscape for Intersectionality

JASON C. GARVEY

Within the fields of higher education and student affairs, there are a select number of national surveys that provide data for a considerable amount of empirical analyses. Because of their wide recognition and publication volume, findings from these analyses have the potential to shape the discourse of research on students in higher education and student affairs. Pascarella and Terenzini (2005) wrote, "[A] number of national data sets, which produce a substantial portion of the evidence on the impact of college on students, have become targets of opportunity for large numbers of social scientists" (p. 15). These national quantitative datasets significantly permeate tier-one journals within the fields of higher education and student affairs and the disciplines of sociology, economics, and political sciences. It is possible that these national surveys not only influence the entire body of literature in these broad fields and disciplines but also policies and administrative practices.

Though these national quantitative datasets heavily permeate research publications, scholarly communities do not have a holistic or transparent understanding of how participant information is collected. With a growing emphasis on intersectional survey research (Cole, 2009; Davis, 2008; McCall, 2005), there is a need to examine the ways in which these influential surveys collect demographic information across various social identities.

Sanlo (2002) wrote, "I am concerned about the language we as professionals still use on our campuses...these words violate boundaries of race, gender, and sexual identity, and serve to perpetuate a climate of exclusion and marginalization" (p. 171). Notably, the tension between recognizing intersectional and fluid identities while quantitatively categorizing responses is a continual struggle for survey methodologists. These assertions beget the question, how can researchers embrace a more inclusive and intersectional understanding of social identities and incorporate these strategies when collecting demographic information?

LITERATURE REVIEW

Students' social identities play a central influence in their higher education experiences (Astin, 1970a, 1970b, 1991; Pascarella, 1985; Tinto, 1975, 1987, 1993; Weidman, 1989). In their examination of how colleges impact students, Pascarella and Terenzini (2005) discussed that "diversity in the faculty and student body is a potentially powerful force in shaping important cognitive and noncognitive outcomes" (p. 631). Social identities are fundamentally important within higher education and student affairs scholarship, yet there are few established guidelines for contextualizing demographic variables into empirical analyses, particularly within quantitative research.

Intersectionality is a research paradigm that offers new ways to understand the complexity of social identities. Cole (2009) wrote, "Rather than prescribing—or proscribing—any particular research or data analysis technique, the concept of intersectionality entails a conceptual shift in the way researchers understand social categories" (p. 178). The following sections briefly outline the main tenets of intersectionality and discuss its relevance to quantitative analyses in higher education and student affairs.

Intersectionality

Developed through Black feminist thought and originally coined by Crenshaw (1989), intersectionality refers to the interaction between gender, race, and other categories of difference and the outcomes of these interactions as they relate to power. Intersectionality began in feminist and critical scholarship to acknowledge differences among women and deconstruct a history of exclusion within the field of women's studies (Davis, 2008). Davis (2008) commented, "As a concept, intersectionality is, without a doubt, ambiguous and open-ended" (p. 77). Nonetheless, scholars understand intersectional approaches to research as the relationship between people and their social locations, paying particular attention to power within social spaces (Mahalingam, 2007). Intersectionality encourages scholars to understand how systems of oppression intersect to create structures, political systems, and cultural contexts that shape the experiences of individuals with oppressed identities. More specifically, intersectional scholars are interested in the relationships among social groups defined by the inclusion of all groups in each social category (McCall, 2005).

McCall (2005) provided commentary on intersectionality from a methodological standpoint. She discussed that there are no established guidelines for empirically addressing research questions informed by an intersectional framework and recognized that the current restriction on intersectional research comes down primarily to methods. As a new frame of understanding, intersectionality has introduced new methodological difficulties. Nevertheless, Cole (2009) discussed that "[t]o translate the theoretical insights of intersectionality into psychological research does not require the adoption of a new set of methods; rather, it requires a reconceptualization of the meaning and consequences of social categories" (p. 176). Although a large portion of intersectional work employs qualitative methods, intersectional theorists must utilize quantitative techniques to advance intersectionality as a research paradigm. Dubrow (2008) wrote that "[w]e need to stop wondering whether quantitative analysis of survey data is appropriate for accounting for intersectionality. The challenge now is to strengthen the bond between intersectionality theory and quantitative techniques" (p. 99).

Regarding higher education and student affairs research, Stage (2007) described two broad tasks for quantitative scholars. First, researchers should use data to represent and uncover large-scale processes and outcomes that perpetuate systemic social or institutional inequities. Second, scholars must question quantitative models, measures, and analytic practices in order to propose competing models, measures, and analytic practices that more appropriately describe minority individuals and communities. An intersectional theorist can achieve these tasks set forth by Stage, providing a more nuanced understanding of demographic variables and recognizing power and cultural differences as influential and evolving.

The purpose of this chapter is to examine the national landscape of higher education and student affairs survey instruments in regard to demographic information collection utilizing intersectionality as a theoretical lens. The chapter addresses the following questions:

1. How prevalent are studies using quantitative methods in tier-one higher education and student affairs journals?
2. Which demographic variables do higher education and student affairs researchers include in quantitative analyses?
3. Which survey instruments are most widely used by higher education and student affairs researchers? What demographic variables are included in these widely used survey instruments?
4. (How) do current demographic data collection techniques inhibit or promote intersectional research?

METHOD

To answer the aforementioned research questions, I began by reviewing five tier-one higher education and student affairs journal volumes from 2010 to 2012. These journals included *The Journal of Higher Education, Review of Higher Education, Research in Higher Education, Journal of College Student Development,* and *Higher Education* (Bray & Major, 2011).

I first categorized the primary methods used for each article within the journals, noting whether they were quantitative, qualitative, mixed-methods, or nonempirical. Within articles that used quantitative methods, I tracked the demographic variables that researchers included in the analyses. These demographic variables included the following: gender (male/female), race/ethnicity, age, class/socioeconomic status (SES), immigration status/nationality, religion/spirituality, sexual identity, transgender identity, and ability (Adams et al., 2013). From this information, I determined the proportion of quantitative studies from 2010 to 2012 that included each demographic variable.

Also for all quantitative articles, I noted which survey instruments the researchers used in their studies. From this information, I identified the most widely used survey instruments in these top-tiered journals for the past three years. For this study, I was most interested in survey instruments that were used in analyses for three or more studies published in the aforementioned journals from 2010 to 2012. Upon identifying the most widely used survey instruments, I gained copies of the instruments by either contacting the survey distributors or downloading the survey online. After collecting the instruments, I conducted a detailed assessment of demographic information included in the surveys. For each demographic variable, I examined the prevalence across all survey instruments.

RESULTS

Figure 17.1 presents the primary analyses used across tier-one higher education and student affairs journals from 2010 to 2012. *The Journal of Higher Education* had 87 articles published from 2010 to 2012, with 47 (52.02%) using quantitative methods. *Review of Higher Education* had 65 total articles published, and of those, 29 (44.62%) used quantitative methods. In *Research in Higher Education,* there were 113 total articles and 108 (95.58%) used quantitative methods. For the *Journal of College Student Development,* 83 of the 154 total (53.90%) used quantitative methods. Finally, in *Higher Education,* there were 272 articles published from 2010 to 2012 and of those, 106 (38.97%) used quantitative methods. There were 691 articles published among all five journals from 2010 to 2012 and of those, 373 (53.98%) used quantitative methods.

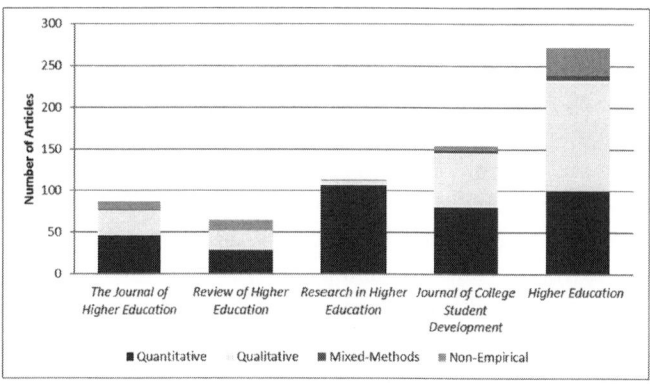

Fig 17.1. Primary Analyses Used across Tier-One Higher Education and Student Affairs Journals from 2010 to 2012.

Figure 17.2 presents the percentage of quantitative articles in tier-one higher education and student affairs journals that included demographic variables. Regarding demographic variable use in quantitative studies, a significant percentage of articles included gender (male/female; N = 201; 53.89%) or race/ethnicity (N = 157; 42.09%) in their analyses. About one in five articles included age (N = 74; 19.84%) or class/SES (N = 73; 19.57%). Fewer articles included immigration status/nationality (N = 23; 6.17%), religion/spirituality (N = 16; 4.29%), or sexual identity (N = 7; 1.88%). Finally, only two quantitative studies (0.54%) included transgender identity, and no quantitative articles included ability. Interestingly, across all five tier-one journals, only the *Journal of College Student Development* published quantitative articles that included sexual identity or transgender identity.

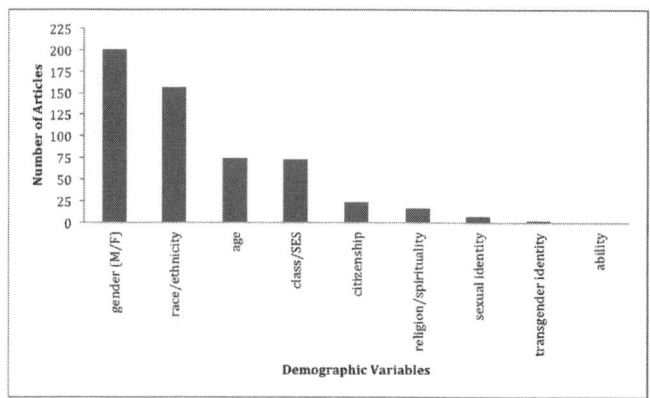

Fig 17.2. Percentage of Quantitative Articles in Tier-One Higher Education and Student Affairs Journals that Included Demographic Variables.

Results in Table 17.1 provide a list of higher education and student affairs survey instruments used three or more times across the tier-one journals from 2010 through 2012. In total, there were 19 instruments used three or more times in these journals. Of the total 373 articles that used primarily quantitative analyses, these instruments were used 135 times in 124 articles (a select number of articles used more than one instrument in their analyses). In other words, one-third of all the quantitative articles published in tier-one higher education and student affairs journals from 2010 to 2012 used data from these 19 survey instruments. From 2010 through 2012, scholars who published quantitative studies in *Research in Higher Education* used 18 of the 19 surveys for a total of 62 times. For all studies that used quantitative methods in *Research in Higher Education*, these 19 survey instruments were utilized 45.93% of the time.

Among the 19 widely used survey instruments, six were U.S. federal government surveys and 13 were administered by education nonprofit organizations. The most widely used U.S. federal government surveys were the National Education Longitudinal Study (N = 21) and the Integrated Postsecondary Education Data System (N = 19). The most used surveys from education nonprofit organizations were the Wabash National Study of Liberal Arts Education (N = 17) and the National Survey of Student Engagement (N = 12).

Table 17.1. Higher Education and Student Affairs Survey Instruments Used Three or More Times Across Tier-One Journals from 2010 through 2012.

	Research in HE	TJHE	JCSD	Review of HE	HE	Total
National Education Longitudinal Study*+	11	5	-	5	-	21
Integrated Postsecondary Education Data System*+	7	6	1	1	4	19
Wabash National Study of Liberal Arts Education	5	2	7	2	1	17
National Survey of Student Engagement	7	-	3	2	-	12
Freshman Survey	4	2	2	-	-	8
College Students' Beliefs and Values Survey*	3	1	3	-	-	7
National Student Clearinghouse*	5	1	-	1	-	7
Beginning Postsecondary Students Longitudinal Study*+	2	2	-	1	1	6
National Study of Postsecondary Faculty*+	2	1	-	1	2	6

	Research in HE	TJHE	JCSD	Review of HE	HE	Total
Faculty Survey	1	1	-	1	1	4
Survey of Earned Doctorates	1	2	-	-	1	4
Current Population Study*+	2	-	-	1	-	3
Postsecondary Education Transcript Study*+	1	1	-	1	-	3
Faculty Survey of Student Engagement	3	-	-	-	-	3
Gates Millennium Scholars Tracking and Longitudinal Study	2	1	-	-	-	3
Multi-Institutional Study of Leadership	-	-	2	1	-	3
National Study of Living-Learning Programs	1	1	1	-	-	3
The College Student Experiences Questionnaire	2	-	1	-	-	3
National Association of State Student Grant and Aid Program*	3	-	-	-	-	3
Total	62	26	20	17	10	135

Note. Research in HE = *Research in Higher Education;* TJHE = *The Journal of Higher Education;* JCSD = *Journal of College Student Development;* Review of HE = *Review of Higher Education;* HE = *Higher Education.*
*not evaluated.
+federal government survey.

For the purposes of this chapter, I only assessed survey demographic information collection from education nonprofit organizations. Among the 13 survey instruments administered by education nonprofit organizations, three were from the Cooperative Institutional Research Program (Freshman Survey [N = 8], College Students' Beliefs and Values Survey [N = 7], and Faculty Survey [N = 4]); two were from the National Survey of Student Engagement (National Survey of Student Engagement [N = 12] and Faculty Survey of Student Engagement [N = 3]); and two were from the National Opinion Research Center (Survey of Earned Doctorates [N = 4] and Gates Millenium Scholars Tracking and Longitudinal Study [N = 3]). The remaining surveys were from other education nonprofit organizations, including the Center of Inquiry (Wabash National Study of Liberal Arts Education, N = 17), the National Student Clearinghouse (N = 7), the College Student Experiences Questionnaire Assessment Program (N = 3), the Multi-Institutional Study of Leadership (N = 3), the National Study of Living-Learning Programs (N = 3), and the National Association of State Student Grant and Aid Program (N = 3).

Three education nonprofit organization survey instruments were not included in the analyses for specific reasons. First, the College Students' Beliefs and Values Survey is administered by the Cooperative Institutional Research Program as a follow-up to their Freshman Survey. Participants' survey responses are linked across both instruments by a personal identifier. Therefore, although the only demographic question included in the College Students' Beliefs and Values Survey is religion/spirituality, researchers are able to include other demographic variables into analyses that were asked in the Freshman Survey. Second, the National Association of State Student Grant and Aid Program survey was not included because it assessed information from the programmatic level and did not include individual-level variables. Lastly, the National Student Clearinghouse Research Center does not publish and did not make available the National Student Clearinghouse survey for this study.

Table 17.2 details the demographic questions included across the 10 survey instruments utilized in the analysis. All 10 surveys included gender (male/female) and race/ethnicity in their questionnaires. Nine out of 10 included age, four included sexual identity and ability, three included religion/spirituality, and two included transgender identity. Worth noting is that the Multi-Institutional Study of Leadership was the only instrument to include all demographic questions examined in this study.

Table 17.2. Demographic Questions Included within 10 Widely Used Higher Education and Student Affairs Survey Instruments.

	Gender (M/F)	Race/ Ethnicity	Age	Citizenship	Religion/ Spirituality	Sexual Identity	Transgender Identity	Ability
Wabash National Study of Liberal Arts Education	yes	yes	yes	yes	no	no	no	no
Freshman Survey	yes	yes	yes	yes	yes	no	no	no
Faculty Survey	yes	yes	yes	no	no	no	no	no
Multi-Institutional Study of Leadership	yes	yes	yes	yes	yes	yes	yes	yes

	Gender (M/F)	Race/ Ethnicity	Age	Citizenship	Religion/ Spirituality	Sexual Identity	Transgender Identity	Ability
Survey of Earned Doctorates	yes	yes	yes	yes	no	no	no	yes
Gates Millennium Scholars Tracking and Longitudinal Study	yes	yes	yes	no	no	no	no	no
National Study of Living-Learning Programs	yes	yes	no	yes	yes	yes	yes	yes
National Survey of Student Engagement	yes	yes	yes	yes	no	yes	no	yes
Faculty Survey of Student Engagement	yes	yes	yes	yes	no	yes	no	no
The College Student Experiences Questionnaire	yes	yes	yes	no	no	no	no	no
Percentage	100.00%	100.00%	90.00%	70.00%	30.00%	40.00%	20.00%	40.00%

Given the variability and difficulty in determining how survey instruments operationalized class/SES, I consciously decided to remove this demographic question from this portion of my analyses. Though all 10 surveys included proxy measures for class/SES (e.g., parents' education and income, Pell Grant status), I was unable to determine how specific instruments quantified the variable. Whereas

I was able to determine in analyses for individual articles based on authors' variable descriptions, I could not with certainty verify the ways in which survey instruments constructed class/SES.

Finally, Table 17.3 provides a side-by-side comparison of demographic variables included in the most widely used higher education and student affairs instruments from education nonprofit organizations with demographic variables included in articles across the tier-one journals from 2010 through 2012.

Table 17.3. Comparison of Demographic Variables Included within 10 Widely Used Higher Education and Student Affairs Survey Instruments with Quantitative Articles in Tier-One Journals That Included Demographic Variables.

	Included within Survey Instruments	Included within Quantitative Articles
Gender (M/F)	100.00%	53.89%
Race/Ethnicity	100.00%	42.09%
Age	90.00%	19.84%
Class/Socioeconomic Status	-	19.57%
Citizenship	70.00%	6.17%
Religion/Spirituality	30.00%	4.29%
Sexual Identity	40.00%	1.88%
Transgender Identity	20.00%	0.54%
Ability	40.00%	0.00%

DISCUSSION

Results from the analyses help to examine the national landscape of higher education and student affairs survey instruments in regard to demographic information collection. The following paragraphs highlight how current demographic data collection techniques inhibit or promote intersectional research.

Regarding demographic variable use across the tier-one journals, only two quantitative articles included transgender identity in their analyses. In both studies, the researchers employed the Multi-Institutional Study of Leadership as their survey instrument. Not surprisingly, sexual identity was included in both of these analyses as well. As previously stated, seven quantitative articles included sexual identity and two quantitative studies included transgender identity. The only tier-one higher education and student affairs journal to publish quantitative articles with sexual and transgender identity was the *Journal of College Student Development*. The general omission of sexual and transgender identities is highly problematic given the scope of our field. Among all the tier-one journals, the *Journal of College Student Development* is the only functional-specific publication. It concentrates largely on student development and learning, whereas the other tier-one journals are general higher education publications (Bray & Major, 2011). Renn (2010) wrote the following:

> Higher education scholars frequently divide their work into categories of students (experiences, outcomes, demographics, development), faculty (preparation, tenure, satisfaction), administrative leaders (career tracks, leadership style), organization (culture, structures, change), governance and finance (state oversight, boards of trustees, faculty governance), policy (national, state, institutional), and teaching (curriculum, pedagogy, technology). (p. 133)

Given that sexual and transgender identities were only included in two articles within the student-centered journal publication, it is clear that we are limiting the scope of quantitative research across social identities. Nowhere in these journals is there quantitative research that examines faculty, administration, organization, finance, policy, or teaching through the lens of sexuality or transgenderism. Furthermore, none of the 373 quantitative studies in the tier-one higher education journals included ability in their analyses.

These findings are astonishing and unacceptable given the importance of quantitative scholarship in advancing institutional, state, and national policies in higher education and student affairs (Stage, 2007). Sexual, transgender, and disability identities permeate all facets of higher education, including all constituents (students, faculty, administration, alumni), policy, and teaching. The five aforementioned tier-one journals in higher education and student affairs are the leading scholarly voices in our fields. Unfortunately, due to the subject and content of quantitative analyses, these journals are in essence erasing the experiences of several large groups of individuals, namely people with disabilities, transgender individuals, and sexual identity minorities. Consequently, institutional advocacy, policy reform, and resource allocation are all hindered by the absence of quantitative studies that closely examine these populations. Intersectionality calls for scholars to understand the relationship between people and their social locations with specific focus on power and privilege (Mahalingam, 2007). As a scholarly community, we have caught ourselves in a catch-22, whereby these underrepresented groups are underresearched, yet survey developers do not include these demographic questions because of a lack of empirical research on these populations.

Findings from this study demonstrate the high prevalence and use of certain higher education and student affairs survey instruments. As indicated in the results, the 19 most widely used survey instruments permeated one-third of all quantitative studies in tier-one journals. This alone justifies the need to closely examine the ways in which these survey instruments collect demographic data.

Among the widely used surveys from education nonprofit organizations, 12 of the 13 were individual-level surveys. This finding demonstrates the centrality of examining students, faculty, staff, and other constituents in higher education and student affairs. Clearly, demographic variables are essential to comprehensively understanding individual-level outcomes and relationships. As demonstrated in the results, certain education nonprofit organizations control a majority of the widely used survey instruments. To advocate for a more intersectional approach to higher education and student affairs research, change must begin with these organizations. In particular, the Cooperative Institutional Research Program, the National Survey of Student Engagement, the National Opinion Research Center, the Wabash National Study of Liberal Arts Education, and the College Student Experiences Questionnaire Assessment Program must reform their survey designs to be more inclusive of social identities. Not only will this change the statistical analyses possible with these data, but it will also demonstrate a strong commitment to intersectionality and giving voice to all higher education constituents.

As discussed by Cole (2009), scholars do not have to create a new set of methods for incorporating intersectionality into current research. Rather, researchers must reconceptualize the meaning and consequences of social categories. This process begins with revising and incorporating a broader understanding of individual experiences as framed through demographic information and social identities.

Furthermore, higher education and student affairs researchers must advocate for a wider and more intersectional approach to research among journals. The tier-one journals in this study published articles that included demographic information to varying degrees. Table 17.3 provided a comparison of demographic variables included in the most widely used higher education and student affairs instruments from education nonprofit organizations with demographic variables included in articles across the tier-one journals from 2010 through 2012. These findings are not surprising, leading to an understanding of the absence of certain demographic questions. A side-by-side comparison leads to the possibility that the more regularly demographic variables are included in survey designs, the more likely these demographics will be included in quantitative analyses. Especially in *Research in Higher Education* and *Higher Education,* which published 55.50% of all quantitative studies in tier-one journals, we must advocate for a stronger presence of complex social identities and demographics across all empirical analyses.

LIMITATIONS

As previously discussed, I only assessed demographic information collection from education nonprofit organizations. Though it is important to examine federal government surveys in regard to demographic collection, the inaccessibility of the instruments coupled with the near-impossible difficulty of advocating for change made it difficult to include these survey instruments in the analyses. Future studies should explore quantitative survey instruments in education from federal government agencies and ways in which policy makers and advocacy organizations can promote change for more inclusive demographic information collection.

Additionally, I was unable to include class/SES in portions of my analyses because of the uncertainty in how survey instruments operationalized the construct. Because I did not have code books or variable operationalizations for each instrument, I was unable to determine the ways in which researchers quantified class/SES. Future studies should examine class/SES as a quantitative construct to determine valid and reliable ways to include this construct through an intersectional lens.

The instruments examined in this study were used in only about one-third of all quantitative articles published from 2010 through 2012. I consciously decided to include only the most widely used survey instruments to demonstrate the high impact that these surveys have on the field of higher education and student affairs. Needless to say, though, it is important to advocate for an intersectional understanding of demographic information collection with all survey instruments, regardless of the frequency of use. When we create a culture of change and a stronger affirmation toward intersectional perspectives in quantitative designs, our scholarly community will be better prepared to advocate for all higher education constituents across and within social identities.

IMPLICATIONS

Intersectionality offers researchers new ways to operationalize complex social identities. Survey methodologists can modify demographic collection and analytic techniques to facilitate more intersectional research. Dubrow (2008) discussed that for quantitative scholars who want to incorporate intersectional theory with existing survey data, interaction terms are an appropriate way to measure relationships among social identities. Similarly, McCall (2005) advocated for a research design with demographic information as independent variables with main effects and interactions. She termed this technique as the categorical approach to intersectionality, "focus[ing] on the complexity of relationships among multiple social groups within and across analytical categories.... The subject is multigroup and the method is systematically comparative" (p. 1786). Multiple categories analyze intersections of demographics and categories within, simultaneously examining power and privilege in relation to social identities.

One major issue when conducting survey research is determining the number of participants required to obtain a representative and stable approximation of the population and of subpopulations. There are several risks in using too few participants. Covariation among factor items may not be stable when sample size is low. Further, when the ratio of participants to survey items is low and the sample size is small, chance may influence correlations among items to a fairly substantial degree (DeVellis, 2003). With small samples, a deviant sample has greater influence and presence than with a larger sample due to randomization and representation. Additionally, a small sample size may not adequately detect a significant effect (Kerlinger & Lee, 2000). With an increased sample size, the sampling distribution narrows and the standard error decreases.

If not enough participants are sampled, the entire population for which the instrument is intended may not be represented. To address this concern, both the sample size and participant composition should be a consideration. Nonrepresentative samples can be different from the intended population in two ways: by the level of attribute present in the sample as opposed to the intended population, and with a sample that is qualitatively rather than quantitatively different from the target population. The latter nonrepresentativeness can result when the sample is unlike the population in important ways (i.e., social identities), thus affecting the underlying causal structure relating variables to true scores and ultimately reliability (DeVellis, 2003). Researchers must take extra care in choosing a sample that closely represents the population for which the instrument is being developed (Ajzen & Fishbein, 1980; Nunnally & Bernstein, 1994). Due to the difficulty in recruiting certain subpopulations, survey methodologists may consider oversampling certain constituencies so there is a lesser threat of nonrepresentativeness. Furthermore, oversampling may provide a sufficient participant yield to conduct analyses using the categorical approach to intersectionality.

As evidenced, quantitative intersectional research does not come without difficulties. McCall (2005) discussed that "it is near impossible to publish grandly intersectional studies in top peer-reviewed journals using the categorical approach: the size and complexity of such a project is too great to contain in a single article" (p. 1787). Quantitative intersectional analyses usually require interaction effects through multilevel or hierarchical designs, providing a more complex estimation and interpretation of results. Still, quantitative scholars must not limit themselves in embracing a more intersectional approach to research in both demographic data collection and analyses. By expanding the scope of demographic variables included in higher education and student affairs research, scholars can have data accessible to conduct intersectional research. Without reforming the ways in which survey methodologists include demographic variables, scholars will continue to perpetuate a culture of exclusion in higher education and student affairs research that ignores various communities and social identities.

CONCLUSION

By approaching demographic information collection from an intersectional lens, I hope for this chapter to encourage a new wave and generation of quantitative empirical analyses that examine the intersections of identities and experiences in higher education and student affairs. Such an assertion has the potential to transform the scholarly body of higher education. Though this chapter has only fostered a surface-level dialogue of quantitative intersectional research, these findings and discussions can provide a starting point for higher education and student affairs scholars to advocate for systemic change in quantitative designs and survey instrumentation.

REFERENCES

Adams, M., Blumenfeld, W. J., Castaneda, C., Hackman, H., Peters, M., & Zungia X. (Eds.). (2013). *Readings for diversity and social justice* (2nd ed.). New York, NY: Routledge.

Ajzen, I., & Fishbein, M. (1980). *Understanding attitudes and predicting behavior.* Englewood Cliffs, NJ: Prentice Hall.

Astin, A. (1970a). The methodology of research on college impact (I). *Sociology of Education, 43,* 223–254.

Astin, A. (1970b). The methodology of research on college impact (II). *Sociology of Education, 43,* 437–450.

Astin, A. (1991). *Assessment for excellence: The philosophy and practice of assessment and evaluation in higher education.* New York, NY: Macmillan.

Bray, N. J., & Major, C. H. (2011). Status of journals in the field of higher education. *Journal of Higher Education, 82,* 479–503.

Cole, E. R. (2009). Intersectionality and research in psychology. *American Psychologist, 64,* 170–180.

Crenshaw, K. (1989). Demarginalizing the intersection of race and sex: A black feminist critique of antidiscrimination doctrine, feminist theory and antiracist politics. *The University of Chicago Legal Forum, 139,* 139–167.

Davis, K. (2008) Intersectionality as buzzword: A sociology of science perspective on what makes a feminist theory successful. *Feminist Theory, 9,* 67–85.

DeVellis, R. F. (2003). *Scale development: Theory and applications.* Newbury Park, CA: Sage.

Dubrow, J. K. (2008). How can we account for intersectionality in quantitative analysis of survey data? Empirical illustration for Central and Eastern Europe. *ASK, 17,* 85–100.

Kerlinger, F. N., & Lee, H. B. (2000). *Foundations of behavioral research* (4th ed.). Fort Worth, TX: Wadsworth/Thompson Learning.

Mahalingam, R. (2007). Culture, power and psychology of marginality. In A. Fuligni (Ed.), *Contesting stereotypes and creating identities Social categories, social identities, and educational participation* (pp. 42–65). New York, NY: Sage.

McCall, L. (2005). The complexity of intersectionality. *Signs, 30,* 1771–1800.

Nunnally, J. C., & Bernstein, I. H. (1994). *Psychometric theory* (3rd ed.). New York, NY: McGraw-Hill.

Pascarella, E. T. (1985). College environmental influences on learning and cognitive development: A critical review and synthesis. In J. Smart (Ed.), *Higher education: Handbook of theory and research* (Vol. 1, pp. 1–64). New York, NY: Agathon.

Pascarella, E. T., & Terenzini, P. T. (2005). *How college affects students* (Vol. 2). San Francisco, CA: Jossey-Bass.

Renn, K. A. (2010). LGBT and queer research in higher education: The state and status of the field. *Educational Researcher, 39,* 132–141.

Sanlo, R. (2002). Scholarship in student affairs: Thinking outside the triangle, or Tabasco on cantaloupe. *NASPA Journal, 39,* 166–180.

Stage, F. K. (2007). Answering critical questions using quantitative data. *New Directions for Institutional Research, 13,* 5–16.

Tinto, V. (1975). Dropout from higher education: A theoretical synthesis of recent research. *Review of Educational Research, 45,* 89–125.

Tinto, V. (1987). *Leaving college: Rethinking the causes and cures of student attrition.* Chicago, IL: University of Chicago Press.

Tinto, V. (1993). *Leaving college: Rethinking the causes and cures of student attrition* (2nd ed.). Chicago, IL: University of Chicago Press.

Weidman, J. (1989). Undergraduate socialization: A conceptual approach. In J. Smart (Ed.), *Higher education: Handbook of theory and research* (Vol. 5, pp. 289–322). New York, NY: Agathon.

PART THREE

Praxis

CHAPTER EIGHTEEN

The Women of Color Circle

Creating, Claiming, and Transforming Space for Women of Color on a College Campus

VALERIA SINCLAIR-CHAPMAN, SASHA ELOI,
AND SHARESE KING

We seldom think of conversation as a commitment, but it is. (Imara, as cited in hooks, 1993, p. 16)

Many students often feel that they have no voice, that they have nothing to say that is worthy of being heard. That is why conversation becomes such a vital intervention, for it not only makes room for every voice, it also presupposes that all voices must be heard. (hooks, 2009, p. 15)

In the early hours of January 15, 2011, a Black male student at our small, liberal arts, private university was stabbed to death by a fellow Black male student at a "gansta-" themed White fraternity party. Both the murdered student and his killer were well-known, well-liked members of the student body. Ostensibly, their fight was over the affections of a young Woman whom the first young man had dated for several years, but with whom things had ended a few weeks earlier. In the days immediately following the incident, the Women of Color Circle (WOCC) emerged as a desperate and courageous act of Black women staff and faculty joining together for the first time in an intentionally focused effort to "wrap our arms around" our besieged and mourning Black and Latina young women.

That the WOCC evolved to address new challenges and continued to engage women of color on campus is a testament to its role in filling a void in Black women's social and academic care. The violence between two Black men, the sudden loss of both as members of the academic community, the centrality of male/female relationships, and the contestation over Black women's bodies as sites of social conflict brought the absence of structured, community-based social supports into sharp relief. The consequences of historical divides between the university and the local Black community, along with customary divisions of labor between faculty and staff, distance between students and faculty, and traditional hierarchies and power dynamics in higher education institutions, had converged to leave people of color unprepared, unprotected, and unsupported in a time of grave crisis. Many participants in the WOCC were able to reclaim a sense of belonging and (re)establish a sense of self and safety on campus even as the fallout from the incident continued through much of the following academic year.

The WOCC created a structure for the care of Black women and other women of color built upon traditions of Black women's caretaking at kitchen tables and church meetings, on bus rides and porch steps, and in hair salons (Collins, 2000; Harris-Lacewell, 2004). WOCC participants engaged in intersectional praxis as an organic outcome of their work. There was no master plan or guidebook to which to turn (although, in retrospect bell hooks's [1993] *Sisters of the Yam* could have fit the bill). Drawing on the work of the Combahee River Collective, Townsend-Bell (2009) proposes that Black women's activism is inherently intersectional because "a focus on themselves requires attention to multiple categories of difference… race, class, gender and, to some degree, nationality" (p. 4), and because when Black women fight against their own marginalization, "any achievement they make has a direct and positive impact on every other population" (p. 4).

Intersectional praxis requires alliances across differences internal to the group and the incorporation of difference into the work of the group (Townsend-Bell 2009, p. 5). While not naming what they did "intersectionality," the foundational practices of the WOCC allowed for and encouraged the interrogation of within-group differences in ethnicity, nationality, sexuality, class, religion, occupation, and status. This was accomplished through reading and discussing feminist literature, including portions of Audre Lorde's (1984) *Sister Outsider*, Patricia Hill Collins's (2000) *Black Feminist Thought,* and Cherrie Moraga and Gloria Anzaldua's (1984) edited collection in *This Bridge Called My Back,* to name a few. Scholarship, poetry, music, videos, cultural events, campus speakers, and campus events were all used to foster self-discovery and empowerment in the WOCC.

In what follows, we discuss, as founding members and practitioners, the utility and value of the WOCC as an approach to self-care and empowerment in environments where women of color find themselves confronting entrenched and codified norms of silence and oppression, as in many predominantly White institutions (PWIs). Where appropriate, we include scholarship to buttress our claims. For the most part, however, the perspectives presented are based on our own personal experiences and observations while engaged in the work of the WOCC.

It is fitting at this point, to provide some background on the authors and their relationship to the WOCC. Each of us was a founding member of the WOCC and was present in the very first, hours-long, tear-filled meeting.

In January 2011, I (VSC) was a new, part-time administrator and instructor in the social sciences. I had taught one of the young men involved in the altercation in several courses.

I (SE) was a staff person in a student academic affairs unit with primary responsibility for underrepresented minority (URM), low-income, and first-generation students.

I (SK) was an active student leader, young scholar, and close friend of one of the young men in the altercation.

Two of us have moved on to new positions—VSC to a new academic appointment and SK to graduate school—but we all remain deeply connected to and affected by our shared time in the WOCC.

BACKGROUND

The midsized northeastern university where we worked is an elite PWI, located in an urban area, with a population of URM students comprising a little over 9% of the student body. Extant research shows that the experiences of URM students at PWIs are markedly different from that of majority students (Bennett, Cole, & Thompson, 2000; Karp, O'Gara, & Hughes 2008). Our recent experiences support such claims. At the institution, majority students reported feeling supported by the university in the wake of the incident, including the president of the fraternity where the incident took place, while some URM students reported feelings of alienation and anxiety.

Students of color were simultaneously hyper-visible and invisible. They were being reminded of the negative notions of deviance and difference that hover like specters in shadows on PWIs, waiting for one failed test, one public embarrassment, or one tragic event to confirm that maybe, just maybe, these students really did not belong. Black and Latino students quickly moved into action. They set up tables to raise money and organize meal deliveries for the slain young man's family. They set about marching from the campus to the church for the funeral service, undaunted by the frigid January weather.

In response, faculty and staff were actively trying to figure out next steps. More than 30 women, including students, faculty, and staff, responded to an informal call to gather and stayed for three hours of talking, screaming, cursing, praying, crying, and healing. After several months, the WOCC was solidly established as a site for women's intellectual engagement and activism on campus. Relying on ourselves, we had begun to create what Collins (2000) terms, a *safe space* and what hooks (1990) identified as "a space of radical openness" (p. 145) on the margins. For hooks, the spaces that women claim on the margins are never safe from external threat, though hooks and Collins appear to agree on the necessity for openness and safety among group participants.

By the end of that first semester, the students were impatient with the WOCC's focus on the underlying social and structural origins of the January 15th altercation. A vocal contingent of students pushed the WOCC to transition into an organization engaged not only in addressing issues such as the lack of a permanent physical space for minority students to gather on campus and the unequal policing of minority students, but also in addressing the current concerns of women of color on campus, such as life after graduation, relationships, gender pay equity, and personal finances. Participants, especially students, wanted discussions whose outcomes they could apply directly to improving their own lives and well-being.

The WOCC mission statement (2012), developed by students at the end of the second year, reflected the roots of our convening and the focus on the empowerment and well-being of Black and Latino women. It read as follows:

> The Women of Color Circle (WOCC) is comprised of [university] students, staff, and faculty focused on Community Awareness, Research, Education, and Service (CARES). The purpose of WOCC-CARES is to raise awareness of the experiences of Black women and Latinas and to facilitate their inclusion, voice, and leadership in the [university] community.

CREATING SAFE SPACE

In *Black Feminist Thought*, Collins (2000) fittingly asks the question, "How do U.S. Black women identify the specific issues associated with controlling images of Black Womanhood without safe spaces where we can talk freely?" (p. 110). Safe spaces are arenas where Black women (and for us, Latinas, women of mixed-race, and global women of color) define and redefine themselves and their circumstances, potentially developing what Cohen (1999) referred to as an *alternative worldview*. Cohen observed that through formal and informal interactions in indigenous organizations, marginalized individuals may be able to "transform and redefine" (p. 52) issues in ways that contribute to collective mobilization to change their own circumstances. In constructing the WOCC, conveners immediately faced three related issues of membership, each requiring an answer to the question, "Who belongs?" In a nutshell, these concerns engaged three sites of intersectionality for women of color: gender, race, and class/status. We discuss each in turn.

While WOCC conveners acknowledged the shared vulnerability of all students of color, we also recognized that the young men and women had somewhat different work to do, somewhat different conversations to be had. We decided to organize as women, inviting the men to one or two open events during the year. It was important that the young women be reminded that they alone have the right to give or refuse consent in relationships with others. Husbands, boyfriends, and lovers have no claims of ownership over women's bodies, and thus, fighting to claim a Woman's affections holds no merit. The necessity for this approach became more evident as the young women began taking sides. Therefore, a primary task of our group was to lay the foundation for healing. For us, this healing came through voicing our fear, hurt, anger, disappointment, and shame. Our chief task was to break the silence that threatened to smother us.

As the WOCC was organized, we also had to confront issues of race. Would this initial Circle be a meeting of only Black and Latino women? Certainly, White female colleagues showed support and expressed interest in joining the WOCC as allies, friends, and family. As Hazel Carby (1996) points out, it is not unusual for Black women and women of color to grapple with the tensions between inclusion and racial justice on the one hand and self-determination and self-definition on the other. Kimberle Crenshaw (1991) warns against color-blind approaches that risk reproducing social inequities by treating all people the same. Other scholars have noted that Black women's safe spaces can be misinterpreted as "separatist" (Collins, 2000, p. 110), particularly as colleges and universities become more diverse. Because women of color have gained uneven entry into predominantly White social institutions, including institutions of higher education, Collins (2000) argues that in these environments, we encounter "new forms of racism and sexism that require equally innovative responses" (p. 202). Our response was to establish the WOCC as a safe space explicitly centered on the well-being, empowerment, and safety of women of color. Women of all racial and ethnic backgrounds were welcome to—and did—participate; however, our mission remained squarely focused on bringing the issues and interests of women of color from the margins to the center. The racial and ethnic composition of the Circle generated heated discussions over an appropriate name for the new group. Despite the debates, we stuck with the Women of Color designation, noting its inclusivity of Black women and Latinas, as well as its capacity to include indigenous peoples and Black and Brown women from across the globe.

After addressing gender and race, conveners also had to deal with differences in status and power. With the Circle as an organizing framework, we deliberately sought to flatten out hierarchies in our gathering. Recognizing the need to create a familial environment also required addressing the potential for family dysfunctionality, including patriarchy, the modeling of constrictive gender roles, and power differentials based on age, status, and so forth (McDonald, 2007). The academy presents power dynamics and embedded hierarchies that could impede our objectives of candid, truthful conversations (Collins, 2000). We recognized that those at or near the top of university leadership faced cross-pressures in their commitments to a university-centered versus student-, women-centered agenda, should conflict arise. We also acknowledged that our own behavior could change when someone with the power to evaluate us was in the room. To mitigate the challenges presented by academic hierarchies, top administrators were kept in the loop but not invited to attend the early meetings. Like hooks's (1993) *Sisters of the Yam,* our objective was healing, not policymaking. We wanted to open opportunity to honest engagement, not professional performance.

A final concern was how to conduct this meeting just a few days after the incident in the absence of an established women of color network, when emotions might run high and feelings were still raw. Not only might many of the women in the room not know each other, several of them would arrive from different and potentially opposing camps. Some of the women were friends or relatives of the slain student, others were friends of the accused, while still others were uncertain but hurt and angry. In an unscripted environment, things could easily spiral out of control. Restorative justice circles (RJC) provided a framework for bringing a variety of individuals with potentially conflicting perspectives to the table. A counselor from the university's counseling center proposed RJC as a tool to allow people to come together, ensure that potentially conflicting views could be shared, and open the pathway to a healing rather than blaming exchange. The basic tenets of RJC for our purposes included a focus on people and restoring relationships rather than punishment or blame, the use of inclusive processes, and mutual respect (Hansen, 2005). RJC was indispensable for the work of the WOCC in promoting real conversation, disrupting superficial norms of self-presentation, and allowing women to move into and out of multiple experiences and categories.

THE CIRCLE IN PRACTICE

In the WOCC, we unapologetically and collectively set about reclaiming our sense of self and safety as Black women and women of color in a new and evolving reality. We found that the Circle became a sacred space, taking on a life of its own. Literally and practically, organizing our seats in a circle reinforced the mission of sister-work. In a sense, we developed what Murguía, Padilla, and Pavel (1991) referred to as "ethnic enclaves" (p. 436). Their research found that participation in ethnic organizations enabled Hispanic and Native American students to scale down the larger campus environment by forming smaller "enclaves" through which students felt more comfortable exploring and integrating into the larger campus community. Physically organizing our seats into the Circle symbolically marked entry into an ethnic enclave.

The Circle itself had a mystical effect. For example, on the handful of occasions when space limitations required that the Circle deviate from its loosely circular layout and women sat on the sidelines, the tone and nature of the conversation changed. The positioning of women in the room impacted the discussions, and, as a new periphery was created, side conversations emerged. Discussion shifted from egalitarian mutual engagement to some women, typically older women in the group (professors, graduate students, staff), giving advice to younger women. The objective of our monthly gathering was not to teach but rather to share. Participants needed to listen and speak as co-equals, peers, and sisters. In this way, the WOCC approach encouraged bounded conversations around predetermined themes or topics but open-ended dialogue.

After the initial meeting, the Circle gained momentum and developed its own rhythm. We began to convene once monthly, typically the last Friday of the month at 6 or 6:30 p.m., early enough to allow students to attend and still enjoy weekend plans. Each meeting opened with a simple meal. At the start of the Circle, a welcome was extended to everyone along with "rules" about how the Circle would operate. The rules included allowing each participant the opportunity to speak, listening actively and without judgment, and honoring confidentiality.

To facilitate egalitarian exchange, we used a "totem" or a meaningful item that was passed to each individual in the Circle. The totem can be just about anything, but preferably should be something symbolically meaningful and/or physically weighty to serve as a useful reminder of the significance of the moment. The individual holding the totem also "holds the floor" and has the right to speak, sing, pray, scream, or simply keep silent with the full attention of all of the people in the room. It was through this process that participants became familiar with their own voices and the rich diversity of expression and experience that the group collectively embodied. Thus, the WOCC began a process of "coming to voice" or the empowering recognition that each of us has a right and responsibility to honor her own story in the telling and in the hearing, no matter how dark or joyous, painful or celebratory (Collins, 2000, p. 100).

The Circle also served to invert traditional educational norms—students could be teachers, teachers could be students; staff as experts, faculty as learners (hooks, 2009). The meetings included discussions of intimate partner violence, girlhood molestation, loneliness, racist roommates and professors, failing or stellar grades, romantic relationships, Black-Latino relations, new jobs, graduations, and agenda-setting for change. African American students at PWIs experience considerably higher levels of stress related to their perceptions of campus climate and feelings of isolation (Steele, 2010). The Circle interrupted students' internalization of their experiences of isolation, discrimination, and oppression in classrooms and campus social life by creating a space where students, as well as staff and faculty, could openly discuss their feelings.

As Imara observed in the opening epigraph, "We seldom think of conversation as commitment, but it is" (as cited in hooks, 1993, p. 16). Confidentiality was an important practice in the Circle, and its significance was emphasized at the opening and closing of every meeting. Not once did word get back that someone was using what was said in the Circle against someone else. Although participants did not always agree with each other, the women practiced listening with openness and not judgment. The flattening of hierarchies, range of discussion topics, inclusive norms around both speaking and listening, and the value participants placed on keeping the work of the Circle private created a space where participants could begin to see themselves anew. After only a few months together, the women in the Circle began to envision new ways to engage the campus as legitimate stakeholders and from a position of strength.

MAINTAINING A SAFE SPACE

As one might imagine, beginning the Circle involved widespread support across units, administrative levels, generations and professional positions. In contrast, maintaining the Circle over time relied on a small, dedicated handful of mostly Black female staff. When the WOCC might have been allowed to lapse due to competing demands or what appeared to be waning interests, students requested that it be revived. The staff and faculty were not compensated for the work of maintaining the Circle. In fact, despite its importance, this work was largely invisible, and when it was acknowledged was viewed as purely voluntary—in addition to the jobs faculty and staff were being paid to do. That Black women's care work is largely unrecognized and uncompensated is not unusual (Jordan-Zachery, 2013; Nzinga-Johnson, 2013). The unconventional membership of the Circle also came at a price. The WOCC was neither a student organization nor a staff organization. Because the Circle did not "belong" to any department or affinity group, it therefore did not have a budget for the first several years. Although the Circle requested and received occasional support for cultural outings or conferences, a handful of faculty and staff provided most of the necessary financial support needed to maintain the Circle.

Participation in the Circle was voluntary and fluid. There was an expectation from students that the WOCC meet monthly, even if participation was unpredictable. Attending a circle was all that was required to join the WOCC, which amounted to adding participants' names to a central e-mail distribution list. Those who received the e-mailed invitations were encouraged to share the invitation with others in their circle of friends. In that way, the Circle was available to those who needed it. Some women would attend all meetings, helping to plan topics or generating a longer-term agenda. Other women might only attend a meeting if the topic struck a chord with them. Both regular and sporadic attendees were important contributors to the utility and longevity of the group.

The WOCC helped many students manage diversity-related conflicts on the college campus. The Circle presented itself as a space where students could comfortably voice their authentic perspectives. The nurturing space of the Circle allowed students the opportunity to gain a better understanding of themselves in relation to and as a part of a deep and wide, if numerically small, group of women on campus. This cross-generational meeting of women drew on Black women's self-care traditions: raising uncomfortable issues, solving problems, celebrating triumphs, encouraging women to claim and transform their own lives. Women in the WOCC envisioned change and took action. They shared the benefits of participation in the WOCC through presentations on creating safe spaces at gender studies conferences, including one national conference for women student leaders. Several young women from the WOCC fundamentally transformed the campus with a successful proposal for a residential leadership house, the first student-led, minority-focused physical space at the university.

The Women of Color Circle represented an attempt to model the sister-work of Black and Latina communities within the confines of an institution of higher education. The Circle operated as a "kitchen table" where participants could converse, argue, cry, and share their truths with the aim of teaching and learning who we say we are. Committing to the practice of the Circle flattened hierarchies in ways that deconstructed and challenged power structures embedded in many male-dominated Western institutions, including PWIs. This egalitarian forum, while disconcerting to many, including, occasionally, its own participants, created the infrastructure for safe space and the pathway to coming to voice. Safe spaces need not be precipitated by tragedy. Here, we suggest that women of color at PWIs serve themselves and their institutions well by carving out space for themselves from which they can challenge and transform the environments where they learn, work, and live.

ACKNOWLEDGMENTS

The authors wish to thank Julia Jordan-Zachery and Elizabeth Daniele for their instructive feedback on versions of this manuscript.

REFERENCES

Bennett, C., Cole, D., & Thompson, J. (2000). Preparing teachers of color at a predominantly white university: A case study of project TEAM. *Teaching and Teacher Education, 16,* 445–464.

Carby, H. (1996). White Woman listen! Black feminism and the boundaries of sisterhood. In H. A. Baker, Jr., M. Diawara, & R. H. Lindebor (Eds.), *Black British cultural studies: A reader* (pp. 61–86). Chicago, IL: University of Chicago Press.

Cohen, C. J. (1999). *The boundaries of blackness: AIDS and the breakdown of black politics.* Chicago, IL: University of Chicago Press.

Collins, P. H. (2000). *Black feminist thought: Knowledge, consciousness, and the politics of empowerment* (2nd ed.). New York, NY: Routledge.

Crenshaw, K. (1991). Mapping the margins: Intersectionality, identity politics, and violence against women of color. *Stanford Law Review, 43*, 1241–1299.

Hansen, T. (2005). *Restorative justice practices and principles in schools.* Saint Paul, MN: Center for Restorative Justice & Peacemaking, School of Social Work, University of Minnesota.

Harris-Lacewell, M. V. (2004). *Barbershops, bibles, and BET: Everyday talk and black political thought.* Princeton, NJ: Princeton University Press.

hooks, b. (1990). *Yearning: Race, gender, and cultural politics.* Boston, MA: South End.

hooks, b. (1993). *Sisters of the yam: Black women and self-recovery.* Boston, MA: South End.

hooks, b. (2009). *Teaching critical thinking: Practical wisdom.* New York, NY: Taylor & Francis.

Jordan-Zachery, J. S. (2013). Black women occupying the academy: Merging critical mothering and mentoring to survive and thrive. In. S. Nzinga-Johnson (Ed.), *Laboring positions: Black women, mothering, and the academy* (pp. 273–291). Bradford, Ontario, Canada: Demeter.

Karp, M., O'Gara, L., & Hughes, K. (2008). *An exploration of Tinto's integration framework for community college students* (CCRC Working Paper No. 12). Retrieved from Columbia University Academic Commons website: http://academiccommons.columbia.edu/catalog/ac%3A145016

Lorde, A. (1984). *Sister outsider: Essays and speeches by Audre Lorde.* Freedom, CA: Crossing Press.

McDonald, K. B. (2007). *Embracing sisterhood: Class, identity, and contemporary black women.* Lanham, MD: Rowman & Littlefield.

Moraga, C., & Anzaldua, G. (Eds.). (1984). *This bridge called my back* (2nd ed.). New York, NY: Kitchen Table Women of Color Press.

Murguía, E., Padilla, R. V., & Pavel, M. (1991). Ethnicity and the concept of social integration in Tinto's model of institutional departure. *Journal of College Student Development, 32*, 433–439.

Nzinga-Johnson, S. (2013). Introduction: Extending the boundaries. In. S. Nzinga-Johnson (Ed.), *Laboring positions: Black women, mothering, and the academy* (pp. 1–32). Bradford, Ontario: Demeter Press.

Steele, C. (2010). *Whistling Vivaldi: And other clues to how stereotypes affect us.* New York, NY: W. W. Norton.

Townsend-Bell, E. E. (2009, August). *Intersectional praxis.* Paper presented at the 2009 annual meeting of the American Political Science Association, Toronto, Ontario, Canada.

Women of Color Circle. (2012). *Mission statement.* Unpublished document, University of Rochester, Rochester, NY.

CHAPTER NINETEEN

Utilizing Intersectionality to Engage Dialogue in Higher Education

BETTY JEANNE TAYLOR, RYAN A. MILLER,
AND CLAUDIA GARCÍA-LOUIS

Discussions of social identity intersections are critical in examining systems of privilege and oppression and engaging social justice dialogue throughout academia. In praxis, conceptual models can become useful mechanisms for delivering interactive educational sessions where participants build awareness about their own social identities, as well as perspectives different than their own. This chapter introduces an adapted model of Intersections of Identities (Taylor, 2011) that can be utilized in the facilitation of social justice training programs with faculty, staff, students, and community members to advance understandings of our multiple, intersecting social identities.

The Intersections of Identities model presents the concept of intersectionality as a tangible, practical catalyst for self-reflection and dialogue. The model is useful in establishing the training foundation before discussing context and salience of identities, historical and current systems of oppression, power and privilege, and participants' individual and collective roles in perpetuating and interrupting those systems. Utilized in practice, the model encourages self-reflections on identity and is based on the conceptual framework presented by the Model of Multiple Dimensions of Identity (Jones & McEwen, 2000) as well as the Social Identity Wheel (Alimo & Treviño, 2000). This chapter reviews the relevant literature on identity intersectionality, outlines a process for facilitating dialogue using the Intersections of Identities model, and offers implications for practice.

INTERSECTIONALITY AND HIGHER EDUCATION

While not named as such, the concept of intersectionality was first expressed by notable scholars including Du Bois (1920/2003), Baldwin (1963), hooks (1981), and Anzaldúa (1987), to name only a few. In "Demarginalizing the Intersection of Race and Sex," Crenshaw (1989) brought greater visibility, naming the concept of intersectionality and discussing the "tendency to treat race and gender as mutually exclusive categories of experience and analysis," which results in Black women being "theoretically erased" (p. 139). Collins (2000) explained that Black feminist thought "challenges additive analyses of oppression" and instead views each system of oppression as a unique component of an overarching, interlocking "matrix of domination" (p. 270). Early theorists examining marginalized and underrepresented populations have implied (often by omission) that individuals experience only one identity at a time, as identity group labels have reduced the complexity of multiple intersecting identities. While the concept of intersectionality has roots in sociology and Black feminist scholarship, intersectionality has over time become an interdisciplinary approach for considering and analyzing societal structures of power. A prominent, contemporary strain of research within identity development is acknowledging the intersectional nature of multiple identities, asserting that each individual possesses many personal and social identities that operate simultaneously in a complicated landscape informed by privilege and oppression (Berger & Guidroz, 2009; Dill & Zambrana, 2009; Josselson & Harway, 2012; Pliner & Banks, 2012). Groups at the intersections face distinct experiences of privilege and oppression based on their own intersectionality of identities.

In higher education, intersectionality as concept and practice has only recently become part of the social identity development scholarship. Many theories of college student development, and identity development in general, tend to present a stair-step or stage model that foregrounds one particular aspect of identity, such as race, gender, sexual orientation, or disability. These models may imply linearity and idealize a particular final stage, while neglecting to acknowledge the role that other identities play in development. Students undergo dynamic identity transformations during the span of their college careers, and simplistic identity models do not adequately capture such changes (Harper, 2011). Calling for an intersectional approach to higher education scholarship, Museus and Griffin (2011) asserted that studying students along a single dimension of identity at a time prevents scholars from understanding and responding to the changing educational landscape.

The Model of Multiple Dimensions of Identity (Jones & McEwen, 2000) offers one intersectional departure from such linear models, proposing that various aspects of one's identity may shift in salience and importance depending on the changing context and time period of a person's life. The Reconceptualized Model of Multiple Dimensions of Identity (Abes, Jones, & McEwen, 2007) includes the addition of a meaning-making filter, indicating the importance of considering the impact of contextual influences within multiple intersecting identities. Expanding on their previous work, Jones and Abes (2013) discussed anecdotal evidence that the Model of Multiple Dimensions of Identity is being used in practice and specified that published accounts of these uses are rare. This chapter offers one example of how the concepts introduced in Jones and McEwen (2000) are used in diversity education sessions at the University of Texas at Austin for student, faculty, staff, and community participants. The Intersections of Identities model encourages participants to reflect on personal and social identities as a comprehensive representation of oneself, creating a connection among identities, privilege, and oppression. Practical use of the Intersections of Identities model, created in 2011 and based on Jones and McEwen's (2000) Model of Multiple Dimensions of Identity, has been further informed by revisions in Abes et al. (2007) as well as Jones and Abes (2013), which have influenced the continued development of the facilitation and discussion processes. Thus, the Intersections of Identities model is offered as one practical application of the concepts addressed by the Model of Multiple Dimensions of Identity.

As institutions of higher education become more diverse, there is a heightened obligation to implement educational programs that prioritize reflective learning about self as well as learning about perspectives other than one's own. This is done so that institutions develop and sustain campus climates that are inclusive, accessible, and welcoming (Hurtado, Milem, Clayton-Pedersen, & Allen, 1998). Faculty, staff and university administrators, in particular, have the obligation to reflect on their own perspectives and challenge themselves to become catalysts for change. Critically assessing how individuals' experiences affect their sense of belonging on college campuses and how one's own actions affect campus climate will provide a critical lens through which to examine oneself (Pérez Huber, 2010). Individual experiences are based on many considerations, including the intersection of identities and contextual factors. Acknowledging that identities are complex is critical in conceptualizing how over time, lived experiences are compounded and materialize into individual realities.

Hytten and Bettez (2011) found that student programs with an emphasis on social justice increase awareness of self and initiate the critical process of engaging difficult conversations. This is particularly important when members of populations that have historically been marginalized have a heightened sense of awareness regarding how they present themselves and are perceived by others in various educational spaces. For example, students of color undergo a process of identity mediation, in which the way they position themselves in different settings is influenced by expectations and environment (Nasir, McLaughlin, & Jones, 2009; Romo, 2011). Accordingly, students with dominant group identities are often unaware of their privilege: "The ease of not being aware of privilege is an aspect of privilege itself, what some call 'the luxury of obliviousness'" (Johnson, 2006, p. 22).

INTERSECTIONS OF IDENTITIES MODEL DESIGN AND GOALS

Effective social justice education programs encourage participants to reflect on their own social identity positionalities and the impact of positionalities in terms of power and privilege. It is critical to recognize that how we are socialized and positioned as "outsider" or "insider" has a profound influence on attitudes and behaviors (Collins, 1986). Integrating intersectionality in social justice education programs helps participants develop awareness about themselves and others, in terms of considering the complexities of multiple identities as well as empowering participants to be heard.

Social justice education programs in practice vary widely, though many social justice education pedagogies are rooted in academic and activist traditions with the overarching goal of education for positive social change. In designing the Intersections of Identities model, elements were combined from the Social Identity Wheel (Alimo & Treviño, 2000; Zúñiga, Cytron-Walker, & Kachwaha, 2004), utilized in practice and first introduced via Intergroup Relations Center curriculum for Intergroup Dialogue courses at Arizona State University, as well as elements from the Model of Multiple Dimensions of Identity (Abes et al., 2007; Jones & McEwen, 2000), a conceptual model of multiple dimensions of identity that evolved from a grounded theory study conducted by Jones and McEwen (2000). Essentially, the design of the Intersections of Identities model utilizes the practical application of the Social Identity Wheel, while incorporating a more literal representation of identity intersections, via intersecting ovals representing multiple intersecting identities. Through reflective questions and facilitated conversations in small and large groups, facilitators also introduce the concepts of context, salience, privilege, and systems of oppression. These elements are not represented visually in the model but are introduced at various lengths depending on the particular group and educational session being facilitated.

The Intersections of Identities model (see Figure 19.1) serves as an interactive component of social justice education programs (Taylor, 2011). At the University of Texas at Austin, the Diversity Education Initiatives unit has facilitated programs using these concepts with faculty and staff in departmental workshops including a professional development series; with undergraduate and graduate students in spaces such as academic courses, first-year peer mentoring workshops, and sessions preparing teaching assistants and assistant instructors for classroom instruction; and with community members external to the university in contexts such as K-12 teacher and counselor training sessions as well as new student orientation at a seminary. The program goals encourage participants to do the following:

1. Develop awareness regarding their own intersecting identities.
2. Develop awareness regarding perspectives different from their own.

3. Identify and analyze individual, social/cultural, and institutional systems of oppression.

4. Develop capacity and strategy to interrupt those systems of oppression.

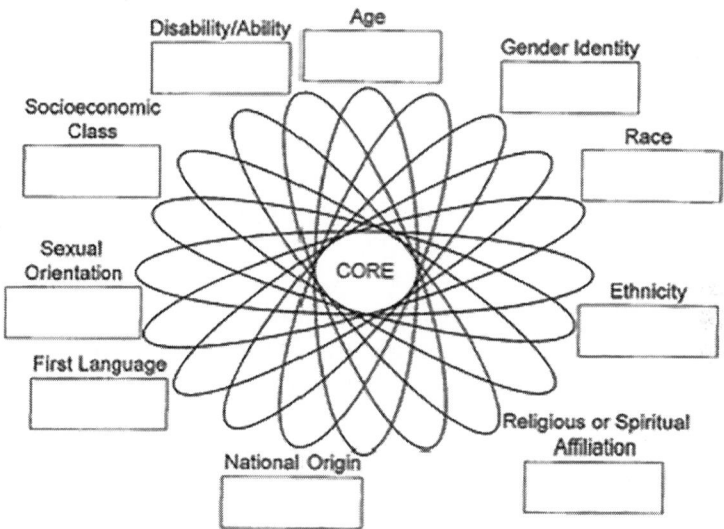

Fig 19.1. Intersections of Identities Model. Adapted from "A Conceptual Model of Multiple Dimensions of Identity," by S. R. Jones and M. K. McEwen, 2000, *Journal of College Student Development, 41,* 405–414. Copyright by the American College Personnel Association (ACPA). Adapted with permission.

FACILITATION OF INTERSECTIONS OF IDENTITIES MODEL

Utilizing the Intersections of Identities model, participants can reflect on their own individual identities within broader social identity categories. Given the opportunity to name each identity, which corresponds with each intersecting oval, participants can consider a representation of their whole selves in relation to their multiple identities. Participants are also asked to consider the role of identity salience (Tajfel & Turner, 1979) by responding to reflective questions regarding the significance of their own intersecting identities at the given point in time. Identity salience may change depending on contextual influences at the point in time, as indicated by Jones and McEwen (2000): "The particular salience of identity dimensions depended upon the contexts in which they were experienced. Therefore, both difference and privilege worked to mediate the connection with and salience of various identity dimensions" (p. 410).

The social identity categories represented in the Intersections of Identities model are each connected to systems of oppression, privilege, and power; however, those listed are not exhaustive, and facilitators can offer participants the chance to discuss other social identities. While participants are asked to write in how they identify regarding each category—a decision-making process that suggests a series of choices, which is ideally unpacked later in the facilitation—they are not asked to check a box or select an option from a predefined list of identities. This has provided a freedom for which some participants have voiced appreciation. If not presented with these categories, many participants may consider only a few salient social identities and may often neglect those identities that afford them a degree of privilege. The act of naming identities that are in positions of privilege (or not) may make visible those identities that are not often considered in the daily lives of participants. Indeed, we have found that some participants without disabilities have experienced expressed uncertainty in naming an identity in the disability/ ability category, just as some White participants have been unsure how to identify their race and ethnicity. Each of these points can become an opportunity for dialogue and continued learning in-group debriefing.

Understanding multiple social identities is beneficial in establishing a foundation of self-awareness in social justice education. Drawing on the Social Identity Wheel, participants are asked to reflect in writing about the identities they think about most often and least often, the identities that most affect how they perceive themselves and how others perceive them, and their own identity intersections that are most significant. These questions are not presented as formulaic or as items on a checklist; skilled facilitators must repeatedly consider the space, assessing the questions and tensions that arise for participants and make adjustments as needed. Gaining perspective on one's own multiple identities is a helpful first step before engaging in learning about others' perspectives. As Adams, Bell, and Griffin (2007) asserted, participants who engage in such reflection "can learn to identify and challenge what are often unexamined beliefs about themselves and others and understand how these beliefs have been established through an unequal system based on hierarchies of privilege and power" (p. 70). Once participants have named their own social identities within provided social identity categories, they explore positionality of those groups related to privilege and power before engaging in an interactive dyad with another participant and processing in the larger group.

Further reflective questions encourage participants to explore the impact specifically related to the intersectionality of two or more identities. Extending the session, the facilitators introduce concepts related to power and privilege and ask participants to consider the ways in which they have privilege and/or do not have privilege based on their identities. Documenting their own identities, reflecting on individual privileges related to group membership, and having the opportunity to reflect and share perspectives with others is an effective format for introducing concepts such as social identities, intersectionality, privilege, and oppression: "What 'develops' is a person's increasingly informed, differentiated, and inclusive understanding of within-group and between-group commonalities and differences, and a personalized awareness of how these understandings bear on one's everyday behaviors" (Adams et al., 2007, p. 18). When asked to evaluate their experiences at the conclusion of educational sessions, participants reflected on what they found most beneficial. Some examples of statements from participants in sessions facilitated by University of Texas at Austin staff include the following:

- "Identity intersections; [I] never considered myself from so many directions."
- "Internal processing—noticing/learning about my own perspectives that I've never previously spent time thinking about."
- "Hearing others' perspectives; talking about saliency."

CONSIDERATIONS IN ADAPTING MODELS FOR PRACTICE

Translating intersectionality theory to practice in diversity education necessarily involves a number of decisions about how to represent theoretical models and encourage participants to consider their own identities in meaningful and constructive ways. There is a tension undeniably present when facilitators introduce these models in practice: Each participant in the room has a perspective and will make decisions about how to share that perspective via verbal engagement and even body language. Further, it would be difficult to introduce sweeping concepts such as identity, salience, context, intersectionality, privilege, and oppression in one or several educational sessions of several hours in length. Semester or quarter-long academic courses may provide opportunities to delve more deeply into each of these concepts. Regardless of course offerings, there are routinely one-time training sessions and workshops with faculty, staff, and students that diversity education professionals in higher education are sought out to facilitate.

With this complexity as well as practical realities in mind, sessions must be carefully designed and led by skilled facilitators. Even the most experienced educators will need to tailor their sessions to the needs of participants on the spot in real time. Specific participants and the goals, length, content, and follow-up may be a negotiation between the facilitator(s) and the person requesting a session, but many of these factors may be partially or completely out of the facilitators' control. A facilitator may have a detailed plan of content for a two-hour session, which may be completely upended by a triggering comment or insightful reflection that steers group conversations in a different direction.

It is in this dynamic group process that the Intersections of Identities model can be used as a starting point for discussing social identities and intersectionality. Deepening the session, concepts of contextual influences and salience of identities can be introduced and considered by participants on a personal level using a number of tools, such as written reflection, paired discussions, and conversations in the large group. Depending on the prior knowledge and composition of the group, a significant portion of the session may be spent on developing foundational concepts of personal and social identities. These conversations can prepare participants for deeper conversations in future sessions. Groups for which these concepts are familiar or discussed on a regular basis may benefit from increased time discussing specific intersections of identities that are salient to participants and how these intersections are influenced by contextual factors. Even with limited time and practical demands, facilitators ideally introduce concepts that remain in participants' minds and are reinforced and expanded through other curricular, co-curricular, and programmatic offerings on campus.

IMPLICATIONS FOR DIVERSITY EDUCATION

The Intersections of Identities model offers a variety of implications for social justice education in colleges and universities. Use of the model can be framed within a need for increased diversity and social justice education on campus. Further, this increased education must be sustained and interwoven in various campus contexts. Moving beyond a one-time conversation, use of the model can facilitate deeper understandings of individuals' identity intersections and how those intersections affect their experiences on campus and in the world. For instance, many campuses host training sessions and courses that examine identity along a singular dimension, such as a program that promotes safer and more welcoming campus cultures for students with disabilities or for students of color, but intersectionality is often neglected in these conversations. Intersectionality as a practice for social justice education can create spaces where participants can name and contemplate lived experiences that may be unnamed or misrepresented. Educators, in particular, have a responsibility to engage this conversation, as Accapadi (2007) implored:

> Our responsibility as educators committed to social justice, is to reframe our "standard of humanity," so that we are asking different questions, treating the actual cause of the conflicts presented to us and not their external symptoms, and challenging our own notions of "normal." (p. 214)

Practitioners utilizing this model should carefully plan for its use and view the model as a foundation for facilitating dialogue and understanding the implications of power, privilege, and oppression. When separate from the context of power relations, discussion of social identities and intersectionality can inadvertently support a discourse that situates diversity merely as surface-level differences to be tolerated, accepted, or celebrated. Naming and examining identities and the impact of individual and collective intersecting identities in addition to exploration of privilege and socialization is critical for initiating reflection and engaging dialogue. According to Accapadi (2007), "The notion of privilege is complex, especially whether we have privilege or we do not have privilege positions us to act in conflicting manners regarding oppression" (p. 208). In short, the Intersections of Identities model is a starting point for exploring social justice, privilege, and oppression, not an ending point.

There is often a temptation among higher education practitioners to focus on diversity and social justice education for students, without a critical examination of faculty and staff attitudes toward an understanding of identity, intersectionality, and social justice. We suggest that faculty and staff members should not encourage students to have conversations or take risks in which they themselves, as educators and administrators, have not engaged (Jones & Abes, 2013). As such, it is crucial to "start at home" by having these dialogues among campus professionals, particularly since numerous qualitative studies have found that educators' unspoken expectations of students influence student performance (Nasir et al., 2009). An example of an effective program where staff engages this dialogue is the Social Justice Conversation Series implemented by and for the professional leadership within the Division of Diversity and Community Engagement at The University of Texas at Austin (Blair, 2013). The professional development series is largely based on engaging dialogue about social justice issues affecting education and drawing from staff members' individual perspectives, experiences, and reflections.

Just as courses or student-centered educational programs should be carefully planned, any opportunities for faculty and staff to have these conversations must be attuned to creating a safer space for discussion (e.g., faculty and staff may be more willing to be open among their colleagues than in discussions with students) and must consider power dynamics of supervisory relationships and positional authorities on campus. Faculty and staff who have reflected on their own identities and positionalities, and engaged in dialogue with others about these topics, will be better prepared to facilitate use of the Intersections of Identities model and encourage students to reflect similarly. In this way, faculty and staff are poised to become role models for discussing intersectionality on campus. Once this conversation begins, it is important to move beyond interpersonal relationships and conversations to examine ways in which institutional structures and discourses presume that identity is experienced singularly and in a segmented, isolated fashion. Students, faculty, and staff might begin to question how diversity is framed within the rhetoric of the institution and how structures such as programs serving underrepresented populations might essentialize the experience of individuals and neglect unique identity intersections.

CONCLUSION

The Intersections of Identities model creates a space where individuals are invited to explore their own identities and reflect on the intersection of those identities.

Intersections need to be understood in the macrolevels (systemic, institutional, and cultural) and the microlevels (interpersonal and individual), acknowledging how historical and current disparities affect these intersections and help us understand our own experiences. We cannot say that all people of color experience racism in the same way, as individual experiences are influenced by numerous factors, including intersecting identities. Nevertheless, the marginalization of subordinated groups has a compound effect on its members. Those who belong to marginalized groups rarely need reminders of their group memberships, and members of dominant groups do not always realize their privilege or the effects of their individual and collective actions on others. The model assists participants in drawing the connection among social construction of identities, intersectionality, and systems of oppression.

The Intersections of Identities model emphasizes the important distinction between social and personal identities. Participants often find it more comfortable to talk about their personal identities because it provides a safe space to speak from, but the true challenge arises when they are pushed to think more critically about their own social identities. Higher education administrators who understand the intersections of their own identities will be better apt to serve a diverse, growing student population. Engaging in a constant practice of self-assessment and discernment is an initial step on the path to implementing a social justice framework on campus.

REFERENCES

Abes, E. S., Jones, S. R., & McEwen, M. K. (2007). Reconceptualizing the model of multiple dimensions of identity: The role of meaning-making capacity in the construction of multiple identities. *Journal of College Student Development, 48*, 1–22.

Accapadi, M. M. (2007). When white women cry: How white women's tears oppress women of color. *College Student Affairs Journal, 26*, 208–215.

Adams, M., Bell, L. A., & Griffin, P. (2007). *Teaching for diversity and social justice.* New York, NY: Routledge.

Alimo, C., & Treviño, J. (2000). *Intergroup relations center curriculum.* Phoenix: Arizona State University.

Anzaldúa, G. (1987). *Borderlands/La frontera: The new mestiza.* San Francisco, CA: Spinsters/Aunt Lute.

Baldwin, J. (1963). *The fire next time.* New York, NY: Dial Press.

Berger, M. T., & Guidroz, K. (Eds.). (2009). *The intersectional approach: Transforming the academy through race, class, and gender.* Chapel Hill: The University of North Carolina Press.

Blair, L. D. (2013, Fall). DDCE "starts at home" with social justice conversation series. *The Social Justice Leader, V,* 12–13.

Collins, P. H. (1986). Learning from the outsider within: The sociological significance of black feminist thought. *Social Problems, 33*(6), S14.

Collins, P. H. (2000). *Black feminist thought: Knowledge, consciousness, and the politics of empowerment* (2nd ed.). New York, NY: Routledge.

Crenshaw, K. (1989). Demarginalizing the intersection of race and sex: A black feminist critique of antidiscrimination doctrine, feminist theory and antiracist politics. *University of Chicago Legal Forum, 1989*, 139–167.

Dill, B. T., & Zambrana, R. E. (Eds.). (2009). *Emerging intersections: Race, class, and gender in theory, policy and practice.* New Brunswick, NJ: Rutgers University Press.

Du Bois, W. E. B. (2003). *Darkwater: Voices from behind the veil.* New York, NY: Prometheus. (Original work published 1920)

Harper, C. (2011). Identity, intersectionality, and mixed-methods approaches. In S. D. Museus & K. A. Griffin (Eds.), *Using mixed-method approaches to study intersectionality in higher education: New directions for institutional research* (No. 151, pp. 103–115). San Francisco, CA: Jossey-Bass.

hooks, b. (1981). *Ain't I a Woman: Black women and feminism.* Boston, MA: South End.

Hurtado, S., Milem, J. F., Clayton-Pedersen, A., & Allen, W. R. (1998). Enhancing campus climates for racial/ethnic diversity: Educational policy and practice. *Review of Higher Education, 21,* 279–302.

Hytten, K., & Bettez, S. C. (2011). Understanding education for social justice. *Educational Foundations, 25,* 7–24.

Johnson, A. G. (2006). *Privilege, power, and difference* (2nd ed.). New York, NY: McGraw-Hill.

Jones, S. R., & Abes, E. S. (2013). *Identity development of college students: Advancing frameworks for multiple dimensions of identity.* San Francisco, CA: Jossey Bass.

Jones, S. R., & McEwen, M. K. (2000). A conceptual model of multiple dimensions of identity. *Journal of College Student Development, 41,* 405–414.

Josselson, R., & Harway, M. (Eds.). (2012). *Navigating multiple identities: Race, gender, culture, nationality, and roles.* New York, NY: Oxford University Press.

Museus, S. D., & Griffin, K. A. (2011). Mapping the margins in higher education: On the promise of intersectionality frameworks in research and discourse. In S. D. Museus & K. A. Griffin (Eds.), *Using mixed-method approaches to study intersectionality in higher education: New directions for institutional research* (No. 151, pp. 5–13). San Francisco, CA: Jossey-Bass.

Nasir, N. S., McLaughlin, M. W., & Jones, A. (2009). What does it mean to be African American? Constructions of race and academic identity in an urban public high school. *American Educational Research Journal, 46,* 73–114.

Pérez Huber, L. (2010). Using Latina/o critical race theory (LatCrit) and racist nativism to explore intersectionality in the educational experience of undocumented Chicana college students. *Educational Foundations, 24,* 77–96.

Pliner, S. M., & Banks, C. A. (Eds.). (2012). *Teaching, learning and intersecting identities in higher education.* New York, NY: Peter Lang.

Romo, R. (2011). Between black and brown: Blaxican (black-Mexican) multiracial identity in California. *Journal of Black Studies, 42,* 402–426.

Tajfel, H., & Turner, J. C. (1979). An integrative theory of intergroup conflict. In W. G. Austin & S. Worchel (Eds.), *The social psychology of intergroup relations* (pp. 33–47). Monterey, CA: Brooks-Cole.

Taylor, B. J. (2011). *Intersections of identities.* Austin: The University of Texas at Austin, Division of Diversity and Community Engagement.

Zúñiga, X., Cytron-Walker, A., & Kachwaha, T. (2004). *Dialogue across differences* (Unpublished curriculum). University of Massachusetts, Amherst, MA.

CHAPTER TWENTY

Huntley House

A "Post-Black" Living-Learning Community for African American Men

PATRICK N. TROUP AND WALTER R. JACOBS

Equity and diversity initiatives on university campuses not only include gender, race, ethnicity, sexual orientation, religion, national origin, and disability, but they also have been expanded to understand that these identities reflect invisible ranges of perspectives, ideas, and epistemologies that have the ability to enhance innovation and creativity that is central to excellence in higher education. There must be more than lip service to equity; intentional strategies to increase the value and retention of diversity as an integrated process by faculty, administration, and staff require explicit policies that can be monitored, evaluated, and internalized for new strategies. This is especially true for those students at the intersection of two identities: African American and male. An overwhelming body of research highlights poor retention and graduation rates in higher education of those with this intersectionality. (For example, see Shaun Harper's [2012] *Bibliography on Black Undergraduate Men: Books, Reports, and Peer-Reviewed Journal Articles*). New strategies are needed to raise the graduation and retention rates of these students.

Dara Strolovitch (2008) noted, "[P]roactive efforts and extra resources [can] overcome entrenched but often subtle biases that persist against marginalized groups" (p. 10). Often when African American students arrive at predominantly White institutions (PWIs), they are faced with various academic and social stresses that may impede their commitment to the institution and matriculation (Harper, 2006). Further, African American males face one of the lowest graduation rates (DeAngelo, Franke, Hurtado, Pryor, & Tran, 2011). Although African American males experience social and academic barriers, the conversation of their success in higher education must move from a deficit framework to sustainable transformation of campus resources in retaining and graduating these students (Harper, 2009). This is the shared responsibility of departments, administration, faculty, and communities to support collegiate African American men in their retention, persistence, identity development, campus experiences, and academic matriculation. Higher education institutions must be held accountable to their commitment to social justice and the necessity of diversity to promote academic excellence.

BARRIERS TO AFRICAN AMERICAN MALE PERSISTENCE AND OPPORTUNITIES FOR RETENTION

Campus climate, social integration, and institutional services affect academic and social experiences of African American males at PWIs (Harper, 2009). In fact, students of color generally experience culture shock with the lack of diversity at PWIs, evidenced in social climate, interracial interactions, racism, discrimination, in-group dynamics, and academic outcomes (Harper, 2009). Alienation and isolation often result in a lack of social and academic integration because of the unavailability of affinity groups or a critical mass of students of color who can provide peer support, coping mechanisms, and psychological adjustment (Harper, 2009). Students of color leave higher education because of financial problems, personal issues, academic unpreparedness, lack of fit with field of study, dissatisfaction with experience, lack of effective coping mechanisms or maturity, and flawed decision making (Davies & Elias, 2003). While realizing that there are personal and societal factors at play, we now address some of the institutional factors that exist.

Institutional factors broadly include the need for male African American students to adjust to a stressful and new environment that intensifies the relevance and awareness of their minority status. These students have desires to see the campus as an inclusive and affirming culture without scrutiny inside and outside the classroom; they seek to avoid *stereotype threat* in which social identity becomes linked to negative performance or lower standards, causing marginalized groups to underperform due to anxiety about perception (Steele, 2011). Racially mixed environments in which messages about lower performance are prevalent reinforce the status quo, instead of reframing the message to empower African American males and speak to the intellectual capacity of all students. By combating institutional assumptions and messages implicit about behavior toward African American males, one can reverse the trend of underachievement with higher standards and higher expectations and reinforce their initial high level of commitment to the institution, which often initially match or exceed that of their White counterparts (Griffin & Pollak, 2009).

To maximize persistence to graduation, short-term and long-term goals for African American males must be aligned to both academic and social dimensions of the institution. Campus climate and institutional support fit into this paradigm of integration; students of color often feel ill-fitted to their institution, thus negatively affecting their performance and potential to persist and graduate. Student support service professionals, staff, faculty, and administration need to understand that perception is often reality for students of color, thus there must be a greater effort to reach out though services and support to students of color. Programs to retain African American males should include programmatic elements such as summer bridge programs for incoming freshmen, campus living-learning communities, research opportunities, and mentoring by faculty and staff to minimize alienation. College programs that emphasize institutional fit, academically and socially, are able to develop students who persist by supplementing initial commitment with intentional integration mechanisms through workshops, programming, social activities, and academic acclamation (Peltier, Laden, & Matranga, 1999). In the case of living communities, African American males often benefit from another African American male roommate in terms of grade point average (Peltier et al., 1999).

Examining African American males through the lens of intersectionality provides a framework to examine the experiences of African American males, because it not only places race at the center of its analysis, but it also examines other forms of oppression. The U.S. educational system has negatively impacted African American males in complex and harmful ways through the intersections of race, gender, and class (Polite & Davis, 1999). The Huntley House was created to aid in mitigating the harmful impact on African American males in higher education.

THE FORMATION OF HUNTLEY HOUSE

To address the barriers to postsecondary education retention and graduation for African American male students, numerous departments, organizations, and individuals at the University of Minnesota have created a multilayered framework based on best practices and innovative strategies to assist in increasing the recruitment and retention of African American male students to the University of Minnesota. A cohort of African American male students was provided with a comprehensive support system and sense of community that will increase their likelihood of retention and graduation. Launched in the fall of 2012, Huntley House is a living-learning community, an arrangement where students with a closely linked set of interests live together in a residence hall and participate in group curricular, cocurricular, and extracurricular activities. The goal of establishing Huntley House was to provide a sense of community and connectedness for

African American males and opportunities for personal and academic growth in a supportive atmosphere to ensure their success in college and beyond. Students have the opportunity to explore issues of ethnicity, identity, and leadership, while receiving vital academic support and actively participating in and contributing to campus student life. In the inaugural 2012–2013 year, Huntley House was open to incoming first-year male students, and it attracted six student participants.

Huntley House is named in honor of Dr. Horace Huntley, a member of the first graduating class from the University of Minnesota Department of African American & African Studies in 1970, who went on to earn a PhD from the University of Pittsburgh and become a professor of history at the University of Alabama at Birmingham. Dr. Huntley was one of the leaders in the Morrill Hall Takeover in the spring of 1969, when a small group of African American students occupied the University of Minnesota's administration building. This action led to the fall 1969 founding of the university's African American & African Studies Department, one of the first in the nation. The action also saw the creation of increased scholarship and on-campus student support opportunities for African American students.

While the six initial students in Huntley House were all African American, the community was open to any male student. A few women applied but were directed to other opportunities. At the University of Minnesota, there are many organizations devoted to the success of African American women (such as "Black Motivated Women," an organization that serves as an educational vehicle about challenges and opportunities of Black women). Huntley House was formed to enable community building for male African American students, especially those who were not student athletes or fraternity members.

Huntley House Programming

Academic course. The inaugural Huntley House students had the opportunity to attend a class together during the fall 2012 semester. All students were required to take a seminar entitled "Black Men: Representation and Reality," offered through the Department of African American & African Studies. In the seminar, students explored the African American male experience by examining labor force participation and employment outcomes and representations of Black masculinity in popular culture and exploring academic dilemmas associated with primary and secondary educational pursuits and issues of law, incarceration, and criminal justice. In addition, they analyzed the complex relationships between African American men and African American women, African American men and White women, and African American men and other African American men, looking closely at African American roles in traditional and nontraditional family structures. They explored questions such as, "What have other people said about being a Black male, and what have Black men imagined and constructed for themselves?" The curriculum of this class was designed so students could work in small or large groups and produce work that interwove what they were learning regarding African American and male issues in the United States.

Unfortunately, only one of the students signed up for the course. The students attended orientation sessions in the summer before moving into the residence halls during Welcome Week prior to the first week of classes. We e-mailed the students and their advisors to inform them of the requirement, but we did not have a system in place to ensure that they registered for the class when meeting with their counselors during the orientation sessions. By the time we had our initial face-to-face meeting with the students during Welcome Week, many classes were closed, so it would have been difficult to rearrange their schedules. Going forward, we decided to move the required class to the spring semester so that we could more closely monitor the process to ensure that students register.

In the 2013–2014 year, 17 African American men are participating in Huntley House. In the spring of 2014, the students will be taking the "Black Minnesota History Project" course, which is also taught in the Department of African American & African Studies. This course explores the local history of African American activism in Minnesota between the 1920s and the 1950s. Placed at the center of a collaborative inquiry will be the history of Minnesota's African American railroad porters, as well as these porters' family members and allies active in the organizing activity of the Brotherhood of Sleeping Car Porters. Working closely with a social service agency called Model Cities, the students will help create a public history space in their new building. A major goal of the course is to produce and present historical knowledge in a way that allows St. Paul's community members and others with deep ties to this community—the young and the old—to remember the rich local history of African American activism between the 1920s and 1950s. Equally important to the course's objective of community outreach is the development of an effective strategy to transform what the students produce into a teaching resource for the K-12 public education system.

Community engagement. Astin (1985) believed that student involvement is a key element of social integration. We encouraged the Huntley House students to be active in African American student organizations. Two students now serve as officers in the Black Student Union, and two students are active in the Black Men's Forum. We also encouraged students to interact with other students of color on campus. In the spring semester of 2013, Huntley House cohosted a screening and discussion of the film, *Black Indians: An American Story* (2001), with members of the Native American living-learning community, American Indian Cultural House.

We introduced the inaugural cohort of Huntley House students to the director of a local alternative high school, with the hope that they would be interested in mentoring high school students. While interested, the Huntley House students were a bit overwhelmed by other responsibilities, so we decided to work on integrating this aspect of programming into the second year of Huntley House. In the current year, the second cohort of Huntley House students are tutoring and mentoring youth through the University YMCA in Minneapolis. They are also working with 20 eighth-grade African American students at Battle Creek Middle School in St. Paul.

Academic and social support. African American male campus leaders should be encouraged to reach out to incoming freshman to show them the benefits of engagement (Harper, 2006). To support their retention, African American faculty and staff provided students with guidance, referrals, and support as the students navigated their first year at the University of Minnesota. Huntley House students regularly met with authors Troup and Jacobs, a peer mentor, a community advisor who lived with them in the residence hall, and other professional staff. The peer mentor was the president of the Board of Governors on campus, a tutor in the Multicultural Center for Academic Excellence's instructional center, and a board member in the African Student Association. The community advisor was the president of his fraternity and an active member of the Black Student Union.

The inaugural class of Huntley House was provided with academic support primarily through the peer mentor. As a group, students met with the peer mentor for approximately two hours per week on Mondays in a study hall. The peer mentor also helped each house member create and follow a weekly individual study plan. Additionally, each house member participated in at least one formal mentoring/tutoring activity during the semester, such as the development of an academic success action plan with the university's Multicultural Academic Excellence Center. Each Huntley House member is required to maintain a 3.0 grade point average. Four of the six inaugural members achieved that goal in the first year; Troup worked with those who fell short to raise their grades.

The inaugural community advisor organized many social activities for the first cohort of Huntley House students, such as weekly basketball games and a fantasy football league. The students also attended a football game with Horace Huntley while he was on campus for grand opening activities. The initial community advisor is again serving Huntley House in its second year and works closely with another community advisor who was a member of the first cohort of Huntley House students.

A discussion of post-Blackness. Although the students were assigned numerous readings and participated in a variety of discussions, we chose to highlight the discussion of post-Blackness. In the spring of 2013, Troup and Jacobs assigned the students a reading: the first chapter of Touré's (2012) book, *Who's Afraid of Post-Blackness? What It Means to Be Black Now*. The chapter entitled "Forty Million Ways to Be Black" opens with the author's story of enjoying sky diving, even after being confronted by middle-aged African American men: "Brother, Black people don't do that" (p. 1). Touré goes on to argue that African Americans should be allowed to have an expansive view about what it means to be Black and should resist efforts from other African Americans as well as from non-African Americans to police those understandings.

Touré (2012) argued that, "we are in a post-Black era, which means simply that the definitions and boundaries of Blackness are expanding in forty million directions—or really, into infinity" (p. 12). He is adamant that being post-Black does not equate with "post-racial" (which is understood to be the state where race is irrelevant); race still matters today, but how we understand the meaning of race is now more fluid. Touré closes the chapter with the following: "If Blackness is, like an ocean, too high to get over and too low to get under, then how could any Black person ever not be Black?" (p. 17).

Exploring the intersectionality of being an African American male in a more nuanced way is vital. Henry Louis Gates Jr. (1997) addressed the diversity and complexity of what it means to be African American and male in the United States, noting the following: "We agree that the notion of a unitary black man as imaginary (and as real) as Wallace Stevens' blackbirds are; and yet to be a black man in the twentieth century is to be heir to a set of anxieties: beginning with what it means to be a black man" (p. xvii). Gates spoke to the complexity of the African American male identity, which is both located in a collective identity, yet influenced by individual experiences. African American males find themselves in perpetual negotiation as they seek to reconcile their own individual lived experiences with prescribed societal expectations. This negotiation can prove exhausting mentally, physically, and emotionally, and may impact their social and academic outcomes in school.

The Huntley House students enthusiastically discussed the article, and many shared stories of how their Blackness was called into question, where they were charged with "acting White" for studying too much or for preferring swim team membership instead of joining the basketball team. They shared strategies for dealing with questions about their Blackness and also discussed how their understandings of masculinity and social class affected their intersectional articulations. We were especially pleased when some of the students wanted to read additional chapters. Going forward, we believe that *Who's Afraid of Post-Blackness? What It Means to Be Black Now* (Touré, 2012) is an important text to share with future Huntley House students. It is an excellent text for stimulating discussion of intersectional identities.

REPLICATING HUNTLEY HOUSE

Jacobs is in the process of proposing a living-learning community for African American men at his new institution, the University of Wisconsin-Parkside. As is the case for Huntley House, the proposed "Fearn House" will be open to any male student, but it is specifically designed to build community by exploring the shared experience of African American males in and out of the classroom. Fearn House is named in honor of Isom Fearn, Jr., the first African American graduate of the University of Wisconsin-Parkside. For 32 years Mr. Fearn served as the director of the Access Opportunity Program at the State University of New York at Geneseo, which provided academically and economically disadvantaged students an opportunity to attend college.

At the University of Wisconsin-Parkside, Jacobs convened meetings of African American male leaders to discuss the possibility of a living-learning community for African American males. The leaders have appointments in multiple areas of the university: faculty, student services, and senior administration. Surprisingly, one leader expressed strong reservations about the possibility of creating an African American male living-learning community, and his "Blackness" was questioned by others: "Are you a real Black man? Why do you not want to help out the brothers?" Jacobs introduced Touré's (2012) post-Blackness formulation, however, which reminded the group that there are multiple ways to understand African American identity, especially at the intersection of male identity. The dissenter wanted to make sure that scarce resources were spent on programs that maximize student success, while engaging students in discussions identifying those programs before any commitments were finalized.

By the beginning of the fall 2014 semester, Fearn House should be up and running. At the same time, the third year of Huntley House at the University of Minnesota will begin. We are excited that these two living-learning communities for African American men allow those students to explore the intersections of multiple identities in the pursuit of success in the classroom and beyond. We encourage the development of similar living-learning communities on other campuses.

REFERENCES

Astin, A. W. (1985). *Achieving educational excellence.* San Francisco, CA: Jossey-Bass.

Davies, R., & Elias, P. (2003). *Dropping out: A study of early leavers from higher education.* London, England: DFES.

DeAngelo, L., Franke, R., Hurtado, S., Pryor, J. H., & Tran, S. (2011). *Completing college: Assessing graduation rates at four-year institutions.* Los Angeles, CA: University of California, Los Angeles, Higher Education Research Institute.

Gates, H. L., Jr. (1997). *Thirteen ways of looking at a black man.* New York, NY: Vintage.

Griffin, E., & Pollak, D. (2009). Student experiences of neurodiversity in higher education: Insights from the BRAINHE project. *Dyslexia, 15,* 23–41.

Harper, S. R. (2006). *Black male students at public flagship universities in the U.S.: Status, trends and implications for policy and practice.* Washington, DC: Joint Center for Political and Economic Studies.

Harper, S. R. (2009). Niggers no more: A critical race counternarrative on black male student achievement at predominantly white colleges and universities. *International Journal of Qualitative Studies in Education, 22,* 697–712.

Harper, S. R. (2012). *Bibliography on black undergraduate men: Books, reports, and peer-reviewed journal articles.* Philadelphia: University of Pennsylvania.

Peltier, G. L., Laden, R., & Matranga, M. (1999). Student persistence in college: A review of research. *Journal of College Student Retention, 1,* 357–375.

Polite, V., & Davis, J. E., (1999). *African American males in school and society: Practices and policies for effective education.* New York, NY: Teachers College Press.

Steele, C. N. (2011). *Whistling Vivaldi: How stereotypes affect us and what we can do.* New York, NY: W. W. Norton.

Strolovitch, D. Z. (2008). *Affirmative advocacy: Race, class and gender in interest group politics.* Chicago, IL: University of Chicago Press.

Touré. (2012). *Who's afraid of post-blackness? What it means to be black now.* New York, NY: Atria.

CHAPTER TWENTY-ONE

Theory to Practice

Problematizing Student Affairs Work through Intersectionality

MARIA OROPEZA FUJIMOTO AND MIGUEL U. LUNA

I call myself a mixture of different things. I don't think anybody is one particular self...one particular group...there is a lot of hidden things in people's backgrounds. They might look one way, but that has absolutely little or no bearing on their actual [experiences].... I think a lot of people want to limit and kind of put people into boxes. (Sonic, a Latina college graduate reflecting on her identities)

For many students, their social identities are far more complex than signifiers imply, yet they are typically labeled based on just *one* of their social identities. For example, many student affairs practitioners understand the lived experiences and struggles of students from one particular social identity but may not necessarily consider students' multiple social identities that are interlocking and intersecting. Unfortunately, working with students based on just one of their social identities has not resulted in increased levels of academic success. Intersectionality provides an important lens to examine both the complexity of individual identities grounded in multiple oppressions (Reynolds & Pope, 1991) *as well as* a framework for understanding educational inequities and pursuing social justice (Dill & Zambrana, 2009). This social justice agenda requires a challenging of essentialized and deficit-based understandings of social identities. More specifically, community cultural wealth (CCW) holds that individuals from nondominant communities draw on nondominant forms of knowledge, skills, and resources (or forms of capital) to counteract barriers, thereby enabling them to achieve academically. CCW provides a conceptual reframing of these entrenched notions that can lead to theorizing as well as advocacy to enhance the success of students from nondominant groups.

This chapter begins by defining intersectionality and how it is used as a guiding framework and then continues by contextualizing Latino/a and first-generation college students as intersecting identities. Finally, two programs are presented as examples that focus on the complex and intersecting identities present among Latino/a and first-generation students. The first example draws on intersectional identities to serve two distinct, yet overlapping populations—Latinas (Hispanic females) and female students from small towns. The second example examines the parent component of a community-based project that utilizes intersectionality as an analytical tool, and CCW as a framework to create a college-going culture. The chapter concludes with a discussion about how intersectionality can provide a more nuanced and accurate understanding of students and their communities and highlights how CCW can be used to help professionals understand the strengths of the students and communities they work with on college campuses.

GUIDING FRAMEWORK: INTERSECTIONALITY

In student affairs, intersectionality tends to be used to understand individual students and their development. Less often is intersectionality seen as a tool "to examine social problems that most affect those most harmed by inequalities" (Collins, as cited in Dill & Zambrana, 2009, p. viii.). Intersectionality in this latter sense is also an analytical tool to better understand the complexity of social oppression and how it operates. In this chapter, intersectionality is used as a way to understand both individual development as well as structures of social oppression. Clearly, these two ways of defining intersectionality are intertwined. Intersectionality reveals how social structures limit the range of opportunities available to a particular individual's identity (Collins, 2000). But can intersectionality help us understand how to take action toward social justice, such as change policy, or know how and when to provide advocacy? For example, scholars (Crenshaw, 1991; Delgado & Stefancic, 2012) point to the ways in which discrimination against women of color, that is not clearly race or gender based, may go unrecognized and unpunished by a legal system that falls short of addressing discrimination that is intersectionally more complex than racism or sexism alone. But what steps can we take to remedy this and similar examples in higher education?

Students with multiple social identities are often misunderstood due to the common belief that a true essence of a particular group can be named. When these beliefs are rooted in social oppression, particular groups such as the poor, women, and people of color, are generally seen through a very narrow lens that is typically framed by deficit conceptions to explain their relative place in our socially and racially stratified system. CCW (Yosso, 2005) can be used to complement intersectional analysis, to reframe deficit explanations of educational inequities. CCW draws on critical race theory and recognizes the intercentricity (Yosso, 2005) of race, acknowledging the centrality of race but that this also intersects with gender, class, and other oppression-based social identities. Similar to intersectionality, CCW goes beyond being a theoretical construct to being action oriented and emphasizing social justice as a primary goal.

More specifically, CCW is composed of forms of community-based capital that are typically not valued by the dominant culture, including our institutions of higher education, for example, aspirational capital, navigational capital, social capital, resistant capital, and so forth. These forms of capital become ways to transform communities and lives and challenge individualistic, dominant explanations of inequity based in deficit. CCW can be an important tool for practitioners to identify barriers and take steps to support students' academic success.

Intersecting Identities: First-Generation and Latino/a

Latinos/as are the fastest growing ethnic group in the United States (Yosso, 2006). They represent approximately 15% of the undergraduate population and are expected to increase to 22% within the next two decades (Gonzalez, Olivas, & Calleroz, 2004). For many of these students, they will be the first in their families to attend college. Programs and services have been created to educate them, yet only 7% of Latinos/as who begin in elementary school graduate from college (Yosso, 2006). There are many contributing factors to this statistic, but with the growing population of Latinos/as in the United States, it is clear that change is needed to improve the retention and degree attainment of these students. Student affairs professionals must not only take a deeper look into practices but must also better understand this diverse student subpopulation to create truly holistic programs and services.

To understand students is, in part, to stop looking through a singular lens and comprehend varying identities of Latino/a and first-generation college students. Much of the literature to date is single-identity-specific, such as examining students as Latinos/as *or* as first-generation college students, but rarely are students' experiences as first-generation Latinos/as taken into account. Current literature on Latinos/as describes how they encounter various barriers in high school and increasingly enroll in two-year institutions, and are more likely to attend part time (Fry, 2002; Gamboa & Vasquez, 2006). As first-generation college students, they and their families have less knowledge and access to resources about college. Yet, despite their first-generation status, parents, siblings, and relatives are very important in the college decision-making process. They are also integral to students' success and are an important support system while in college (Perez & McDonough, 2008).

Practices utilizing a singular lens often result in comparing populations or may assume that the families of first-generation students have little to offer in helping a student succeed. These assumptions can lead to missed opportunities for programs to connect with families and ultimately promote Latino/a students' success.

In the rare cases where research attempts to understand multiple identities, there is a tendency to box Latino/a first-generation students into one group. Often this approach fails to see the differences within the subpopulation. For example, gender representation of Latino/a first-generation college students has changed over the years. Currently there are more female students attending college than male students (Saenz & Ponjuan, 2009). The many cultural and social layers that are at play can affect the type of services we provide. Also varying to a significant degree may be generational status in the United States and socioeconomic status. Thus, as we create and implement our practices, we fail to be more inclusive and holistic in our approach to support today's Latino/a students. The two examples that follow illustrate both the problems and the possibilities.

Intersectionality: Student Affairs Practices

Example no. 1: Latinas and women from small towns. The Leaders in the Midwest (LM) program originally intended to serve the needs of rural female students, recognizing the "new poor" who were affected by the "farm crisis" of the 1980s and Latinas as a growing, yet underserved population (White, 1996). It evolved to focusing on two growing but "invisible" populations—female students from small towns (largely White; approximately 80% to 90% of the participants) and Latinas (largely not from small towns). It was reasoned that students from both these groups shared close ties with their families, benefited from protective factors of close knit-neighborhoods or communities, and were attending college at lower rates than other women (White, 1996). Based on meetings with educators and community leaders as well as the literature on best practices, LM identified the following needs of these populations: (a) academic preparation, (b) financial resources, (c) college aspirations, and (d) links to leadership development within their communities. The program attempted to address these needs through (a) tutoring, (b) scholarships (up to $5,000 based on need), (c) outreach programs for middle and high school students, and (d) leadership programs and mentoring (White, 2001).

A strength of the LM program was that it recognized commonalities across multiple and intersecting identity groups (Latinas and women from small towns). These two groups of students were mixed based on common needs to form "clusters." For example, in the mentoring program, students were "clustered" in groups of three to five, with a student affairs practitioner or faculty member available to provide a system of support; Latinas were largely with those not of their own racial/ethnic group. At the same time, opportunities for Latinas to interact with someone from the same or similar racial/ethnic group were formed as well, recognizing the need to develop support systems based on this common experience. This recognition of the need for Latina participants to build relationships with other Latinas, White rural students, and college personnel was important and offered a way to develop the multiple social identities of these Latina students. For example, low-income Latinas who were from urban areas had the opportunity to interact with those from similar racial/ethnic and socioeconomic backgrounds and with those from similar-size towns. The retention and graduation rates from the program showed that Latina LM participants and LM participants from small towns, overall, were generally retained and graduated at rates comparable to or higher than the rest of the student population. To delve deeper into these issues, here is Ann, one of the students who participated in the LM program.

Ann entered Saint Mary's College after taking four advanced placement classes. She described herself as a "second/third-generation Mexican-American, first in my family to go to college [who never] got anything lower than an A or A-." However, she struggled academically in college: "Academically, [my school] wasn't really good…it is a low-income area, and the teacher's aren't paid well. [The city I grew up in] goes back and forth with Detroit for being the murder capital [of the U.S.]."

Ann, a high achieving Latina from a working-class/poor background, realizes after the first week of classes that she is underprepared compared to other students. She feels disadvantaged because of her economic background, yet she does not want to receive any scholarships for being a racial minority. She feels that to do so is to admit that she is less than White students. Ann feels that race-based scholarships are unfair and that to receive money for being a minority means that she is inferior, further discrediting her academic background. Ultimately, Ann does not utilize tutoring services, changes majors from bio-chemistry to psychology, and initially refuses scholarship money.

Ann's racial identity trumps all others when she initially decides to forgo scholarship money because she does not want to be associated with any race-based benefits that might be perceived as her being less academically qualified than her White classmates. This occurred in spite of the fact that the vast majority of the LM scholarship money went to White students, many with similar or lower academic qualifications than Ann. Her story exemplifies some of the complications in coordinating such a program like LM. Ann is a poor/working-class, first-generation Latina college student. She is admitted to the program based on being Latina, a historically underrepresented group on campus. As mentioned earlier, the program works to affirm her Latina identity and to provide support services in recognition of her low-income background and first-generation status.

It is important to consider that students such as Ann, who would have benefited from such support, do not want to be associated with the aspects of the program that mark her as lacking (such as academic support and financial assistance), and she rather chooses to utilize the mentorship aspect of the program, which helps her build connections to campus. Rendón (1992) explained that often, students of color and women

> enter higher education consumed with self-doubt.... This doubt is reinforced by the subtle yet powerful messages that higher education institutions communicate.... We hear loud and clear that only white men can do science and math, that only the best and brightest deserve to be educated, that white students are inherently smarter than nonwhites, and that allowing people of color to enter a college diminishes its academic quality. (pp. 60–61)

This begs the question: How can student affairs practitioners effectively meet the needs of students like Ann? One way to do this is to affirm students' multiple identities—especially those that are sources of strength. Ann is capable of completing academic work, yet her identity as a high achiever goes unrecognized after she is admitted to college. In considering students like Ann, it is especially important for practitioners to recognize that higher education perpetuates a culture of inequality as described earlier by Rendón (1992). In working for social justice, it is important that practitioners draw on analytic tools such as intersectionality to deconstruct educational inequality and critique deficit frameworks that advantage some groups over others. Through intersectionality, practitioners can challenge internalized deficit-based understandings of social identities (such as race/ethnicity) and help students understand themselves in more complicated ways and realize that inequalities are maintained through systems.

Example no. 2: Maywood Educational Fair: Parent workshop. The Maywood Educational Fair was started by a student affairs graduate student who felt that there was a lack of college information and resources. The city of Maywood's population is largely Latino/a, low income, has low high school graduation rates, low college-going rates, and many social and political barriers. Now in its fifth year, the Maywood Educational Fair includes workshops for varying age groups. This section discusses a workshop specifically focused on the parents of the community.

The need for a parent workshop comes from research that shows that family is very influential in the college attendance and academic success of Latino/a students (Auerbach, 2004). Further, student organizers who examined the history of oppression in education informed the implementation of the workshop. Recognizing that most research draws on deficit frameworks that blame Latino/a parents for their student's low achievement (Valencia, 1997), the student organizers examined other studies that revealed a more complex picture of Latino/a student achievement. These studies showed that Latino/a families tended to value academic success more than non-Latino White parents (Ryan, Casas, Kelley-Vance, Ryalls, & Nero, 2010). Family support can come in different ways and through culturally different means than how support is usually defined by the dominant culture.

With the Maywood Educational Fair and the parent workshop, there was con-scious effort to avoid a deficit approach in planning the event. Instead, a CCW model was used (Yosso, 2006), allowing a focus on the strengths of the Latino parents. For example, after reading sources on critical consciousness (Freire, 1990), critical race theory, and CCW, the organizing group met with a local parent group to better understand the community. From this meeting, the group came to understand this particular community in terms of intersecting identities—parents, Latinos/as, immigrants, primarily Spanish speakers, low-income families, with first-generation college-bound students. To understand nondominant forms of knowledge, skills, and resources (or capital) that the community possessed, the organizers studied the intersectional and interlocking forms of oppression that the community faced with their educational system, water pollution, and "safe haven" statuses for undoc-umented immigrants, among many others. If the various forms of oppression that exist had not been examined, there would have been no recognition that it is through this very process of social marginalization that forms of CCW were developed.

With the knowledge of the resources within the community *and* the barriers they faced, a parent panel was developed. Three Latina mothers whose children were attending or had graduated from college served on the panel. The panel offered ways parents used their different forms of capital to respond to misinformation and oppression. The workshop also provided a space where genuine dialogue among parents, panelists, and facilitators took place. Through the safe space and creation of dialogue, the parent attendees became very involved in the workshop and freely shared personal stories about their experiences and the barriers they have had to overcome. They also shared their aspirations for their children, ways they have supported them, and how they have navigated the U.S. higher education system.

CCW provided the opportunity to reframe the deficit explanations and use these reframes as tools to create spaces where individuals can feel safe, appreciated, and empowered. This workshop's panel format and space for dialogue allowed the parents to see that they were not alone in facing racism, challenges, and oppression within their community. By listening to other parents of the community, partic-ipants came to a new understanding of their various forms of navigational and aspirational capital. These participants became empowered through listening to one another and identifying how, despite the many challenges, parents continued to support their children.

DISCUSSION AND RECOMMENDATIONS

"When we [work with] a group…we should think about the ethics of our action, considering whether or not our work will be used to reinforce and perpetuate domination" (hooks, 1984, p. 43).

In higher education there is increasing awareness that students from nondominant groups, such as people of color, women, low-income and first-generation college students, are less likely to be academically successful. These students are typically labeled based on just *one* of their social identities, and these labels influence policies as well as practices by student affairs professionals and often determine which programs or services are deemed necessary for these students to be academically successful. There are several problems with focusing on single identities of students: this narrow focus (a) has not resulted in increased levels of academic success; (b) incorrectly assumes that social identities are singular, separate, and independent from one another, instead of overlapping, interlocking, and intersecting; (c) has reinforced stereotypes, essentializing an entire group through a single social identity by focusing on a "deficient" aspect of that identity; (d) denies the full humanity of students; and (e) does not address the need for systemic change.

This chapter presented intersectionality as a tool for practitioners to better serve students' multiple identities and how they experience multiple oppressions. It highlighted the intersecting identities of first-generation and Latino/a students and their families. From a practical standpoint, it illustrated how one college coupled the needs of two groups with intersecting identities to provide services under the LM program. Ann's story also highlights a challenge in working with students, specifically, how students may negotiate their identities in ways that are counterproductive to their educational achievement.

Intersectionality was also utilized in the Maywood Educational Fair to move beyond labels that define individuals and communities in terms of their deficits, toward an analytical tool to understand how social problems (specifically a low-college-going culture) are created and maintained through broader social inequities. The Maywood project helped student affairs professionals recognize the intersectional and interlocking nature of oppression, understand how dominant forms of capital operate, and realize that people from nondominant groups also possess forms of capital, which they use to counter inequities. Drawing on CCW helps new practitioners see beyond the typical deficits associated with notions of poor communities of color and provides a framework to work for social justice.

The following recommendations are presented for student affairs professionals who are interested in working for social justice and using intersectionality as an analytical tool.

Start by Increasing Awareness

All college campuses face challenges with the retention and graduation rates of students from nondominant backgrounds. The widespread failure to educate these students is a failure of the educational system as a whole and not individual students. Create professional development opportunities for practitioners on social justice and intersectionality. It would be appropriate to include training about deficit versus asset frameworks to understand inequalities.

Develop Knowledge

Avoid trying to find "*the* missing link" to the student success puzzle. There is no single reason why students succeed academically. Instead, understand that students' identities are multiple and complex and study policies and practices using disaggregated data in examining multiple, intersecting identities such as race, gender, *and* class to identify, analyze, and deconstruct the impact of policies and practices that perpetuate inequalities.

Create Spaces Where "Transforming Ideas and Institutions Inform One Another" (Collins, as cited in Dill & Zambrana, 2009, p. vii).

This may take the form of a department, division, or college-wide dialogue in which participants not only identify challenges to serving students but where data is used to inform policy decisions and practices and ultimately can transform the institution.

In sum, the use of intersectionality must move beyond the individual students toward institutional change. In this sense, it can be a very useful tool for student affairs practitioners to understand and work toward equitable student outcomes.

REFERENCES

Auerbach, S. (2004). Engaging Latino parents in supporting college pathways: Lessons from a college access program. *Journal of Hispanic Higher Education, 3*, 125–145.

Collins, P. H. (2000). *Black feminist thought: Knowledge, consciousness, and the politics of empowerment.* New York, NY: Routledge.

Crenshaw, K. (1991). Mapping the margins: Intersectionality, identity politics, and violence against women of color. *Stanford Law Review, 43*, 1241–1299.

Delgado, R., & Stefancic, J. (2012). *Critical race theory: An introduction.* New York: New York University Press.

Dill, B.T. & Zambrana, R. E. (2009). *Emerging intersections: Race, class, and gender in theory, policy, and practice.* New Brunswick, NJ: Rutgers University Press.

Freire, P. (1990). *Pedagogy of the oppressed.* New York, NY: Continuum.

Fry, R. (2002). *Latinos in higher education: Many enroll, too few graduate.* Washington, DC: Pew Hispanic Center.

Gamboa, E., & Vasquez, S. Y. (2006). Latino/a/Hispanic students. In L. A. Gohn & G. R. Albin (Eds.), *Understanding college student subpopulations: A guide for student affairs professionals* (pp. 313–348). Washington, DC: NASPA.

Gonzalez, K. P., Olivas, L., & Calleroz, M. (2004). Transforming the post-secondary experiences of Latinos. In L. I. Rendón, M. Garcia, & D. Person (Eds.), *Transforming the first year of college for students of color* (Monograph No. 38, pp. 23–35). Columbia: University of South Carolina, National Resource Center for the First-Year Experience and Students in Transition.

hooks, b. (1984). *Feminist theory: From margin to center.* Boston, MA: South End.

Perez, P. A., & McDonough, P. M. (2008). Understanding Latina and Latino college choice: A social capital and chain migration analysis. *Journal of Hispanic Higher Education, 7,* 249–265.

Rendón, L. I. (1992). From the barrio to the academy: Revelations of a Mexican American "scholarship girl." *New Directions for Community Colleges, 80,* 55–64.

Reynolds, A. L., & Pope, R. L. (1991). The complexities of diversity: Exploring multiple oppressions. *Journal of Counseling and Development, 70,* 174–180.

Ryan, C. S., Casas, J. F., Kelly-Vance, L., Ryalls, B. O., & Nero, C. (2010). Parent involvement and views of school success: The role of parents' Latino and white American cultural orientations. *Psychology in the Schools, 47,* 391–405.

Saenz, V. B., & Ponjuan, L. (2009). The vanishing Latino male in higher education. *Journal of Hispanic Higher Education, 8,* 54–89.

Valencia, R. C. (1997). *The evolution of deficit thinking: Educational thought and practice.* New York, NY: Routledge.

White, P. (1996). *Leaders of a new Indiana: A proposal.* Manuscript submitted to the Lilly Special Initiative Program, Notre Dame, Indiana, Saint Mary's College.

White, P. (2001). *Leaders of a new Indiana project: Creating inclusive spaces at Saint Mary's College. New Indiana: Recruiting and retaining Latinas and students from small communities: The faculty perspective.* Notre Dame, IN: Saint Mary's College.

Yosso, T. J. (2005). Whose culture has capital? A critical race theory discussion of community cultural wealth. *Race, Ethnicity and Education, 8,* 69–92.

Yosso, T. J., (2006). *Critical race counterstories: Along the chicana/chicano educational pipeline.* New York, NY: Routledge.

CHAPTER TWENTY-TWO

PhD Pathways Mentoring Program

A Site to Build Intersectional Praxis

ROBIN PHELPS-WARD AND THALIA M. MULVIHILL

In 2012, Ball State University and its Office of Institutional Diversity embarked on a journey to pilot a formal mentoring program to guide minority students to the professoriate. Since then, the PhD Pathways mentoring program has formed and continues to evolve as a site for experimenting with intersectional praxis. As a public, four-year, predominantly White, Midwestern university, Ball State University works to recruit and retain diverse students and faculty as part of its strategic, institutional goals. PhD Pathways exists among the various actions the university has taken to proactively foster a diverse campus climate as it embraces a model of mentoring and supporting current students with the hope that they will return to motivate and mentor future students. Although the mission of the PhD Pathways program was designed within a specific campus culture, the idea of mentoring programs for underrepresented students seeking graduate education is not new (e.g., Southern Regional Education Doctoral Scholars Program, Ronald E. McNair Postbaccalaureate Achievement Program), and the higher education literature has steadily placed attention on related research questions (see Holley & Caldwell, 2012; Keith & Russell, 2013; Warnock & Appel, 2012).

Through initiatives designated as formal mentoring programs (FMPs), higher education institutions have addressed issues of recruitment, retention, academic performance, college satisfaction, and matriculation to foster communities of institutional diversity, yet they are often created with narrow understandings of how identity issues impact mentoring experiences (Crisp & Cruz, 2009; Gershenfeld,

2014; Girves, Zepeda, & Gwathmey, 2005). Although affirmative action once served as the impetus for FMPs established in the past (Edwards, 1995), today's FMPs require more theoretically grounded rationale for serving the increasingly diverse American college student population. With the growing number of students labeled as low-socioeconomic status, first-generation, nontraditional, disabled, LGBTQ (Lesbian, gay, bisexual, transgender, queer), multiracial, and international, the need for institutions to reassess and evaluate academic programs—in terms of race, class, gender, and other identity markers—is especially relevant (Renn, 2012). We argue for institutional application of intersectional theories and approaches, which may assist those planning and delivering FMPs, especially those designed to guide future diverse faculty at colleges and universities.

In this chapter, the PhD Pathways program is described and examined as a representative case to demonstrate the benefits of moving away from essentializing identity theories and moving toward recognition of a larger range of identity shapers. Before delving into the specific case of the PhD Pathways program, we begin with an overview of mentoring in higher education and the research that has informed FMPs' best practices. We also review college student development theories that have traditionally informed the mentoring of minority students and present intersectionality perspectives that might inform the new practices regarding FMPs. We conclude with recommendations for practitioners, educators, and administrative leaders.

FORMAL MENTORING PROGRAMS IN HIGHER EDUCATION

Since the 1964 Civil Rights Act, institutions have spent more than 50 years attempting to ameliorate the lasting effects of discrimination, prejudice, and exclusion of ethnic and racial minority citizens to higher education. Through affirmative action and diversity-related programs, colleges and universities have worked to rectify injustices by providing increased access to higher education for all. Among these initiatives, FMPs serve as tools to address diversity-related concerns like low enrollment, retention, matriculation, job placement, and minority faculty representation (Davis, 2008).

Mentoring programs have taken many forms to address the needs of the diverse college student populations through peer mentoring initiatives that rely on slightly more experienced students to assist the less experienced, and faculty-student mentoring projects, which require faculty willing to add to their uncompensated workload (e.g., departmental and university service, which is typically minimally rewarded in promotion and tenure; Long, 1997). In contrast to informal mentoring, formal mentoring relationships are governed by aspects of initiation and structure whereby a third party matches two individuals and establishes the guidelines and duration of the relationship (Eby, Rhodes, & Allen, 2007). As a labor-intensive endeavor, due to their reliance on institutional support and resources, diversity initiatives in the form of FMPs take time and commitment by many in order to grow, and they seem to thrive best when connected to administrative support (Girves et al., 2005).

RACIAL AND ETHNIC MINORITY MENTORING PROGRAMS

Research dedicated to the topic of racial and ethnic minority FMPs has investigated numerous psychosocial (e.g., competence and learning) and career (e.g., exposure and career development) functions (Kram, 1983). Such formalized mentoring has led to outcomes of increased academic engagement, success, goal attainment, graduate school interest, awareness of educational and career opportunities, value of professional relationships, college persistence, and graduate school readiness (Hu & Ma, 2010; Willison & Gibson, 2011). For racial and ethnic minority students—especially those attending predominantly White institutions (PWIs)—access to supportive mentoring relationships that cultivate psychosocial and career functions is challenging (Thomas, Willis, & Davis, 2007). This challenge is amplified for the African American male college student population, which represents a group with the most dismal outcomes in academic achievement (Harper, 2012). Others also have examined the unique challenges African American males experience (e.g., Mitchell & Means, 2014; Strayhorn & Terrell, 2007).

IDENTITY THEORIES AND COLLEGE STUDENT DEVELOPMENT

College student development theories offer further insight into the theoretical perspectives that guide FMP processes. Though traditional theories have informed the evolution of college student development theories, a broader array of identity development theories is needed to further inform our discussion of conceptualizing mentoring as an act of intersectionality praxis. Jones and McEwen (2000), Renn (2003), and Torres, Jones, and Renn (2009) have adopted more holistic views of college students by addressing the multiple dimensions of their identity, interactions with and within the campus environment, and the intersections of students' identities. These perspectives provide a social-constructionist framework that recognizes the need to understand students' identities as more than additive qualities but rather "the tension of examining both the whole student and his or her constituent parts" (Torres et al., 2009, p. 590). The Model of Multiple Dimensions of Identity (Jones & McEwen, 2000) veered from stage and phase developmental models and adopted a less static illustration of the college student identity. The model provides a much-needed focus on the complexities of students' current selves, which may vary greatly from the self who entered freshman year or returned to college after military tour. Renn's (2003) use of a developmental ecology lens focused on the campus environment in relation to students' racial identities and recommended that faculty facilitate postmodern and social constructionist discussions concerning race, race relations, and racial identity, and provide students with the linguistic and cognitive capital to engage in productive, intellectual discussions.

Torres et al. (2009) and Renn's (2012) work called for student affairs practitioners and research scholars to focus on a holistic view of the college student and adopt a more "fluid approach" (Torres et al., 2009, p. 591) that enmeshes race, class, and gender categories while situating each in microlevel and macrolevel contexts. This approach requires that colleges and universities cease overessentializing concepts of race, class, and gender, and conceptualize FMPs as opportunities to enhance individual understanding of the self; engage in dialogues about power and privilege; and evolve the larger campus diversity climate. Moreover, this approach compels practitioners to move our discussion toward combining theoretical perspectives—as Renn (2011) and Abes (2009) suggested—and employ intersectional frameworks for implementing programming, understanding students' development, and constructing evaluations that make new contributions to the body of research on FMPs. Renn and Reason's (2013) most recent work sets the stage for a reconceptualization of the next phases of theorizing about student development, and together with other research, such as Baxter Magolda's (2008) ongoing studies involving the concept of self-authorship, the focus on identity intersections holds great promise as a guiding framework for FMPs.

INTERSECTIONAL PERSPECTIVES

Crenshaw (1991) believed that through intersectionality, individuals would be able to "better ground the differences among us to negotiate the means by which these differences will find expression in constructing group politics" (p. 1299). Later, Cole (2009), McCall (2005), and Yuval-Davis (2006) added methodological, conceptual, and psychological perspectives and presented several ideas related to how scholars should address concepts of categorization, social divisions, and inequality in intersectional research. Though most intersectional research exists as anticategorial, intercategorical, or intracategorical (McCall, 2005), Yuval-Davis (2006) addressed the concept of "triple oppression" (p. 195) and explained how such notions of intersectionality reify additive and essentialized identity models.

The intersectionality literature on higher education mentoring has alluded to the debated categorical issues of the approach and has focused on classroom teaching and learning (e.g., Grant & Zwier, 2011), faculty mentoring experiences (e.g., Griffin & Reddick, 2011), and multidimensional analyses of intersectionality in mentoring research (e.g., Museus & Griffin 2011). With a focus on the context of higher education, scholars have grappled with intersectionality and asked three key questions. First, how can educators incorporate intersectional dialogues to encourage discussions of privilege and oppression in the classroom space? Second, how can administrators better understand how faculty's multiple identities support or burden their ability to effectively mentor? Third, how can scholars implement research that reflects the demographic diversity in the field, presents the voices and realities of those on the margins, garners understanding of how identities contribute to inequality, and avoids the perpetuation of inequalities? We argue that building understanding about the complexities of intersecting identities will lead to meaningful opportunities for innovative practices in the area of higher education and FMPs—particularly those like PhD Pathways.

PHD PATHWAYS: A SITE TO BUILD INTERSECTIONAL PRAXIS

Designed to serve academically high-achieving underrepresented racial and ethnic minority undergraduate and graduate students, the PhD Pathways program relies on faculty/staff-student relationships to recruit, encourage, guide, and prepare students for graduate education, particularly doctoral programs, and careers as professors. Through a matching process, program coordinators pair the dyads based on academic and research interests, personality similarities, and student interest in working with a specific mentor.

Student and Faculty Demographics

In its first year, the PhD Pathways program included undergraduate and graduate students in the College of Communication, Information, and Media (CCIM), and was comprised of 10 students who identified as female and 3 who identified as male (13 students total). Additionally, all students belonged to a self-reported racial or ethnic group (i.e., African American or of African descent, Asian American, or biracial). During this same year, 12 faculty and staff within the academic college volunteered to become mentors (nine female and three male faculty and staff). This group included 12 faculty and staff who self-identified as White and one who self-identified as belonging to a racial minority group. In its second year, the program expanded to include the university's Teachers College and was comprised of 20 students and 19 faculty total.

Programming and Interactions

Participation in all aspects of the program is voluntary for both students and faculty. Through biweekly meetings between mentoring pairs, social gatherings with the larger PhD Pathways group, and university-sponsored programming facilitated by university offices (i.e., the Career Center, University Libraries, Graduate School, Student Life, Multicultural Center, and academic colleges), the program encourages students to engage with the campus environment on multiple levels. A memorandum of understanding informs students and mentors of program expectations and processes. Although such structures help encourage and guide productive relationships between students and their faculty mentors, the tone and tenor of the conversations might be further enhanced by being more intentional about the role multiple intersecting identities play in the decision-making process about graduate school and careers. For example, intersectional praxis could take the form of purposeful and direct conversations—initiated by mentors—that allow students to reflect and articulate ideas about how their identity impacts and influences their ways of knowing and understanding the world.

Program Challenges and Triumphs

As a voluntary program reliant on student and faculty participation without a tangible reward, the livelihood of the program is driven by interpersonal relationships. Yet, for our protégés assuming roles as campus leaders, sorority and fraternity members, local volunteers, and employees, their ability to attend events and meet face-to-face with their mentors is challenged. Nonetheless, the program's strengths are based in the mentoring partnerships. Initial conversations about students' goals, a written agreement about the expectations of the relationship, and concrete plans facilitate the academic focus of the relationship.

While all PhD Pathways students may not choose to attend graduate school immediately after graduation, the goal is for all students in the program to leave with a plan for applying to graduate school—a plan they did not have before. This goal is made possible through dedicated mentors who guide students through the process of understanding the culture of academe and support them throughout the decision-making task of considering graduate school as an option. PhD Pathways mentors have offered psychosocial and career support by making students aware of scholarly opportunities and providing guidance through norms and process. Mentors have also offered high levels of socioemotional support in the form of relationship advice. Further, mentors have sought resources outside of the program to assist them with mentee conversations about social justice and psychological and physical health issues. The PhD Pathways program is ripe for making good use of what intersectionality ideas about identity development hold for those planning programs for the next generation of academics. By thoughtfully creating opportunities for students to express their multiple identities, FMPs may make a larger impact on students' educational journeys influenced by numerous internal and external factors entangled with their complex selves.

INTERSECTIONAL APPLICATIONS AND FUTURE DIRECTIONS

An intersectional focus has the ability to equip practitioners, educators, and administrative leaders with awareness, understanding, and the means to benefit individuals and institutions on multiple levels. It is our belief that thoughtful applications of the intersectional approach will ultimately lead to more congenial and proactive strategies that eliminate barriers. We proceed with recommendations for each group. Further, we envision a future that includes FMPs and other student services programs that work to make students feel completely, and not partially, known.

Implications for Practitioners

For practitioners in student and academic affairs, we recommend a more integrated approach in FMPs that includes opportunities for students to share new and more complete stories of their identities. Allowing spaces for dialogue impacts students and FMPs in reciprocal ways and leads to centers that promote more fine-tuned student development. Such spaces can take the form of open and safe venues for discussing challenging topics concerning how students experience all aspects of their growing identities in a way that helps them consider the possibilities of shaping a professional identity such as a university faculty member.

Implications for Educators

Faculty who work with students in the classroom and meet regularly with them through FMPs enter new territory with each interaction. Yet, in order to build on the relationship embedded in FMPs and elevate the level of learning, we support a pedagogical approach to the structure that both acknowledges and incorporates the socialization challenges and social capital issues diverse students must overcome as they enter the culture of academe as future faculty. We propose a more direct, conscious, and intersectional approach that promotes collaboration with multiple constituents represented at the university (e.g., academic affairs, student affairs, academic colleges, etc.) and builds relationships with faculty adept at constructing and implementing curricula to prevent racist, sexist, and classist curricular designs and to incorporate diverse perspectives that actively support students as they pursue the professoriate (Wijeyesinghe, Griffin, & Love, 1997). Figure 22.1 offers more insight into the multiple forms of collaborations useful in FMPs and illustrates the types of interdependent relationships that might promote pedagogical practice that embraces students' multiple identities. We encourage this model of collaboration in FMP practice because it demonstrates the need to involve the entire campus community in the mentoring of individual students.

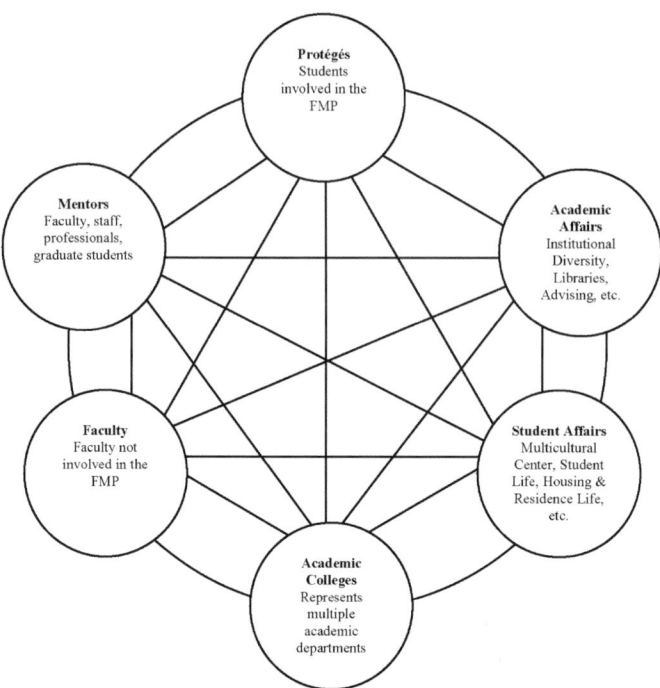

Fig 22.1. Formal Mentoring Program Collaborative Constituent Model.

Implications for Administrators

Administrative leaders in higher education have the most arduous task of incorporating an approach to FMPs that honors the intersecting identities of the participants. Through decision making and lobbying power, administrators in this context have the efficacious ability to move student voices away from the margins and to the forefront of institutional goals, plans, and missions. As Taylor (2013) explained, institutions should feel more than compelled by external factors to include and consider diversity, and as Gurin, Dey, Hurtado, and Gurin (2002) pointed out, administrators must intentionally construct diverse campus communities. The power of intersectionality lies within an institution's ability to discern the voices and experiences of students and mentors involved in the bounded system of FMPs.

The PhD Pathways program represents one of numerous diversity initiatives and mentoring programs at colleges and universities that work as conduits to achieve institutional diversity, equity, and inclusion goals. The extent to which such goals are achieved will depend on institutional leaders' ability to apply approaches that recognize and integrate students' intersectional identities. As PhD Pathways moves into its third academic year, the program will embrace intersectional praxis by coaching mentors to initiate thought-provoking conversations with their protégés, listen to the experiences of *both* individuals in the dyadic mentoring partnership, and cultivate open spaces for students to dialogue about their identities in tandem with future academic careers. Ultimately, we believe that the more mindful institutions are about the impact of students' multiple identities, the more able FMPs like PhD Pathways will be to achieve objectives.

REFERENCES

Abes, E. S. (2009). Theoretical borderlands: Using multiple theoretical perspectives to challenge inequitable power structures in student development theory. *Journal of College Student Development, 50*, 141–156.

Baxter Magolda, M. B. (2008). Three elements of self-authorship. *Journal of College Student Development, 49*, 269–284.

Cole, E. R. (2009). Intersectionality and research in psychology. *American Psychologist, 64*, 170–180.

Crenshaw, K. (1991). Mapping the margins: Intersectionality, identity politics, and violence against women of color. *Stanford Law Review, 43*, 1241–1299.

Crisp, G., & Cruz, I. (2009). Mentoring college students: A critical review of the literature between 1990 and 2007. *Research in Higher Education, 50*, 525–545.

Davis, D. J. (2008). Mentorship and the socialization of underrepresented minorities into the professoriate: Examining varied influences. *Mentoring & Tutoring: Partnership in Learning, 16*, 278–293.

Eby, L. T., Rhodes, J., & Allen, T. D. (2007). The definition and evolution of mentoring. In T. D. Allen & L. T. Eby (Eds.), *Blackwell handbook of mentoring: A multiple perspectives approach* (pp. 7–20). Oxford, UK: Blackwell.

Edwards, J. (1995). *When race counts: The morality of racial preference in Britain and America.* London, England: Routledge.

Gershenfeld, S. (2014). A review of undergraduate mentoring programs. *Review of Educational Research, 84*, 1–27.

Girves, G. E., Zepeda, Y., & Gwathmey, J. K. (2005). Mentoring in a post-affirmative action world. *Journal of Social Issues, 61*, 449–479.

Grant, C. A., & Zwier, E. (2011). Intersectionality and student outcomes: Sharpening the struggle against racism, sexism, classism, ableism, heterosexism, nationalism, and linguistic, religious, and geographical discrimination in teaching and learning. *Multicultural Perspectives, 13*, 181–188.

Griffin, K. A., & Reddick, R. J. (2011). Surveillance and sacrifice: Gender differences in mentoring patterns of Black professors at predominantly white research universities. *American Educational Research Journal, 48*, 1032–1057.

Gurin, P., Dey, E. L., Hurtado, S., & Gurin, G. (2002). Diversity in higher education: Theory and impact on educational outcomes. *Harvard Educational Review, 72*, 330–366.

Harper, S. R. (2012). Black male student success in higher education: A report from the National Black Male College Achievement Study. Philadelphia: University of Pennsylvania, Center for the Study of Race and Equity in Education.

Holley, K. A., & Caldwell, M. L. (2012). The challenges of designing and implementing a doctoral student mentoring program. *Innovative Higher Education, 37*, 243–253.

Hu, S., & Ma, Y. (2010). Mentoring and student persistence in college: A study of the Washington State Achievers Program. *Innovation in Higher Education, 35,* 329–341.

Jones, S. R., & McEwen, M. K. (2000). A conceptual model of multiple dimensions of identity. *Journal of College Student Development, 41,* 405–414.

Keith, N. R., & Russell, J. A. (2013). Creating a climate of organizational diversity: Models of best practice. *Kinesiology Review, 2,* 190–202.

Kram, K. E. (1983). Phases of the mentor relationship. *The Academy of Management Journal, 26,* 608–625.

Long, J. (1997). The dark side of mentoring. *The Australian Educational Researcher, 24,* 115–133.

McCall, L. (2005). The complexity of intersectionality. *Signs: Journal of Women in Culture and Society, 30,* 1771–1800.

Mitchell, D., Jr., & Means, D. (2014). "Quadruple consciousness": A literature review and new theoretical consideration for understanding the experiences of Black gay and bisexual men at predominantly white institutions. *Journal of African American Males in Education, 5,* 23–35.

Museus, S. D., & Griffin, K. A. (2011). Mapping the margins in higher education: On the promise of intersectionality frameworks in research and discourse. In S. D. Museus & K. A. Griffin (Eds.), *Using mixed-method approaches to study intersectionality in higher education: New directions for institutional research* (No. 151, pp. 5–13). San Francisco, CA: Jossey-Bass.

Renn, K. A. (2003). Understanding the identities of mixed-race college students through a developmental ecology lens. *Journal of College Student Development, 44,* 383–403.

Renn, K. A. (2011, November). *Intersectionality as a theoretical perspective for examining faith and race in higher education.* Paper presented at the annual meeting of the Association for the Study of Higher Education, Charlotte, NC.

Renn, K. A. (2012). Creating and re-creating race: The emergence of racial identity as a critical element in psychological, sociological, and ecological perspectives on human development. In C. L. Wijeyesinghe & B. W. Jackson, III (Eds.), *New perspectives on racial identity development: A theoretical and practical anthology* (2nd ed., pp. 11–22). New York: New York University Press.

Renn, K. A., & Reason, R. D. (2013). *College students in the United States: Characteristics, experiences, and outcomes.* San Francisco, CA: Jossey-Bass.

Strayhorn, T. L., & Terrell, M. C. (2007). Mentoring and satisfaction with college for Black students. *The Negro Educational Review, 58,* 69–83.

Taylor, Y. (2013). Compelling diversities, educational intersections: Policy practice, parity. *Gender and Education, 25,* 243–250.

Thomas, K. M., Willis, L. A., & Davis, J. (2007). Mentoring minority graduate students: Issues and strategies for institutions, faculty and students. *Equal Opportunity International, 26,* 178–192. doi:10.1108/02610150710735471

Torres, V., Jones, S. R., & Renn, K. A. (2009). Identity development theories in student affairs origins, current status, and new approaches. *Journal of College Student Development, 50,* 577–596.

Warnock, D. M., & Appel, S. (2012). Learning the unwritten rules: Working class students in graduate school. *Innovative Higher Education, 37,* 307–321.

Wijeyesinghe, C. L., Griffin, P., & Love, B. (1997). Racism in curriculum design. In L. A. Bell & P. Griffin (Eds.), *Teaching for diversity and social justice: A sourcebook* (pp. 82–109). New York, NY: Routledge.

Willison, S., & Gibson, E. (2011). Graduate school learning curves: McNair scholars' postbaccalaureate transitions. *Equity & Excellence in Education, 44,* 153–168.

Yuval-Davis, N. (2006). Intersectionality and feminist politics. *European Journal of Women's Studies, 13,* 193–209.

CHAPTER TWENTY-THREE

Beyond Identity Politics

Equipping Students to Create Systemic Change

COLETTE SEGUIN BEIGHLEY, CARRIE SIMMONS,
AND EMILY WEST

In the second year of the Lesbian, Gay, Bisexual and Transgender (LGBT) Resource Center at Grand Valley State University, we began to understand that our work must go beyond identity politics to include the many social justice issues that impact students. We wanted to expand our analysis beyond individual acts of discrimination to understanding larger intersecting systems of oppression that perpetuate injustice. "Change U: Social Justice Training" was created to provide both the intersectional analyses and the skills necessary to participate in transformational change that moves beyond individual activism to collective liberation. Collaborating with community partners, this semester-long social justice training engages students around work to dismantle systems of oppression.

SHIFT FROM IDENTITY POLITICS TO A SYSTEMIC ANALYSIS

It was students who led us on a journey away from identity politics to a more systemic analysis. In 2010, two years after the opening of the LGBT Resource Center, a sophomore who self-identified as queer and Chicano challenged our center staff to support the National Equality March for LGBT Rights. At that time, the major national LGBT organizations had not yet signed on to support that action, and our political view was still very much tied to a mainstream gay rights agenda. This student held several marginalized identities and had participated in activist work in his hometown of Chicago around the intersections of immigration, labor, and LGBT justice. He had experience doing direct action and understood the efficacy of grassroots mobilization. He also understood how justice issues were connected and that the singular view of identity politics did not create a full view of the systems creating harm. Hearing this critique from a student with whom we were in close relationship caused us to question our analysis and better understand the larger justice issues at play. This moment was one of many that sparked our journey from identity-based politics to a collective liberation frame.

Another shift happened that fall when the Matthew Shepard and James Byrd Jr. Hate Crimes Prevention Act was signed into law after over a decade of work by activists. This new legislation became the first federal protection on the basis of sexual orientation and gender identity. In the LGBT Resource Center, we celebrated this momentous event with a party for students and members of the campus administration. Yet, after reading critiques of this legislation, our staff began to see how pursing identity politics could undergird systems of oppression and exacerbate harm (Mogul, Ritchie, & Whitlock, 2011). The hate crimes law actually expanded the Prison Industrial Complex (PIC), which disproportionly impacts communities of color, immigrants, and queer and transgender (trans) youth (Mogul, Ritchie, & Whitlock, 2011). We came to understand the ways in which transphobia and racism were legitimized by this legislation (Sylvia Rivera Law Project et al., 2002). For the first time, it was clear to us that the kinds of "wins" that mainstream gay organizations were pursuing (e.g., hate crimes legislation, marriage equality, the repeal of the "Don't Ask, Don't Tell" law) reinforced systems of oppression. We knew we needed a more critical analysis if we were to truly engage in justice work.

Throughout this journey, students generously shared about their lived experiences and the ways they encountered institutionalized oppression. They experienced struggles on campus from lack of access to gender-inclusive restrooms to police profiling; however, their experiences of these harmful systems extended beyond campus. Their challenges included mounting student debt, the increased targeting of undocumented people in our area, food insecurity, and ongoing hassles with slumlords.

Trans students were challenging us to see patriarchy as a system that does harm to people of all genders. Many of our queer students were involved in the campus Socialist organization and began to educate staff and students on the injustices embedded in our neoliberal economic system. Queer students involved in the campus environmental student organization were making the connections among racism, gentrification, and environmental injustice. Learning these more complex analyses of social justice issues was the start of an acute departure from our previous thinking. We realized how incorporating the full lived realities of students radically transformed what justice looked like. We moved from serving students as only having one identity to acknowledging the complexities of how intersecting systems of oppression impacted their daily lives. Once we understood this, a rights-based framework no longer made sense.

PREPARING FOR THE WORK: THE DAILY PRACTICE OF PRIVILEGE INTERROGATION

As an all-White staff at a predominantly White institution (PWI), our frame for understanding LGBT justice was through a White lens. Unfortunately, this White framework was in alignment with many mainstream LGBT organizations. Our first task was to examine how Whiteness was dominating our work and begin to deconstruct our racist practices. There were two facets to this deconstruction: first, examining our own individual, internalized White supremacy; and second, understanding that becoming a "nicer, less racist" White person would not create a racially just world. We had to come to terms with the fact that individual actions would not dismantle unjust systems.

Deconstructing Whiteness in our work led our staff to confront privilege not only around race but also around class, sexuality, cisgender identity, citizenship, and ability. As staff, we were learning how to "do the work." This deconstruction process was and is often painful; however, we learned there is a cost involved in seeing how we, as people with tremendous privilege, can perpetuate these systems that value some lives over others. For many people, there is just too much at stake for them to participate in this process: being "nice" or liked, pursuing career aspirations or remaining in relationships with others who resent a social justice critique. Additionally, there is often pain in learning how to "get it right." Through this process, it has become clear that, unless we are willing to do this kind of thorough (sometimes painful) and constant examination, it is impossible to understand how we participate in and benefit from these systems of harm. This interrogation of our personal ways of being in the world as well as the kinds of work we produce became and remains a daily practice.

"WHY IS THE LGBT RESOURCE CENTER DOING SOCIAL JUSTICE TRAINING?"

The main criticism we receive comes in the question of why the LGBT Resource Center is doing social justice work. There are three "identity centers" at Grand Valley State University—the Office of Multicultural Affairs, the Women's Center, and the LGBT Resource Center. The general assumption is that each center focuses on the "marginalized population" their name represents and that the work will end there. The problem with this assumption is that students have complex identities that require more complicated support structures. Additionally, in the absence of federal and state protections, injustice disproportionately impacts queer students.

Once we saw students interfacing with interwoven webs of oppression on multiple levels, we realized that understanding intersectionality in both its interpersonal and systemic manifestations would be key to our work. We understood that we could not eradicate heterosexism, homophobia, cissexism, or transphobia if we were not challenging the cis-hetero patriarchy and the other systems buttressing straight and cisgender supremacy (Pharr, 1997).

Our understanding was informed by intersectional Black feminist thought, including the work of the Combahee River Collective, Angela Davis, Kimberlé Crenshaw, and bell hooks. Just as bell hooks used the phrase "white supremacist capitalist patriarchy" (hooks, 1994, p. 6) to articulate the intersecting systems of oppression, our social justice training developed "Points of Unity" to name harmful systems and enumerate our shared values. In 2013, the LGBT Resource Center Advisory Council unanimously accepted these Points of Unity as our center's values:

- We believe in grassroots, participatory democracy as a group and will use consensus as a model for both learning and decision-making.
- We are opposed to oppression in all its forms: racism, sexism, ageism, ableism, homophobia/biphobia/transphobia, religious intolerance, etc.
- We are opposed to violence, both personal and institutional.
- We believe that the current economic system does not serve the interests of the majority of people and that economic justice must be part of all of our social justice work for the future.
- We believe in ecological integrity, environmental justice and the urgent need for humanity to prevent catastrophe from global warming.
- We are committed to creating more dialogue and collaboration between social justice sectors and practicing the intersectionality of all social justice efforts in West Michigan.
- We are committed to understanding how state, national and international policies impact the social justice work being done at the local level.
- We are committed to the transformation of relationships with one another.
- We are committed to systemic change.

As long as systems of oppression exist, identity or culture centers can provide "sites of resistance" (hooks, 1990, p. 151). Our social justice training is an effort to create this space for queer students as well as other justice-minded students, faculty, staff, and community members. For hooks, a "site of resistance" is a space on the margins, a space for honest conversations and for resisting normative cultural assimilation. hooks (1990) pointed out, "[w]e know better the margin as site of deprivation.... We know less the margin as site of resistance" (p. 151). Students with marginalized identities can be empowered, but as hooks argued, the margin "is not a 'safe' place. One is always at risk. One needs a community of resistance" (p. 149). If we want students to have a site of resistance, it has to be intentionally created. Change U seeks to create that community and space.

CREATION OF A SOCIAL JUSTICE TRAINING

In creating a social justice training that was rooted in the rich social movements of U.S. history, we needed to go beyond individual rights to collective liberation. To move beyond some of these common frames that focus on individual actions and not on dismantling systems of oppression, we wanted to look more deeply at each of these common terms and expand their definitions to include the ways that they may undergird unjust systems of power.

What We Are Not Doing: Diversity

It is now common for major institutions (e.g., the academy, the military, corporate America) to hold diversity as a value. This manifests in the number of trainings offered on diversity, cultural competence, and multiculturalism. These concepts are related to but not the same as social justice. The following set of definitions makes explicit the limits of diversity, inclusion, and cultural competence. In creating a social justice training, we felt it was important to clarify how our work was different from other higher education inclusion and equity trainings. We also wanted to demonstrate the ways that operationalizing these terms can serve to reinforce injustice if we do not also learn to critique larger systems of oppression.

Diversity is simply the presence of individual differences. These differences can be highly visible (e.g., race, ethnicity, sex, age, physical ability) or less visible (e.g., culture, ancestry, language, religious beliefs, sexual orientation, gender identity, socioeconomic status, mental ability). Still, the presence of diversity is not an indicator of the presence of justice. Organizations and institutions engaging in social responsibility (such as diversity strategies) often engage in even greater oppressive practices (Ormiston & Wong, 2013, p. 862).

Inclusion is the concept of individuals with different identities being incorporated into specific environments. Inclusion means having members of nondominant groups present and heard. Yet, the "inclusion" of diverse voices does not mean those voices will carry the same weight and value as dominant voices. The incorporation of diverse identities does not change who holds the power in our "white supremacist, capitalist patriarchy" (hooks, 1994, p. 6).

Cultural competence refers to an ability to understand the norms and mores of an identity group of which you are not a part. While cultural competence can lead us to a larger worldview, it does not address the systems of oppression that privilege some and marginalize others. Through a justice lens, it becomes important to understand how cultural competence has been used as a tool of U.S. imperialism/colonialism (Saunders, 1999). Diversity, inclusion, and/or cultural competence can be paradoxical, causing us to believe an institution is engaging in just practices when, in fact, these practices may be preventing us from engaging in deeper critiques.

What We Are Doing: Collective Liberation

The first three years of Change U: Social Justice Training were made possible through a grant from the Arcus Foundation Gay and Lesbian Fund. This grant allowed the training series to be free and open to university students, faculty, and staff, as well as members of the greater community. These community connections were important for a number of reasons. Working with community members allowed students to build relationships and participate in important intergenerational learning. These connections consistently led to opportunities for internships, practica, volunteer experience, and jobs. Finding ways for community members to participate free of charge also reflected our value of creating greater access for people directly experiencing systemic oppression. In addition, the Change U pedagogical framework, which values open discussion and the lived experience of participants, created an opportunity for people to engage in organic intellectualism (Gramsci, 1971).

In 2011, the first year of Change U, 105 participants included 36 community members, 24 university faculty and staff, and 45 university students. That first year, approximately 10% of the participants self-identified as members of the disabilities community; 50% identified as queer, gender queer, or trans; 25% identified as people of color; and 37% came from a low socioeconomic background. Not all the participants were U.S. citizens. The participants' range of identities was especially important, because the training series centers participants' lived experiences and knowledge. We wanted to create a civic engagement experience for students that educated and empowered them to engage in the kind of direct democracy that they learn about by exploring historic justice movements. During the training, students were often engaging in autonomous actions for social change, which created opportunities to weave in praxis.

From the abolitionist movement to work for immigrant justice, the Change U curriculum examines U.S. social movements that demonstrate that change comes from below, from the grassroots (Zinn, 2003). Students are often taught that creating positive change is simply a matter of engaging in electoral politics, improving policy, and/or becoming policymakers. Our goal in this examination of social movements was to juxtapose individual rights with collective liberation. When students encounter the strategies and tactics of the abolition movement, the Black power movement, women's liberation movement, or the gay liberation movement, they respond with questions similar to this: "Why didn't I know about this before?" This high-impact learning experience has often created huge paradigm shifts for participants. Such transformational learning can be described as "radical," a return to the root of the problem. In this case, we were engaging in a radical deconstruction of injustice in order to understand the system of oppression producing harm.

On the first night of the second year of Change U, we studied the freedom movement and examined Dr. Martin Luther King Jr.'s "Beyond Vietnam" speech (1967). This presentation included an analysis of King's shift from a civil rights discourse to a critique of what he called "the evil triplets" (p. 9): militarism, capitalism, and racism. One major theme that came out of collective discussion was that we could not just engage in small, individual acts of charity when faced with human suffering. In his speech, Dr. King said the following:

> On the one hand, we are called to play the good Samaritan on life's roadside; but that will be only an initial act. One day we must come to see that the whole Jericho road must be transformed so that men and women will not be constantly beaten and robbed as they make their journey on life's highway. True compassion is more than flinging a coin to a beggar.…
> *It comes to see that an edifice which produces beggars needs restructuring* [emphasis added]. (p. 9)

For the last part of that session, participants engaged in an intersectional analysis of U.S. militarism today in the same spirit of King's "Beyond Vietnam" speech. After this exercise, one student stated, "I've learned more in these three hours than I learned in four years of high school." Statements like this have not been uncommon, as participants report being profoundly impacted in their learning from one another and from learning about history from a nondominant perspective. The omission of narratives from the margin is not an accident. Students recognize that their ways of seeing have been orchestrated by the dominant narrative. They come to understand that this purposeful negligence creates harm to others and protects systems of power.

Through developing a shared critique, engaging local history, learning from one another's community organizing and other lived experiences, participants form relationships with one another. These relationships often provide campus and community participants with opportunities to learn from others who have been working on local, national, and international justice issues for years and sometimes decades. As participants learn from people who have directly experienced injustice and/or participated in campaigns to end injustice, the relationships serve as a vehicle for transformational learning.

RELATIONAL ORGANIZING MODEL

Inspired by the work of Southerners on New Ground (SONG; 2014), Change U is firmly grounded in a relational organizing model. This model views justice in terms of collective liberation based on the trust and mutual respect developed through relationships. We recognize that we are in relationship with one another and our struggles are interwoven and inseparable; therefore, we must do social justice work together. This approach is in contrast to organizing models that prioritize single identities and incremental reforms like identity-based rights. Relational organizing is unlike an Alinsky-style of organizing, which puts the cause above care for both self and one another (Alinsky, 1971).

Change U also acknowledges mutual teaching and learning between staff and students, in contrast to more hierarchical learning relationships common to the academy (Freire, 1993). While this type of mutual relationship may not be as common in the student development literature, we noticed that our relationships with students were characterized by increased mutual respect and intimacy. Students told us they felt empowered in this learning environment. As the students were learning to value the lived experience of others, they were in turn having their own lived experience validated. We were inspired by their passion and sense of urgency; it was a gift to watch them experience their own power.

For example, several of the Change U students challenged what they considered to be injustice in the funding of budgets among the three identity centers. They requested that the university provide budgets for all diversity work on campus. When the students were met with a perceived lack of transparency, they became very vocal and refused to tolerate a public institution withholding information. The students felt they had a right to know, and they were persistent until their demands were met. The students' expectations and demands were an engagement in direct democracy. They were utilizing tactics and strategies from social movements found to be effective in creating change. At times, we felt there was an expectation for us to "manage" the students by redirecting their actions. Administrators described the students' persistence as overly aggressive and impolite. These students were seen as unwilling to work within the system. We were questioned about our role in these students' requests. While trying to support our students in their efforts to name inequity among university diversity efforts, we were also navigating our colleagues' reactions to our students. Even though their tactics were negatively received, the students secured the information requested and, as a result, Student Senate passed a resolution calling for resource equity among the three identity centers.

Student development theory could be understood to say that we as professionals are farther along in our developmental journeys. The mutual learning model of Change U required a "queering" of student development theory. To queer something is to do the impossible. As Halberstam (1998) explained, "queer methodology attempts to combine methods that are often cast as being at odds with each other, and it refuses the academic compulsion toward disciplinary coherence" (p. 13). For us, this meant flipping on its side the familiar "challenge and support" model (Sanford, 1962, 1966). While participants were challenging and supporting one another in their learning, our staff was learning and growing along with them. We were transparent about our own struggles with the paradigm shifts we were experiencing, as well as how our own ways of seeing were being both shattered and reconstructed. We were taking the journey with the participants as opposed to leading them. The result has been transformational relationships with students, as together we develop deeper understandings of the work. As we prepare to begin the fourth year of Change U, many participants have stayed connected with both staff and the program. Some have gone on to be small group facilitators as well as co-creators of the curriculum and large group facilitators. This capacity building has allowed us to sustain the training beyond the grant funding.

EMPOWERING STUDENTS TO CREATE CHANGE

Under the rules of neoliberalism, the education system is exploited as a training ground for future laborers (Giroux, 2013). In the aforementioned climate, students are simply workers in training. In Change U, students are present and future movement builders and visionaries of a more just world. One particular example happened during the first year of Change U, when a group of campus residents organized an informational meeting to discuss the possibility of bringing Gender-Inclusive Housing (GIH) to our campus. The campus newspaper ran a story about the meeting along with a poll asking students if they felt GIH was needed. The majority of students polled felt this housing option was unnecessary. This response was not unexpected in our very conservative community. The publication of this poll caused a group of Change U student participants to organize in support of the implementation of GIH on our campus.

Students began by going out in pairs to gather signatures in support of GIH. This effort allowed students an opportunity to engage and educate their peers. After hundreds of signatures were gathered, these student organizers began to meet with campus administrators. Their strategy included bringing large groups of students to the meetings and telling stories of how their lives had been impacted by the current housing policy. On National Day of Silence, these students and others gathered for a silent march around campus, which ended with around 30 students finishing their march in the office of the director of Housing and Resident Life. The director met with these students and heard why they wanted this policy implemented and how their time on campus had been negatively impacted by sex-segregated housing.

Administrators were impacted by the organization of these students, the number of students involved in the meetings, the number of petitions signed, and the students' stories. It was clear that implementing this policy would positively affect retention as well as serve as a recruitment device. In the fall of that year, after six months of organizing, GIH was implemented on our campus. A story highlighting the successful organizing campaign of these students was featured on the front page of our student newspaper. This student campaign was an exercise in collective self-realization and grassroots organizing.

Another example of students and community members taking action occurred during the time frame when many austerity measures, including antiworker legislation, were being implemented at the state level. Some of the Change U participants attended demonstrations at the state capitol to protest these measures. They began to realize that the main reason these demonstrations were not effective was that the groups doing the organizing were putting their hope in electoral politics and not in the power of grassroots social movements like the ones participants had been studying in Change U. On one such occasion, there were an estimated 12,000 people at the state capitol to protest right-to-work legislation. This was one of the largest protests in Lansing. Some of the participants chose to engage in direct action by joining a sit-in inside the capitol building.

After a few hours of sitting in the Capitol rotunda, the legislation was passed and the crowd dispersed. The Change U participants realized that if more of the protesters joined the occupation inside the building, they might have been able to stop the legislation. Instead, what they heard from other protestors was, "Wait until the next election." These were transformative moments for the participants in many ways. First, it was the process itself that changed how participants viewed themselves in the world, and it was their relationships with one another that allowed them to take action to create the kind of just spaces they envisioned. Secondly, the failures of this action led participants to have a conversation about not only movement tactics but the importance of prefigurative politics. For example, the labor movement spent over $20 million to pass the worker rights legislation in Michigan that failed. What if this money had been spent to support working-class families who were experiencing poverty? Such an action might have gained new members for the labor movement; but, more importantly, it would have had the potential to develop class solidarity and build relationships. This is an example of prefigurative politics, where people put into practice the kinds of changes they want to see in a more just world. Social justice is as much a process as it is a goal (Spade & Gosset, 2014).

CONCLUSION

Student affairs has examined student development along identity lines as opposed to critiquing the systems that create harmful material realities for students. The complexities begin with students holding multiple identities: they are queer and undocumented, trans and Black, gender queer and members of the disabilities community (Jones & McEwen, 2000). And the complexities expand as we examine larger systems maintaining injustice. We realized that understanding the injustice impacting students' lived experiences was imperative to our ability to support their development and persistence. In order to best serve students, we must acknowledge the fullness of their identities, as well as the harmful systems impacting their lives. From there, we felt it was our obligation to understand with students how harmful systems were creating injustice. We also wanted to educate them in regard to the rich history of social movements in the United States as well as the strategies used to create change. Change U: Social Justice Training was designed to help students develop a shared critique of intersecting systems of oppression and to experience the transformative nature of relational organizing.

REFERENCES

Alinsky, S. D. (1971). *Rules for radicals: A pragmatic primer for realistic radicals.* New York, NY: Random House.

Freire, P. (1993). *Pedagogy of the oppressed.* New York, NY: Continuum.

Giroux, H. A. (2013). *Neoliberalism and the politics of higher education: An interview with Henry A. Giroux.* Retrieved from http://truth-out.org/news/item/15237-predatory-capitalism-and-the-attack-on-higher-education-an-interview-with-henry-a-giroux

Gramsci, A. (1971). *Revolutionary intellectual* (Q. Hoare & G. N. Smith, Trans.). In Roger S. Gottlieb (Ed.), *An anthology of western Marxism: From Lukács and Gramsci to socialist-feminist* (pp. 112–119). New York, NY: Oxford University Press.

Halberstam, J. (1998). *Female masculinity.* Durham, NC: Duke University Press.

hooks, b. (1990). *Yearnings: Race, gender, and cultural politics.* Boston, MA: South End.

hooks, b. (1994). *Outlaw culture: Resisting representations.* New York, NY: Routledge.

Jones, S. R., & McEwen, M. K. (2000). A conceptual model of multiple dimensions of identity. *Journal of College Student Personnel, 41,* 405–413.

King, M. L., Jr. (1967, April 4). Beyond Vietnam [Transcript]. *The King Center.* Retrieved from http://www.thekingcenter.org/archive/document/beyond-vietnam

Mogul, J. L., Ritchie, A. J., & Whitlock, A. (2011). *Queer (in)justice: The criminalization of LGBT people in the United States.* Boston, MA: Beacon.

Ormiston, M. E., & Wong, E. M. (2013). License to ill: The effects of corporate social responsibility and CEO moral identity on corporate social irresponsibility. *Personnel Psychology, 66,* 861–893.

Pharr, S. (1997). *Homophobia: A weapon of sexism.* Berkeley, CA: Chardon.

Sanford, N. (1962). *The American college.* New York, NY: Wiley.

Sanford, N. (1966). *Self and society: Social change and individual development.* New York, NY: Atherton.

Saunders, F. S. (1999). *Who paid the piper? The CIA and the cultural cold war.* London, England: Granta.

Southerners on New Ground. (2014). Beliefs. Retrieved from http://southernersonnewground.org/about/beliefs-agreements/

Spade, D. (Interviewer) & Gosset, R. (Interviewee). (2014). Part 1: Prison abolition + Prefiguring the world you want to live in [Video interview]. Retrieved from http://bcrw.barnard.edu/event/no-one-is-disposable-everyday-practices-of-prison-abolition/#videos

Sylvia Rivera Law Project, FIERCE, Queers for Economic Justice, Peter Cicchino Youth Project, & Audre Lorde Project. (2002). *SRLP announces non-support of the Gender Employment Non-Discrimination Act* [Press release]. Retrieved from http://srlp.org/genda/

Zinn, H. (2003). *A people's history of the United States: 1492-present.* New York, NY: HarperCollins.

Editor Biographies

EDITOR

Donald Mitchell, Jr., PhD

Donald Mitchell Jr.'s scholarship theoretically and empirically explores the effects of race, gender, and underrepresented identity intersections in higher education contexts, with a particular interest in historically Black fraternities and sororities and historically Black colleges and universities as microsystems and macrosystems of analysis.

He was awarded the Center for the Study of the College Fraternity's 2012 Richard McKaig Outstanding Doctoral Research Award for his dissertation, "Are They Truly Divine? A Grounded Theory of the Influences of Black Greek-Lettered Organizations on the Persistence of African Americans at Predominantly White Institutions." He also was awarded the Multicultural/Multiethnic Education Special Interest Group of the American Educational Research Association's 2014 Dr. Carlos J. Vallejo Memorial Award for Emerging Scholarship, the American College Personnel Association's Standing Committee for Men and Masculinities 2014 Outstanding Research Award (with Dr. Darris Means), and the Michigan College Personnel Association's 2013 John Zaugra Outstanding Research/Publication Award.

Mitchell is assistant professor of higher education at Grand Valley State University in Grand Rapids, Michigan. In addition, he currently serves as managing editor and editorial board member of the *Journal of African American Males in Education* and editorial board member for the *Journal of Ethnographic & Qualitative Research* and *Oracle: The Research Journal of the Association of Fraternity/Sorority Advisors*. He also is lead editor of *Student Involvement and Academic Outcomes: Implications for Diverse College Student Populations* (with Krista Soria, Elizabeth A. Daniele, and John Gipson; Peter Lang, in press).

Mitchell earned a bachelor of science in chemistry from Shaw University, the first historically Black institution in the South; a master of science in educational leadership from Minnesota State University, Mankato; and a PhD in educational policy and administration with a concentration in higher education from the University of Minnesota–Twin Cities.

ASSOCIATE EDITORS

Charlana Y. Simmons

Charlana Y. Simmons served as associate managing and technical editor of *Intersectionality & Higher Education: Theory, Research and Praxis.* She earned her BA in English literature and MS in adolescent English education at the University of Rochester in 2002 and 2004, respectively. She currently serves as director of student success and diversity in the College of Natural Sciences at the University of Massachusetts–Amherst. She also serves as an editorial board member for *Annuals of the Next Generation,* a graduate student–led journal.

Previously, Simmons served as associate director of college programs for the David T. Kearns Center at the University of Rochester, which included the Ronald E. McNair Post-Baccalaureate Achievement program, National Science Foundation STEM & STEP programs, Kearns Scholars program, and Xerox Engineering Fellows programs. Her research interests focus on cultural issues in education including, but not limited to, community change initiatives, urban education, and intersectionality, particularly as it relates to Black males in U.S. public schools. Her work is traditionally grounded in the following theories: critical race theory, Black feminist theory, grounded theory, and the Africanist presence.

Lindsay A. Greyerbiehl

Lindsay A. Greyerbiehl served as associate managing and technical editor of *Intersectionality & Higher Education: Theory, Research and Praxis.* She earned her BAA in family studies and women's studies at Central Michigan University and her MEd in higher education, emphasizing in college student affairs leadership at Grand Valley State University. Greyerbiehl serves as inaugural editor in chief of *College Student Affairs Leadership,* a peer-reviewed journal for graduate students in college student affairs and higher education.

Greyerbiehl received Grand Valley State University's 2013 Graduate Dean's Citation for Excellence in Leadership and Service, Grand Valley State University's 2014 Outstanding Student in the Major for Higher Education, and American College Personnel Association's Standing Committee for Graduate Student and New Professionals 2014 Outstanding Master's Student Award. Greyerbiehl's research interests include critical feminist and queer theory, neoliberalism, structural inequity/violence, and intersectionality.

Author Biographies

Tara L. Affolter, PhD

Tara Affolter is assistant professor of education studies at Middlebury College. Prior to Middlebury, she spent over 15 years teaching high school English and theater while working for social justice within the public schools. Dr. Affolter has research and teaching experience in antiracist and social justice education, culturally relevant pedagogy, and critical race theory. Her current research explores experiences of students of color at predominantly White liberal arts colleges in order to find more effective ways to build, support, and sustain diverse communities of learners. Her work seeks to support communities in disrupting inequitable education practices.

Allison D. Anders, PhD

Allison Daniel Anders is assistant professor in Educational Foundations and Inquiry in the Department of Educational Studies at the University of South Carolina. She earned her doctorate in education from the University of North Carolina at Chapel Hill. She studies the everyday experiences of targeted youth and the K-20 educational settings they navigate, contexts of education, systemic inequities, and qualitative methodologies. Her research includes work with incarcerated youth, children with refugee status, and LGBT (Lesbian, gay, bisexual, and transgender) youth.

Colette Seguin Beighley

Colette Seguin Beighley became director of the Grand Valley State University (GVSU) LGBT Resource Center in 2010 after two years as assistant director. Prior to her work at GVSU, Seguin Beighley was director of communications for Triangle Foundation (now Equality Michigan). She has co-chaired the Great Lakes Region of the National Consortium of LGBT Resource

Professionals in Higher Education. She also has served on the board of Equality Michigan. Seguin Beighley is a recipient of the West Michigan Pride ACE Advocacy Award and the GVSU's Maxine Swanson Advocacy Award. She received a master's degree in counseling from California State University, Hayward.

James M. DeVita, PhD

James M. DeVita is assistant professor of higher education in the Department of Educational Leadership in the Watson College of Education at the University of North Carolina, Wilmington. He earned both his doctorate in higher education administration and MS in college student personnel from the University of Tennessee, Knoxville, where his dissertation included three research projects on the experiences and development of gay male college students. His research is focused on the educational experiences of marginalized and targeted populations in higher education, issues of identity development, access and success during college, and the transition from secondary to postsecondary institutions.

Majorie L. Dorimé-Williams, PhD

Marjorie Dorimé-Williams earned her doctorate in education policy, organization, and leadership at the University of Illinois at Urbana–Champaign. She specializes in educational research and evaluation. Prior to receiving her PhD, she earned a bachelor of science in sociology from Saint Joseph's University and a dual-master's in social work and social policy from the University of Pennsylvania. Dr. Dorimé-Williams's research interests include assessment and evaluation in education; identity intersectionality with a focus on race, gender, and class; and, access, persistence, and retention of historically underrepresented students in postsecondary education. She currently serves as Baruch College's director of academic assessment.

Sasha Eloi

Sasha Eloi advises and counsels first-generation and underrepresented minority undergraduates at the University of Rochester. Dedicated to helping students achieve academic success while navigating unfamiliar spaces, she worked with students to found the Women of Color Circle and the Frederick Douglass Leadership House. She received a BA in Linguistics from the University of Rochester and an MA in Linguistics from Syracuse University. Eloi is pursuing her doctorate in higher education at the Warner School of Education at the University of Rochester.

Claudia García-Louis

Claudia García-Louis is a research associate for Project MALES at The University of Texas at Austin (UT Austin). Her responsibilities include researching Latino male attrition in higher education, program development, and student support. Prior to attending graduate school, García-Louis worked at Linfield College as director of multicultural programs, conducting trainings on social justice, upholding safe spaces and group facilitation. She received a BA in psychology and a BS in anthropology from Oregon State University and an MA in student development administration from Seattle University. Currently she is pursuing a doctoral degree in the Higher Education Administration program at UT Austin. Her research interests include AfroLatino identity development, race relations in higher education, and education access and equity.

Jason C. Garvey, PhD

Jason C. Garvey is assistant professor of higher education in the Department of Educational Leadership, Policy, and Technology Studies at the University of Alabama and a research associate with Campus Pride's Q Research Institute for Higher Education. Dr. Garvey's research combines statistical methods and survey design with critical epistemological approaches (i.e., intersectionality, queer theory) with intentions of maintaining complex and fluid understandings of social identities and experiences. Most of his studies explore issues related to campus and classroom climate, philanthropy and fundraising for higher education alumni, and LGBTQ individuals. Dr. Garvey is the recipient of the 2014 AERA Queer Studies SIG Scholar-Activist Dissertation of the Year Award.

Diane Goodman, EdD

Diane J. Goodman has been educating about diversity and social justice issues for over 30 years. As a trainer and consultant, Dr. Goodman has worked with a wide range of organizations, community groups, schools, and universities. She has been a professor at several universities in the areas of education, psychology, social work, and women's studies. In addition, she was the director of human relations education and the interim affirmative action officer at the University of Rhode Island. Dr. Goodman is the author of the book *Promoting Diversity and Social Justice: Educating People from Privileged Groups* (2nd ed.) and other publications.

Sheri C. Hardee, PhD

Sheri C. Hardee is assistant professor of education and Social Foundations program coordinator at the University of North Georgia. Much of her research has centered on college access and retention and the experiences of underrepresented students at predominantly White institutions with a conceptual framework focused on intersectionality, postcolonial theories, and critical multicultural education. She also is program coordinator on a Federal Near Peer Service-Learning Grant, pairing preservice educators with underrepresented high school students in a weekly mentoring program, and her research with this project focuses on youth empowerment, intersectionality, identity development, and critical multicultural education for both mentors and mentees.

Susan V. Iverson, EdD

Susan V. Iverson is associate professor of higher education administration and student personnel at Kent State University and holds affiliate faculty status with both women's studies and LGBT (Lesbian, gay, bisexual, transgender) studies. Dr. Iverson's research interests focus on equity and diversity, status of women in higher education, and feminist pedagogy; she co-edited *Reconstructing Policy Analysis in Higher Education: Feminist Poststructural Perspectives* (Routledge, 2010). She holds a BA in English from Keene State College, an MA in higher education administration from Boston College, an MEd in counseling from Bridgewater State College, and an EdD in higher educational leadership at the University of Maine.

Walter R. Jacobs, III, PhD

Walter R. Jacobs, III, serves as founding dean of the College of Social Sciences and Professional Studies at the University of Wisconsin–Parkside. Dr. Jacobs earned his master's degree and doctorate in sociology from Indiana University. He received his bachelor's degree in electrical engineering from the Georgia Institute of Technology. His current research explores personal and social possibilities of undergraduate students' generation of creative digital nonfiction.

Susan R. Jones, PhD

Susan Robb Jones is professor and program director in the Higher Education and Student Affairs program in the Educational Studies Department at The Ohio State University and previously served as associate professor and director of the College Student Personnel program at the University of Maryland–College Park. Her research interests include psychosocial perspectives on identity, intersectionality and multiple social identities, service-learning, and qualitative research methodologies. She is the co-author of books titled *Identity Development of College Students* (with Elisa S. Abes; Jossey-Bass, 2013) and *Negotiating the Complexities of Qualitative Research: Fundamental Elements and Issues* (with Vasti Torres & Jan Arminio; Routledge, 2006, 2nd ed. published in 2014). Dr. Jones is one of the co-editors of the fifth edition of *Student Services: A Handbook for the Profession* (with John Schuh and Shaun Harper; Jossey-Bass, 2011).

Sharese King

Sharese King attended the University of Rochester for her undergraduate studies and graduated in 2012. While there, she majored in linguistics and minored in American Sign Language. She is currently a graduate student at Stanford University pursuing a PhD in linguistics. She has investigated topics relevant to children's acquirement of syntactic and pragmatic knowledge and currently examines the social and psychological effects of being a speaker of African American English, a stigmatized dialect.

Miguel U. Luna

Miguel U. Luna is a student affairs practitioner that has worked in both public and private institutions. He has experience in admissions and outreach, student ambassadorship, student life, and first-year seminar programs. He holds a bachelor's degree in psychology from the University of Notre Dame and a master's of science in higher education from California State University, Fullerton.

Carmen L. McCrink, PhD

Carmen L. McCrink serves as associate professor and director of the PhD Program in Leadership and Education and coordinator of the MS in higher education administration specialization at Barry University. Prior to her employment with Barry University, Dr. McCrink worked for Miami–Dade College, serving as associate dean and executive director of federal- and state-funded grant programs. Given her tenure as an administrator and faculty member at the community college and university levels, Dr. McCrink has interest and expertise in areas such as community colleges; teaching and learning; curriculum development; reading, writing, and literacy studies; and Hispanic research issues.

Ryan A. Miller

Ryan A. Miller is associate director of campus diversity and strategic initiatives in the Division of Diversity and Community Engagement at The University of Texas at Austin, where he works with constituencies across campus on strategic planning, diversity education initiatives, campus climate assessment and incident response, and diversity planning. Previously, Miller directed the

Lesbian, Gay, Bisexual and Transgender Resource Center at the University of North Florida, where he also served as an adjunct faculty member in education, designing and teaching intergroup dialogue courses. He received his master's degree from the Harvard Graduate School of Education and bachelor's degree in journalism *cum laude* from The University of Texas at Austin, both as a Point Scholar, and he is currently pursuing a PhD in educational administration at the University of Texas at Austin.

Thalia M. Mulvihill, PhD

Thalia M. Mulvihill is professor of social foundations and higher education and an affiliate faculty member in Women's and Gender Studies and the Honors College. Dr. Mulvihill is also the director of the Adult, Higher and Community Education Doctoral Program at Ball State University. Her areas of research/teaching include qualitative research methods, innovative pedagogies, history and sociology of higher education with a focus on women and gender issues. Her awards and recognition include the following: University Excellence in Teaching Award, Virginia B. Ball Center for Creative Inquiry Fellowship, Department Award for Outstanding Research, University Diversity Associate, GLACUHO Consultant in Residence, Williams Academic Affairs Award/Outstanding Higher Education Faculty, and the Multicultural Center Faculty Award.

Samuel D. Museus, PhD

Samuel Museus is associate professor of higher education at the University of Denver. He has produced over 100 publications and national conference presentations on the racial, cultural, and structural factors affecting the experiences and outcomes of diverse student populations. His work has appeared in the *Harvard Educational Review, Teachers College Record, The Review of Higher Education,* and *Journal of Higher Education.* His books include *Creating Campus Cultures: Fostering Success among Racially Diverse Student Populations* (with Uma Jayakumar, 2012) and *The New Majority and Higher Education: A Synthesis of Research on College Students of Color* (with Kimberly Griffin, in press).

Mitsu Narui, PhD

Mitsu Narui currently serves as assistant director for academic initiatives at The Ohio State University in the Student Life Multicultural Center. Dr. Narui has done research on the experiences of Asian international and Asian American gay, Lesbian, and bisexual college students and the experiences of Asian American doctoral students in education programs. Dr. Narui's research currently focuses on the impact of social justice programming on the undergraduate student experience. Dr. Narui earned her BS in physical therapy from The Ohio State University, MA in college student personnel from Bowling Green State University, and PhD in higher education administration from The Ohio State University.

Z Nicolazzo

Z Nicolazzo is a doctoral candidate in the Student Affairs in Higher Education program at Miami University in Oxford, Ohio. Nicolazzo earned hir MS in college student personnel from Western Illinois University and hir BA in philosophy from Roger Williams University. Hir dissertation study is an ethnographic study of trans* student resilience at a large public institution in the Midwest and focuses specifically on the ways in which trans* college students navigate, confront, push back, and resist genderism on campus. Nicolazzo's research interests include trans* college students, activism in higher education, and alternative epistemologies, methodologies, and representations of knowledge.

Maria Oropeza Fujimoto, PhD

Maria Oropeza Fujimoto teaches in the Master's of Higher Education program at California State University, Fullerton. Her experience as a student affairs practitioner includes the areas of leadership development, multicultural affairs, academic advising, and women's issues at four different campuses, both public and private. She has worked with numerous academic and administrative departments to foster a better understanding of the complex identities and issues students face on campus. Dr. Oropeza Fujimoto received her master's degree from the University of Iowa and doctorate from the University of Washington.

Shelly Perdomo, EdD

Shelly A. Perdomo is director of the Center for Multicultural Advancement and Student Success at the University of Massachusetts Amherst. Dr. Perdomo is a passionate educator and university administrator. Her theoretical interests include Black feminist theory, Latina feminism, identity development theory, student development theory, and critical race theory. Dr. Perdomo is a native of Harlem, New York City, and a first-generation Dominican American. She received her doctorate and master's in educational policy, research, and administration from the University of Massachusetts–Amherst and her bachelor's in Latin American studies from Mount Holyoke College.

Robin Phelps-Ward

Robin Phelps-Ward is a doctoral student at Ball State University in the Department of Educational Studies studying adult, higher, and community education with an emphasis in higher education. She is the director of the PhD Pathways mentoring program at Ball State University within the College of Communication, Information and Media. Her research focuses on organizational socialization, minority student mentoring, instructional classroom technology, and diversity initiatives at American, public universities. She received her master's degree from Ball State University in communication studies and her bachelor's degree from Murray State University in journalism and mass communications and organizational communication.

Stephen John Quaye, PhD

Stephen John Quaye is a faculty member in the Student Affairs in Higher Education Program at Miami University. He is a 2009 ACPA Emerging Scholar and was awarded the 2009 NASPA Melvene D. Hardee Dissertation of the Year Award. His research focuses on understanding how to enable students to engage difficult issues (e.g., privilege, oppression, power), civilly and honestly, as well as how storytelling is used as an educational tool to foster reflection and learning across differences. He also is interested in the strategies educators use to facilitate these dialogues and what they learn about themselves in the process.

Leah Reinert

Leah Reinert is a higher education PhD candidate in the Department of Organizational Leadership, Policy, and Development at the University of Minnesota. Her research interests include faculty issues, equity and diversity in higher education, LGBT (Lesbian, gay, bisexual, transgender) issues in higher education, and multicultural teaching and learning. She has worked as a research assistant at the Midwestern Higher Education Compact since 2011. Reinert earned a BS and MS in education at Southern Illinois University, Carbondale.

Nicole Alia Salis Reyes

Nicole Alia Salis Reyes (Kanaka Maoli) is a doctoral student in the Department of Educational Leadership and Policy Studies at The University of Texas at San Antonio. Her research interests are centered on the college experiences and college success of Kanaka Maoli (Native Hawaiian) students, Indigenous students, and other students of color. She holds a bachelor's degree in comparative studies in race and ethnicity and a master's degree in policy, organization, and leadership studies from Stanford University.

Claire Kathleen Robbins, PhD

Claire K. Robbins is assistant professor of higher education at Virginia Tech. Her research focuses on social identities, ally behaviors, and developmental experiences among students and educators, with an emphasis on qualitative methodologies and critical theoretical frameworks. She was the recipient of the Southern Association for College Student Affairs' 2013 Dissertation of the Year Award and runner-up for the 2012 NASPA Melvene D. Hardee Dissertation of the Year Award for her dissertation, "Racial Consciousness, Identity, and Dissonance among White Women in Student Affairs Graduate Programs."

Rebecca Ropers-Huilman, PhD

Rebecca Ropers-Huilman is professor and chair in the Department of Organizational Leadership, Policy, & Development, and an affiliate of the Gender, Women & Sexuality Studies program at the University of Minnesota. She has published four books and more than 50 scholarly works related to equity, diversity, and change in higher education contexts. Having served as director of a women's center, editor of the interdisciplinary and international journal *Feminist Formations,* and head of both women's studies and educational leadership academic units, Dr. Ropers-Huilman grounds her work in an understanding of the social role of higher education in creating inclusive and engaged communities.

Natasha Saelua

Natasha Saelua is a graduate student at the University of Denver's Morgridge College of Education, pursuing a doctoral degree in higher education. She has extensive experience in student affairs, most recently serving as associate director for University of California, Los Angeles's (UCLA) Community Programs Office and also as a community advocate at the local, state, and national level. Her research interests revolve around access to higher education for Pacific Islanders from the continental United States, Pacific Territories, and nations under the Compact of Free Association. She completed her master of arts degree from UCLA's Asian American Studies program in 2012.

Gabriel R. Serna, PhD

Gabriel Ramón Serna is assistant professor of higher education and student affairs leadership at the University of Northern Colorado. His research interests include higher education economics and finance with emphasis on the impacts of price barriers on college-going and choice as well as student price responsiveness. His interest in intersectionality stems from both personal experiences and scholarly examination of the relationships between social constructions of identity and economic theory and methodology. He holds a PhD in education policy from Indiana University Bloomington, an MPP in public finance from the Martin School of Public Policy & Administration at the University of Kentucky, and a BBA in economics from New Mexico State University.

Carrie Simmons

Carrie Simmons is the program coordinator for the LGBT Resource Center at Grand Valley State University. Simmons has been at the center since it opened in the fall of 2008. In her role as program coordinator, Simmons helped conceptualize and produce Change U: Social Justice Training. Previously, her student services career was focused in housing and residence life. Simmons received the 2013 Grand Valley State University Student Senate's Laker of the Year Award. She holds a master's degree in college student affairs and a bachelor's degree in elementary education, both from Western Michigan University.

Valeria Sinclair-Chapman, PhD

Valeria Sinclair-Chapman is associate professor of political science at Purdue University. Her research examines legislative politics, minority representation in Congress, and minority political participation. Her research and advocacy are driven by a fundamental interest in uncovering and understanding the institutions, processes, and practices that foster the inclusion of marginalized groups. She is author or co-author of several journal articles, book chapters, and an award-winning book, *Countervailing Forces in African-American Political Activism, 1973–1994* (Cambridge University Press, 2006). She has facilitated workshops on diversity and inclusion for faculty, graduate students, and undergraduates, and spearheaded new organizations for women and students of color. She earned her PhD from The Ohio State University in 2002 and her BA from the University of North Carolina–Asheville in 1991.

Betty Jeanne Taylor, PhD

Betty Jeanne Taylor is director of diversity education initiatives in the Division of Diversity and Community Engagement at The University of Texas at Austin. Her responsibilities include development and facilitation of comprehensive diversity education programs, with an emphasis on sustained learning environments for university students, staff, faculty, and community organizations. Dr. Taylor also assists with strategic planning, campus climate, bias incident response, and diversity planning. She holds a BS in communication and an MS in higher education from Florida State University, as well as a PhD in higher education administration from The University of Texas at Austin. Her research focuses on racial identity development.

Traci Thomas-Card

Traci Thomas-Card earned her bachelor's degree in comprehensive English literature and her master's degree in English from the University of Wisconsin–Eau Claire. She is currently pursuing her EdD in higher education through the Department of Organizational Leadership, Policy, and Development at the University of Minnesota–Twin Cities. Thomas-Card is the prevention program coordinator for The Aurora Center for Advocacy & Education/Boynton Health Service at the University of Minnesota and is responsible for providing education and training on bystander intervention, sexual assault, relationship violence, and stalking. Her current research interests include the LGBTQ (Lesbian, gay, bisexual, transgender and transsexual, queer and questioning) college student population, intersectionality, student development, and violence prevention.

Daniel Tillapaugh, PhD

Dan Tillapaugh is a postdoctoral fellow in the higher education programs at the University of Maine. He graduated with a PhD in leadership studies at the University of San Diego and an MEd in counseling and personnel services from the University of Maryland, College Park. Dr. Tillapaugh's research interests are related broadly to intersectionality within higher education, particularly intersections of sexuality and gender on student development. He currently serves as chair of the Standing Committee on Men and Masculinities for ACPA–College Student Educators International.

Patrick N. Troup

Patrick Troup has worked in higher education for 11 years. After graduating from the University of Wisconsin–Madison, he went on to graduate school at Howard University. After completing advanced graduate coursework at the Catholic University of Leuven in Belgium, he returned to the United States to serve as assistant director of the Multicultural and International Programs and Services office and to teach ethics at the College of St. Catherine's for four years. He then took a position as the founding director of the Multicultural Center for Academic Excellence at the University of Minnesota. He is now the director of retention initiatives for the Office for Equity and Diversity.

Emily West

Emily West serves as grant coordinator for the LGBT Resource Center at Grand Valley State University. West graduated from Hope College in 2010 with a bachelor of arts in English literature and women's studies. At Hope, West was involved in extensive campus organizing. She completed a year of service with AmeriCorps at Goodwill Industries of Grand Rapids, working in the Youth Services Department. Most recently, West worked as a field organizer for both Holland is Ready and Unity Michigan, focused on amending Michigan's Elliott-Larsen Civil Rights Act of 1976 to be inclusive of perceived sexual orientation and gender identity.

Heidi Whitford, PhD

Heidi Whitford is assistant professor at Barry University in the PhD Program in Leadership and Education, specializing in higher education administration. In addition, she teaches graduate level courses in the Organizational Learning and Leadership program. Prior to her appointment at Barry University, she taught at LaGuardia Community College and New York University. Her research interests include student activism, college student development, teaching and learning, civic engagement in higher education, and international higher education.

Charmaine L. Wijeyesinghe, EdD

Charmaine L. Wijeyesinghe, EdD, has worked in social justice education for 30 years. She held numerous positions in higher education administration at the University of Massachusetts, Amherst; served as dean of students at Mount Holyoke College; and was national program consultant for the National Conference of Christians and Jews. Dr. Wijeyesinghe lectures and writes on multiracial identity, the use of racial identity models in various areas of practice, and the connection between intersectionality and social identity models. She co-edited *New Perspectives on Racial Identity Development: A Theoretical and Practical Anthology* and *New Perspectives on Racial Identity Development: Integrating Emerging Frameworks* (with Bailey Jackson; New York University Press) and has written book chapters and journal pieces on racial identity and intersectionality.